INTELLECTUAL PROPERTY

THIRD EDITION

Margreth Barrett

Professor of Law
University of California Hastings College of the Law

The *CrunchTime*® Series

Published by Wolters Kluwer Law & Business in New York.

Wolters Kluwer Law & Business serves customers worldwide with CCH, Aspen Publishers, and Kluwer Law International products. (www.wolterskluwerlb.com)

To contact Customer Service, e-mail customer.service@wolterskluwer.com, call 1-800-234-1660, fax 1-800-901-9075, or mail correspondence to:

Wolters Kluwer Law & Business
Attn: Order Department
PO Box 990
Frederick, MD 21705

Printed in the United States of America.

1 2 3 4 5 6 7 8 9 0

ISBN 978-0-7355-9807-2

Library of Congress Cataloging-in-Publication Data
Barrett, Margreth, 1951-
  Intellectual property / Margreth Barrett, Professor of Law, University of California Hastings College of the Law. — Third edition.
    pages cm — (The CrunchTime series)
  ISBN 978-0-7355-9807-2 (perfectbound)
  1. Intellectual property — United States — Outlines, syllabi, etc. 2. Law examinations — United States — Study guides. I. Title.
  KF2980.B3893 2012
  346.7304'8 — dc23
                                    2012030339

This book is intended as a general review of a legal subject. It is not intended as a source for advice for the solution of legal matters or problems. For advice on legal matters, the reader should consult an attorney.

About Wolters Kluwer Law & Business

Wolters Kluwer Law & Business is a leading global provider of intelligent information and digital solutions for legal and business professionals in key specialty areas, and respected educational resources for professors and law students. Wolters Kluwer Law & Business connects legal and business professionals as well as those in the education market with timely, specialized authoritative content and information-enabled solutions to support success through productivity, accuracy and mobility.

Serving customers worldwide, Wolters Kluwer Law & Business products include those under the Aspen Publishers, CCH, Kluwer Law International, Loislaw, Best Case, ftwilliam.com and MediRegs family of products.

CCH products have been a trusted resource since 1913, and are highly regarded resources for legal, securities, antitrust and trade regulation, government contracting, banking, pension, payroll, employment and labor, and healthcare reimbursement and compliance professionals.

Aspen Publishers products provide essential information to attorneys, business professionals and law students. Written by preeminent authorities, the product line offers analytical and practical information in a range of specialty practice areas from securities law and intellectual property to mergers and acquisitions and pension/benefits. Aspen's trusted legal education resources provide professors and students with high-quality, up-to-date and effective resources for successful instruction and study in all areas of the law.

Kluwer Law International products provide the global business community with reliable international legal information in English. Legal practitioners, corporate counsel and business executives around the world rely on Kluwer Law journals, looseleafs, books, and electronic products for comprehensive information in many areas of international legal practice.

Loislaw is a comprehensive online legal research product providing legal content to law firm practitioners of various specializations. Loislaw provides attorneys with the ability to quickly and efficiently find the necessary legal information they need, when and where they need it, by facilitating access to primary law as well as state-specific law, records, forms and treatises.

Best Case Solutions is the leading bankruptcy software product to the bankruptcy industry. It provides software and workflow tools to flawlessly streamline petition preparation and the electronic filing process, while timely incorporating ever-changing court requirements.

ftwilliam.com offers employee benefits professionals the highest quality plan documents (retirement, welfare and non-qualified) and government forms (5500/PBGC, 1099 and IRS) software at highly competitive prices.

MediRegs products provide integrated health care compliance content and software solutions for professionals in healthcare, higher education and life sciences, including professionals in accounting, law and consulting.

Wolters Kluwer Law & Business, a division of Wolters Kluwer, is headquartered in New York. Wolters Kluwer is a market-leading global information services company focused on professionals.

Summary of Contents

Table of Contents

FLOW CHARTS

CAPSULE SUMMARY

EXAM TIPS

Preface

The *CrunchTime®* series is intended for students who want Emanuel quality but don't have the time to buy and use the full-length *Emanuel® Law Outline* on a subject. We've designed the series to be used for review purposes in the last few weeks (or less) before your final exams.

This book includes the following features, most of which have been extracted from the *Emanuel® Law Outline* on *Intellectual Property*:

- ■ Flow Charts — We've reduced many of the key principles of intellectual property law to a series of flow charts, created especially for this book and never published elsewhere. We think these will be especially useful for reviewing for exams. The charts provide an overview of the most important points in a format that demonstrates the relationship of the points visually. The figures will be especially handy for use in open-book exams, because they give a step-by-step guide for thoroughly addressing in each subject area (1) whether there are enforceable rights and (2) whether there is a cause of action. We used boldface in each chart box to assist you in quickly locating the box that addresses the particular issue you need. A list of all the flow charts is printed on p. 3.

- ■ Capsule Summary — This is an 86-page summary of intellectual property law. We've carefully crafted it to cover the main issues that are likely to be covered on the exam. It enables you to review the key points without getting bogged down in the more minor details and exceptions to the exceptions. The Capsule Summary starts on p. 59.

- ■ Exam Tips — We've compiled these Exam Tips based on dozens of actual past essay and short-answer questions asked in law school exams, focusing on the issues that surface most often in exams. The Exam Tips start on p. 145.

- ■ Short-Answer Questions — Most of these questions are actual questions asked on law school exams. We also provide sample answers (written by the professor who asked the questions). The Short-Answer Questions start on p. 163.

- ■ Essay Exam Questions — These questions are actual questions asked on law school exams. We also provide sample answers (written by the professor who asked the questions). The Essay Questions start on p. 227.

We hope you find this book helpful and instructive.

Good luck.

Margreth Barrett
Professor of Law, University of California,
Hastings College of the Law
June 2012

FLOW CHARTS

FLOW CHARTS

SUMMARY OF CONTENTS

FIGURE 1

IS THERE A CAUSE OF ACTION FOR TRADE SECRET MISAPPROPRIATION?

Use this chart to determine whether a trade secret misappropriation cause of action exists under a given fact setting.

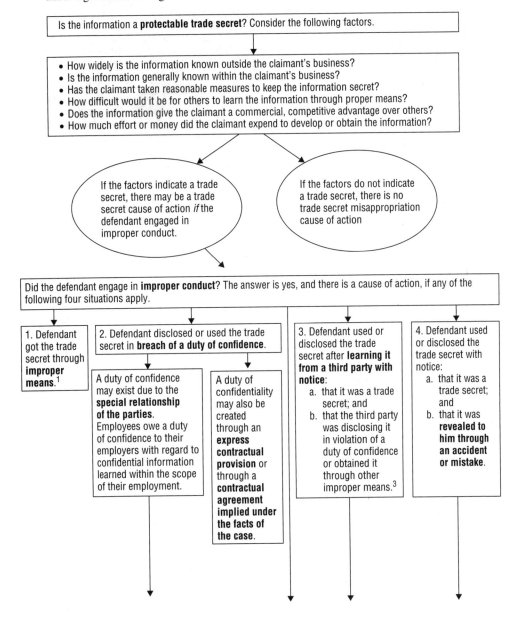

Is the information a **protectable trade secret**? Consider the following factors.

- How widely is the information known outside the claimant's business?
- Is the information generally known within the claimant's business?
- Has the claimant taken reasonable measures to keep the information secret?
- How difficult would it be for others to learn the information through proper means?
- Does the information give the claimant a commercial, competitive advantage over others?
- How much effort or money did the claimant expend to develop or obtain the information?

If the factors indicate a trade secret, there may be a trade secret cause of action *if* the defendant engaged in improper conduct.

If the factors do not indicate a trade secret, there is no trade secret misappropriation cause of action

Did the defendant engage in **improper conduct**? The answer is yes, and there is a cause of action, if any of the following four situations apply.

1. Defendant got the trade secret through **improper means**.[1]

2. Defendant disclosed or used the trade secret in **breach of a duty of confidence**.

A duty of confidence may exist due to the **special relationship of the parties**. Employees owe a duty of confidence to their employers with regard to confidential information learned within the scope of their employment.

A duty of confidentiality may also be created through an **express contractual provision** or through a **contractual agreement implied under the facts of the case**.

3. Defendant used or disclosed the trade secret after **learning it from a third party with notice**:
   a. that it was a trade secret; and
   b. that the third party was disclosing it in violation of a duty of confidence or obtained it through other improper means.[3]

4. Defendant used or disclosed the trade secret with notice:
   a. that it was a trade secret; and
   b. that it was **revealed to him through an accident or mistake**.

Chart continues on next page.

See notes after final page of chart.

FIGURE 1 *(cont.)*

IS THERE A CAUSE OF ACTION FOR TRADE SECRET MISAPPROPRIATION?

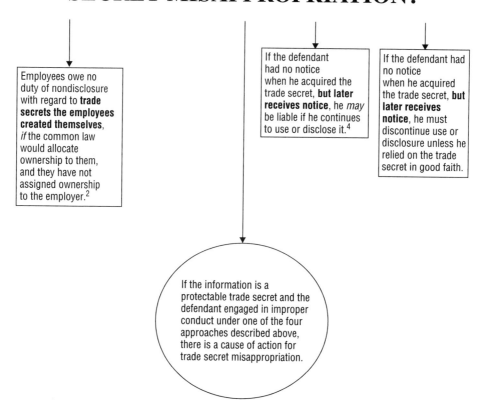

Employees owe no duty of nondisclosure with regard to **trade secrets the employees created themselves**, *if* the common law would allocate ownership to them, and they have not assigned ownership to the employer.[2]

If the defendant had no notice when he acquired the trade secret, **but later receives notice**, he *may* be liable if he continues to use or disclose it.[4]

If the defendant had no notice when he acquired the trade secret, **but later receives notice**, he must discontinue use or disclosure unless he relied on the trade secret in good faith.

If the information is a protectable trade secret and the defendant engaged in improper conduct under one of the four approaches described above, there is a cause of action for trade secret misappropriation.

NOTES TO FIGURE 1

IS THERE A CAUSE OF ACTION FOR TRADE SECRET MISAPPROPRIATION?

1 Improper means include unlawful conduct and conduct that is below reasonable standards of commercial morality.

2 If the employee was especially hired or directed to create information of the type involved, and the employer has placed time and resources at the employee's disposal for that purpose, then the resulting trade secret created by the employee generally belongs to the employer. On the other hand, if the employee was not hired or directed to create information of the type involved, but nonetheless creates the trade secret during the course of employment, the trade secret will be deemed to belong to the employee, and the employee will owe no duty of confidentiality. However, if the employee used the employer's work time, facilities, or supplies to develop the trade secret, then the employer will probably have a **shop right** in it—a nonexclusive license to use the employee's trade secret.

3 The recipient will be deemed to have the requisite **notice** if a reasonable person under similar circumstances would know or if the reasonable person would be led to make further inquiry and a reasonable inquiry would reveal the information.

4 Under the Uniform Trade Secrets Act, he is liable for continuing use or disclosure without a license. Under the Restatement of Torts §758, he is liable for continuing unless he paid value for the trade secret in good faith or changed his position in reliance on it, making it inequitable to make him discontinue use.

FIGURE 2

ANALYZING THE PATENTABILITY OF AN INVENTION

Use this chart to determine whether an invention is patentable or whether a patent that has been granted is valid. (All statutory references are to the Patent Act, 35 U.S.C. §1 *et seq.*) **This figure demonstrates the U.S. patent law that applies to applications, and patents resulting from applications, whose effective filing date is prior to March 16, 2013**. Applications and patents granted on applications filed on or after March 16, 2013, are subject to significant changes in U.S. patent law introduced by the Leahy-Smith America Invents Act. The amended patent law that will govern these later-filed applications and patents will be demonstrated in Figure 2A, *infra*.

1. The invention must fall into one of the categories of **statutory subject matter**: process, machine, article of manufacture, composition of matter, or any improvement thereof.[1]

Only **"man-made" discoveries** qualify. However, a patent may be granted for living matter that has been altered to have characteristics it would not have naturally.

Exception for tax strategies: Effective Sept.16, 2011, patent protection does not extend to "**any strategy for reducing, avoiding, or deferring tax liability,** whether known or unknown at the time of the invention or application for patent."[2]

Natural phenomena, laws of nature and abstract ideas are not themselves patentable subject matter, though a particular *application* of a law of nature or abstract idea can be patented.

To be patentable, a claimed specific application of a law of nature or abstract idea must add something significant—beyond routine, conventional actions or elements that would normally accompany any application of that law of nature or abstract idea. The claim must not "wholly preempt" use of the law of nature or abstract idea, even in a single technological environment or field of use.

Mathematical algorithms constitute abstract ideas and are not patentable by themselves. Likewise **mental processes,** by themselves, are unpatentable abstract ideas. However, one might combine use of a mathematical algorithm or mental process with additional steps to claim a patentable process, or combine them with elements of hardware to claim a machine.

Business methods can be patented as processes, if the method at issue does not constitute an abstract idea. It is useful to ask whether the claimed method is tied to a particular machine or apparatus, or transforms a particular article into a different state or thing. If not, it is likely to constitute an abstract idea. However, this "machine or transformation" test is not the sole test. One might also ask whether the claim could be stated as a mathematical algorithm, and whether the claim would wholly preempt use of such an algorithm, even in a single technological field.

2. The invention must be **novel**: On the date the patent applicant **made the invention**, there must not have been an earlier invention that **contained all the same elements** as the applicant's claimed invention, **arranged in the same way**, which falls within the terms of §102(a), (e), or (g).

Under **§102(a)**, the earlier invention will disqualify the applicant if, prior to the applicant's invention date:

1. it was known[3] or used[4] in the United States; or
2. it was patented[5] or the subject of a printed publication[6] anywhere in the world.

Under **§102(e)**, the earlier invention will disqualify the applicant if, before the applicant's invention date:

1. it was described in an application for patent that was pending in the PTO; and
2. the pending application was ultimately published and/or granted.

Under **§102(g)**, the earlier invention will disqualify the applicant if it was made in the United States prior to the applicant's invention date,[7] and was not abandoned, suppressed, or concealed at the time the applicant invented.[8]

An earlier foreign invention can also invalidate if not abandoned, suppressed, or concealed, as long as the foreign invention date is established in a patent interference proceeding.

3. The invention must not be the subject of a **statutory bar** under **§102(b), (c), or (d)**.

Chart continues on next pages.   *See notes after final page of chart.*

FIGURE 2 *(cont.)*

ANALYZING THE PATENTABILITY OF AN INVENTION

Under **§102(b)**, a patent must be denied if, more than **one year prior to the date the application was filed,** the invention was:

1. in public use[9] or on sale[10] in the United States; or
2. patented or the subject of a printed publication anywhere in the world.

Section 102(c) prohibits a patent if the applicant abandoned her invention.[11]

Section 102(d) prohibits a patent if:

1. the applicant filed a patent application in a foreign country more than 12 months before he filed his U.S. application; and
2. the foreign patent was granted before the U.S. filing date.

A public use or sale that is made for the purpose of testing the operability of claimed aspects of the invention (not for the purpose of testing the market) is deemed an **experimental use** or **experimental sale** and will not trigger the **§102(b)** statutory bar.

4. The applicant must be the **inventor.**[12]

5. The invention must be **non-obvious**. That is, **at the time the invention was made**, it must not have been obvious to a person of ordinary skill in the pertinent art who has knowledge of all the pertinent prior art.

To make this legal determination, one must ascertain:

1. the scope and content of the prior art;
2. the differences between the pertinent prior art and the invention; and
3. the ordinary level of skill in the pertinent art.

A court may also consider **objective factors** as **circumstantial evidence** of obviousness:

1. the commercial success of the invention;
2. how long the need for the invention was felt;
3. others' acquiescence to the patent;
4. movement of persons skilled in the art in a different direction;
5. the existence of skepticism on the part of experts regarding the approach taken by the inventor; and
6. the fact that others copied the invention, rather than existing alternatives.

Once an otherwise patentable invention becomes obvious (because of the disclosure of new pertinent art), the **application to patent it must be filed within one year**, or the right to a patent will be lost. The new art must fall within the terms of §102(b).[14]

The **prior art** consists of prior inventions that fall within the terms of §102(a), (e), (f), and (g).[13]

Prior art is **pertinent** if it is in the same field of endeavor as the invention, regardless of the problem to be solved, or if it is reasonably related to the particular problem with which the inventor was concerned.

While lack of novelty can only be demonstrated through a single prior-art reference that includes all the elements of the invention in the same arrangement, obviousness can be **demonstrated by combining two or more prior-art references**, if it would be obvious to combine them.

FIGURE **2** *(cont.)*

ANALYZING THE PATENTABILITY OF AN INVENTION

6. The invention must be **useful**. An invention will have the requisite usefulness (or "utility") if there is a current, significant, beneficial use for the invention or, in the case of a process, the product of the process.

Included in the usefulness requirement is the requirement that the invention be **operable**—that is, that it operate as claimed in the application.

7. The invention must be **fully disclosed**, as provided in **§112**. The disclosure requirement consists of four parts: the "claiming" requirement, the "enablement" requirement, the "best mode" requirement, and the "written description" requirement.

Claiming: The patent must include one or more claims that clearly and distinctly describe the invention, setting forth its constituent elements. The **claims are the official definition of the invention** and establish the "metes and bounds" of the patent monopoly.

Enablement: The patent specification must describe how to make and use the invention with sufficient clarity, precision, and detail to **enable a person skilled in the relevant art to make and use the invention** without undue experimentation.

Best mode: The patent specification must set forth the **best mode that the applicant contemplates for carrying out his invention** as of the application filing date.[15]

Written description: The application must demonstrate that the applicant had possession of the invention, as ultimately claimed, at the time he filed the application.

If all of the seven requirements above are satisfied, the invention is patentable (or if a patent has already issued, it is valid).

NOTES TO FIGURE 2

ANALYZING THE PATENTABILITY OF AN INVENTION

[1] This is the subject matter of utility patents. **Design patents** protect the ornamental design of an article of manufacture. An "article of manufacture" includes most tangible objects that are man-made. The design patent protects the article's appearance, but not its operation. The design is only protectable if at some point in the life of the article its appearance is a matter of concern. **Plant patents** are available to persons who discover a distinct and new variety of plant and asexually reproduce it. Cultivated sports, mutants, hybrids, and newly found seedlings may qualify for a plant patent (once asexually reproduced).
Most aspects of design and plant patent protection are similar to those of utility patent protection. However, there are some important deviations. **This figure does not undertake to demonstrate those differences.**

[2] Pub. L. No. 112-29 §14(a), 125 Stat. 327 (2011). Subsection (b) defines tax liability as "any liability for a tax under any Federal, State, or local law, or the law of any foreign jurisdiction."

[3] The earlier invention was **known** if it was (1) reduced to actual or constructive practice and (2) accessible to the public.
Actual reduction to practice entails building an operable prototype (or, in the case of a process, carrying out the physical steps of the process) as described in the applicant's patent claims, and ascertaining that the invention works for its intended purpose. **Constructive reduction to practice** entails creating and filing an application for patent. In the Patent Act §102(a) context, courts have held that, in addition to reducing the invention to practice, as defined above, the earlier inventor may satisfy the disclosure requirement by creating a writing, other than a patent application, that describes the invention in sufficient detail to enable a person with ordinary skill in the art to make it without undue experimentation.

[4] The earlier invention was **used** if (1) it was reduced to actual practice, (2) it was used in the manner its inventor intended, and (3) the use was accessible to the public.

[5] The earlier invention was **patented** for purposes of §102(a) if (1) it was the actual subject of the patent monopoly, (2) the patent granted rights effective prior to the applicant's invention date, and (3) the patent disclosure was available to the public before the applicant's invention date.

[6] The earlier invention was the subject of a **printed publication** for purposes of §102(a) if a description of the invention (1) was reduced to a discernible, tangible, permanent form; (2) set forth sufficient information to enable a person with ordinary skill in the art to make or practice the invention without further experimentation; and (3) was reasonably available to an interested American exercising reasonable diligence to find it.

[7] Invention involves conception and reduction to practice. In **deciding which of two inventors invented first**, it is presumed that the first inventor to reduce the invention to practice was the first to invent. However, an inventor who was first to conceive of the invention but last to reduce it to practice may rebut that presumption if she can show that she was diligent in reducing the invention to practice from a time prior to the other inventor's conception date.

[8] An earlier inventor will not **abandon, suppress, or conceal** the invention as long as she is engaged in reasonable efforts to bring the benefit of the invention to the public. She may bring the benefit to the public by introducing the invention to the market, by publishing a description of it, or by filing an application for a patent.

[9] The invention will be **in public use** if someone other than the inventor/applicant used the completed, operable invention in the manner for which it was intended, with no restriction or obligation of secrecy.

[10] The invention will be deemed **on sale** if it is (1) "ready for patenting" and (2) the subject of a "commercial offer to sell." According to the Supreme Court, an invention may be "ready for patenting" if it has been reduced to actual practice, or if the inventor has prepared drawings or other descriptions of the invention that are sufficiently specific to enable a person skilled in the art to make or practice the invention. *Pfaff v. Wells Electronics,* 525 U.S. 55 (1998). A commercial offer to sell for this purpose is an offer that satisfies the formal standards for an offer under the Uniform Commercial Code.

[11] Unlike "abandonment" for purposes of §102(g), §102(c) focuses on whether the applicant evidenced an intent to abandon her right to a patent (as opposed to an intent to abandon the invention itself).

[12] The **inventor** is the person who conceived of the specific invention claimed in the application. If more than one person makes a mental contribution to the final invention concept, then each is a joint inventor.

[13] Patent Act **§102(f)** has been construed to provide that an earlier invention or other information that was *actually revealed* to the applicant prior to his invention date may be deemed prior art in evaluating the obviousness of the applicant's later invention.

[14] To fall within the terms of **§102(b)**, the new pertinent art must be in public use or on sale in the United States, be patented, or be the subject of a printed publication anywhere in the world.

[15] The Leahy-Smith America Invents Act provides that, while applicants must disclose the best mode, failure to do so will not be a ground for invalidating an issued patent. Failure to comply with the other disclosure requirements may still be a ground for invalidating an issued patent.

FIGURE 2A

ANALYZING THE PATENTABILITY OF AN INVENTION WHEN THE EFFECTIVE FILING DATE IS ON OR AFTER MARCH 16, 2013

Use this chart to determine whether an invention is patentable or whether a patent that has been granted is valid. **This figure demonstrates the U.S. patent law that applies to applications and patents resulting from applications whose effective filing date[1] is on or after March 16, 2013,** reflecting important changes to the novelty and non-obviousness determinations made by the Leahy-Smith America Invents Act. While pre–Leahy-Smith law (reflected in Figure 2, *supra*) continues to govern all patents granted on applications effectively filed before March 16, 2013, use this chart to evaluate applications and patents with later effective filing dates. (All statutory references are to the Patent Act as amended by the Leahy-Smith America Invents Act, 35 U.S.C. §§1 *et. seq.*)

---

1. The invention must fall into one of the categories of **statutory subject matter**: process, machine, article of manufacture, composition of matter, or any improvement thereof.

Only **"man-made" discoveries** qualify. However, a patent may be granted for living matter that has been altered to have characteristics it would not have naturally.

Exceptions for tax strategies: Effective Sept. 16, 2011, patent protection does not extend to **"any strategy for reducing, avoiding, or deferring tax liability,** whether known or unknown at the time of the invention or application for patent."

Natural phenomena, laws of nature and abstract ideas are not themselves patentable subject matter, although a particular *application* of a law of nature or abstract idea can be patented.

To be patentable, a claimed specific application of a law of nature or abstract idea must add something significant—beyond routine, conventional actions or elements that would normally accompany any application of that law of nature or abstract idea. The claim must not "wholly preempt" use of the law of nature or abstract idea, even in a single technological environment or field of use.

Mathematical algorithms constitute abstract ideas and are not patentable by themselves. Likewise **mental processes,** by themselves, are unpatentable abstract ideas. However, one might combine use of a mathematical algorithm or mental process with additional steps to claim a patentable process, or combine them with elements of hardware to claim a machine.

Business methods can be patented as processes, if the method at issue does not constitute an abstract idea. It is useful to ask whether the claimed method is tied to a particular machine or apparatus, or transforms a particular article into a different state or thing. If not, it is likely to constitute an abstract idea. However, this "machine or transformation" test is not the sole test. One might also ask whether the claim could be stated as a mathematical algorithm, and whether the claim would wholly preempt use of such an algorithm, even in a single technological field.

---

2. The invention must be **novel**. On the **effective filing date of the application to patent the claimed invention,[2]** there must not have been any disclosure of an invention that **contained all the same elements** as the applicant's claimed invention, **arranged in the same way.** In order to disqualify the claimed invention for lack of novelty, the disclosure must fall within the terms of §102(a)(1) or (2) and must not be excepted from the prior art under §102(b).

Chart continues on next pages.   *See notes after final page of chart.*

FIGURE 2A *(cont.)*

ANALYZING THE PATENTABILITY OF AN INVENTION WHEN THE EFFECTIVE FILING DATE IS ON OR AFTER MARCH 16, 2013

Under **amended §102(a)(1)**, a claimed invention will be "disclosed" and disqualified for lack of novelty if that invention was *patented, described in a printed publication, in public use, or on sale anywhere in the world*,[3] or was *otherwise available to the public*[4] prior to the claimed invention's effective filing date.

Under **amended §102(a)(2)**, a claimed invention will be disqualified for lack of novelty if that invention is:
i. described in a U.S. issued patent, or in a published application for patent;
ii. the patent or published application names a different inventor; and
iii. the patent or published application was effectively filed prior to the claimed invention's effective filing date.

Exclusions: Under **amended §102(b)(1)**, disclosed subject matter will not be prior art for evaluating the novelty of the claimed invention if the disclosure occurred **one year or less** before the claimed invention's effective filing date, **and:**
i. was made *by the inventor of the claimed invention*, a joint inventor, or someone who derived the information from that inventor or joint inventor; or
ii. was made by an unrelated person, but only *after the persons listed in i, above, had already publicly disclosed the claimed invention*.[5]

Exclusions: Under **amended §102(b)(2)**, disclosures appearing in applications and patents will not be disqualifying prior art to a claimed invention under §102(a)(2) if:
i. the disclosed subject matter was *derived from* the inventor or a joint inventor of the claimed invention;
ii. prior to the effective filing date of the patent or application disclosing the subject matter, the persons in i, above, had *already disclosed* the claimed invention; or
iii. no later than the effective filing date of the claimed invention, the disclosed subject matter and the claimed invention were *owned by the same person, or subject to an obligation to assign to the same person*.[6]

3. The invention must be **non-obvious**. That is, on the claimed invention's **effective filing date**, it must not have been obvious to a person of ordinary skill in the pertinent art who has knowledge of all the pertinent prior art.

To make this legal determination one must ascertain (as of the effective filing date):
1. the scope and content of the pertinent prior art;
2. the differences between the pertinent prior art and the claimed invention; and
3. the ordinary level of skill in the pertinent art.

A court may also consider **objective factors** as circumstantial evidence of obviousness:

1. the commercial success of the invention;
2. how long the need for the invention was felt;
3. others' acquiescence to the patent;
4. movement of persons skilled in the art in a different direction;
5. the existence of skepticism on the part of experts regarding the approach taken by the inventor; and
6. the fact that others copied the invention, rather than existing alternatives.

The **prior art** consists of disclosures falling within the terms of Patent Act §102(a)(1) and (2), that do not fall within the exceptions set forth in Patent Act §102(b). These provisions of the Patent Act, as amended by the Leahy-Smith America Invents Act, are discussed above.

Prior art is **pertinent** if it is in the same field of endeavor as the invention, regardless of the problem to be solved, or if it is reasonably related to the particular problem with which the inventor was concerned.

While lack of novelty can only be demonstrated through a single prior-art reference/disclosure that includes all the elements of the invention in the same arrangement, obviousness can be demonstrated by **combining two or more prior-art references/disclosures**, if it would be obvious to combine them.

4. The invention must be **useful**. An invention will have the requisite usefulness (or "utility") if there is a current, significant, beneficial use for the invention or, in the case of a process, the product of the process.

FIGURE 2A *(cont.)*

ANALYZING THE PATENTABILITY OF AN INVENTION WHEN THE EFFECTIVE FILING DATE IS ON OR AFTER MARCH 16, 2013

Included in the usefulness requirement is the requirement that the invention be **operable**—that is, that it operate as claimed in the application.

5. The invention must be **fully disclosed**, as provided in **§112**. The disclosure requirement consists of four parts: the "*claiming*" requirement, the "*enablement*" requirement, the "*best mode*" requirement, and the "*written description*" requirement.

Claiming: The patent must include one or more claims that clearly and distinctly describe the invention, setting forth its constituent elements. The **claims are the official definition of the invention** and establish the "metes and bounds" of the patent monopoly.

Enablement: The patent specification must describe how to make and use the invention with sufficient clarity, precision, and detail to **enable a person skilled in the relevant art to make and use the invention** without undue experimentation.

Best mode: The patent specification must set forth the **best mode that the applicant contemplates for carrying out his invention** as of the application filing date.

Written description: The application must demonstrate that the applicant had possession of the invention, as ultimately claimed, at the time he filed the application.

If all of the five requirements above are satisfied, the invention is patentable (or if a patent has already issued, it is valid).

ANALYZING THE PATENTABILITY OF AN INVENTION WHEN THE EFFECTIVE FILING DATE IS ON OR AFTER MARCH 16, 2013

[1] The "effective filing date" under the Leahy-Smith America Invents Act is the actual filing date of a U.S. patent application containing a claim to the invention, unless the patent/application is entitled to an earlier filing date by virtue of international treaty provisions (see 35 U.S.C. §§119, 365) or a continuation or division of earlier-filed claims (see 35 U.S.C. §§120, 121).

[2] While the United States has traditionally given priority to the first inventor, the Leahy-Smith America Invents Act harmonizes U.S. patent law with that of other countries by adopting what is essentially a "first to file" system of priority among competing inventors, and focusing the novelty evaluation of the applicant's *filing date*, rather than her *invention date*. However, the Leahy-Smith Act retains a form of grace period (somewhat similar to that created under the pre–Leahy-Smith §102(b) statutory bar) by creating *exceptions to anticipatory prior art* in new §102(b).

[3] The issues of whether the invention was "patented," disclosed in a "printed publication" or in "public use" or "on sale" should be resolved in the same manner that they were prior to the Leahy-Smith America Invents Act. Note, however, that the amended §102(a) **imposes no geographic limitations on where a public use or on-sale event takes place**. Under pre–Leahy-Smith law, the only relevant public uses and on-sale events were those that took place in the United States. Under Leahy-Smith, any public use or on-sale event anywhere in the world can serve as prior art to defeat the novelty of the applicant's invention.

[4] The catchall phrase "or otherwise available to the public" has no counterpart in pre–Leahy-Smith §102. Presumably this phrase will give the P.T.O. and the courts some flexibility to find anticipation and reject or invalidate a patent, even if the disclosing activity at issue fails to fall within one of the earlier listed categories, as long as the activity renders the invention "available to the public" prior to the applicant's effective filing date.

[5] This exception effectively gives the inventor/applicant a year to file after disclosing the invention to the public himself, but unlike the pre–America Invents Act grace period, it does not give the inventor an opportunity to file after disclosure is made by an independent third party, **unless** the inventor/applicant has already publicly disclosed before the third party disclosure. In other words, if the inventor discloses the invention to the public under subsection 102(a) within the year preceding his application date, he is immunized from **subsequent** independent disclosures made by third parties. So, as a practical matter, priority under the Leahy-Smith America Invents Act goes to the first inventor to file an application **or** to the first inventor to publicly disclose the invention, **assuming** that the first inventor to disclose files an application within a year of his disclosure.

[6] Under amended §102(c), disclosed subject matter and the claimed invention will be deemed owned by the same person or subject to an obligation to assign to the same person if both were developed by or on behalf of a party to a joint research agreement that was in effect on or before the effective filing date of the claimed invention; the claimed invention was made within the scope of the joint research agreement; and the application for patent for the claimed invention discloses or is amended to disclose the names of the parties to the joint research agreement.

Figure 3

IS THERE A CAUSE OF ACTION FOR PATENT INFRINGEMENT?

Use this chart to determine whether a patentee has a likely cause of action for direct or indirect infringement. (All statutory references are to the Patent Act, 35 U.S.C. §1 *et seq.*)

Regardless of the theory of infringement asserted, the **alleged infringing product or process must constitute the patented invention**. This issue is resolved through construction of the patent claims and a comparison of the defendant's product or process with the express claim language.[1] To constitute the patented invention, a product or process must have an element that corresponds (is literally the same or is equivalent) to each element in the patent claim.

Literal infringement may occur if the defendant's product or process literally falls within the language of one or more of the patent claims, incorporating each of the elements set forth in the claim.[2]

Infringement may occur under the **doctrine of equivalents** if the defendant's product or process literally lacks an element set forth in the claim, but has another element that is equivalent to it. Equivalency is judged from the perspective of a person with ordinary skill in the art at the time of the infringement.[3]

The doctrine of equivalents is limited by the **doctrine of prosecution history estoppel**.[4]

When an applicant makes a narrowing amendment to claim language during prosecution to satisfy a requirement of the Patent Act,[5] he is prevented from using the doctrine of equivalents to regain the relinquished scope in a later infringement action.[6]

If the defendant's product or process constitutes the patented invention, under the test for literal infringement or under the doctrine of equivalents as described above, then consider whether the defendant can be held liable under any of the theories of liability described in §271(a)-(g).

If the alleged infringing product or process does not constitute the patented invention, because it lacks one or more of the claim elements, or an equivalent, then there can be no cause of action for patent infringement.

1. Direct infringement: Section 271(a) provides that a person who makes,[7] uses, sells, offers to sell, or imports the patented invention in the United States during the patent term without the patentee's authorization will be liable for direct infringement.[8]

FIGURE 3 *(cont.)*

IS THERE A CAUSE OF ACTION FOR PATENT INFRINGEMENT?

While the Supreme Court has stated that one cannot make an infringing **"sale"** of a product until the product is "made," the Federal Circuit has held that a contract between two U.S. companies for sale of a patented product constitutes an infringing "sale" in itself, even if the product actually delivered pursuant to the contract is altered and does not itself infringe.[9]

Under the **doctrine of exhaustion (or doctrine of first sale)**, once the patentee sells or authorizes sale of an embodiment of the patented invention in the United States, she loses the right to control subsequent resales and uses of it, absent an express, binding contractual restriction. While a process is not generally sold, sale of a product that practices a process will exhaust the patent rights in both the product and the process.[10]

An **offer to sell** the patented invention is an offer in which the sale will occur prior to the expiration of the patent term. There is some authority that the offer must also be for a sale that will take place **in the United States**, rather than abroad. Apply regular contract principles to determine whether defendant's actions constitute an "offer."

It will violate the patentee's **importation** right to import products that the U.S. patentee first sold abroad because the doctrine of exhaustion only applies to products first sold in the United States.

---

2. Indirect infringement: Even if the defendant did not directly infringe under §271(a), she may be held liable for the direct infringement of others under §271(b) or (c).

Inducement to infringe: Section 271(b) imposes liability for inducing infringement if the defendant actively and knowingly solicits or assists a third party to directly infringe, and the third party does so infringe. The defendant must know of the patent and specifically intend to encourage or assist infringement. However, willful blindness may suffice.[11]

Contributory infringement: Under **§271(c)**, a person who sells, offers to sell, or imports a **material component** of the patented invention, which has **no substantial use other than use in the patented invention**, will be liable if:

1. he knows that the component is especially made or adapted for use in the patented invention and has no other substantial use; and
2. the buyer in fact uses the component to directly infringe.

The defendant must know of the patent and know that the buyer's use is likely to constitute infringement.

---

3. Additional means of infringement: Even if a defendant's acts do not fall within the provisions of §271(a)-(c), the defendant may be liable under two more recent provisions that Congress enacted to plug perceived "loopholes" in patent protection.

Patent Act §271(f) prohibits persons in the United States from **supplying all or a substantial portion of the components** of a patented invention in a manner that induces combination of the components into the patented invention abroad.

Patent Act §271(g) prohibits persons from **importing, selling, or offering to sell products made by a U.S. patented process**, regardless of whether the patented process was employed to make the products in the United States or abroad.

FIGURE 3 *(cont.)*

IS THERE A CAUSE OF ACTION FOR PATENT INFRINGEMENT?

Subsection (f) also prohibits persons in the United States from **supplying a material component** of a U.S. patented invention that has no substantial use aside from use in the invention if:

1. they know that the component is especially adapted for use in the patented invention and has no substantial noninfringing use; and
2. they intend that the component will be combined with other components abroad in a manner that would infringe the patent if such combination occurred within the United States.[12]

There will be no liability under this section if:

1. the product has been materially changed by subsequent processes; or
2. the product has become a trivial or nonessential component of another product.

Additional exceptions and limitations are made to shelter innocent infringers, noncommercial users, and retail sellers from liability.[13]

If the defendant's actions do not fall within one of the infringement provisions described above (§271(a)-(g)), then the defendant is not liable for patent infringement.

If the defendant's actions do fall within §271(a)-(g), then he is likely to be liable for patent infringement, if none of the following special patent defenses apply.

The special patent defenses include (1) patent invalidity, (2) patent misuse, (3) inequitable conduct, (4) the experimental-use defense, and (5) the prior-use defense.

Patent invalidity	Patent misuse	Inequitable conduct	The experimental-use defense	The prior-use defense
Patent invalidity: A patent is presumed valid, but the defendant may overcome the presumption by proving with clear and convincing evidence that a condition of patentability was not satisfied and the patent should not have been granted.	**Patent misuse:** A patentee will be deemed to have misused his patent if he uses it unreasonably to extend his market power beyond what Congress intended. If the defendant is able to demonstrate patent misuse, the patentee will be denied enforcement of his patent until the misuse ceases and the patentee no longer enjoys any benefits from his prior misuse.[14]	**Inequitable conduct:** A patent will be unenforceable if the defendant proves, with clear and convincing evidence, that the patentee misrepresented or omitted material information during the application process, with the specific intent to deceive the P.T.O.[15]	**The experimental-use defense:** A person may make or use a patented invention without authorization if his purpose is only to satisfy his scientific curiosity or to amuse himself as an intellectual exercise, and he has no commercial or other practical motivation.[16]	**The prior-use defense:** §273 provides a defense to a claim that the defendant infringed a patented **business method**. The defendant must prove by clear and convincing evidence that he: 1. actually reduced the patented business method to practice, in good faith, at least one year before the effective filing date of the plaintiff's patent application; and 2. commercially used the patented business method before the effective filing date. Congress has significantly **expanded** the prior use defense in connection with **patents issued on or after September 16, 2011.**[17]

NOTES TO FIGURE 3

IS THERE A CAUSE OF ACTION FOR PATENT INFRINGEMENT?

[1] The patent claims define the scope of the invention and of the patent rights. Do not confuse the claims with the specification. The patent specification must provide sufficient information to enable a person with ordinary skill in the art to practice or make the invention and must set forth the best mode contemplated by the inventor for carrying out his invention. The specification is not intended to define the scope of the invention. However, the specification may be consulted in the course of construing the claims, for example, to find definitions of terms used in a claim. **The court construes the patent claims in a "Markman" hearing.** After the court construes the claims, the finder of fact determines whether the defendant's product or process falls within the scope of any of those claims, as construed.
The standards and means for evaluating infringement of design and plant patents differ from those relevant to utility patent infringement and are not covered in this chart.

[2] The fact that the defendant's product or process contains **additional elements** not included in the claim will not prevent a finding of infringement unless the additional elements so drastically change the defendant's product or process that the doctrine of reverse equivalents applies.

[3] The standard for equivalency is either (1) whether the defendant's differing element performs substantially the same function in substantially the same way to obtain the same result as the element in the patent claim or (2) whether the difference between the elements is "insubstantial." Important considerations in determining whether elements are equivalent include:

- whether persons reasonably skilled in the art would have known that the differing elements were interchangeable at the time of the infringement;
- whether finding the defendant's element equivalent would give the patentee rights that he would not have been able to obtain through broader claim language; and
- how great a departure the patentee's invention is from the prior art.

[4] The doctrine of prosecution history estoppel (also called "file wrapper estoppel") requires that the scope of the patent claims be interpreted in light of what happened in the application process in the P.T.O. If the applicant took a position with regard to the scope of coverage of the claims, he or she will not be allowed in a later infringement action to take an inconsistent position. The doctrine of prosecution history estoppel thus limits the doctrine of equivalents, and allows competitors to rely on the record generated in the course of a patent's prosecution to construe the patent's scope.

[5] When the purpose of the amendment is not clear, it will be presumed to have been made to satisfy a statutory requirement, unless the applicant can prove otherwise.

[6] When a narrowing claim amendment is made in order to satisfy the statutory requirements for patentability, it will be **presumed that all equivalence arguments are barred** as to the narrowed claim element. However, the patentee may **rebut that presumption** by showing that:

- the equivalent was unforeseeable at the time the narrowing amendment was made;
- the rationale underlying the amendment bears no more than a tangential relation to the equivalent in question; or
- there is some other reason suggesting that the patentee could not reasonably be expected to have described the insubstantial substitute in question in the amended claim language.

[7] In the case of combination patents, the defendant will only "make" the patented invention if he makes an operable assembly of all the claimed components.
Reconstruction of a patented product constitutes an infringing "making," but repair does not. Generally reconstruction occurs only when the product as a whole is spent, and the owner essentially makes a whole new one.

[8] The patent term is measured from the application date, even though patent rights do not commence until the patent is granted (or published—patentees have "provisional rights" during the time between publication of the application (generally 18 months after application) and issuance of the patent, 35 U.S.C. §154(d)). Thus, the term lasts 20 years from the application date, although the patentee may actually enjoy rights for only 17 or so years of the term.

[9] See *Deepsouth Packing Co., Inc. v. Laitram Corp.*, 406 U.S. 518 (1972); *Transocean Offshore Deepwater Drilling, Inc. v. Maersk Contractors U.S.A., Inc.*, 617 F.3d 1296 (Fed. Cir. 2010). In *Transocean*, two U.S. companies made the contract to sell outside the United States, but performance and delivery of the contract were to take place in the United States. The Federal Circuit held that the sale could be understood to have taken place in the United States.

[10] Even when the sold product has to be combined with other components in order to perform the patented process, its sale may exhaust the patentee's rights in the process if (1) the product's only reasonable and intended use is to practice the patented process, and (2) the product embodies the essential features of the patented process. (That is, the omitted components of the process are standard, generic, or fungible.) *Quanta Computer, Inc. v. LG Electronics, Inc.*, 533 U.S. 617 (2008).

[11] A defendant is "willfully blind" if he (1) subjectively believes that there is a high probability that the induced acts constitute infringement, and (2) takes deliberate actions to avoid learning of that fact. Put another way, to be willfully blind, the defendant must take deliberate actions to avoid confirming a high probability of wrongdoing. *Global-Tech Appliances, Inc. v. SEB S.A.*, 131 S. Ct. 2060 (2011).

[12] The Supreme Court has held that the §271(f) provisions should be construed strictly, since they entail extraterritorial application of U.S. law. Thus, supplying software on master disks to overseas computer manufacturers, who then made individual copies of the software to install on the computers they manufactured and sold, did not infringe subsection (f). The Court held that the defendant must supply the individual copies of the software from the United States to be liable. *Microsoft Corp. v. AT&T Corp.*, 550 U.S. 437 (2007).

[13] Congress recognized that it may be difficult for retailers and others to avoid infringing §271(g) because it is often hard to ascertain whether products were made by patented processes. To avoid inequitable results, Congress channeled infringement claims toward persons practicing the patented process and those controlling them and toward persons having prior knowledge of infringement. **Patent Act §287(b)** limits remedies against innocent infringers and allows them to sell off or use any inventory that they accumulated prior to notice that the inventory infringes. **Section 271(g)** also withholds a remedy against noncommercial users or retail sellers unless no remedy is available against importers or commercial users or sellers.

[14] A patentee who commits a violation of the antitrust laws through use of the patent generally will be subject to the misuse defense. However, the misuse defense is not expressly limited to antitrust violations.

Patent Act §271(d) provides that it will **not** be patent misuse for a patentee to:

     a. derive revenue from acts that would constitute contributory infringement if performed by others without a license;

     b. license others to perform acts that if done without a license would constitute contributory infringement;

     c. seek to enforce his rights against infringement or contributory infringement; or

     d. refuse to license or use any rights in the patent.

[15] In *Therasense, Inc. v. Becton, Dickinson & Co.*, 649 F.3d 1276 (Fed. Cir. 2011), the Federal Circuit clarified that in a case involving non-disclosure of information, clear and convincing evidence must show that the applicant made a deliberate decision to withhold a known material reference—that is, the accused infringer must prove by clear and convincing evidence that the applicant knew of the reference, knew that it was material, and made a deliberate decision to withhold it. The materiality required to establish inequitable conduct is "but for" materiality. Non-disclosed material is "but for" material if the P.T.O. would not have allowed a claim had it been aware of the undisclosed prior art. There is an exception to the "but for" materiality requirement when the patentee has engaged in "affirmative acts of egregious misconduct," such as filing an unmistakably false affidavit.

[16] Developers of drugs and veterinary biological products must perform numerous tests of their products' safety and efficacy and submit the results of these tests to the Food and Drug Administration (FDA) or other regulatory agencies in order to obtain approval to put them on the market. Particularly in the case of generic drugs, the developers may need to make or use drugs that are still under patent to perform their tests and generate the necessary data to be ready to enter the market once the patent expires. The Court of Appeals for the Federal Circuit has ruled that such making and use does not qualify for an "experimental use" defense, because the developers using the patented drugs in their experiments have a commercial motivation. Congress enacted Patent Act §271(e) in response to the Federal Circuit's ruling. Subsection (e) permits persons, under limited circumstances, to make, use, sell, offer to sell, or import certain patented inventions in the course of developing information to submit to federal agencies regulating the manufacture, use, or sale of drugs or veterinary biological products.

[17] The Leahy-Smith America Invents Act, which moves the United States to a "first-to-file" priority system, creates a **broader "prior commercial user" defense** against **patents issued on or after September 16, 2011**, making the defense available against patents for processes, machines, articles of manufacture, and compositions of matter used in manufacturing or other commercial processes. This expanded defense is available when a defendant proves by clear and convincing evidence that it commercially used the subject matter of the patent in the United States in good faith at least a year before the earlier of two dates: (1) the effective filing date of the patent claims, or (2) the date on which the claimed invention was disclosed to the public in a manner that qualified for the exception from prior art under Patent Act §102(b), as amended.

FIGURE 4

ANALYZING COPYRIGHTABILITY

Use this chart to consider whether material is copyrightable subject matter and the scope of the copyright protection. (All statutory references are to the Copyright Act, 17 U.S.C. §101 *et seq.*)

The subject matter of copyright: Copyright extends to "**original works of authorship fixed in any tangible medium of expression**, now known or later developed, from which they can be perceived, reproduced, or otherwise communicated, either directly or with the aid of a machine or device." §102(a). Thus, to be protected, material must constitute a "work of authorship" that is "original" and "fixed."

---

1. The work must be a "work of authorship." "Works of authorship" include (1) literary works;[1] (2) musical works;[2] (3) dramatic works; (4) pantomimes and choreographic works; (5) pictorial, graphic, and sculptural works;[3] (6) motion pictures and other audiovisual works;[4] (7) sound recordings;[5] and (8) architectural works.[6] Derivative works[7] and compilations[8] can constitute protectable works of authorship.

Copyright does not extend to **works of the U.S. government**.[9] The Copyright Act **does not prohibit state and local government entities from claiming copyright** in works of authorship created by their officials or employees. However, case law indicates that judicial opinions, statutes, city ordinances, and other state and local laws and regulations with the force and effect of law must be accessible to the public because of **due process considerations**.

---

2. The work must be "original." For a work of authorship to be "original:" (1) the author must have engaged in some intellectual exercise of her own, as opposed to copying from a preexisting source; and (2) the author's work must demonstrate at least minimal creativity.

***De minimis* works**, such as words, short phrases, and slogans, are not protected.	When the alleged copyrightable expression consists of selection and arrangement of preexisting elements, the selection-and-arrangement judgment must be more than merely rote, "obvious," or "expected." Even when this minimum threshold of creativity is demonstrated, if the work's overall level of originality is low, **courts may treat the copyright as "thin,"** meaning that only a "bodily appropriation of protected expression" or "virtual identicality" will infringe.	In the case of **derivative works**, the derivative-work author's expression **must constitute a substantial, not merely trivial, variation** from the preexisting work.	Because **facts** are "discovered" rather than "created," they are **not proper subject matter for copyright**. Only the author's original means of expressing the facts can be copyrighted.

Chart continues on next pages.   *See notes after final page of chart.*

FIGURE **4** *(cont.)*

ANALYZING COPYRIGHTABILITY

3. The original work of authorship must be "fixed." A work is fixed in a tangible medium of expression "when its embodiment in a copy or phonorecord, by or under the authority of the author, is sufficiently permanent or stable to permit it to be perceived, reproduced, or otherwise communicated for a period of more than transitory duration." §101.[10]

Temporary copies: Bringing a work of authorship into the **random-access memory** (RAM) of a computer for more than a very brief time may "fix" the work, because it allows the work to be "perceived, reproduced, or otherwise communicated" for a period of more than transitory duration.[11]

Even though federal copyright protection does not extend to **unfixed works**, states may provide **common-law copyright** protection for unfixed works.[12]

If the work falls within one of the enumerated categories of copyrightable subject matter and is original and fixed, as described in boxes 1-3 above, it qualifies for federal copyright protection unless there are notice problems.

If the work fails to satisfy one or more of the requirements discussed in boxes 1-3 above, it does not qualify for federal copyright protection.

Proper notice of copyright: Prior to March 1, 1989, all published copies of a work had to bear proper notice of federal copyright protection.[13] If authorized copies were published without this notice, the work lost any copyright protection that it otherwise might have enjoyed. This notice requirement was eliminated effective March 1, 1989, but the amendment making this change was **not retroactive** in effect. Thus, if there was an authorized publication of any copies of a *domestic* work[14] without proper notice prior to March 1, 1989, the work may be unprotected today.[15]

Notice requirements prior to the Copyright Act of 1976: Prior to January 1, 1978, almost all publications of copies without notice would result in a **forfeiture of copyright**.

Notice requirements between commencement of the 1976 Act and March 1, 1989: Effective January 1, 1978, the Copyright Act of 1976 provided some **savings provisions** that, if satisfied, would prevent a forfeiture of copyright for those copies published without notice between January 1, 1978, and March 1, 1989.[16]

FIGURE 4 *(cont.)*

ANALYZING COPYRIGHTABILITY

Even assuming that the work otherwise qualifies for copyright, if it is a domestic work and authorized copies were published without proper notice, there probably is no copyright today, unless the publication occurred (1) after March 1, 1989, or (2) between January 1, 1978, and March 1, 1989, and one of the savings provisions described above applies.

Assuming that there are no notice problems and that the work otherwise qualifies for copyright, consider whether the original elements in the work are excluded from protection under the **idea/ expression dichotomy** or because they are **functional**.

Unprotectable elements: Even if the work of authorship qualifies for copyright protection, the **copyright will only extend to the author's original expression**. The copyright owner obtains no rights in material that is copied from other sources or that constitutes *scènes à faire*.[17] Moreover, §102(b) specifies that the copyright will not extend to "any idea, procedure, process, system, method of operation, concept, principle, or discovery" contained in a work of authorship, regardless of how it is expressed or explained. This is known as the "idea/expression dichotomy."

The **idea/expression dichotomy**:

1. squares copyright protection with the First Amendment;
2. ensures that the basic building blocks of expression remain available to future authors; and
3. draws a line between the subject matter of patent law and the subject matter of copyright law.

The **merger doctrine** provides that, whenever there is only one or a very limited number of ways to express a particular idea, the expression "merges" with the underlying idea and is not protected.

Courts frequently use the **abstractions test** to distinguish the unprotectable ideas underlying a work from the author's copyrightable expression of those ideas.[18]

In the software context, courts have adopted an "abstraction" exercise as part of a three-step process for identifying the protectable elements in a computer **program's structure**. First, the structure is abstracted. Then, at each level of abstraction, the following unprotectable elements are filtered out: (1) elements that constitute an idea or that merge with the idea, (2) elements required by factors external to the program itself, and (3) elements taken from the public domain. After these elements are filtered out, whatever remains is protectable expression.

Circuits have disagreed about whether to protect **expression that is part of a process, system, or method of operation**. The First Circuit has held that such expression is unprotectable,[19] while the Tenth Circuit has held that it can be protected.[20]

Figure 4 *(cont.)*

ANALYZING COPYRIGHTABILITY

Functionality: Copyright law also prohibits protection for the **designs of useful articles**[21] unless the design elements are either **physically or conceptually separable**[22] from the utilitarian function of the useful article.

Even though two-dimensional plans or drawings of useful articles are protected as "graphic works," it will **not infringe the graphic work copyright to build the useful article that the graphic work depicts.** This rule ensures that functional designs of useful articles are evaluated under the standards of patent law, rather than copyright law.

Architectural works created prior to the effective date of the AWCPA (December 1, 1990)[23] are treated under the rules regarding useful articles and technical plans, described above.

Architectural works created after December 1, 1990, are treated as a separate category of copyrightable subject matter, protectable in both their two-dimensional and three-dimensional forms. It may infringe the architectural work copyright to build a building from plans, to copy the building directly, or to copy the plans. While architectural works are not subject to the physical or conceptual separability requirement, Congress specified that architectural **design elements that are dictated by functional considerations** should not be protected.

If the work is not within the subject matter of copyright; lacks originality, is not fixed, was the subject of a disqualifying publication without proper notice; or if the copied elements constitute only *scènes à faire*, ideas, procedures, processes, systems, methods of operation, concepts, principles, or discoveries, or merge with idea(or, in the case of useful articles or architectural works, are inseparable from function or dictated by function), then there is no copyright protection.

If the work is within the subject matter of copyright, is original and fixed, and was not the subject of a disqualifying publication without notice prior to March 1, 1989; and if the copied elements do not constitute *scènes à faire*, ideas, procedures, processes, systems, methods of operation, concepts, principles, or discoveries, or merge with idea (or, in the case of useful articles or architectural works, are separable or not dictated by function), then there is copyright protection.

NOTES TO FIGURE 4

ANALYZING COPYRIGHTABILITY

[1] Copyright Act §101 provides that "**literary works**" are "works, other than audiovisual works, expressed in words, numbers, or other verbal or numerical symbols or indicia, regardless of the nature of the material objects, such as books, periodicals, manuscripts, phonorecords, film, tapes, disks, or cards, in which they are embodied."

[2] **Musical works** consist both of the musical composition and any accompanying words. Note that a musical work is a work of authorship separate and apart from any sound recordings that may be made of it, and is protectable in both its written (sheet music) and recorded forms.

[3] Copyright Act §101 provides:

> **[P]ictorial, graphic, and sculptural works** include two-dimensional and three-dimensional works of fine, graphic, and applied art, photographs, prints and art reproductions, maps, globes, charts, diagrams, models, and technical drawings, including architectural plans. Such works shall include works of artistic craftsmanship insofar as their form but not their mechanical or utilitarian aspects are concerned; the design of a useful article, as defined in this section, shall be considered a pictorial, graphic, or sculptural work only if, and only to the extent that, such design incorporates pictorial, graphic, or sculptural features that can be identified separately from, and are capable of existing independently of, the utilitarian aspects of the article.

[4] Copyright Act §101 provides that "**audiovisual works**" are "works that consist of a series of related images which are intrinsically intended to be shown by the use of machines or devices, such as projectors, viewers, or electronic equipment, together with accompanying sounds, if any, regardless of the nature of the material objects, such as films or tapes, in which the works are embodied."

[5] Copyright Act §101 provides that "**sound recordings**" are "works that result from the fixation of a series of musical, spoken, or other sounds, but not including the sounds accompanying a motion picture or other audiovisual work, regardless of the nature of the material objects, such as disks, tapes, or other phonorecords, in which they are embodied." It is important to note that the copyright in a sound recording is separate and independent from any copyright in the recorded material (e.g., the recorded literary or musical work).

[6] Copyright Act §101 provides that "an '**architectural work**' is the design of a building as embodied in any tangible medium of expression, including a building, architectural plans, or drawings. The work includes the overall form as well as the arrangement and composition of spaces and elements in the design, but does not include individual standard features."

[7] Section 101 defines a "derivative work" as follows:

> A "derivative work" is a work based upon one or more preexisting works, such as a translation, musical arrangement, dramatization, fictionalization, motion picture version, sound recording, art reproduction, abridgment, condensation, or any other form in which a work may be recast, transformed, or adapted.

Section 103 provides that the copyright in a derivative work "extends only to the material contributed by the author of such work, as distinguished from the preexisting material employed in the work, and does not imply any exclusive right in the preexisting material. The copyright in such work is independent of, and does not affect or enlarge the scope, duration, ownership, or subsistence of, any copyright protection in the preexisting material."

[8] Section 101 defines a "compilation" as:

> a work formed by the collection and assembling of preexisting materials or of data that are selected, coordinated, or arranged in such a way that the resulting work as a whole constitutes an original work of authorship. The term "compilation" includes collective works.

As in the case of derivative works, §103 limits copyright protection to the expression contributed by the compilation author, which generally will consist of selection and arrangement judgment and any introductory or explanatory material.

[9] U.S. government works are works "prepared by an officer or employee of the U.S. government as part of that person's official duties." Copyright Act §101. Government agencies that arrange for **independent contractors** to create works for the U.S. government may require the independent contractors to waive their right to copyright in some cases, when it is in the public's interest that they do so.

[10] Under the 1976 Act, all copyrightable works of authorship are fixed either in copies or in phonorecords. Phonorecords are "material objects in which sounds, other than those accompanying a motion picture or other audiovisual work, are fixed." Copyright Act §101. All other material objects in which works of authorship are fixed are copies. Section 101 defines "copies" as:

> Material objects, other than phonorecords, in which a work is fixed by any method now known or later developed, and from which the work can be perceived, reproduced, or otherwise communicated, either directly or with the aid of a machine or device. The term "copies" includes the material object, other than a phonorecord, in which the work is first fixed.

[11] Some courts have hesitated to apply the RAM copying rule strictly in the case of Internet service providers, whose computers and related equipment automatically make RAM or other temporary duplicates of digital works posted or transmitted on their systems by Internet users. For example, the Fourth Circuit has held that whether a RAM or similar temporary duplicate is "of more than a transitory duration" (and thus is "fixed" and a potentially infringing copy) should be judged on both a quantitative and a qualitative basis. If the temporary RAM duplicate *serves* the ISP or other computer owner's purposes, it should be deemed to be

"of more than transitory duration" and thus a potentially infringing "copy." On the other hand, if the RAM duplication does not serve the ISP or other computer owner's purposes (and the ISP or computer owner is indifferent as to its content), then it is not of more than transitory duration and thus does not constitute a reproduction. *CoStar Group, Inc. v. LoopNet, Inc.*, 373 F.3d 544 (4th Cir. 2004).

[12] Under the Copyright Act of 1909, state common-law copyright protected works, fixed or unfixed, prior to their publication. Upon publication, the state common-law copyright ended. If proper notice was included on each published copy, federal statutory copyright commenced. If proper notice was omitted, the work fell into the public domain. The Copyright Act of 1976 consolidated copyright for all *fixed* works under federal law, and preempted state common-law copyright protection except for unfixed works.

[13] Proper notice consists of an indication of copyright—generally ©—accompanied by the name of the copyright owner and the date of first publication. Under the Copyright Act of 1909, federal copyright generally commenced upon publication with proper notice. While the Copyright Act of 1976 provided that copyright would commence upon fixation, rather than publication, it still required that all published copies and phonorecords of a work bear proper notice of copyright, and provided that failure to provide the notice could result in a forfeiture of copyright in the work.

[14] **Domestic works** (those whose country of origin is the United States) whose copyright was lost because of publication without proper notice prior to March 1, 1989, remain uncopyrighted. **Foreign works** whose copyright was lost because of publication without proper notice **may have their copyrights restored** under the conditions set forth in Copyright Act §104A. (A work's country of origin is the United States if it was first published in the United States, was simultaneously published in the United States and another country, or, in the case of unpublished works, was created entirely by U.S. authors.)

Publication does not occur simply because the work has been made public or commercially exploited. As a general matter, publication requires physically distributing tangible copies of the work to members of the public. Courts have sometimes distinguished between "investive" and "divestive" publications. In the case of divestive publications (publications that divest the author of common-law copyright), they distinguish and overlook a "limited publication"—a distribution of copies to a selected group of people for a limited purpose.

[15] There are other formalities that U.S. law may impose on copyright owners. The owner of copyright or the publication rights in a published work must **deposit** two copies or phonorecords of the best edition of the work with the Copyright Office within three months of publication. Failing to comply with the deposit requirement is punishable by fine, but not by forfeiture of copyright. In addition, in the case of domestic works, the owner of copyright must **register** her copyright, or show that she attempted to register and was refused, before she can bring suit for infringement.

[16] These savings provisions apply if:

a. only a relatively small number of copies or phonorecords was distributed to the public without notice;

b. the work was registered with the Copyright Office within five years of the public distribution without notice, and the owner made reasonable efforts to add notice to all of the copies distributed to the public in the United States after the omission was discovered; or

c. notice was omitted in violation of an express, written agreement conditioning authorization to publish on provision of notice.

Copyright Act §405.

[17] *Scènes à faire* are incidents, characters, settings, or other elements of the work that are indispensable, or at least standard, in the treatment of the work's topic. They are basic building blocks of expression and must remain in the public domain for other authors to use.

[18] Under the abstractions test, the work should first be described in full detail and then repeatedly restated, omitting more of the detail with each restatement, until the final restatement constitutes only a very broad, general description of the work. The court must then determine the proper point in the progression of restatements at which to draw the line between the idea and the protectable expression (which consists of the details the author chose to express the general idea), keeping in mind the purposes of the prohibition against copyright protection for ideas.

[19] In *Lotus Development Corp. v. Borland International, Inc.*, 49 F.3d 807 (1st Cir. 1995), *aff'd*, 516 U.S. 233 (1996), the First Circuit held that the menu command hierarchy of a computer program constituted a method of operation (a method of operating the computer program) and that any expressive elements contained within the method of operation (in that case, selection and arrangement of menu command terms) was unprotectable. The court reasoned that once the menu command hierarchy was found to constitute a method of operation, it would be inappropriate to apply an abstraction/filtration analysis to determine whether it contained any copyrightable expression.

[20] The Tenth Circuit expressly disagreed with the *Lotus* reasoning, holding that while something may constitute a system or process or method of operation on one (more general) level of abstraction, expressive elements found on a lower (more detailed) level of abstraction can be protected. *Mitel, Inc. v. Iqtel, Inc.*, 124 F.3d 1366 (10th Cir. 1997).

[21] A **useful article** is "an article having an intrinsic utilitarian function that is not merely to portray the appearance of the article or to convey information." Copyright Act §101.

[22] **Physical separability** exists if the pictorial, graphic, or sculptural element of the useful article could be physically separated from the useful article and still be recognizable as a pictorial, graphic, or sculptural work. **The leading approach for determining conceptual separability** (from the Second Circuit) focuses on the design process. If the design features were significantly influenced by utilitarian considerations, then the features are "inextricably intertwined" with the utilitarian function of the useful article and are not conceptually separable. If the design features were not significantly influenced by the utilitarian function of the article, but reflect purely aesthetic choices, then the design features are conceptually separable.

[23] This is the Architectural Works Copyright Protection Act, which became effective December 1, 1990.

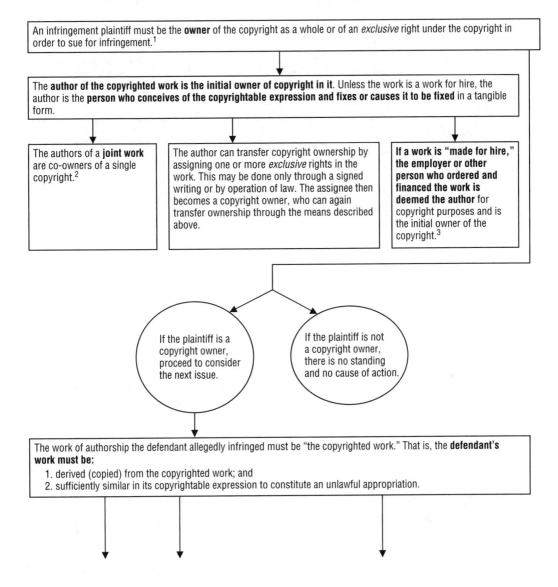

FIGURE 5

IS THERE A CAUSE OF ACTION FOR COPYRIGHT INFRINGEMENT?

An infringement plaintiff must be the **owner** of the copyright as a whole or of an *exclusive* right under the copyright in order to sue for infringement.[1]

The **author of the copyrighted work is the initial owner of copyright in it**. Unless the work is a work for hire, the author is the **person who conceives of the copyrightable expression and fixes or causes it to be fixed** in a tangible form.

The authors of a **joint work** are co-owners of a single copyright.[2]

The author can transfer copyright ownership by assigning one or more *exclusive* rights in the work. This may be done only through a signed writing or by operation of law. The assignee then becomes a copyright owner, who can again transfer ownership through the means described above.

If a work is "made for hire," the employer or other person who ordered and financed the work is deemed the author for copyright purposes and is the initial owner of the copyright.[3]

If the plaintiff is a copyright owner, proceed to consider the next issue.

If the plaintiff is not a copyright owner, there is no standing and no cause of action.

The work of authorship the defendant allegedly infringed must be "the copyrighted work." That is, the **defendant's work must be:**

1. derived (copied) from the copyrighted work; and
2. sufficiently similar in its copyrightable expression to constitute an unlawful appropriation.

Chart continues on next pages.

See notes after final page of chart.

FIGURE 5 *(cont.)*

IS THERE A CAUSE OF ACTION FOR COPYRIGHT INFRINGEMENT?

There are three ways to demonstrate that the **defendant copied:**

1. direct evidence (e.g., eyewitnesses or a defendant's admission);
2. circumstantial evidence that the defendant had access to the work and the defendant's work is substantially similar to the plaintiff's;[4] and
3. circumstantial evidence that the defendant's work is strikingly similar to the plaintiff's.

A finding of **unlawful appropriation** generally turns on whether the defendant's work is **substantially similar to the copyrightable expression in the plaintiff's work**. This evaluation is made from the overall subjective standpoint of an average member of the intended audience for the copyrighted work, considering both works as a whole.

Similarities in uncopyrighted elements cannot support a finding of unlawful appropriation/substantial similarity, but similarities in the selection and arrangement of uncopyrightable elements can. Because the finder of fact must consider similarities of selection and arrangement, or the overall "look and feel" of the works,[5] both works are usually considered as a whole, **without dissection**. However, there are exceptions.

The Ninth Circuit and a few other courts have adopted an **extrinsic/intrinsic** test to determine infringement, which combines both an objective and a subjective evaluation of similarities in expression.[6]

When a plaintiff's copyrighted work contains a **large proportion of uncopyrightable elements**, courts sometimes change their method of evaluation:

1. In the case of **nonliteral software infringement claims**, in particular, courts have applied the highly analytical **abstraction-filtration-comparison test**.[7]
2. The Second Circuit applies a **"more discerning" test** in other cases of works with a high proportion of uncopyrightable elements.[8]
3. In cases of "thin copyright," usually involving factual or highly utilitarian works, or works in which the expression consists mostly of selection and arrangement of uncopyrightable elements, the courts sometimes raise the standard for infringement from "substantial similarity" to "virtual identicality" or "bodily appropriation of copyrightable expression."

If the defendant's work was **not derived** (copied) from the plaintiff's or **does not constitute an unlawful appropriation** because the works are not sufficiently similar, then there is no infringement.

If the defendant's work was **derived** from the plaintiff's and **constitutes an unlawful appropriation**, then the next step is to determine whether the defendant has infringed any of the copyright owner's **exclusive economic or moral rights**, which are separately listed and discussed below.

FIGURE 5 *(cont.)*

IS THERE A CAUSE OF ACTION FOR COPYRIGHT INFRINGEMENT?

1. The exclusive right to reproduce the work is the right to make material copies or phonorecords of it. To infringe, the defendant must have fixed the work in a material object in a manner that is "sufficiently permanent or stable to permit it to be perceived, reproduced, or otherwise communicated for a period of more than transitory duration." §101.

Loading, downloading, or typing a work in the **random-access memory** (RAM) of a computer constitutes potentially infringing "reproduction" as long as the work is fixed sufficiently to constitute a "copy" (see Figure 4).	While imitating the copyright owner's expression is sufficient to infringe the reproduction right in most cases, §114 provides that **sound recordings** are only "reproduced" by mechanical reproduction of the actual sounds fixed in the plaintiff's copyrighted recording.	There are **numerous exceptions to the reproduction right**, which authorize various members of the public to make specific, narrowly defined types of reproductions without the copyright owner's authorization. Some of the more important ones are listed in note 9.

2. The exclusive right to make derivative works (This right is also known as the "adaptation" right.) Section 101 defines a "derivative work" as "a work based upon one or more preexisting works, such as a translation, musical arrangement, dramatization, fictionalization, motion picture version, sound recording, art reproduction, abridgment, condensation, or any other form in which a work may be recast, transformed, or adapted."

Some (but not all) courts have suggested that to constitute an infringing adaptation, the defendant's alleged derivative work must constitute a "**substantial variation**" from the plaintiff's copyrighted work.	Courts often consider the **potential economic impact** of the defendant's acts on potential markets for the plaintiff's work in deciding whether the defendant has infringed the adaptation right.	The right to adapt a **sound recording** is only infringed if the defendant mechanically recaptures sounds from a copy or phonorecord of the copyrighted sound recording and alters or mixes them with other sounds.	**Statutory exceptions** permit certain unauthorized adaptations of a copyrighted work. Some of them are listed in note 10.

The Ninth Circuit has held that even though one need not reproduce a copyrighted work in order to infringe the adaptation right, the defendant's work must **incorporate the copyrighted work in a concrete or permanent form**.

Figure 5 *(cont.)*

IS THERE A CAUSE OF ACTION FOR COPYRIGHT INFRINGEMENT?

3. The exclusive right to distribute copies or phonorecords of the work to the public by sale or other transfer of ownership, or by rental, lease, or lending: Traditionally, to violate this right, one must **physically transfer** a copy or phonorecord of the work to a member of the public without authorization. Section 602 provides that unauthorized **importation** of copies or phonorecords into the United States also constitutes infringing distribution.

Recent case law erodes the "physical transfer" rule. **Transmission of an electronic (digital) copy** is likely to constitute a distribution. Likewise, some precedent indicates that **posting a copyrighted work on a Web site** or holding an unlawful copy of a work **available to the public in a library collection** (regardless of whether the work is actually visited or checked out) can be an infringing distribution to the public.

The **chief limitation** on the distribution right is the **doctrine of first sale**, which provides that once the copyright owner authorizes transfer of title to a copy or phonorecord of the copyrighted work, the transferee and his successors in interest are entitled to retransfer or otherwise dispose of that copy or phonorecord without further authorization.[11] The doctrine of first sale may apply whenever a plaintiff alleges infringement of the §106(3) distribution right or the §602 importation right.[12]

Because **Internet transmissions** generally entail reproducing the sender's copy and sending the reproduction, the doctrine of first sale will seldom apply to permit purchasers of digital works to transfer them to others via the Internet. (The doctrine of first sale does not authorize reproduction or resale of unauthorized (unlawful) copies.)

4. The exclusive right to perform the work publicly: To "perform" a work is "to recite, render, play, dance, or act it, either directly or by means of any device or process or, in the case of a motion picture or other audiovisual work, to show its images in any sequence or to make the sounds accompanying it audible." §101. The initial rendition and any further act by which that rendition is made to recur is a performance. The copyright owner only enjoys the right of **public** performance.

Unauthorized private performances do not infringe. Section 101 describes four ways in which a performance may be deemed **public** and infringing:

1. the performance occurs at a **place open to the public**;
2. the performance occurs at any place where a **substantial number of persons outside the normal circle of a family** and its social acquaintances is gathered;
3. the performance is **transmitted** to a place described in items 1 and 2 above; or
4. the performance is **transmitted** or otherwise communicated **to the public** by means of any device, regardless of whether the public receives it in the same or separate places or at the same or different times.

Sound-recording copyrights do not provide a general right of public performance. However, §106(6) provides sound-recording copyright owners a more limited **"right to perform publicly by means of a digital audio transmission."**[13]

Pursuant to the TRIPS Agreement, Congress enacted **anti-bootlegging** provisions giving performers "neighboring rights" in their **live musical performances**.[14] These rights are separate from any rights in the musical compositions being performed.

FIGURE 5 *(cont.)*

IS THERE A CAUSE OF ACTION FOR COPYRIGHT INFRINGEMENT?

There are a number of narrowly drawn **statutory exceptions** that permit certain unauthorized public performances. Some of the more important ones are described in note 15.

5. The exclusive right of public display: Section 101 provides that to display a work is "to show a copy of it, either directly or by means of a film, slide, television image, or any other device or process, or, in the case of a motion picture or other audiovisual work, to show individual images nonsequentially." Copyright owners only enjoy the right of **public** display.

A display is **public** under the same circumstances that a performance is. (See above.)	Copyright Act **§109(c)** provides that the owner of a lawfully made copy of a work may display that copy publicly, either directly or by the projection of no more than one image at a time, to viewers present at the place where the copy is located.[16] Some of the other more important **exceptions** to the public display right are listed in note 15.	Providing a **link** to copyrighted material on the Internet does not constitute a public display of the material. Only the person storing a digital copy on his server can display the copy.

6. Moral rights: The Berne Convention requires its members to protect **authors'** moral rights of integrity and attribution. However, to date, the United States has only extended express moral-rights protection to a very narrow category of copyrightable subject matter: works of visual art. The limited U.S. moral-rights provisions were enacted in the **Visual Artists Rights Act** (VARA) in 1990.

Works of visual art include: • paintings, drawings, prints, or sculptures that exist in a single copy or in a limited edition of 200 or fewer signed, numbered copies; and • **still photographs** that were produced for exhibition purposes only and exist in a single, signed copy or in a limited edition of 200 or fewer signed, numbered copies. The moral rights provided under VARA **only apply to the original and signed, limited edition copies** described above.	The §106A **right of attribution** gives the author the right: 1. to be identified as the author of the work; 2. to prevent attribution to him of works that he did not create; and 3. to prevent use of his name in connection with a work that has been modified in a way that will injure his honor or reputation.	The §106A **right of integrity** enables the author to prevent intentional distortion, mutilation, or other modification of her work if it is prejudicial to her honor or reputation as an artist. In the case of works of **recognized stature**, the right of integrity enables the author to prevent intentional or grossly negligent destruction of the work.[17]

Works made for hire and works that do not qualify for copyright are *not* protectable "works of visual art."	Moral rights **accrue in the author of the work and are not transferable**. The author may **waive** her moral rights, but only under narrow circumstances.

FIGURE 5 *(cont.)*

IS THERE A CAUSE OF ACTION FOR COPYRIGHT INFRINGEMENT?

Even if the defendant did not directly infringe one of the exclusive rights of the copyright owner or an author's moral right, he may be indirectly liable for the direct infringement of others, under one of the copyright law's indirect liability theories.

Indirect-infringement liability: One may be held indirectly liable for the direct infringement of others through a finding of **contributory infringement, vicarious infringement**, or **inducement of infringement** as recognized by the Supreme Court in the *Grokster* case.

One who knowingly induces, causes, or materially contributes to the infringing conduct of another is liable for **contributory infringement**. The defendant must:

1. know or have reason to know of another's directly infringing activity; and
2. actively participate in it by inducing, materially contributing to, or furthering it.

Vicarious liability may be found whenever the defendant has:

1. the right and ability to control or supervise the direct infringer; and
2. a direct financial interest in the infringement.

In the ***Sony* case**,[18] the Supreme Court held that merely distributing a device with knowledge that some purchasers may use it to infringe copyrights will not give rise to contributory liability, as long as the device is **capable of substantial, noninfringing uses**.

In ***Napster*** and ***Grokster***,[19] the Ninth Circuit construed *Sony* to provide that if the defendant **receives actual notice of specific acts** of infringement through use of the device or service it distributes, it may incur a **duty to take action to stop** the infringement, even though the device or service is capable of substantial, noninfringing uses. Failure to act to stop the infringement after receiving such notice will result in contributory infrigement liability.

Section 512 provides a series of safe harbors to insulate Internet service providers from both direct and indirect liability for user-initiated infringement, if various conditions are met.

In *Grokster*, the Supreme Court held that while the *Sony* rule protects a defendant who merely distributes a device that it knows **may be used to infringe**, it does not apply to shelter a defendant who is clearly distributing the device with the **intent that it be used to infringe** or who **actively, intentionally promotes** the infringing use. Contributory infringement under these circumstances is sometimes called **inducement infringement**

FIGURE 5 *(cont.)*

IS THERE A CAUSE OF ACTION FOR COPYRIGHT INFRINGEMENT?

If the plaintiff is the owner of exclusive rights, and the defendant has infringed one or more of the exclusive rights (or can be held liable for the infringing acts of others under one of the indirect infringement theories described above), then the defendant will be liable, if there are no applicable defenses. The following special defenses may be raised against claims of copyright infringement.

If the plaintiff has not infringed any of the exclusive rights, either because necessary elements of the cause of action are missing or one of the statutory exceptions to liability applies, then there is no cause of action for copyright infringement.

1. The fair-use defense: The fair-use defense is available once a *prima facie* showing of copyright infringement or violation of moral rights has been made. It is applied on a case-by-case basis to **identify and permit unauthorized uses of copyrighted works that further the purposes of copyright law without significantly undercutting authors' incentive to create.**[20]

Section 107 provides **four factors** that courts should consider in determining whether a defendant's use was fair. Courts must always consider all four factors and may consider additional factors that appear relevant under the particular circumstances of the case.

1. **The purpose and character of the defendant's use**, including whether the use is of a commercial nature or is for nonprofit educational purposes.[21]
2. **The nature of the copyrighted work.**[22]
3. **The amount and substantiality of the portion used** in relation to the copyrighted work as a whole.[23]
4. **The effect of the use on the potential market** for or value of the copyrighted work.[24]

Under the *Sega* decision,[25] the **intermediate copying of object code** that takes place in the course of reverse engineering (decompiling) a computer program may be excused as a fair use when reverse engineering is the only means of gaining access to unprotected ideas and functional elements embodied in the object code, and the defendant has a legitimate interest in gaining such access.

2. The copyright misuse defense is an equitable defense that renders a copyright unenforceable if the copyright owner has **engaged in misconduct in licensing or enforcing the copyright, thereby enlarging the scope of his monopoly beyond that intended by Congress**. Under the misuse doctrine, the plaintiff's copyright will be unenforceable until the misuse ends and its effects have dissipated. Some court opinions indicate that acts that do not constitute an antitrust violation may nonetheless constitute copyright misuse.

If no defenses apply, the plaintiff should prevail in his copyright infringement claim.

IS THERE A CAUSE OF ACTION FOR COPYRIGHT INFRINGEMENT?

[1] Copyright ownership is divisible. Any person who owns an exclusive right under the copyright is considered a copyright owner and has the right to sue to enforce the right she owns against others. A person who has only a nonexclusive right is a licensee and has no standing to sue for infringement.

[2] A joint work is "a work prepared by two or more authors with the intention that their contributions be merged into inseparable or interdependent parts of a unitary whole." §101. Each joint author must have intended to contribute a part to a unitary whole at the time he created his portion. Moreover, each joint author must have contributed copyrightable expression, not just ideas or facts.

[3] Copyright Act §101 describes two ways in which a work can be deemed a work for hire. First, it is a work for hire if it was **prepared by an employee within the scope of his employment**. Common-law agency principles should be used to determine whether someone is an employee for this purpose. As a general matter, if the hiring party has the **right to control the manner and means by which the worker creates the work**, then the worker probably is an employee.

Second, a work is a work for hire if it was created by an independent contractor, fits into one of nine categories of works enumerated in §101, and the parties have expressly agreed (as evidenced in a written, signed instrument) that the work is a work made for hire. The nine categories of work are: (1) a contribution to a collective work, (2) a part of a motion picture or other audiovisual work, (3) a translation, (4) a supplementary work, (5) a compilation, (6) an instructional text, (7) a test, (8) answer material for a test, or (9) an atlas.

[4] All similarities between the parties' works may be considered, regardless of whether the similarities involve copyrightable expression or uncopyrightable elements, such as facts or ideas. Expert testimony may be used in identifying and evaluating the similarities.

[5] An author's combination of elements may create a kind of *synergy*, a distinctive mood. In the case of nonfactual, nonutilitarian works, such as photographs, greeting cards, or paintings, this synergy or mood is sometimes called the work's "total concept and feel" and may be treated as copyrightable expression in itself.

[6] The extrinsic test examines the similarity of the parties' expression from an **objective** standpoint, with the help of dissection and expert testimony. If the defendant's work is substantially similar under the extrinsic test, the finder of fact then applies the intrinsic test, which is essentially the same as the "**subjective**, overall impression of the average viewer/listener, without dissection" test described above. A cause of action can only be found if the work is deemed substantially similar under both the extrinsic standard and the intrinsic standard. This allows the court to ensure that the finder of fact has considered selection-and-arrangement expression and the "total look and feel" of the works, but has not had to rely on uncopyrightable elements in finding infringement.

[7] The work is abstracted (repeatedly restated in increasing generality), and all the uncopyrightable elements are identified and filtered out on each level of abstraction. The finder of fact then compares the remaining expression with the defendant's work. Under this approach, the programmer or other author's selection and arrangement of uncopyrightable elements is protected, because individual elements that are filtered out on one level of abstraction may nonetheless be considered and protected as part of an aggregate of elements at a higher level of abstraction.

[8] One simultaneously considers similarity from an objective and subjective standpoint, to ensure that there are similarities of copyrightable expression. However, there is no formal dissection and filtration (as in the abstraction-filtration-comparison test), in order to ensure that the finder of fact considers the work's "total concept and feel."

[9] **Copyright Act §117** permits **the *owner* of a lawful copy of a computer program** to reproduce the program if she does so as an essential step in using the program in a computer or for archival purposes. While most software transactions purport only to convey a license, rather than ownership of the copy, courts will sometimes examine the circumstances of the transaction to determine whether the "licensee" should be treated as an "owner" for purposes of §117. Section 117 permits both owners and licensees of programs to reproduce the program to the extent necessary to service or repair the computer on which it is installed.

Copyright Act §115 provides a compulsory license allowing persons to record ("cover") copyrighted **musical compositions** if the composition has already been recorded and distributed to the U.S. public under the copyright owner's authority, and the compulsory licensee complies with specified notice and royalty requirements. **Copyright Act §113** permits others to make pictures or photographs of **useful articles** for advertisements, commentaries, or news reports.

Copyright Act §120 permits others to make pictorial representations of **works of architecture** if the building is visible from a public place.

Copyright Act §108 provides limited safe harbors for **public libraries, archives, and their employees** to reproduce works for noncommercial purposes.

Copyright Act §§1001-1010 permit noncommercial digital and analog audiotaping of copyrighted **sound recordings**, and the **musical compositions** recorded in them, if certain requirements are met.

[10] **Copyright Act §117** permits the owner of an authorized copy of a **computer program** to adapt it if making the adaptation is an essential step in utilizing the program in a computer or for archival purposes. (See note 9, *supra*, for comments about the exception's limitation to *owners* of lawful copies.)

Copyright Act §120 permits the owner of a building embodying a copyrighted **architectural work** to make alterations to the building without the copyright owner's permission.

[11] Special exceptions to this rule allow owners of copyright in sound recordings of music, the recorded music, and software to prohibit commercial rental of copies and phonorecords of these works (§109(b)).

[12] Courts have disagreed over whether the doctrine of first sale applies to copies and phonorecords *made abroad* by the U.S. copyright owner for sale in foreign markets, and then imported into the United States. The U.S. Supreme Court has granted certiorari to decide this issue. *Kirtsaeng v. John Wiley & Sons,* 132 S.Ct. 1905 (2012).

[13] The digital audio transmission performance right does not extend to FCC-regulated over-the-air radio or television broadcasts (though it does apply to webcasts), and it does not apply to digital transmissions of audiovisual works, such as music videos, or to forms of digital performances that do not constitute transmissions, such as playing a CD of the recording in a public place. There are a number of other limitations on the right, including compulsory licenses that permit certain performances through non-interactive digital transmissions, upon payment of a statutorily prescribed royalty. §114(d)-(j).

[14] These provisions prohibit unauthorized broadcasts of live musical performances; unauthorized fixations of such performances; and reproduction, distribution, offers to distribute, and trafficking of unauthorized fixations. Violators are subject to civil copyright infringement remedies. Copyright Act §1101.

[15] **Copyright Act §110(4)** permits **nonprofit direct** (non-transmitted) **performances** of **nondramatic literary or musical works** if there is no purpose of direct or indirect commercial advantage; the performers, promoters, and organizers are not paid specifically for the performance; and there is no direct or indirect admission charge (unless the proceeds go to charity).

Copyright Act §110(5) permits **performance and display** of works by transmission to a place open to the public or where the public is gathered (primarily, it allows businesses to play radio or television broadcasts on their premises), if the performance or display complies with certain limitations on the type and number of receivers, and certain other restrictions are satisfied. (A TRIPS dispute resolution panel has found much of the §110(5) exception to violate U.S. obligations under the TRIPS Agreement, leaving the future of this exception in doubt.)

Copyright Act §110(1) permits certain **performances and displays** of works by instructors or pupils in the course of **face-to-face teaching activities** in a classroom or similar place devoted to instruction. This exception applies to all kinds of copyrighted works. However, the educational instruction must be nonprofit, and some other restrictions apply.

Copyright Act §110(2) permits certain **transmissions** of **performances and displays** of copyrighted material **in educational programs** directed to students or governmental employees. This **distance-learning provision** extends to performances of nondramatic literary or musical works, "reasonable and limited" performances of other works, and displays of any work by transmission, as long as the performance or display is made by or at the direction of an instructor, is offered as an integral part of a class session or as a regular part of the systematic instructional activities of a governmental body or an accredited nonprofit educational institution, and other requirements are met.

Copyright Act §110(3) permits **performances** of nondramatic literary and musical works and dramaticomusical works of a religious nature as well as **displays** of works in the course of **services at a place of worship or other religious assembly**.

Copyright Act §§111 and 119 provide for compulsory licenses to enable **cable systems** and **satellite retransmission** companies to make secondary transmissions of broadcast signals and authorize secondary transmissions in a number of other situations.

[16] The primary value of the public display right lies in displays of copyrighted works in television broadcasts, movies, and over the Internet, which are not subject to the §109(c) exception.

[17] Under Copyright Act §113(d), the owner of a building into which a work of visual art is incorporated may, under limited circumstances, remove the work from the building even though removing it will destroy, distort, mutilate, or otherwise modify the work.

[18] *Sony Corp. of America v. Universal City Studios, Inc.,* 464 U.S. 417 (1984).

[19] *A & M Records, Inc. v. Napster, Inc.,* 239 F.3d 1004 (9th Cir. 2001); *Metro-Goldwyn-Mayer Studios, Inc. v. Grokster, Ltd.,* 380 F.3d 1154 (9th Cir. 2004), *vacated & remanded,* 545 U.S. 913 (2005).

[20] Examples of fair use, provided in §107, include uses "for purposes such as criticism, comment, news reporting, teaching (including multiple copies for classroom use), scholarship, or research." The fact that the defendant's use fits within one of these categories, however, creates no presumption of fair use.

[21] Under this factor, a **commercial use weighs against** a finding of fair use. Additional considerations include whether the defendant's use was **productive or transformative in nature,** and whether the defendant was acting in **good faith.**

[22] If the plaintiff's work was **unpublished,** this **weighs against** a finding of fair use. If the plaintiff's work was **factual, functional, or otherwise heavily laden with uncopyrightable elements,** the courts typically give the defendant **more leeway to copy,** to the extent the copying is necessary in order to access and use the work's uncopyrightable elements.

[23] This factor examines both the **quantity** of material taken and its **overall importance** to the plaintiff's work. It also considers whether the defendant took more than necessary, given his purpose in copying, as determined under factor 1.

[24] Under this factor, courts consider whether the defendant's acts **could potentially harm any market** for the plaintiff's copyrighted work or for adaptations of it. However, it must appear that the defendant's work supplanted demand for the plaintiff's. A showing that it suppressed demand, for example, by criticizing or ridiculing it, is not relevant.

[25] *Sega Enterprises v. Accolade, Inc.,* 977 F.2d 1510 (9th Cir. 1992).

FIGURE 6

THE DIGITAL MILLENNIUM COPYRIGHT ACT ANTI-CIRCUMVENTION PROVISIONS

Use this chart to evaluate alleged violations of the Digital Millennium Copyright Act (DMCA) anti-circumvention provisions, 17 U.S.C. §§1201, 1203. (All statutory references are to the Copyright Act, 17 U.S.C. §1201.)

The Digital Millennium Copyright Act (DMCA) facilitates copyright owners' use of **two types of technological measures** to prevent unauthorized access to and use of their works:

1. technological measures that effectively control **access** to a copyrighted work ("access control measures"); and
2. technological measures that effectively control **exercise of rights** in a copyrighted work ("use control measures").

An **access control measure** is a technological measure that, in the ordinary course of its operation, requires the application of information, or a process or treatment, with the authority of the copyright owner, to gain access to a copyrighted work.

A **use control measure** effectively protects rights in a work if, in the ordinary course of its operation, it prevents, restricts, or otherwise limits the exercise of a right of a copyright owner (i.e., limits reproduction, adaptation, distribution, public performance, or public display of the copyrighted work).

While an access control measure must **"effectively"** control access to a work, courts have routinely rejected arguments that access control measures are unprotected if they can be easily circumvented. However, the Sixth Circuit has held that access control measures must restrict **all** forms of access to the work, rather than just one, in order to qualify for protection.[1]

The DMCA grants copyright owners three rights:

1. the right to prohibit **circumvention** of **access** control measures;
2. the right to prohibit manufacture, importation, offer, provision, and trafficking of ("**trafficking in**") devices or services for circumventing **access control measures**; and
3. the right to prohibit **trafficking in** devices or services for circumventing **use control measures**.

Circumvention: The DMCA only prohibits circumvention of **access control measures**. Thus, in cases of alleged circumvention, first ascertain whether the technological measure at issue is an access control measure or a use control measure.

Trafficking: The DMCA prohibits trafficking in technologies, products, services, devices, or components ("devices or services") for use in circumventing **both access control measures and use control measures**. However, the device or service must meet one of the following three criteria:

- it must be primarily designed or produced for the purpose of circumvention;
- it must have only limited commercially significant purposes or uses other than to circumvent; or
- it must be marketed for use in circumventing.

Chart continues on next page.
                                            See notes after final page of chart.

FIGURE 6 *(cont.)*

THE DIGITAL MILLENNIUM COPYRIGHT ACT ANTI-CIRCUMVENTION PROVISIONS

If the technological measure is an access control measure, apply the following **definition** to see if it has been circumvented in violation of §1201(a)(1): "**circumvention**" means "to descramble a scrambled work, to decrypt an encrypted work, or otherwise to avoid, bypass, remove, deactivate, or impair a technological measure, without the authority of the copyright owner."

If the technological measure is a use control measure, circumvention is not actionable in itself. The defendant's liability, if any, will be for copyright infringement. Apply the regular rules for copyright infringement and determine if any defenses, such as fair use, apply.

Relationship to copyright infringement: Courts have disagreed about the meaning of §1201(c)(1), which provides that §1201 does not affect "rights, remedies, limitations, or defenses to copyright infringement, including fair use."

The Court of Appeals for the Second Circuit has construed §1201 to operate independently of the copyright infringement provisions, and thus to create a separate cause of action that may be available to copyright owners regardless of whether the §1201 defendant's actions infringed or facilitated copyright infringement by others.[2] It is irrelevant that circumvention may have been committed in order to engage in a noninfringing fair use.

The Court of Appeals for the Federal Circuit has held that, in order to be liable under §1201, the defendant's actions must infringe or facilitate infringement of copyright. The court reasoned that to hold otherwise would interfere unduly with fair uses of copyrighted works and overwrite the Copyright Act's careful balance of competing interests.[3]

Exceptions to §1201 liability: Section 1201 sets forth several very narrow, limited exceptions to liability, none of which is broad or flexible like the fair-use defense to infringement liability.[4]

THE DIGITAL MILLENNIUM COPYRIGHT ACT
ANTI-CIRCUMVENTION PROVISIONS

[1] *Lexmark International, Inc. v. Static Control Components, Inc.*, 387 F.3d 522 (6th Cir. 2004).

[2] *Universal City Studios, Inc. v. Corley*, 273 F.3d 429 (2d Cir. 2001).

[3] *Chamberlain Group, Inc. v. Skylink Technologies, Inc.*, 381 F.3d 1178 (Fed. Cir. 2004), *cert. denied*, 544 U.S. 923 (2005).

[4] These exceptions include:

- a very limited exemption for nonprofit libraries, archives, and educational institutions (§1201(d));
- an exception for law enforcement, intelligence, and other government activities (§1201(e));
- an exception to allow reverse engineering of software in order to identify and analyze program elements necessary to achieve program interoperability (§1201(f));
- a limited exception for encryption research (§1201(g));
- an exception allowing disablement of cookies and other devices that collect and disseminate personal information (§1201(i)); and
- a very limited exception for network security testing (§1201(j)).

FIGURE 7

ANALYZING RIGHTS IN INDICATIONS OF ORIGIN

Use this chart to determine whether a word, name, symbol or device can be protected as an indication of origin (mark, trade dress, or trade name) under the Lanham Act. (Because the same rules usually apply to all indications of origin, the term "mark" is often used in the chart to refer to all kinds of indications of origin. All statutory references are to the Lanham Act, 15 U.S.C. §1051 *et seq*.)

Protectable subject matter: Any **word, name, symbol, or device** (or any combination thereof) can qualify for protection as an indication of origin[1] as long as the following requirements are satisfied:

- it is **distinctive**;
- it is **not deceptive, scandalous, or disparaging**;
- it is **not functional**; and
- its claimant has taken the actions necessary to establish **ownership and priority**.

The rest of this chart can be used as a checklist for these and related factors.[2]

A combination of two or more words, names, symbols, or devices is called a **composite mark** and is evaluated as a unit, rather than as separate elements.

Distinctiveness: To be protected, a mark must be distinctive—it must **notify consumers of the source of the good or service with which it is used** and enable consumers to distinguish the user's goods or services from those of other producers. Marks are often divided into **three categories** according to their distinctiveness.

- Highest in the hierarchy are **arbitrary, fanciful, and suggestive marks**,[3] which are deemed *inherently distinctive* and protectable upon use in trade and commerce.
- Lower in the hierarchy are **common, descriptive, and surname marks**, which are merely *capable of becoming distinctive*. This category of marks can only be protected upon a showing of **acquired distinctiveness, or "secondary meaning."**
- At the bottom of the hierarchy are "**generic words or symbols**," which are *incapable of becoming distinctive* and cannot be the subject of rights.

The "common, descriptive, and surname" mark category includes:

- marks that appear to describe the product or service they identify;
- marks that appear to describe the geographic location from which the goods or services emanate;
- marks that are primarily merely a surname; and
- other marks that are **commonly used** in connection with the relevant type of good or service.

A mark is descriptive if consumers encountering the mark are *likely to think* that the mark describes the product. It does not matter whether the mark does, in fact, provide accurate information about the product.[4]

The **standard** for determining whether an alleged mark is or has become **generic** is whether its **primary significance** to consumers is to indicate the class or genus of product or service itself or to indicate the product or service's source.

Chart continues on next pages.   *See notes after final page of chart.*

FIGURE 7 *(cont.)*

ANALYZING RIGHTS IN INDICATIONS OF ORIGIN

Rules to observe in evaluating the distinctiveness of a mark:

- Marks must always be evaluated in light of the **particular good or service** they identify.
- Consider the **overall commercial impression** the mark would make on the average prospective customer.
- **Misspelled words** must be treated as though they were properly spelled, as long as the phonetic identity between the misspelled word and the properly spelled word is clear.
- **Foreign words** are generally translated into English and then evaluated to determine if their translation is descriptive of the product or service, geographically descriptive, or generic.

The Supreme Court has ruled that **color, by itself,** and **product features** may **never be deemed inherently distinctive**. They must always be shown to have secondary meaning before they can be protected. **Product packaging** (as distinguished from product features) may be inherently distinctive, as long as the combination of elements as a whole is not descriptive of the product, commonplace for that type of product, or a trivial variation on a combination that is commonplace.

A mark is **primarily merely a surname** if its overall impact on the consuming public is a surname meaning and nothing more.

- If the mark has no meaning to the public, surname or otherwise, then it is not primarily merely a surname.
- If the mark has both a surname meaning and some other reasonably known meaning, such as "King" or "Miller," then it generally will not be deemed primarily merely a surname and thus will not require a showing of secondary meaning.

Marks are considered **primarily geographically descriptive** if:

- the mark conveys to a meaningful segment of the purchasing public primarily or immediately a geographical connotation; and
- those persons are likely to think that the goods or services, in fact, come from that place.[5]

Primarily geographically descriptive marks require a showing of secondary meaning. If the mark **inaccurately** communicates geographic origin, it may be deemed **geographically deceptively misdescriptive** and unprotectable regardless of secondary meaning.[6]

Words or symbols that are **commonly used** in connection with the particular goods or services may not be understood to indicate source and therefore require a showing of secondary meaning. Likewise, **common, basic designs**, such as circles, squares, or stripes, are so commonly used that consumers are unlikely automatically to assume that they indicate source.[7]

Secondary meaning is attained when the relevant consuming public learns (through extensive exposure to the claimant's use) to understand the word or symbol not in its primary, common, descriptive, or surname sense, but as an indication of the product or service's source.[8]

FIGURE 7 *(cont.)*

ANALYZING RIGHTS IN INDICATIONS OF ORIGIN

Deceptiveness and related §1052(a) limitations: Lanham Act §1052(a) prohibits **registration** of marks that:

- are immoral or scandalous;[9]
- are deceptive;[10]
- falsely suggest a connection with persons, living or dead, institutions, beliefs, or national symbols;[11] or
- are composed of matter that may disparage others.[12]

The Supreme Court has held that these §1052(a) prohibitions are also relevant in evaluating the protectability of **unregistered** marks under §1125(a).

Deceptive marks (which cannot be registered or protected pursuant to §1052(a)) and **deceptively misdescriptive marks** (which can be registered and protected with a showing of secondary meaning pursuant to §1052 (e) and (f)) can be **distinguished on the basis of materiality**. If the mark misrepresents a characteristic, consumers would be likely to believe the misrepresentation, and the misrepresentation would be material to consumers in making their purchasing decision, the mark is deceptive. If the misrepresented characteristic would not be material, then the mark is deceptively misdescriptive.

Functionality: Functionality may prevent registration and/or protection of product features or packaging trade dress. The functionality doctrine prevents use of Lanham Act claims to circumvent the higher standards of patent protection and more generally prevents anticompetitive use of Lanham Act claims.

In the *TrafFix* case,[13] the Supreme Court set forth a **two-part test for functionality**.

1. First, the court/P.T.O. must apply the *Inwood Laboratories* standard: Is the claimed feature essential to the use or purpose of the article, or does it affect the cost or quality of the article? If so, the feature is functional and cannot be the subject of trade dress protection.
2. If not, then the court/P.T.O. must apply the *Qualitex* standard: Would the exclusive use of the feature "put competitors at a significant, non-reputation-based disadvantage"? If so, there is "aesthetic functionality," and the feature cannot be protected.

Only if a claimed feature is non-functional under both standards can it be protected as trade dress.

The Supreme Court has held that if product features are **encompassed** in the claims of a **utility patent**, this constitutes strong evidence of functionality.

Prior use: In keeping with the rules of **ownership and priority** discussed below, Lanham Act §2(d) prohibits registration of a mark that, when used in connection with the applicant's goods or services, is confusingly similar to a mark or trade name that another party began using before the applicant and has not abandoned. However, an applicant's mark can be registered if the P.T.O. determines that both the earlier mark or trade name and the applicant's mark can be used concurrently without causing a likelihood of consumer confusion, as when, for example, each party restricts his use to a portion of the country that is remote from the other. This rule is consistent with the common-law rule for unregistered marks and other indications of origin.

FIGURE 7 *(cont.)*

ANALYZING RIGHTS IN INDICATIONS OF ORIGIN

If the mark or other indication of origin lacks distinctiveness, is deceptive, is functional, is in prior use, or falls under one of the other objections set forth in §1052, it cannot be the subject of rights under the Lanham Act.

If the mark or other indication of origin is distinctive, nonfunctional, and does not fall under any of the other objections set forth in §1052, it is a protectable mark, **assuming that** its claimant has established **ownership rights** in it and has **priority** over other users.

Ownership of marks and priority: One acquires common-law ownership in inherently distinctive marks through **use of the mark in trade**. In the case of marks that are merely capable of becoming distinctive, one acquires ownership through **acquisition of secondary meaning**. The **first to use a mark in trade** (in the case of inherently distinctive marks) or **to acquire secondary meaning** in it (in the case of marks that are not inherently distinctive) has seniority and **priority** over subsequent uses within his geographic territory.

To use the mark in trade is to use it in a way that allows consumers to rely on it for its ultimate purpose—to identify the source of the user's goods or services and distinguish them from others. The use must be "in the ordinary course of trade"—not merely a token use made for the purpose of reserving the mark.[14]

Part of the "use" requirement entails **affixation**. In the case of **goods**, the mark must be:

- placed on the goods themselves;
- placed on their containers;
- placed on tags or labels attached to the goods or containers;
- prominently featured in a conspicuous display associated with the goods; or
- placed on documents associated with the goods or their sale.

In the case of **services**, use or display of the mark in connection with the sale or advertising of the services is sufficient, as long as the mark is used in direct, explicit reference to the services being offered.

Geographic boundaries and the remote, good-faith user: Under the common law and §1125(a), the first person to use a mark (or acquire secondary meaning in it, in the case of marks that are not inherently distinctive) has priority over subsequent users. However, if a second person later uses (or acquires secondary meaning in) a confusingly similar mark in a **remote geographic area in good faith** (i.e., with no notice that another person has made an earlier use that is ongoing in the United States), the second person will have superior rights in the mark in that remote area, by virtue of the remote, good-faith user defense. Thus, there may be **concurrent owners** of the same mark in different geographic locations.

FIGURE 7 *(cont.)*

ANALYZING RIGHTS IN INDICATIONS OF ORIGIN

Ownership and priority in a qualifying mark gives rise to limited rights against infringement, dilution (in the case of "famous" marks), and cybersquatting, as will be discussed in the next charts. It is not necessary to register the mark: Rights in unregistered marks and other indications of origin exist under the common law and are federally protected under Lanham Act §1125.[15]

A person with ownership and priority in a qualifying mark (even if it is just ownership and priority in part of the country, under the remote, good-faith user rule) may **register the mark** on the Lanham Act Principal Register.

Federal registration: While it is not necessary to register a mark in order to own and enforce it, there are several **important benefits** that arise from registering the mark on the Lanham Act Principal Register. These are listed in boxes 1-5 below.

1. Registration provides **greater geographic rights** than are available to mark owners under common law.

Under §1072, registration on the Principal Register **creates constructive notice** of the registrant's use. This prevents subsequent users from demonstrating that they commenced their use in good faith and thus deprives them of the remote, good-faith user defense discussed above. The effect is to give the registrant **superior rights in all parts of the country not already occupied** as of its *registration* date.

For **marks registered on applications filed on or after November 16, 1989**: Section 1057(c) provides that, upon completion of the registration process, the registrant receives the benefit of **constructive use throughout the country, as of its application date**. Thus, even though the registrant did not actually use the mark until after filing (in the case of an intent-to-use application) and/or only used the mark in a limited part of the country, she is treated as though she used the mark throughout the country as of her application date. She thus has priority over anyone who commences use in the United States after that date (or who has an effective registration filing date after that date).

To register, the applicant must not only have made a use in trade (necessary to obtain ownership rights in the mark) but also a **use in commerce** (which is necessary in order to bring the mark within Congress's Commerce Clause power). Use in commerce is usually easy to demonstrate: It only must appear that the sales "affected" interstate commerce.

FIGURE 7 *(cont.)*

ANALYZING RIGHTS IN INDICATIONS OF ORIGIN

↓

2. Registration **shields the registrant from state dilution claims**.

↓

3. Registration provides a **right to assistance from the U.S. Customs Service** in preventing the importation of infringing goods.

↓

4. Registration provides a **presumption of mark ownership and validity** that eases the registrant's burden both in lawsuits that challenge her rights and in lawsuits seeking to enforce her rights.

↓

5. A mark in continuous use for five consecutive years following its registration qualifies for **incontestability status**, if the registrant files an affidavit as specified in Lanham Act §1065. Incontestability status prevents others from raising two important claims, either offensively or as a defense:

1. that the mark is not inherently distinctive and lacks secondary meaning; and
2. that the challenger/defendant used the mark before the registrant (except that this challenge/defense can still be made with regard to the actual geographic area in which the challenger/defender used the mark prior to the incontestable registrant's registration or application to register).

NOTES TO FIGURE 7

ANALYZING RIGHTS IN INDICATIONS OF ORIGIN

[1] The term "indications of origin" is used from time to time as a reminder that things other than trademarks may indicate source to consumers. As a general matter, the same rules apply to protect all indications of origin. Although this book tends to refer to marks, the rules discussed in the book will generally apply to other indications of origin, too. Following is a summary of the different kinds of indications of origin.

a. **Trademark:** A trademark is a word, name, symbol, or device, or any combination thereof that is used to distinguish the goods of one person from goods manufactured or sold by others and to indicate that the goods come from a particular source.

b. **Service mark:** A service mark is the same as a trademark except that it identifies and distinguishes services, rather than products. To qualify for protection as a service mark, the mark must be used to identify a service that is sufficiently separate from the sale of goods. This will not be the case if the service is normally expected and routinely rendered in furtherance of the sale of the goods.

c. **Certification mark:** Certification marks are words, names, symbols, or devices used by one person to certify that the goods or services of others have certain characteristics. Unlike other kinds of indications of origin, they do not indicate the source of goods or services as such, but that the goods or services have satisfied standards set by a third party.

d. **Collective mark:** Collective marks fall into two categories. First, **collective membership marks** are marks adopted for the purpose of indicating membership in an organization. Neither the organization nor its members use the mark to identify and distinguish goods or services. Second, **collective trademarks and service marks** are trademarks or service marks adopted by a collective organization, such as a co-op, for use by its members in selling their individual goods or services to distinguish their goods or services from those of nonmembers.

e. **Trade name:** The term "trade name" used to be used to identify a mark that is not inherently distinctive and requires a showing of secondary meaning to qualify for protection. However, this usage has been discontinued. In modern usage, "trade name" refers to the name of a company, partnership, or other business. Unlike marks, trade names cannot be registered on the Lanham Act Principal Register. However, they can be protected at common law, and pursuant to Lanham Act §1125(a), on the same basis, and pursuant to the same rules, as unregistered marks.

f. **Trade dress:** The term "trade dress" generally refers to:

- a product's packaging (generally, a combination of elements creating an overall impression);
- features of the product itself (typically, a number of features in combination, which give the product an overall appearance; however, sometimes individual elements of the product may be claimed and protected as trade dress); or
- the overall look and feel of a business establishment (e.g., the combination of signs, worker uniforms, layout, and decoration, along with particular methods of doing business).

Trade dress falls within the definition of trademarks and service marks and may be registered on the Lanham Act Principal Register as such. However, more often trade dress is protected under common law or as an unregistered indication of origin under Lanham Act §1125(a).

[2] Lanham Act §1052(b) and (c) also prevent registration or protection of marks that consist of:

- the flag or coat of arms or other insignia of any U.S. or foreign governmental body;
- the name, portrait, or signature of a living individual, unless the individual consents in writing; or
- the name, signature, or portrait of a deceased U.S. president during the life of his widow, unless the widow consents.

[3] **Arbitrary marks** generally are words or symbols that have a meaning, but the meaning has no apparent descriptive or other relationship to the product or service the mark identifies. **Fanciful marks** have no meaning other than their trademarked meaning. **Suggestive marks** are marks that indirectly describe the product or service they identify. The consumer must engage in a mental process to appreciate that the mark describes the good or service being identified.

[4] **Laudatory marks** (like "best" or "supreme") are generally included in the descriptive category. To gain rights, a claimant must demonstrate secondary meaning.

[5] This second condition may turn on the nature of the claimant's goods or services and whether the indicated place is generally understood to be a place where such goods or services are produced.

[6] Prior to this date, the United States protected "primarily geographically deceptively misdescriptive" marks on the same basis as it protected "primarily deceptively misdescriptive" marks. As long as they were not "deceptive," within the meaning of Lanham Act §1052(a), they could be registered and/or protected with a showing of secondary meaning. In 1993, Congress amended Lanham Act §1052(e) and (f) to provide that marks that are "primarily geographically deceptively misdescriptive" may not be registered at all, unless they obtained secondary meaning prior to December 8, 1993.

In *In re California Innovations, Inc.*, 329 F.3d 1334 (Fed. Cir. 2003), the Court of Appeals for the Federal Circuit undercut the 1993 amendment by holding that a mark could not be deemed "primarily geographically deceptively misdescriptive" under Lanham Act §1052(e) unless the misdescribed geographical origin would be a material factor to consumers in making the purchase decision. This makes the Lanham Act §1052(e) "primarily geographically deceptively misdescriptive" finding equivalent to the Lanham Act §1052(a) "deceptive" finding.

[7] **Design or symbol marks** that are striking and unusual in connection with the class of goods or services they are used to identify are more likely to be found inherently distinctive.

[8] Lanham Act §1052(f) provides that proof of substantially exclusive and continuous use of a descriptive mark for five years in connection with the product or service can be *prima facie* **evidence** that the mark has attained secondary meaning.

[9] Marks are **scandalous or immoral** if they give offense to the conscience or moral feelings or are shocking to the sense of decency or propriety. Most of the cases in which registration has been denied on this basis have involved vulgar imagery, such as a defecating dog.

[10] A mark is **deceptive** if:

a. it falsely indicates that the product or service has a characteristic;

b. prospective purchasers are likely to believe that the misdescription correctly describes the product or service; and

c. the misrepresented characteristic would be **material** to a reasonable consumer in deciding whether or not to purchase the product or service.

[11] To disqualify a mark on the ground that it **falsely suggests a connection with persons, living or dead, institutions, beliefs, or national symbols**, it must be clear that consumers will associate the mark with the person or institution at issue. This provision may be used to protect state **publicity interests**, enabling celebrities to prevent the unauthorized use of their identities to sell products.

[12] Whether a mark **disparages a group of persons or brings them into contempt or disrepute** is evaluated from the standpoint of a substantial component of the persons who allegedly are disparaged, not from the standpoint of the general public.

Another §1052(a) limitation prohibits registration of marks that consist of a "**geographical indication**" used in connection with wines or spirits, which identifies a place other than the origin of the goods (but only if the mark was first used in this fashion on or after January 1, 1996). A mark will constitute a "geographical indication" for this purpose if it identifies wines or spirits as originating in the territory of a member of the World Trade Organization, and the indicated territory has a reputation for wines or spirits, so that the wine or spirits at issue will be assumed to have the characteristics associated with the indicated territory.

[13] *TrafFix Devices, Inc. v. Marketing Displays, Inc.,* 532 U.S. 23 (2001).

[14] In order to protect a mark under Lanham Act §1125(a) or to register it, the proprietor must also demonstrate that the trademark use was "**in commerce**." This is to bring the matter within Congress's power to legislate, under the U.S. Constitution's Commerce Clause, Article I, Section 8, Clause 3. A demonstration of use in commerce is not required to protect the mark under the common law.

Jurisdictions have varied in the **quantity of trademark use** they will require of the claimant of an inherently distinctive mark before recognizing ownership rights. Even within a jurisdiction, courts may vary their requirements to some extent to accommodate the equities and circumstances of each case. Some courts hold that a mark claimant must **achieve sufficient market penetration to pose a meaningful risk of consumer confusion** if a competitor commences use of a similar mark. Others have suggested that the use must be sufficient **to give notice of the use** to other potential users. Still others require only a **single *bona fide* use** (even if it is very small), as long as the mark is **continuously used thereafter**. Some courts have applied a **four-factor test** to evaluate whether the claimant's market penetration was sufficient to warrant recognition of rights:

1. the volume of sales of the trademarked product;
2. the growth trends (both positive and negative) in the area;
3. the number of persons actually purchasing the product in relation to the potential number of customers; and
4. the amount of product advertising in the area.

[15] However, any form of protection under the Lanham Act requires that the parties use the mark "in commerce."

FIGURE 8

DOES THE OWNER OF THE INDICATION OF ORIGIN HAVE A CAUSE OF ACTION FOR INFRINGEMENT?

Use this chart to determine whether a plaintiff/owner of an indication of origin has a cause of action for infringement. (All statutory references are to the Lanham Act, 15 U.S.C. §1051 *et seq.*, unless otherwise indicated. The term ''mark'' may be used as a general term for all indications of origin.)

A plaintiff's indication of origin (mark, trade name, or trade dress) will be **infringed** if:

1. the defendant has made an **actionable use** of the indication of origin; and
2. that use has created a **likelihood of consumer confusion about the source, sponsorship, or affiliation of the parties' goods or services**.

Actionable use: The Lanham Act registered and unregistered mark infringement provisions say two things about the kind of use the defendant must make. First, the use must be a **use in commerce**; and second, the use must be **in connection with** goods or services. Particularly in the Internet context, courts have disagreed over which language is relevant and what the language requires.

Some courts have looked to the phrase "**use in commerce**," and the Lanham Act's definition of that phrase in §1127, to hold that the defendant must make a "trademark use" of the mark. That is, the defendant must closely associate the mark with goods or services that the defendant is distributing or offering for sale, in a manner that allows consumers to associate the mark with the **defendant's goods or services** and assume that the mark indicates their source.

Other courts have assumed that the phrase "use in commerce" only requires a connection with interstate commerce sufficient to provide federal jurisdiction to regulate. They have focused instead on the "**in connection with**" language to hold that the defendant's use of the mark need only have *some* connection with *someone's* goods or services or occur in a commercial context. Under this decidedly more liberal approach, some courts have found actionable "use" when the defendant was engaged in no commercial activities itself, but nonetheless "affected" the plaintiff's sales of goods or services or linked its Web site to another Web site that engaged in commercial activities. Some courts have even found actionable "use" when the defendant's use was invisible to consumers, as is the case when marks are inserted into web site metatags, or are used in proprietary software to trigger advertising.

Courts have provided a number of **factors to consider in determining whether a defendant's use of its mark is likely to confuse consumers**. They include:

- the similarity of the marks' appearance, sound, and meaning;
- the similarity (or possible overlap) of prospective purchasers;
- the similarity of the parties' marketing channels;[1]
- the sophistication of prospective purchasers and the cost of the goods or services;
- evidence of actual confusion;[2]
- the manner in which the parties present the mark;
- the strength of the plaintiff's mark;[3]
- the similarity of the parties' products or services;
- the defendant's intent;[4] and
- whether the plaintiff is likely to "bridge the gap."[5]

To find infringement, it is only necessary that a "significant number" of consumers are likely to be confused.

Chart continues on next pages.   *See notes after final page of chart.*

FIGURE 8 *(cont.)*

DOES THE OWNER OF THE INDICATION OF ORIGIN HAVE A CAUSE OF ACTION FOR INFRINGEMENT?

Traditionally, the likelihood of consumer confusion had to occur at the time of the defendant's sale to consumers.

However, today a likelihood of **post-sale consumer confusion** may suffice to impose infringement liability as well.[6]

Some courts have also found infringement on evidence of **initial (or pre-sale) consumer confusion** that is dissipated prior to the actual purchase.[7]

Reverse confusion: Most trademark infringement cases involve a subsequent (junior) user of a mark who causes purchasers to think that its goods or services come from the prior (senior) user. However, sometimes the subsequent user is so big and famous that it overshadows the prior user. In such cases, the subsequent user's use of the mark may confuse consumers into thinking that the prior user's goods come from the subsequent user. This "reverse" confusion may also give rise to infringement liability.

Concurrent use: Most jurisdictions follow the ***Dawn Donut*** rule, which requires that both plaintiff and defendant use their marks in the same geographic area (or at least enjoy mark recognition in the same geographic area) or have concrete plans to do so soon. The minority rule is that geographic proximity is just one factor to consider in the overall "likelihood of confusion" evaluation.

Trademark counterfeiting entails intentional, knowing use of a spurious mark that is identical to (or substantially indistinguishable from) a registered mark, on the same kind of goods or services for which the mark is registered. Congress has enacted **special remedies** to prevent counterfeiting.[8]

Indirect-infringement liability: A person may be held contributorially liable for another's trademark infringement if he induced or assisted in the infringement.

A defendant may be liable for contributory infringement if he **intentionally suggests, directly or by implication, that the other person infringe** the plaintiff's indication of origin and the other does so infringe.

A defendant may also be liable for contributory infringement if he **sells goods to another, knowing or having reason to know that the buyer will use the goods in a direct infringement** of the plaintiff's indication of origin.

The **owner of real or virtual property** may be liable for others' infringement on its premises if it **knows or has reason to know** of the infringement, yet takes no action to stop it. However, the property owner has has no affirmative duty to seek out or take precautions to prevent infringement.

FIGURE 8 *(cont.)*

DOES THE OWNER OF THE INDICATION OF ORIGIN HAVE A CAUSE OF ACTION FOR INFRINGEMENT?

Collateral uses: Trademark law does not give owners of indications of origin absolute control over others' use of the words or symbols constituting their indications of origin. Many "collateral" uses of marks may be made without liability.[9]

Resale of goods lawfully bearing an indication of origin: The **doctrine of exhaustion (or doctrine of first sale)** provides that once a mark owner sells or authorizes goods to be sold bearing its mark, it cannot prevent subsequent owners from reselling the goods with the mark, as long as their use is *truthful and not misleading* about the nature or immediate source of the goods.

Importation and sale of gray-market goods (also known as "parallel imports")[10] generally will not infringe the domestic mark if the imported **goods do not materially differ from** those sold by the U.S. mark owner, and the U.S. owner and the foreign manufacturer are **the same or related entities**.

Comparative advertising: Competitors may refer to a mark in selling their own goods and services—for example, to inform consumers that their goods are comparable—as long as their use is truthful and does not create a likelihood of consumer confusion about the source of the parties, goods, or services.

Some courts recognized a category of "nominative fair use," which provides leeway for businesses to use a plaintiff's mark to refer to the plaintiff's product for purposes of criticism, comparison, parody, etc. To demonstrate a noninfringing "nominative fair use," the defendant must show that:
- the plaintiff's product was not readily identifiable without using the plaintiff's mark;
- the defendant only used so much of the plaintiff's mark as was reasonably necessary to identify the plaintiff's product; and
- the defendant did nothing that would, in conjunction with use of the mark, suggest sponsorship or endorsement of its product by the plaintiff.[11]

If the defendant did not make actionable "use" of the mark, or if the use did not cause a likelihood of confusion, there is no infringement liability.

If the defendant made the requisite actionable use of a plaintiff's indication of origin and caused a likelihood of consumer confusion, then it is important to consider whether any of the **special trademark infringement defenses** apply.

FIGURE 8 *(cont.)*

DOES THE OWNER OF THE INDICATION OF ORIGIN HAVE A CAUSE OF ACTION FOR INFRINGEMENT?

Infringement defenses include the fair-use defense, abandonment, and other challenges to the validity of the plaintiff's mark.

The **fair-use defense** provides leeway for businesses to use descriptive, geographically descriptive, or surname words or symbols in their nontrademark sense to describe their own products or services, or their geographical origin, or to identify their producer.

In evaluating a fair-use defense, courts will consider several **factors**:

- whether the defendant's use is to **describe** its product or service and does so accurately;
- whether the defendant is acting in **good faith**; and
- the **degree of confusion** the defendant's use is likely to cause.

A defendant may raise a defense that the plaintiff has **abandoned its mark** and thus no longer has rights to assert. Abandonment occurs if the plaintiff has **discontinued use of the mark throughout the country** in connection with the particular good or service, with **no intent to resume use** within the reasonably foreseeable future.[12]

A plaintiff may also abandon its mark through **acts or omissions that cause the mark to lose its significance as a mark**. One such act is **assigning the mark in gross**.[13] Another act is **licensing others to use the mark without adequate supervision**, so that products bearing the mark lack consistency and frustrate consumer expectations.[14]

A defendant may raise a number of other **defects in the plaintiff's indication of origin or its ownership rights**.

Such challenges to the plaintiff's mark include:

- lack of distinctiveness;
- lack of priority;[15]
- functionality;
- fraudulent registration;
- use of mark to violate antitrust laws;
- equitable principles, such as *laches*, estoppel, and acquiescence.

DOES THE OWNER OF THE INDICATION OF ORIGIN HAVE A CAUSE OF ACTION FOR INFRINGEMENT?

[1] Are the plaintiff's and defendant's goods or services **likely to be sold in the same or a similar kind of store**? If so, this increases the likelihood of confusion.

[2] **Evidence of actual confusion** is *not necessary* to prove that the defendant's use causes a likelihood of confusion. If available, however, such evidence can be highly persuasive.

[3] The **stronger** the plaintiff's mark (i.e., the greater the mark's distinctiveness and the public's recognition of it as an indication of origin of a particular good or service), the more likely it is that consumers, seeing the defendant's allegedly similar mark, will associate it with the plaintiff's mark and be confused about the source of the defendant's goods.

[4] Evidence that the defendant **intended** to confuse the public is circumstantial evidence that he succeeded and leads to a finding of infringement. In some jurisdictions, evidence of intent to confuse may give rise to an inference, or even a presumption of, confusion.

[5] When the parties' products or services **differ**, a court may consider how likely the plaintiff is to begin selling the same products or services as the defendant.

[6] Even if immediate purchasers are not confused about the source of the goods they purchase, other persons who receive the goods from the immediate purchaser, or see the goods in the purchaser's possession, may be confused, thinking that the defendant's good came from the plaintiff. This confusion may injure the plaintiff's business goodwill.

[7] A defendant's use of a mark that is confusingly similar to the plaintiff's may divert consumers who are seeking the plaintiff. Once they arrive at the defendant's door or web site, it becomes evident that the defendant is not the plaintiff and is not affiliated with the plaintiff. However, the defendant's initial use of the plaintiff's mark gives the defendant the opportunity to make its pitch to consumers who meant to visit the plaintiff, and possibly divert sales that otherwise would have gone to the plaintiff.

[8] These remedies include attorney fees, treble damages, statutory damages, *ex parte* orders to seize goods bearing counterfeit marks, and criminal sanctions against persons who intentionally traffic or attempt to traffic in goods through use of marks they know to be counterfeit.

[9] Mark parodies often are found not to infringe. If the parody takes place in non-commercial speech (commercial speech is speech that "does no more than propose a commercial transaction"), then First Amendment considerations may require courts to balance the competing trademark interests with the public's interest in freedom of speech and uphold the use. Even if the parody is made in commercial speech, the use may not cause a likelihood of consumer confusion: Parody, by its nature, does not seek to confuse consumers about source. If the parody is to be successful, consumers must be aware of the differences in the marks so that they can appreciate the humor of the defendant's parody.

[10] **Gray-market goods** are goods that are manufactured abroad for sale in foreign markets that the foreign manufacturer properly, legally marks with a trademark that is registered in the United States. After these goods are released into foreign markets, parties buy them and import them into the United States for resale in competition with the U.S. mark registrant.

[11] The Ninth Circuit uses this three-factor test **instead of the regular multifactor test** for likelihood of confusion in nominative situations.

[12] The Lanham Act provides that **nonuse for three consecutive years is** *prima facie* evidence of an intent to abandon. 15 U.S.C. §1127.

[13] A mark is **assigned in gross** if it is not accompanied by the business goodwill associated with the mark. Under modern law, this will be the case if the assignee uses the mark to sell different products or services than the assignor did.

[14] **Failure to police** the licensees' use of the mark to ensure consistent quality and uniform characteristics may deceive consumers who rely on the mark for information about quality and characteristics. This will constitute an abandonment because the mark will have lost its informative significance.

[15] But note that challenges to distinctiveness and priority are **limited by incontestability status**. See Figure 7 for more on incontestability status.

FIGURE 9

DOES THE MARK OWNER HAVE A CAUSE OF ACTION FOR DILUTION?

Use this chart to determine whether a plaintiff/owner of an indication of origin has a cause of action for dilution. Note that in 2006, Congress **substantially revised** the federal cause of action for dilution, which is set forth in Lanham Act §1125(a). This chart describes the federal dilution cause of action **as revised** in 2006. (All federal statutory references are to the Lanham Act, 15 U.S.C. §1051 *et seq.*)

Both the **state and the federal dilution causes of action** are statutory creations meant to protect the persuasive or advertising value of famous marks and their owner's investment in creating this value. It is not necessary for the plaintiff to demonstrate that the parties' goods or services are similar or that the defendant's use causes any likelihood of consumer confusion.

↓

The state dilution cause of action: Approximately half the states have antidilution statutes. These statutes have been construed to provide two forms of dilution relief: (1) relief against **blurring**[1] and (2) relief against **tarnishment**.[2] Most state dilution causes of action prohibit a defendant's actions that cause a **likelihood of dilution**. Pursuant to Lanham Act §1125(c), federal registration of a mark immunizes the mark from state dilution claims.

↓

Lanham Act §1125(c) provides a federal cause of action for dilution, enabling the owner of a **famous** mark to enjoin another person's use in commerce of a similar mark or trade name, if such use **began after** the plaintiff's mark became famous and causes a **likelihood of dilution by blurring** or a **likelihood of dilution by tarnishment**.

| **Fame:** Only famous marks qualify for §1125(c) protection. In recent revisions to §1125(c), Congress has clarified that "niche" fame (fame only in a particular segment of the general population) will not suffice for federal dilution protection. To qualify for protection, the plaintiff's mark must be "**widely recognized by the general consuming public**" as a designation of the source of the plaintiff's goods or services. | **Distinctiveness:** Under the 2006 revisions, the plaintiff's mark must be "distinctive," but its distinctiveness may be **either inherent or acquired** through secondary meaning. | **Likelihood of dilution by blurring:** Lanham Act §1125(c) defines blurring as "association arising from the similarity between a mark or trade name and a famous mark that **impairs the distinctiveness** of the famous mark." | **Likelihood of dilution by tarnishment:** Lanham Act §1125(c) defines tarnishment dilution as "association arising from the similarity between a mark or trade name and a famous mark that **harms the reputation** of the famous mark." |

Chart continues on next pages.

See notes after final page of chart.

FIGURE **9** *(cont.)*

DOES THE MARK OWNER HAVE A CAUSE OF ACTION FOR DILUTION?

Section 1125(c) provides that courts should consider "all relevant **factors**" in determining a mark's fame, including:

- the duration, extent, and geographic reach of **advertising and publicity** of the mark;
- the amount, volume, and geographic extent of **sales** made with the mark;
- the extent of actual **mark recognition**; and
- whether the mark is federally **registered**.

Courts should consider "all relevant **factors**" in evaluating a blurring claim, including:

- the **degree of similarity** between the famous mark and the defendant's mark or trade name;
- the degree of the famous mark's **distinctiveness**;
- the extent to which the famous mark owner's use is **exclusive**;
- the degree of the famous mark's **recognition**;
- whether the defendant **intended** to create an association with the famous mark; and
- any **actual association** between the defendant's mark or trade name and the famous mark.

Traditionally, courts have held that the famous mark's reputation can be "harmed," and thus tarnished, if the famous mark is associated with an "**unwholesome context**," such as pornography, or a context that is "**out-of-keeping with the famous mark's high-quality image**," such as a very cheap, tacky, or shabbily made product.

Dilution of trade dress: Federal dilution protection extends to famous trade dress (notwithstanding possible constitutional concerns raised by extending dilution to product feature trade dress).[3] However, §1125(c) provides that when unregistered trade dress is claimed to be diluted, the plaintiff bears the burden of proving that the trade dress is **non-functional**. Moreover, if the trade dress incorporates registered marks, the claimant must prove that the **unregistered portion of the trade dress, taken as a whole, is famous**.

If the plaintiff's mark is not sufficiently famous, or other elements of the dilution cause of action are not satisfied, the plaintiff has no case.

If the plaintiff's mark is sufficiently famous and the other elements of the dilution cause of action can be demonstrated, then it must be determined **whether any of the exclusions to dilution apply**.

Lanham Act §1125(c)(3) provides a number of **exclusions** from dilution protection, to accommodate First Amendment and competition concerns.

FIGURE 9 *(cont.)*

DOES THE MARK OWNER HAVE A CAUSE OF ACTION FOR DILUTION?

Lanham Act §1125(c) expressly prohibits a dilution cause of action against "**any fair use**" of a famous mark "**other than as a designation of source for [the user's] own goods or services**."
This exclusion expressly shelters a number of famous mark uses, including:

- nominative fair use of the famous mark;[4]
- descriptive fair use of the word or symbol constituting the famous mark;[5]
- use of the famous mark in comparative advertising;
- use of the famous mark in identifying, parodying, criticizing, or commenting about the famous mark owner or its goods or services.

These "**fair use**" **exclusions** also extend to persons who **facilitate fair uses** of famous marks.

Lanham Act §1125(c) prohibits dilution claims against all forms of news reporting and news commentary.

Lanham Act §1125(c) also expressly prohibits federal dilution claims against "**noncommercial use**" of famous marks. Courts have routinely construed "noncommercial use" to mean "**noncommercial speech**," and thus to limit the dilution cause of action to uses of marks in commercial speech, as that concept has been defined in First Amendment jurisprudence.

The Supreme Court defines commercial speech as "speech that does no more than propose a commercial transaction."[6] Because dilution claims can only be brought against commercial speech, courts should prohibit dilution claims against unauthorized uses of famous marks in the titles of expressive works, such as books, movies, or songs.

If the plaintiff's dilution claim falls within one of the §1125(c) exclusions, the plaintiff cannot proceed with the cause of action.

If the plaintiff's dilution claim does not fall within one of the exclusions, consider the available remedy for its demonstrated likelihood of dilution.

The remedy in dilution claims is generally limited to an injunction. Plaintiffs can only recover monetary damages if they can demonstrate that:

- the defendant first used its diluting mark in commerce **after** the Trademark Dilution Revision Act of 2006 was enacted; and
- the defendant's actions were **willful**.

The defendant's actions will be deemed **willful** in a **blurring** claim if it "willfully intended to trade on the recognition of the famous mark."

The defendant's actions will be deemed **willful** in a **tarnishment** claim if it "willfully intended to harm the reputation of the famous mark."

DOES THE MARK OWNER HAVE A CAUSE OF ACTION FOR DILUTION?

[1] **"Blurring" dilution** occurs when a defendant uses a mark that is similar to the plaintiff's famous mark and thereby diminishes consumers' automatic, strong association of the mark with the plaintiff and the positive imagery the plaintiff has created through persuasive advertising and promotion.

[2] **"Tarnishment" dilution** occurs when a defendant uses a mark that is similar to the plaintiff's famous mark in a context that is unwholesome or out of keeping with the plaintiff's high-quality or prestigious image, thereby tarnishing the "luster" or selling power of the plaintiff's mark.

[3] Some courts have expressed concern that providing dilution protection for **product features** provides strong, patent-like protection for products that may not qualify for such protection under the high standards of patent law, and that dilution protection, unlike patent protection, is not limited in duration. This could effectively undermine the patent laws and exceed Congress's authority under the Constitution's Patents and Copyrights Clause. (The Patents and Copyrights Clause only authorizes Congress to provide property rights in "inventions" for a "limited duration.") See, for example, *I.P. Lund Trading ApS v. Kohler Co.*, 163 F.3d 27 (1st Cir. 1998).

[4] See Figure 8.

[5] See Figure 8.

[6] In *Bolger v. Youngs Drug Products Corp.*, 463 U.S. 60 (1983), the Supreme Court held that **"mixed speech,"** which *both* proposes a commercial transaction and serves some other purpose, may be treated as commercial speech in some cases. Thus, in *Bolger*, the Supreme Court held that pamphlets, which the defendant conceded to be advertisements, constituted commercial speech even though they linked their promotion of the defendant's product (condoms) to information about prophylactics generally and to prevention of venereal disease. Subsequent decisions have drawn a three-part test from *Bolger* for use in determining whether "mixed messages" constitute commercial speech and thus command a lower level of First Amendment protection: (1) whether the speech is in an advertisement, (2) whether it refers to a specific product or service, and (3) whether the speaker has an economic motivation for the speech.

The Ninth Circuit has construed §1125(c) as limiting the dilution claim to **pure** commercial speech, so that the titles of expressive works (which might be viewed as a form of mixed speech) are sheltered from federal dilution claims. *Mattel, Inc. v. MCA Records, Inc.*, 296 F.3d 894 (9th Cir. 2002),

FIGURE 10

DOES THE MARK OWNER HAVE A CAUSE OF ACTION FOR CYBERSQUATTING?

Use this chart to determine whether a plaintiff/mark owner has a federal cause of action for cybersquatting. (All statutory references are to the Lanham Act, 15 U.S.C. §1051 *et seq.*)

Cybersquatting: Congress enacted the **Anticybersquatting Consumer Protection Act** in 1999. It is codified at Lanham Act §1125(d) and prohibits **bad-faith registration, trafficking in, or use of** a domain name that is identical or confusingly similar to, or dilutive of, another person's mark.

The plaintiff must demonstrate that the **defendant acted with bad-faith intent to profit** from the business goodwill of the plaintiff's mark. §1125(d) provides a nonexclusive list of **factors** to consider in deciding whether a defendant acted with the requisite bad-faith intent.

The **plaintiff's mark must have been distinctive** (i.e., enjoyed trademark status) **at the time the domain name was registered** (or, if the claim is that the defendant's domain name dilutes the plaintiff's mark, the mark must have been famous at the time the domain name was registered).[10]

The **factors for determining bad faith** are as follows:

- Does the domain name registrant have trademark or other rights in the name?[1]
- Is the domain name the same as the registrant's legal name or established nickname?[2]
- Has the defendant used the name in connection with the *bona fide* offering of goods or services?[3]
- Is the defendant making a *bona fide* noncommercial or fair use of the mark in a Web site that is accessible under the domain name?[4]
- Did the defendant intend to divert consumers away from the plaintiff's Web site to a Web site that could harm the mark's goodwill, either for commercial gain or with the intent to tarnish or disparage the mark, by creating a likelihood of confusion?[5]
- Did the defendant make no use of the domain name in *bona fide* offering of goods or services and offer to sell it to the mark owner or others for financial gain?[6]
- Did the defendant engage in a pattern of intentionally providing material and misleading false contact information in applications for domain name registration or failing to maintain accurate contact information?[7]
- Did the defendant acquire multiple domain names that he knew to be identical to, confusingly similar to, or dilutive of others marks?[8]
- To what extent is the mark at issue distinctive and/or famous?[9]

The Anticybersquatting Act provides *in rem* **jurisdiction**, permitting the mark owner to file an action against the domain name itself. To qualify, the mark owner must demonstrate that he **exercised due diligence in trying to locate or obtain personal jurisdiction over** the domain name registrant and was unsuccessful. The relief available in *in rem* actions is limited to an injunction ordering the forfeiture, cancellation, or transfer of the domain name registration.[11]

Chart continues on next page.   *See notes after final page of chart.*

FIGURE 10 *(cont.)*

DOES THE MARK OWNER HAVE A CAUSE OF ACTION FOR CYBERSQUATTING?

Assuming that the plaintiff can demonstrate bad-faith registration, trafficking or use of a domain name that is confusingly similar to or dilutive of its mark, and the other prerequisites discussed above, it may prevail in a §1125(d) anti-cybersquatting claim.

The plaintiff may wish to consider an **administrative alternative** to a §1125(d) claim, however, which may (depending on the circumstances) save it time and money.

The Uniform Domain Name Dispute Resolution Policy (UDRP):[12] This dispute resolution policy, which is binding on all persons who register domain names with ICANN-accredited registrars, requires registrants to submit to administrative proceedings when a third party asserts that:

- the registered domain name is identical or confusingly similar to a trademark or service mark in which the complainant has rights;
- the registrant has no rights or legitimate interest in the domain name; and
- the domain name has been registered and is being used in **bad faith**.

Under the UDRP, a registrant may be deemed to have **registered in bad faith** if he registered and used the domain name:

- primarily to sell or rent the domain name for profit;
- primarily to disrupt a competitor's business;
- intentionally to create a likelihood of confusion with the complainant's mark and thus lure Internet users to her Web site for commercial gain; or
- in order to prevent the mark owner from registering and using the mark as its own domain name (provided that there has been a pattern of such conduct).

The existence of the mandatory UDRP administrative proceeding does not prevent either party from **submitting the dispute to a court for independent resolution**.

The **only relief** under the UDRP is cancellation of the domain name registration or transfer of the registration to the complainant.

A registrant can **rebut** a claim of bad faith by demonstrating that:

- he used or prepared to use the domain name in selling goods or services prior to notice of the dispute;
- he had been commonly known by the domain name; or
- he is making a legitimate, noncommercial, or **fair use** of the domain name, without intent to obtain commercial gain.

In the U.S., mark owners may bring a cause of action against the domain name registrant for cybersquatting or for trademark infringement or dilution. Congress has also provided a **cause of action for domain name registrants** who have had their registrations suspended, canceled, or transferred by order of a UDRP dispute resolution panel. Under Lanham Act §1114(2)(D)(v), such registrants may establish that their registration is **not unlawful** under the Lanham Act and seek injunctive relief ordering **reactivation** of the domain name or **retransfer** of the domain name registration to them.

DOES THE MARK OWNER HAVE A CAUSE OF ACTION FOR CYBERSQUATTING?

[1] For example, does the domain name registrant have a concurrent right to use the word or symbol as a mark for its own, differing products or services? If so, this suggests a lack of bad faith.

[2] If so, this indicates a lack of bad-faith intent.

[3] If so, this would indicate an absence of bad-faith intent.

[4] For example, does the registrant use the mark in comparative advertising, comment, criticism, parody, news reporting, or similar activities on the Web site? This would indicate an absence of bad-faith intent.

[5] For example, did the domain name registrant deliberately use the mark to attract consumers who were looking for the plaintiff's Web site in order to sell them inferior goods, to trick them into providing credit card or other personal information, or to increase the number of "hits" on his site so that he could charge more for advertising? If so, this indicates bad-faith intent.

[6] If so, this indicates bad faith.

[7] This would suggest an attempt to avoid service of process and bad faith.

[8] If so, this suggests mark "warehousing" and bad faith.

[9] The more distinctive and famous the mark, the more likely the owner of the mark deserves relief.

[10] The Anticybersquatting Act also prohibits the registration of a domain name that is, or is substantially and confusingly similar to, **the name of another person** (even though the name does not qualify as a mark). However, this cause of action is narrow: It is limited to situations in which the registrant's specific intent is to profit by selling the domain name to the plaintiff or a third party for financial gain. 15 U.S.C. §1129.

[11] The Court of Appeals for the Fourth Circuit has held that the Anticybersquatting Act's *in rem* jurisdiction provisions **apply in the case of Lanham Act §1125(a) and (c) claims**, as well as to claims under §1125(d). *Harrods Ltd. v. Sixty Internet Domain Names,* 304 F.3d 214 (4th Cir. 2002).

[12] **The Internet Corporation for Assigned Names and Numbers (ICANN)**, a nonprofit, private corporation, administers the Internet name and address system. It contracts with a number of competing domain name registrars and has adopted its dispute resolution policy to assist in resolving disputes between trademark owners and people who register domain names with its authorized registrars. This policy is incorporated into all domain name registration agreements made by ICANN-accredited registrars. Dispute panels to resolve these claims are drawn from dispute resolution organizations approved by ICANN, such as the World Intellectual Property Organization (WIPO).

CAPSULE SUMMARY

CAPSULE SUMMARY

SUMMARY OF CONTENTS

CHAPTER 1

INTRODUCTION TO THE STUDY OF INTELLECTUAL PROPERTY

I. GENERALLY

A. Policy considerations: Intellectual property law seeks to benefit the general public by providing a rich, diverse, efficient, and competitive marketplace. Most intellectual property doctrines (other than trademark and unfair competition law) are crafted to balance two potentially conflicting goals: (1) to provide an incentive to create by giving creators property rights in the products of their creativity, and (2) to provide the greatest possible competitor and public access to products of creativity, in order to promote a progressive and competitive marketplace. In the case of trademark and related unfair competition doctrines, the law provides businesses limited property rights in their indications of origin and/or business good will not as an incentive to create, but in order to promote marketplace efficiency, and to protect consumers from deception.

B. Jurisdiction: Article 1, Section 8, Clause 8 of the U.S. Constitution authorizes Congress to enact patent and copyright laws. The Commerce Clause (Article 1, Section 8, Clause 3) is the basis for Congress's regulation of trademarks and unfair competition. The states retain concurrent jurisdiction to regulate intellectual property under the Tenth Amendment to the Constitution.

CHAPTER 2

THE LAW OF TRADE SECRETS

I. STATUS OF IDEAS OR INFORMATION AS TRADE SECRET

A. General definition: A trade secret is information that (1) derives actual or potential economic value from the fact that it is not known or readily ascertainable by others, and (2) is subject to reasonable efforts to maintain its secrecy.

B. Factors considered in determining trade secret status: In determining whether information constitutes a trade secret, courts will consider: (1) how widely the information is known outside the claimant's business; (2) how widely it is known within the claimant's company; (3) whether the claimant has taken reasonable measures to ensure that the information remains secret; (4) how difficult it would be for others *properly* to acquire or duplicate the information; (5) whether the information gives the claimant a commercial, competitive advantage over others who do not know it; and

(6) how much effort or money the claimant expended in developing or acquiring the information.

II. WHEN ACQUISITION, USE, OR DISCLOSURE OF A TRADE SECRET CONSTITUTES AN ACTIONABLE MISAPPROPRIATION

A. Disclosure or use of a trade secret in breach of confidence: Unauthorized disclosure or use of a trade secret is actionable if it breaches a duty of confidence. A duty of confidence (which requires the defendant to refrain from disclosing or using the claimant's trade secret without permission) arises when the parties are in a special relationship, such as the agent-principal (including employer-employee) relationship, a partnership relationship, or a fiduciary relationship such as lawyer-client or doctor-patient. The parties may also create a duty of confidentiality by expressly or impliedly contracting that the recipient will not disclose or use the secret without permission. An implied contract to this effect may be found if the recipient has notice that the trade secret owner is about to disclose the secret to her in confidence and agrees to hear it.

B. Disclosure or use of a trade secret learned from a third party with notice: If A reveals a trade secret to B under circumstances that impose a duty of confidentiality on B, and B breaches the confidence by revealing the secret to C, C will have a duty not to use or disclose the secret (and will be liable if he does so) if he has notice that the information is a trade secret that is being revealed to him in breach of B's duty. C will be deemed to have notice of this if a reasonable person under similar circumstances would know it or if the reasonable person would be led to make further inquiry and a reasonable inquiry would reveal it. [*Note:* This reasonable person standard is applied in many other situations, *infra*.]

C. Disclosure or use of a trade secret learned by mistake: If A reveals his trade secret to B by accident or mistake and B has notice that the information is a trade secret and is being revealed by mistake, then B has a duty to refrain from using or disclosing the trade secret without permission, and will be liable if he does so. The same reasonable person standard governs the issue of notice as in section B, *supra*.

D. Continued disclosure or use of a trade secret after receipt of notice: If C learns A's trade secret from a third person who was breaching his duty, or if C learns the trade secret by mistake, but at the time of disclosure C has no notice of the secrecy and breach or mistake, then C will not be liable for subsequent disclosure or use of the trade secret. The Restatement of Torts provides that if C later receives such notice, she must stop all further disclosure or use upon receiving notice unless she can demonstrate either: (1) that she paid value for the secret in good faith; or (2) that she otherwise has so changed her position in reliance on the secret that to require her to refrain from further disclosure or use would be inequitable. The Uniform Trade Secrets Act differs somewhat from the Restatement provisions in the case of trade secrets learned through breach of confidence, providing that good-faith users who have materially changed their position or paid value will be liable for continued use or disclosure after receiving notice. The Uniform Act notes, however, that courts may refuse an injunction in such cases, contingent on the defendant's paying a reasonable royalty for continuing use.

E. **Disclosure or use of a trade secret acquired through improper means:** B will be liable for acquisition, disclosure, or use of A's trade secret if she acquired A's trade secret through "improper means." "Improper means" includes illegal conduct and conduct that is below generally accepted standards of commercial morality.

F. **Acquisition, disclosure, or use of a trade secret with notice that the provider acquired it through improper means:** Acquisition of a trade secret through improper means is itself an actionable misappropriation under the Uniform Trade Secrets Act, if the acquirer has reason to know that the means are improper. Moreover, if X acquires Y's trade secret through improper means and gives it to Z, Z will be liable for subsequent disclosure or use if he has notice that it is a trade secret and has been obtained through improper means. The reasonable person standard (discussed above) applies to determine when the defendant will be deemed to have notice.

G. **The effect of the defendant's modification of the plaintiff's trade secret:** The fact that the defendant modified or improved the plaintiff's trade secret before using or disclosing it will not relieve the defendant from liability as long as the plaintiff can demonstrate that the information the defendant used or disclosed was "substantially derived" from the plaintiff's trade secret.

III. PRIVATE OWNERS' RIGHTS IN TRADE SECRET INFORMATION SUBMITTED TO GOVERNMENT AGENCIES

A. **Government agency disclosure of trade secrets and the takings clause:** Many different statutes on the state and federal level require government agencies to publicly disclose trade secret information submitted to them by private parties. Such a disclosure will only be deemed an unconstitutional "taking" if, at the time the private party submitted the trade secret, he had a reasonable, investment-backed expectation of confidentiality. He is unlikely to be deemed to have had such an expectation unless, at the time he submitted the trade secret to the agency, there was a statute expressly prohibiting the agency from disclosing the trade secret.

IV. USE AND DISCLOSURE BY EMPLOYEES AND FORMER EMPLOYEES

A. **In the absence of an express agreement:** An employee owes a duty of confidentiality to his employer, which prohibits him from using or disclosing trade secrets that the employer discloses to him within the scope of his employment. This duty of confidence extends to information that the employee himself creates within the scope of his employment, if the employer especially hired or directed the employee to create the trade secret information and placed substantial time and resources at the employee's disposal for that purpose. In such cases, courts find an implied agreement between the parties that any resulting trade secrets will belong to the employer.

1. **When the trade secret belongs to the employee:** If the employee was not hired or directed to create information of the type involved, but nonetheless creates a trade secret during the course of employment, the trade secret will be deemed to belong to the employee, and the employee will be entitled to use or disclose it as she will. However, if the employee used the employer's work time, facilities, or supplies to develop the trade secret, then the employer will have a "shop right" in it — a nonexclusive, royalty-free license to use the employee's trade secret.

B. **In the case of an express agreement:** An employer and employee may expressly agree that the employee will not disclose the employer's trade secrets (a "non-disclosure agreement") and/or that the employee assigns (in advance) ownership of any trade secrets she creates to the employer (an "advance assignment agreement"). A third type of agreement provides that the employee will not compete with the employer for a specified time in a specified geographical area after leaving the employer. However, courts are less likely to enforce covenants not to compete because they are against public policy. Generally, courts will enforce non-competition agreements only if the employer demonstrates that the employee has the employer's trade secrets or other confidential proprietary information. Even then, courts will hesitate to enforce the agreement unless: (1) it is reasonably necessary to protect the employer; (2) it is reasonable as to the time and geographical area in which the employee is restricted from competing; (3) the restrictions are not harmful to the general public; and (4) the restrictions are not unreasonably burdensome to the employee. Some jurisdictions, such as California, refuse to enforce non-competition covenants.

C. **The doctrine of inevitable disclosure:** Under the doctrine of inevitable disclosure, which some jurisdictions have adopted, the court will enjoin a plaintiff's former employee (at least temporarily) from taking a new position if: (1) the former employee knows the plaintiff's trade secrets; (2) the former employee's new job duties are similar to those of his former position, and it would be difficult for him not to rely on or use the plaintiff's trade secrets in the new position; and (3) there is evidence that the former employee or his new employer cannot be relied on to take adequate precautions to avoid disclosure or use.

V. REMEDIES FOR TRADE SECRET MISAPPROPRIATION

A. **Injunctions:** A defendant may be enjoined from using or disclosing the plaintiff's trade secret. Jurisdictions differ regarding the appropriate length of such injunctions. Most limit the length of the injunction to the duration of the information's secrecy.

B. **Damages:** Damages may be measured by: (1) the profits the plaintiff lost as a result of the defendant's misappropriation; (2) a reasonable royalty for the defendant's use of the trade secret; or (3) profits the defendant made as a result of the misappropriation.

C. **Criminal prosecution:** Many states have made theft of trade secrets a criminal offense. The Economic Espionage Act of 1996 makes it a federal crime in some situations.

CHAPTER 3

PATENTS

I. UTILITY PATENTS

A. The nature and term of a utility patent: A utility patent gives its owner exclusive rights in an invention for a limited term. For many years the term lasted 17 years from the date the patent was issued. However, for patents issued on applications filed after June 8, 1995, the term is measured from the date the application was filed. The term lasts 20 years from the filing date, even though exclusive rights only commence once the patent is granted.

B. Limitations on patents: Patents are available only for those inventions that are non-obvious, novel, useful, and fully disclosed as specified in Patent Act §112. If the Patent and Trademark Office (P.T.O.) grants a patent, this creates a legal presumption that the invention meets these criteria. However, a patent may be challenged in court, either through a declaratory judgment action or through an invalidity defense in an infringement suit. A challenger must demonstrate patent invalidity by clear and convincing evidence. All appeals in patent cases go to the Court of Appeals for the Federal Circuit.

    1. Administrative challenges: There have been various routes for obtaining administrative review of patent scope and validity. These include reissue, *ex parte* reexamination, and *inter partes* re-examination proceedings. The Leahy-Smith America Invents Act provides two new and improved means of obtaining administrative review of a patent's validity: *Inter partes* review (effective September 16, 2012) and post-grant review (effective for patents granted on applications filed on or after March 16, 2013). Both forms of review are adjudicative in nature, are held before the newly reconstituted Patent Trial and Appeal Board, and apply a "preponderance of the evidence" standard for judging patent validity. Each form of review has its own rules regarding when it can be brought, what kinds of invalidity challenges can be made, and its estoppel effect in subsequent litigation.

II. STATUTORY SUBJECT MATTER OF A UTILITY PATENT

Patent Act §101 authorizes utility patents for "any new and useful process, machine, manufacture, or composition of matter, or any new and useful improvement thereof." A newly discovered use for a known process, machine, manufacture, or composition of matter may qualify as a patentable process.

A. Naturally occurring vs. man-made things: Patents may be granted only for "man-made" things, not for naturally occurring things. However, patents are not restricted to inanimate matter—a patent may be granted for living matter that has been altered by the applicant to have characteristics it would not have had naturally. *Diamond v. Chakrabarty,* 447 U.S. 303 (1980).

B. Laws of nature, natural phenomena, and abstract ideas: The Supreme Court has held that laws of nature, natural phenomena, and abstract ideas may not be patented in themselves. Specific applications of laws of nature or abstract ideas can be patented. Thus, for example, mathematical algorithms (of which computer programs are comprised) cannot be patented because they are abstract ideas. However, a process, machine, or article of manufacture that incorporates a mathematical algorithm (or computer program) as one step or element may be patentable, as that would constitute a specific application of the mathematical algorithm. *Diamond v. Diehr*, 450 U.S. 175 (1981).

    1. Processes or methods as abstract ideas: It can be particularly hard to distinguish abstract ideas from patentable processes. The Federal Circuit has held that processes consisting only of steps that can be carried out in the human mind ("mental processes") are unpatentable abstract ideas. In *Bilski v. Kappos*, 130 S. Ct. 3218 (2010), the Supreme Court suggested that the "machine or transformation test" is a valuable tool for determining whether a claimed process is an unpatentable abstract idea, although it is not the sole test. Other considerations include whether the claim would totally preempt use of a mathematical algorithm. Adding field-of-use limitations or "insignificant post-solution activity" will not transform an abstract idea into a patentable process. In its recent decision in *Mayo Collaborative Services v. Prometheus Laboratories*, 101 U.S.P.Q.2d 1961 (2012), the Supreme Court noted that process steps claimed along with an abstract idea or law of nature must add "something significant" to the abstract idea or law of nature and not be merely routine, conventional activity if the combination is to constitute a patentable application of the abstract idea or law of nature.

C. Business methods: Business methods are patentable subject matter. It is not necessary that the claims associate the method with "technological arts." However, many business method claims may constitute unpatentable abstract ideas. Because of this and other perceived weaknesses in issued business method patents, the Leahy-Smith America Invents Act creates a new administrative "transitional post-grant review" proceeding. Persons charged with or sued for infringement of business method patents may invoke this proceeding to review the patent's validity. The Leahy-Smith Act categorically prohibits patents for tax strategies.

D. Medical procedures: Medical procedures are patentable, but infringement remedies against medical practitioners and related health care entities are limited in some cases.

III. THE NOVELTY STANDARD

The novelty requirement is set forth in Patent Act §102. Prior to the Leahy-Smith America Invents Act, the United States tailored its novelty requirement to create a "first-to-invent" system of priority. The Smith-Leahy Act transforms the United States to a "first-to-file" system, with a built-in "grace" period that allows inventors to disclose their inventions up to a year prior to applying for a patent. Applications filed on or after March 16, 2013, and resulting patents will be governed by the Smith-Leahy first-to-file novelty provisions. Applications filed before that date and resulting patents will continue to be governed by the pre–Leahy-Smith novelty and statutory bar provisions.

A. The pre–Leahy-Smith Act novelty provisions: The novelty evaluation under pre–Leahy-Smith §102 focuses on the applicant's *date of invention*. The forms of prior art that may "anticipate" an applicant's invention and render it non-novel are set forth in subsections 102(a), (e), and (g). In each case, the prior art—the earlier embodiment of the invention, written description, publication, patent, or patent application—must include every element stated in the applicant's claim, arranged in the same way.

1. Subsection 102(a): Subsection 102(a) says that a patent must be denied if: (1) the applicant's invention was *known* in the United States before the applicant for patent invented; (2) the applicant's invention was *used* in the United States before the applicant invented; (3) the applicant's invention was *described in a printed publication* in the United States or a foreign country before the applicant invented; or (4) the applicant's invention was *patented* in the United States or a foreign country before the applicant invented. The focus is on the actions of *persons other than the inventor/applicant*, prior to the date the inventor/applicant made the invention.

   a. When an invention is "known" in the United States: To have been "known" in the United States prior to the applicant's invention date, the invention must have been: (1) "reduced to practice," actually or constructively, or otherwise described in a writing sufficiently to enable a person with ordinary skill in the relevant art to make it without undue experimentation; and (2) accessible to the public.

   b. When an invention will be deemed "used" in the United States: To be "used" in the United States prior to the applicant's invention date, the invention must have been: (1) reduced to actual practice, (2) used in the manner for which it was intended by its inventor, and (3) accessible to the public.

   c. When an invention will be deemed "described in a printed publication": To find a "printed publication" that anticipates an applicant's invention, several considerations are relevant. First, the publication must have been "printed." This requirement will generally be satisfied if it was reduced to a discernible, tangible form. Second, there must have been a "publication." A publication generally will be found if an interested American, exercising reasonable diligence, could obtain the information. Third, the alleged printed publication must describe the invention sufficiently to enable a person with ordinary skill in the art to make or practice the invention without undue experimentation. The Federal Circuit has held that when printed matter is displayed but not distributed or indexed, several factors should be considered in determining whether it was sufficiently accessible to constitute a "printed publication": (1) the length of time the matter was displayed or exhibited; (2) the expertise of the targeted audience; (3) the existence of reasonable expectations that the displayed material would not be copied; and (4) the simplicity or ease with which the displayed material could have been copied. *In re Klopfenstein*, 380 F.3d 1345 (Fed. Cir. 2004).

d. **When an invention will be deemed "patented":** For an invention to be anticipated by a prior patent under §102(a), it must appear that: (1) the applicant's invention was the actual subject of the patent monopoly; (2) the patent effectively granted rights in the invention before the §102(a) applicant invented; and (3) the patent disclosure was available to the public before the §102(a) applicant's invention date.

2. **Subsection 102(e):** Subsection 102(e) denies a patent to an applicant if: (1) before she invented, the same invention was described in an application for patent that was pending in the U.S. P.T.O.; and (2) the pending application was ultimately published and/or granted. The pending application is deemed anticipating prior art as of its filing date.

3. **Subsection 102(g):** Subsection 102(g) prohibits B from obtaining a patent if A made the same invention in the United States before B did, and A did not abandon, suppress, or conceal the invention prior to B's invention date.

   a. **Identifying the first person to invent:** Invention entails (1) an inventive concept, and (2) reduction of the inventive concept to actual or constructive practice. It is presumed that the first person to reduce the concept to practice is the first to invent, but this presumption can be rebutted. If the second person to reduce to practice can demonstrates that she was the first to conceive of the invention and was diligent in reducing the concept to practice from a time prior to the other's conception date, she will be deemed the first inventor.

   b. **Abandonment, suppression, and concealment:** A (the first inventor) will not be deemed to have abandoned, suppressed, or concealed the invention as long as she was engaged in reasonable, diligent efforts to bring the benefit of the invention to the public. It is not necessary for A to file for a patent. She may bring the benefit of the invention to the public by introducing it to the market or by publishing a description of it. If A did abandon, suppress, or conceal her invention, but resumed activity with regard to it before B invented, A can rely on her date of resumption as her date of invention, and still prevent B from obtaining a patent.

   c. **Earlier invention abroad:** Section 102(g) also prohibits a patent for B if A's invention was made before B's in a foreign country and was not abandoned, suppressed, or concealed — if A establishes the earlier foreign invention date in a patent interference proceeding consistent with Patent Act §104.

B. **The pre–Leahy-Smith Act statutory bar provisions:** The statutory bars ensure that inventors apply for a U.S. patent in a timely fashion. The statutory bar provisions are set forth in Patent Act §§102(b), (c), and (d). In addition, Patent Act §102(f) requires that the person filing the application be the inventor.

1. **Subsection 102(b):** Subsection 102(b) provides that a patent must be denied if, *more than one year before the application was filed*: (1) the invention was *in public use* in the United States; (2) the invention was *on sale* in the United States; (3) the invention was *described in a printed publication* anywhere in the world; or (4) the invention was *patented* anywhere in the world. Thus, the focus in this

section is on the actions *both* of the inventor/applicant and others more than one year before the application was filed. Subsection (b) may be viewed as a form of statute of limitations that requires an inventor to apply for a patent within a year after the invention enters the public domain in one of the four listed ways. The meanings of "printed publication" and "patented" in this context are similar to the meanings discussed in connection with subsection 102(a), *supra*.

a. **When an invention will be deemed "in public use":** A "public use" in the United States will be found when a person other than the inventor/applicant uses the completed, operable invention in the way the invention was intended to be used, and is under no restriction or obligation to keep the invention secret.

    i. **Experimental use:** A public use that is primarily experimental will not trigger the subsection 102(b) statute of limitations. However, the primary purpose of the use must be experimental—to test the invention from a technological standpoint—not commercial exploitation or development of a market. It is important that the inventor control the use of the invention, test aspects of it that are covered in the patent claims, and systematically collect test results. Courts may also inquire whether it was necessary to test the invention publicly and whether the inventor imposed confidentiality requirements.

    ii. **Indirect public use:** If an invention is put to a commercial use that does not reveal it directly to the public (e.g., the invention is a process used to produce products sold to the public, but the products do not reveal the process), courts will nonetheless find a public use that starts the one-year statute running, if it is *the applicant* who is making this use.

b. **When an invention will be deemed "on sale":** An invention will be deemed "on sale" in the United States if it is offered for sale, regardless of whether it is in fact sold or delivered. While the invention need not be "reduced to actual practice" in order to be found "on sale," the Supreme Court has held (in *Pfaff v. Wells Electronics, Inc.,* 525 U.S. 55 (1998)) that: (1) the invention must be the subject of a commercial offer to sell (according to the Federal Circuit, it must be an offer that satisfies the formal standards for an offer under the Uniform Commercial Code, *Group One Ltd. v. Hallmark Cards, Inc.,* 254 F.3d 1041 (Fed. Cir. 2001), *cert. denied,* 534 U.S. 1127 (2002)), and (2) at the time of the offer, the invention must be "ready for patenting." The Supreme Court specified that the invention may be "ready for patenting" if it has been reduced to actual practice or if the inventor has prepared drawings or other descriptions of the invention that are sufficiently specific to enable a person skilled in the art to make or practice the invention without undue experimentation.

    i. **Processes:** To trigger the statutory "on sale" bar for a process, one must offer to sell a tangible product made through use of the process.

    ii. **Experimental sale:** A sale that is primarily for experimental purposes will not trigger the §102(b) statute of limitations. However, for a sale to be "experimental," the inventor must tell the purchaser that the sale is for purposes of experimentation and maintain control over the purchaser's use.

2. **Subsection 102(c):** Subsection 102(c) prohibits a patent if the applicant abandoned his invention. However, the focus is on whether he *abandoned his right to a patent*, rather than his invention. Abandonment of the right to a patent may be express or implied through conduct that indicates an intent to forgo a patent. In some cases, refraining from applying for a patent for a long period of time may be sufficient evidence of an intent to abandon a patent.

3. **Subsection 102(d):** Subsection 102(d) prohibits a patent if: (1) the applicant filed a patent application in a foreign country more than 12 months before he filed his U.S. application; and (2) the foreign patent was granted *before* the U.S. filing date.

4. **Subsection 102(f):** Subsection 102(f) requires that the applicant for patent be the *inventor*—the person who conceived of the specific invention claimed (as opposed, for example, to that person's employer, who may have directed him to conceive of the invention). If more than one person makes a mental contribution to the final invention concept, then each is a joint inventor.

C. **Novelty under the Leahy-Smith America Invents Act:** In evaluating novelty under the newly amended Patent Act §102, the focus is on the applicant's "*effective filing date*" rather than on her invention date. "Prior art" that can anticipate a patent and render it non-novel is described in amended §102(a), and exceptions to anticipatory prior art are set forth in §102(b). The amended novelty provisions generally recognize priority in the first inventor to file an application, rather than in the first person to invent. However, under certain circumstances, the first inventor to disclose the invention to the public may have priority. (Remember that the amended novelty provisions apply only to applications filed on or after March 16, 2013, and patents granted on those applications.)

1. **Anticipatory prior art under the Leahy-Smith Act:** Under the Leahy-Smith amendments, an applicant's invention is novel unless: (1) the claimed invention was *patented, described in a printed publication, in public use, on sale, or otherwise available to the public* prior to the applicant's filing date (presumably, the terms "printed publication," "patented," "on sale," and "in public use" will continue to retain their pre-amendment meanings); or (2) the claimed invention was described in an earlier-filed application for U.S. patent (or resulting patent), naming another inventor and subsequently published and/or granted. As before, to "anticipate" an applicant's invention, prior art must have all the same elements as the applicant's claimed invention, arranged in the same way. There are no longer any geographical limitations on prior art for purposes of the novelty determination: Foreign public uses and on-sale events have the same anticipatory effect as domestic ones.

2. **Exceptions to anticipatory prior art under the Leahy-Smith Act:** There are three important exceptions to anticipatory prior art under the Leahy-Smith America Invents Act.

a. **Disclosure made by the inventor:** Disclosures made by the inventor and those deriving from him *one year or less* before the application date are excluded from anticipatory prior art. This exception gives the applicant a form of grace period somewhat similar to that provided under pre–Leahy-Smith Patent Act §102(b), allowing him to file within a year of publicly disclosing the invention.

b. **Disclosures by third parties after inventor discloses:** Disclosures made by third parties will not anticipate the applicant's invention *if* the disclosures were made *after* the applicant/inventor or those deriving from him had already disclosed the same subject matter.

c. **Earlier-filed applications/patents:** In the case of patent applications filed before the applicant's (A's) effective filing date and subsequently published and/or granted, there is no anticipatory effect if: (1) the subject matter disclosed in the pending application/patent was derived from the applicant; (2) the applicant/inventor or those deriving from him had already disclosed the same subject matter before the earlier filing; or (3) both the subject matter disclosed in the earlier-filed application/patent and the applicant's claimed invention were owned by the same person or subject to an obligation of assignment to the same person at the time of the applicant's filing date.

3. **Derivation proceedings:** Under the Leahy-Smith amendments, interference proceedings will no longer be necessary. However, a new "derivation proceeding" before the newly constituted and named "Patent Trial and Appeal Board" will be available to determine issues relating to derivation of patent-related information.

IV. THE NON-OBVIOUSNESS STANDARD

Patent Act §103 provides that an invention is not patentable if, at the time it was made (under pre–Leahy-Smith Act law) or at the time of filing (under the Leahy-Smith Act amendments effective for applications/patents filed on or after March 16, 2013), it would have been obvious to a person having ordinary skill in the pertinent art. To determine whether the invention would have been obvious, a court must ascertain: (1) the scope and content of the prior art; (2) the differences between the pertinent prior art and the invention; and (3) the ordinary level of skill in the pertinent art.

A. **The prior art:** The person with ordinary skill in the art, from whose perspective the obviousness determination is made, is presumed to have knowledge of *all* the pertinent prior art. Under pre–Leahy-Smith law, prior art is identified through the provisions of Patent Act §§102(a), (e), (f), or (g). Under the Leahy-Smith Act amendments (effective for applications/patents filed on or after March 16, 2013) prior art is identified through the provisions of Patent Act §102(a) and (b), as amended. However, to be considered in determining whether the person of ordinary skill would find the invention obvious, prior patents, printed publications, and other enumerated forms of prior art need not disclose an invention that is *the same* as the claimed invention. Prior art is "pertinent," and will be considered, if it is in the same field of endeavor as the invention, regardless of the problem to be solved, or if it is reasonably related to the particular problem with which the inventor was concerned. While a lack of novelty, under §102, can only be demonstrated through a single prior reference that includes every element of the invention in the same arrangement, obviousness can be demonstrated by combining two or more prior art references.

B. **The legal determination of non-obviousness:** The non-obviousness determination requires consideration of whether the prior art: (1) would have suggested to the person of ordinary skill that she should pursue the invention; and (2) would have revealed that she had a reasonable chance of success. The determination must be made as of the date of the applicant's invention (in the case of patents filed before March 16, 2013), or as of the applicant's effective filing date (in the case of patents filed on or after that date). The evaluation may not be made with the benefit of hindsight.

C. **Secondary considerations:** In determining non-obviousness, a court may also consider objective factors, including: (1) the commercial success of the invention; (2) the length of time that the need for the invention had been felt before the invention was made; (3) the level of acquiescence of others to the patent; (4) movement of persons skilled in the art in a different direction from that taken by the inventor; (5) the existence of skepticism on the part of experts regarding the approach taken by the inventor; and (6) the fact that the defendant copied the invention, rather than existing alternatives. These factors may provide circumstantial evidence of non-obviousness. However, a nexus must be demonstrated between the objective factor and the issue of non-obviousness.

D. **Combination patents:** A "combination patent" is a patent for an invention that combines old, known elements in a new way. In such cases, it is the combination that constitutes the invention. In determining the obviousness of such inventions it may be relevant to ask whether there is something in the pertinent prior art to suggest the desirability, and thus the obviousness, of making the combination. However, it is not necessary to show precise or explicit prior art teachings that are directed to the specific subject matter of the claims. Courts should adopt an "expansive and flexible" approach to determining obviousness and recognize that market demand, as well as scientific literature, may lead an inventor to try a new combination. The Supreme Court has provided several principles as guidance in *KSR International Co. v. Teleflex, Inc.*, 550 U.S. 398 (2007):

■ When a patent simply arranges old elements with each performing the same function it had been known to perform, and the combination yields no more than one would expect, the combination is obvious.

■ If a technique has been used to improve one device, and a person of ordinary skill in the art would recognize that it would improve similar devices in the same way, using the technique is obvious unless its actual application is beyond his or her skill.

■ When a work is available in one field of endeavor, design incentives and other market forces can prompt variations of it, either in the same field or a different one. If a person of ordinary skill can implement a predictable variation, it is likely to be obvious.

- When there is a design need or market pressure to solve a problem and there are a finite number of identified, predictable solutions, a person of ordinary skill has good reason to pursue the known options within his or her technical grasp. If this leads to the anticipated success, it is likely to be obvious. (In such a case, a combination that was "obvious to try" will be deemed obvious.)

- When prior art teaches away from combining certain known elements, discovery of a successful means of combining them is more likely to be non-obvious and patentable.

E. **Section 103(c)—Secret prior art in collaborative situations:** Pre–Leahy-Smith America Invents Act §103(c) limits the use of "secret prior art" under §102(e), (f) and (g) to evaluate obviousness if that prior art was developed by a person in a collaborative relationship with the applicant. Such a relationship will be deemed to exist if the applicant's invention and the secret prior art were owned by the same person, subject to an obligation to assign to the same person, or generated pursuant to a written joint research agreement between two or more separate research entities. (Some of the exceptions to prior art listed in Leahy-Smith amended §102(b) promote this same interest in protecting inventors from prior art generated in collaborative research endeavors.)

F. **Obviousness as a trigger of the pre–Leahy-Smith §102(b) one-year statute of limitations to file:** The pre–Leahy-Smith America Invents Act §102(b) one-year statute of limitations will begin to run not only when the applicant's precise claimed invention enters the public domain, but also when other information enters the public domain that renders the claimed invention obvious. It is not necessary that the obvious-rendering information be found all in one place. It is sufficient that the new information, when combined with other, already existing, information and/or ordinary skill in the art, renders the invention obvious. Once the new information enters the public domain through one of the means specified in pre–Leahy-Smith §102(b), the applicant must file her application within the one-year grace period.

V. THE UTILITY OR "USEFULNESS" STANDARD

An invention will be "useful" (or "have utility") if there is a current, significant, beneficial use for the invention or, in the case of a process, the product of the process. An invention may be denied a patent for lack of usefulness if it fails to operate as claimed in the application. The Court of Appeals for the Federal Circuit has applied the utility standard liberally in the case of pharmaceutical patents.

VI. THE DISCLOSURE REQUIREMENT

Patent Act §112 requires the patentee to fully disclose his invention as the price of obtaining a patent. The disclosure requirement consists of four parts. First, the applicant must include one or more claims that clearly and distinctly describe the invention. (This is called the "claiming" requirement—the claims are the official definition of the invention and establish the scope of the patent monopoly.) Second, the applicant must describe how to make and use the invention with sufficient clarity and detail to enable a person with ordinary skill in the relevant art to make and use it without undue experimentation. (This is called the "enablement" requirement.) Third, the applicant must set forth the best mode that he contemplates for carrying out his invention as of the application filing date. (This is known as the "best mode" requirement.) Finally, the applicant must demonstrate that he had possession of the invention, as ultimately claimed, at the time he filed his application. (This is called the "written description" requirement.) The enabling, best mode, and written descriptions are made in the patent specification. Traditionally, failure to comply with any of these disclosure requirements could lead to rejection of an application or invalidation of an issued patent. However, the Leahy-Smith America Invents Act provides that failure to comply with the best mode disclosure requirement will no longer be a basis for patent invalidation.

VII. INFRINGEMENT OF UTILITY PATENTS

A. **Suits to enforce patents:** Suits to enforce a patent or to challenge its validity may be brought in any U.S. district court where venue is proper. Appeals from the district courts must be brought to the U.S. Court of Appeals for the Federal Circuit. From there, review may be sought in the U.S. Supreme Court. Claims that infringing goods are being imported into the United States may be taken to the International Trade Commission (I.T.C.). Appeals from the I.T.C. are also taken to the Federal Circuit, and then to the Supreme Court.

1. **Infringement:** Persons may be liable: (1) for directly infringing a patent; (2) for inducing another to infringe a patent; (3) for contributory infringement; (4) for importing, selling, offering to sell, or using a product made through a process protected by a U.S. process patent; or (5) for manufacturing or selling certain components of a patented invention to be assembled abroad.

2. **Claim interpretation and literal infringement:** To determine whether a defendant's product or process infringes the plaintiff's patent, one must look to the patent claims, which describe the scope of the invention. The meaning and scope of the claims is an issue of law, to be decided by the court. (To interpret claims, courts may look at definitions and drawings provided by the applicant in the specification, or to the written prosecution history. Such "intrinsic evidence" is favored over "extrinsic evidence," such as dictionaries, treatises, expert witnesses or technical journals.) If the defendant's product or process literally falls within the description in a patent claim, containing all the elements set forth in the claim in the same relationship, it *literally infringes* the patent. However, if the defendant has made a change, so that his product or process does not literally fall within the wording of any claim, he may still be liable for direct infringement under the *doctrine of equivalents.*

3. **The doctrine of equivalents:** The doctrine of equivalents prevents a defendant from avoiding liability through insubstantial changes that take his device or process outside the literal language of the patent claims. In order to demonstrate infringement under the doctrine of equivalents, the plaintiff must show that for every element in the patent claim, the defendant's device or process includes a corresponding element that is either identical or equivalent to that claimed element. *Equivalency is an objective determination made on an element-by-element basis*

from the perspective of a person with ordinary skill in the art as of the time of the infringement. Warner-Jenkinson Co., Inc. v. Hilton Davis Chemical Co., 520 U.S. 17 (1997). The inquiry may be framed as (1) whether the defendant's differing element performs substantially the same function in substantially the same way to obtain the same result as the claimed element, or (2) whether the difference between the defendant's element and the claimed element is "insubstantial." Important considerations in making this evaluation include: (1) whether persons reasonably skilled in the art would have known that the differing elements were interchangeable at the time of the infringement; (2) whether finding the defendant's invention equivalent, and thus infringing, would give the patentee rights that she would not have been able to obtain initially in the P.T.O., through broader claim language; and (3) how great a departure the patentee's invention is from the prior art (the greater the departure, the greater the scope of infringing equivalents).

4. **The doctrine of prosecution history estoppel:** The doctrine of prosecution history estoppel (or file wrapper estoppel) requires that the scope of the patent claims be interpreted in light of what happened in the application process in the P.T.O. If the applicant took a position with regard to the scope of coverage of the claims, he will not be permitted in a later infringement action to take an inconsistent position. (For example, he may not use the doctrine of equivalents to bring an element relinquished in the course of prosecution back within the scope of the patent's protection.) The Supreme Court has held that any narrowing amendment that the applicant made to satisfy any statutory requirement of the Patent Act will give rise to prosecution history estoppel. When the purpose of the amendment is not clear, it will be presumed to have been made to satisfy a statutory requirement unless the applicant can bear the burden of proving otherwise. *Festo Corp. v. Shoketsu Kinozuku Kogyo Kabushiki Co., Ltd.*, 535 U.S. 722 (2002).

    a. **The extent of the estoppel:** In *Festo,* the Supreme Court held that when narrowing claim amendments are made in order to satisfy the statutory requirements for patentability, courts should presume that all equivalence arguments are barred as to the narrowed claim element. However, the patentee may rebut that presumption by showing that: (1) the equivalent at issue was unforeseeable at the time the narrowing amendment was made; (2) the rationale underlying the amendment bears no more than a tangential relation to the equivalent in question; or (3) there is some other reason suggesting that the patentee could not reasonably be expected to have described the insubstantial substitute in question in the amended claim language. The ultimate question is whether, at the time of the amendment, one skilled in the art could reasonably be expected to have drafted a claim that would have literally encompassed the alleged equivalent. If so, then the equivalent will be barred.

b. **An additional ground for limiting the doctrine of equivalents:** The Court of Appeals for the Federal Circuit has held that when a patent applicant discloses subject matter in her specification, but does not include it in the claims, she dedicates it to the public, and may not rely on the doctrine of equivalents to hold a defendant liable for incorporating that subject matter in the place of claimed elements. See *Johnson & Johnston Associates, Inc. v. R.E. Service Co.*, 285 F.3d 1046 (2002).

B. Direct infringement: Under Patent Act §271(a), as amended in 1996, a person who makes, uses, sells, offers to sell, or imports the patented invention in the United States during the patent term without the patentee's authorization will be liable for direct infringement.

1. **"Making" the patented invention in the case of combination patents:** While there is no statutory category of patents known as "combination patents," the Supreme Court has explained that a combination patent is a patent for an invention comprised of known elements that are combined in a novel, non-obvious fashion. In such cases it is the combination (as opposed to the individual elements) that is the invention and the subject of the patent protection. Supreme Court precedent provides that in order to demonstrate an infringing "making" of the patented invention in such cases, the patentee must prove that the defendant made the patented combination—made an operable assembly of all the claimed components. *Deepsouth Packing Co., Inc. v. Laitram Corp.*, 406 U.S. 518 (1972). However, the U.S. Court of Appeals for the Federal Circuit has found a "making" where the defendant: (1) entered into a contract to sell the patented invention; (2) manufactured all the components; (3) subassembled the components; (4) tested the operation of the various parts in subassembled form; and (5) delivered the subassembled components to its customer in the United States during the patent term. *Paper Converting Machine Co. v. Magna-Graphics Corp.*, 745 F.2d 11 (Fed. Cir. 1984). These actions constituted actionable "making," even though the defendant never combined all the claimed elements into a complete assembly.

2. **Repair vs. reconstruction as a "making":** In the case of a combination patent, since there are no monopoly rights in the individual components, mere replacement of individual components—even key components—is generally permissible repair, and does not constitute actionable "making." Only reconstruction constitutes an impermissible "making" of the patented invention. Reconstruction generally occurs when the entire embodiment of the invention is spent and the owner thus essentially makes a whole new combination. The Court of Appeals for the Federal Circuit has provided four factors to consider in deciding whether a defendant's activities constitute permissible repair or infringing reconstruction: (1) the nature of the defendant's actions (whether complex or simple); (2) the nature of the patented device and its design (are the replaced parts expected to have a shorter useful life than the whole?); (3) whether a market has developed to manufacture or service the part at issue; and (4) objective evidence of the patentee's intent. *Sandvik Aktiebolag v. E.J. Co.*, 121 F.3d 669 (Fed. Cir. 1997), *cert. denied*, 523 U.S. 1040 (1998).

3. **Selling the patented invention:** The Supreme Court has specified that for purposes of subsection 271(a) infringement liability, a patented invention cannot be "sold" until it is "made." *Deepsouth Packing Co., Inc. v. Laitram Corp.*, 406 U.S. 518 (1972). However, the Federal Circuit has loosened this rule, holding that a contract could, in itself, constitute a sale to trigger infringement liability. In that case the contract to sell the patented machine included schematics of the machine. The court held that as long as the machine described in the schematics infringed the patent, the seller would be liable for unauthorized "sale" of the patented invention,

regardless of whether the machine made pursuant to the contract and delivered to the purchaser itself infringed. *Transocean Offshore Deepwater Drilling, Inc., v. Maersk Contractors U.S.A., Inc.*, 617 F.3d 1296 (Fed. Cir. 2010).

    a. The doctrine of exhaustion: The doctrine of exhaustion (or doctrine of first sale) provides that once the patentee authorizes the initial sale of a product that embodies or incorporates the invention, she loses the right to control subsequent resales and uses of that product, absent an express contractual restriction. When a product practices a patented process, sale of the product will exhaust the patent rights in both the product and the process. The purchaser will be able to use the product for its intended purpose—to practice the process. Moreover, even when the product has to be combined with other components in order to perform the patented process, its sale may exhaust the patentee's right in the process if: (1) the product's only reasonable and intended use is to practice the patented process; and (2) the product embodies the essential features of the patented process. *Quanta Computer, Inc. v. LG Electronics, Inc.*, 533 U.S. 617 (2008).

4. Offering to sell the patented invention: An infringing "offer to sell" must offer a sales transaction that will occur prior to the expiration of the patent term. Courts must employ traditional rules of contract law to determine whether an "offer to sell" the patented invention has been made. The offer need not have been accepted, and if it was, it does not matter whether "what was delivered for sale" is the same as what was offered. An offer to sell a patented invention, though made outside the United States, may infringe if the offered sale would occur in the United States. However, it appears that an offer made in the United States to sell a patented invention abroad will not infringe. The focus is not on the location of the offer, but on the location of the future sale that would occur pursuant to the offer.

5. Importing the patented invention: The Court of Appeals for the Federal Circuit has held that the doctrine of exhaustion applies only to goods first sold *in the United States*. Accordingly, if the patentee sells or authorizes foreign sale of goods embodying or incorporating the patented invention, it may assert rights to prevent the importation, use, or sale of those foreign-sold goods in the United States by subsequent owners, even in the absence of contractual restrictions. *Jazz Photo Corp. v. International Trade Commission*, 264 F.3d 1094 (Fed. Cir. 2001), *cert. denied*, 536 U.S. 950 (2002).

C. Inducement to infringe: Patent Act §271(b) imposes liability for inducing infringement if the defendant actively, knowingly solicited or assisted a third party to infringe a patent, and the third party did so infringe. The defendant must know of the patent and have specific intent to cause or encourage infringement. Intent merely to induce the acts that constitute infringement is insufficient in itself. While inducement requires knowledge that induced acts constitute patent infringement, the Supreme Court has held that "willful blindness" will suffice to support a finding of inducement. A defendant is "willfully blind" for this purpose if he: (1) subjectively believes that there is a high probability that the induced acts constitute infringement; and (2) takes deliberate actions to avoid learning that they do. *Global-Tech Appliances, Inc. v. SEB S.A.*, 131 S. Ct. 2060 (2011).

D. **Contributory infringement:** Under Patent Act §271(c), a person who sells, offers to sell, or imports a material component of the patented invention, which has no substantial use other than use in the patented invention, will be liable for contributory infringement if: (1) he knows that the component he sold was especially made or adapted for use in the patented invention and has no other substantial use; and (2) the buyer in fact uses the component to directly infringe. The defendant must know of the patent and that the buyer's use is likely to constitute infringement.

E. **Importing, selling, offering to sell, or using a product made through a process protected by a U.S. patent:** Patent Act §271(g) provides that unauthorized importing, selling, or offering to sell a product made by a U.S.-patented process constitutes infringement of the process patent, unless the product: (1) has been materially changed by subsequent processes; or (2) has become a trivial or nonessential component of another product. Some exceptions and limitations are made to shelter innocent infringers, noncommercial users, and retail sellers from liability.

F. **Manufacturing or selling components of a patented invention to be assembled abroad:** Subsection 271(f) prohibits persons in the United States from supplying all or a substantial portion of the components of a patented invention in a manner that induces combination of the components abroad. It also prohibits persons in the United States from supplying a material component of a U.S.-patented invention that has no substantial use aside from use in the invention if: (1) the person knows that the component is especially adapted for use in the patented invention and has no substantial non-infringing use; and (2) the person intends that the component will be combined with other components abroad in a manner that would infringe the patent if such combination occurred within the United States. However, supplying master disks of software that foreign purchasers then copy and install into the U.S.-patented invention abroad will not constitute infringement under §271(f). *Microsoft Corp. v. AT & T Corp.*, 550 U.S. 437 (2007).

G. **Provisional rights prior to patent issuance:** In 1999, Congress amended the Patent Act, directing the P.T.O. to publish most patent applications 18 months after their filing date. (An exception is made when the applicant requests not to be published and certifies that the invention has not and will not be the subject of an application filed in another country or under a multilateral international agreement that requires publication of applications prior to patent issuance.) Congress afforded provisional rights to patentees against third parties who make, use, sell, offer to sell, or import the invention (or in the case of a process, the product of the claimed process) in the United States during the period between publication and patent issuance. However, the defendant must have actual notice of the published application, and the claims in the published application must also be substantially identical to those in the subsequently issued patent. Recovery is limited to a reasonable royalty.

H. **Defenses to infringement:** There are a number of defenses to a claim of patent infringement. Five that are specific to patent litigation are patent invalidity, patent misuse, inequitable conduct, the experimental use defense, and the prior user defense.

    1. **Patent invalidity:** A patent is presumed valid. However, the defendant may overcome this presumption by proving with clear and convincing evidence that a condition of patentability was not satisfied. If the defendant succeeds, the court will not enforce the patent. Patent licensees are not estopped from challenging the validity of the patent under which they took a license. The Supreme Court has held that the licensee does not have to terminate or breech the license agreement (and thus risk damages for infringement) prior to seeking a declaratory judgment of patent invalidity. *Lear, Inc. v. Adkins*, 395 U.S. 653 (1969). Persons *assigning* patents are estopped from challenging the validity of the patent they assigned.

2. **Patent misuse:** The patentee will be deemed to have misused his patent if he uses it unreasonably to extend his market power beyond what Congress intended. If the defendant is able to demonstrate patent misuse, the patentee will be denied enforcement of his patent until the misuse ceases and the patentee no longer enjoys any benefits from his prior misuse. A patent owner who commits a violation of the antitrust laws through use of the patent generally will be subject to the misuse defense. However, the misuse defense is not expressly limited to antitrust violations.

   a. **Tying arrangements:** Conditioning a license to make, use, sell, or import the patented invention (or conditioning sale of the patented invention itself) on the licensee/purchaser's agreement to purchase another good or license from the patentee will generally constitute patent misuse unless: (1) the item the purchaser/licensee is required to purchase is a material component of the invention and has no substantial non-infringing use; (2) the patentee lacks market power in the relevant market for the patented invention; or (3) in the case of package licensing, the first patented invention cannot be practiced without infringing the second patented invention.

   b. **Activities that will not constitute patent misuse:** Patent Act §271(d) expressly provides that it does not constitute patent misuse for the patentee to: (1) derive revenue from acts that would constitute contributory infringement if performed by another without the patentee's consent; (2) license or authorize others to perform acts that if performed without the patentee's consent would constitute contributory infringement; (3) seek to enforce his rights against infringement or contributory infringement; or (4) refuse to license or use any rights in the patent.

3. **Inequitable conduct:** The inequitable conduct defense renders a patent unenforceable when the defendant proves, with clear and convincing evidence, that the patentee misrepresented or omitted material information during the application process, with the specific intent to deceive the P.T.O. The materiality required to establish inequitable conduct is "but-for" materiality. Nondisclosed material is "but-for" material if the P.T.O. would not have allowed a claim had it been aware of the undisclosed prior art. The only exception to the requirement of "but-for" materiality arises when the patentee has engaged in "affirmative acts of egregious misconduct, such as filing an unmistakably false affidavit." *Therasense, Inc. v. Becton, Dickinson & Co.*, 649 F.3d 1276, 1287-1293 (Fed. Cir. 2011) (*en banc*).

   a. **Supplemental examination:** The Leahy-Smith America Invents Act addresses recent overuse of inequitable conduct allegations by permitting patentees, through a "supplemental examination," effectively to insulate themselves from an inequitable conduct challenge or defense in later litigation. The proceeding is similar to an *ex parte* reexamination. The patentee can submit any form of potentially relevant information that was not considered, was inadequately considered, or was incorrect during prosecution. If the P.T.O. finds that the information does not present a substantial new question of patentability, or that the patent remains valid notwithstanding the information, that information cannot later be asserted in litigation to support an inequitable conduct defense.

4. **The experimental use defense:** A person may make or use a patented invention without authorization if her purpose is only to satisfy her scientific curiosity or to amuse herself as an intellectual exercise, and she has no commercial or other practical motivation.

   a. **Subsection 271(e):** Patent Act §271(e) permits persons, under limited circumstances, to make, use, sell, offer to sell, or import certain patented inventions in the course of developing information to submit to federal agencies regulating manufacture, use, or sale of drugs or veterinary biological products.

5. **Prior use:** The First Inventor Defense Act of 1999 created a "prior user" defense against claims that a defendant has infringed a patented business method. To succeed in the defense, the defendant must prove by clear and convincing evidence that it (1) actually reduced the patented business method to practice, in good faith, at least one year before the plaintiff's filing date; and (2) commercially used the patented business method before the plaintiff's filing date.

   a. **The Leahy-Smith Act expansion of the prior user defense:** The Leahy-Smith America Invents Act expands the prior user defense, making it available against patents for processes, machines, articles of manufacture, and compositions of matter used in a manufacturing or other commercial process. The defense is available when a defendant proves by clear and convincing evidence that it commercially used the subject matter of the patent in the United States, in good faith, at least a year before the earlier of two dates: (1) the effective filing date of the patent claims; or (2) the date on which the claimed invention was disclosed to the public in a manner that qualified for the exception from prior art under Patent Act §102, as amended. The use may be either a commercial internal use or an arm's length sale or transfer of useful end results of commercial use. This expanded prior commercial user defense applies in any case involving a patent issued on or after September 16, 2011. The defense is not available against universities and their associated technical transfer offices.

VIII. REMEDIES FOR PATENT INFRINGEMENT

Both damages and injunctions are available for patent infringement. If the patentee fails to give proper notice of the patent on its products, it may recover damages only for infringement that takes place after the defendant receives notice of the infringement claim.

A. **The proper measure of damages:** Courts may measure infringement damages by calculating a reasonable royalty for the defendant's use of the patented invention (the amount a willing licensee wanting to make, use, sell, or import the patented invention would pay and a reasonable patentee would accept for a license, when negotiating at arm's length) or by calculating the patentee's lost profits attributable to the infringement. Courts may use the incremental income approach in calculating lost profits. Moreover, under the entire market value rule, courts may award lost profits on unpatented components sold with a patented apparatus, if the patented and unpatented components are considered to be parts of a single assembly or constitute a functional unit, operating together to achieve a result. Courts may also award lost profits on products that do not embody the patented invention if the patentee can demonstrate: (1) that it would have sold the unpatented device but for the defendant's infringement; (2) the lost sales were reasonably foreseeable by the infringing competitor; and (3) the unpatented device directly competes with the defendant's infringing product.

   1. **Enhanced damages:** Courts may double or triple the plaintiff's damages upon a showing of willful infringement or bad faith on the part of the defendant. A showing of willfulness requires *at least* a showing of objective recklessness. The Leahy-Smith America Invents Act provides that "the failure of an infringer to obtain the advice of counsel with respect to any allegedly infringed patent, or the failure of the infringer to present such advice to the court or jury, may not be used to prove that the accused infringer willfully infringed the patent."

B. **Other monetary relief:** The Patent Act authorizes awards of reasonable attorney fees to the prevailing party in exceptional cases. Courts award prejudgment interest to prevailing plaintiffs as a routine matter.

C. **Injunctive relief:** Courts may permanently enjoin infringement under the usual four-factor test: (1) Has plaintiff suffered irreparable injury? (2) Are remedies at law inadequate to compensate for the injury? (3) Given the balance of hardships between the parties, is a remedy at equity warranted? and (4) Will the public interest be disserved by a permanent injunction? *eBay, Inc. v. Merchexchange, L.L.C.*, 547 U.S. 388 (2006). Courts grant preliminary injunctions upon a clear showing of irreparable harm *and* likelihood of success on the merits. There can be no presumption of irreparable harm upon finding that the plaintiff is likely to succeed on the merits.

D. **Remedies for infringement through performance of "medical activities":** Patent Act §287(c) provides that there can be no infringement remedies against medical practitioners and related health care entities that directly infringe or induce infringement of a patent through performance of a medical activity. As a general matter, this exception to liability applies only when the defendant performs a patented surgical or medical procedure that does not involve drugs or patented devices.

IX. DESIGN PATENTS

A. **The nature and requirements of design patents:** A design patent gives its owner a 14-year monopoly in the design (appearance) of an article of manufacture. To qualify for a design patent, a design must be novel, non-obvious, and ornamental. The novelty standard is essentially the same for design patents as for utility patents.

1. **Non-obviousness:** The Court of Appeals for the Federal Circuit has held that, to find a claimed design obvious: (1) there must be a primary reference whose design characteristics are basically the same as the claimed design; and (2) the prior art, market trends, or other factors must suggest modifying the primary reference in order to produce the claimed design. The court considers whether a designer of ordinary skill in the field of the patented design would know to combine the primary reference with other prior art references or to modify the primary reference. However, the ultimate issue of obviousness, like anticipation, is determined from the standpoint of the ordinary observer. *Hupp v. Siroflex of America, Inc.*, 122 F.3d 1456 (Fed. Cir. 1997).

2. **Ornamentality:** To be "ornamental," the design must be *primarily* ornamental, not dictated by functional considerations alone. The Federal Circuit has provided the following list of considerations in evaluating the ornamentality of a claimed design: (1) the existence of alternative designs; (2) whether the protected design represents the best design; (3) whether alternative designs would adversely affect the utility of the specified article; (4) whether there are any concomitant utility patents; (5) whether the advertising touts particular features of the design as having specific utility; and (6) whether there are any elements in the design or overall appearance clearly not dictated by function. *Berry Sterling Corp. v. Pescor Plastics, Inc.*, 122 F.3d 1452 (Fed. Cir. 1997).

B. **Infringement of a design patent:** Patent Act §271, defining the various ways a patent may be infringed, applies equally to utility and design patents. However, design patents are not published, so there can be no provisional rights between publication and issuance. A design patent is infringed if, in the eye of an ordinary observer, giving such attention as a purchaser usually gives, the two designs are substantially the same — similar enough to deceive the observer and induce him to purchase one supposing it to be the other. (This is the *Gorham* "eye of the ordinary observer" test. *Gorham Manufacturing Co. v. White*, 81 U.S. (14 Wall.) 511 (1872).) The Federal Circuit has elaborated that the ordinary observer must consider the designs substantially identical *in light of the prior art. Egyptian Goddess, Inc. v. Swisa, Inc.*, 543 F.3d 655 (Fed. Cir. 2008) (*en banc*). Moreover, the ordinary observer should distinguish a design's functional features and ornamental features and "discount" or "factor out" the functional features. *Richardson v. Stanley Works, Inc.*, 597 F.3d. 1288 (Fed. Cir. 2010).

C. **Defenses and remedies for infringement of design patents:** Defenses and remedies available for infringement of utility patents are also available for infringement of design patents. In addition, the Patent Act provides for recovery of the defendant's profits or an alternative minimum statutory damage recovery for certain types of design patent infringement.

X. PLANT PATENTS

A. **The nature of plant patents:** Plant patents are available to persons who discover or invent a distinct and new variety of plant and preserve it through asexual reproduction. Cultivated sports, mutants, hybrids, and newly found seedlings may qualify for a plant patent, but tuber-propagated plants and new plants found in an uncultivated state do not. To qualify for a plant patent, a new variety must be novel, distinct, and non-obvious, and it must have been asexually reproduced.

1. **The novelty requirement:** To be novel, a variety of plant must not have existed before in nature. A plant will not be deemed to have existed in nature unless it existed in a form that was capable of naturally reproducing the new characteristics that set it apart from preexisting varieties. Patent Act §102 provisions apply to plant patents. *Yoder Bros., Inc. v. Cal.-Fla. Plant Corp.*, 537 F.2d 1347 (5th Cir. 1976), *cert. denied*, 429 U.S. 1094 (1977).

2. **The distinctiveness and non-obviousness requirements:** To be distinctive, the new plant variety must have characteristics that are clearly distinguishable from those of existing varieties. In order for the plant to be non-obvious, those new characteristics must be significant.

B. **Infringement of a plant patent:** A plant patent grants the owner the right to exclude others from (1) asexually reproducing the patented plant; (2) selling or using a plant so reproduced or any of its parts; and (3) importing a plant so reproduced or any of its parts.

C. **Utility Patents and the Plant Variety Protection Act:** Utility patents are available for new varieties of plants that are "man-made" and meet the other utility patent requirements. The Plant Variety Protection Act, 7 U.S.C. §§2321-2582, gives patent-like protection to persons who breed new plants by use of seeds (sexual reproduction). Sexually reproduced and tuber-propagated plants other than fungi and bacteria are eligible. To qualify, the new variety must be new, distinct, uniform, and stable. A certificate of plant variety protection, granted by the Department of Agriculture, gives the owner the right to exclude others from selling the variety, offering it for sale, reproducing it, importing or exporting it, or using it in producing (as opposed to developing) a hybrid or different variety.

XI. INTERNATIONAL PATENT TREATIES TO WHICH THE UNITED STATES ADHERES

A. **The Paris Convention:** The Paris Convention for the Protection of Industrial Property (Paris Convention) requires each member nation to extend patent protection to inventors from other member nations on essentially the same basis that it grants protection to its own domestic inventors. (This is known as "national treatment.") It also provides for filing priority: Qualified applicants who file an application for patent in one member nation receive the benefit of their filing date in that nation for all subsequent filings in other member nations made within the next 12 months. With these and a few other exceptions, members of the Paris Convention generally are free to determine the nature and extent of substantive patent protection they will provide for inventions.

B. **The Patent Cooperation Treaty:** The Patent Cooperation Treaty (P.C.T.) provides a centralized filing system to assist inventors applying for patents in a number of different countries simultaneously. An inventor's patent application can be filed, searched, and examined in a centralized fashion, prior to prosecution in the various individual countries' patent offices.

C. The Agreement on Trade-Related Aspects of Intellectual Property Rights: The World Trade Organization's TRIPs Agreement incorporates the provisions of the Paris Convention and builds on them. Among other things, TRIPs imposes minimum disclosure requirements for patent applications, prescribes the subject matter for which WTO members must provide patent protection, the rights they must provide to patentees, and the minimum term of protection.

D. The Patent Law Treaty: The Patent Law Treaty undertakes to harmonize application filing procedures among its members, thus further reducing the complexity and cost of obtaining international patent protection.

CHAPTER 4

THE LAW OF UNDEVELOPED IDEAS

I. THE NATURE OF THE LAW OF UNDEVELOPED IDEAS

The law of undeveloped ideas is a miscellaneous accumulation of state common law decisions addressing claims for compensation for a defendant's unauthorized use of the plaintiff's idea. Courts have recognized five theories of recovery.

A. The express contract theory: Courts have enforced express contracts to pay for an idea. However, some jurisdictions require that the plaintiff demonstrate that the idea was novel. Some also require that the idea be concrete.

B. The contract-implied-in-fact theory: Courts have found and enforced implied contracts to pay for ideas based on the parties' actions and surrounding circumstances, which indicate that they intended to make a binding contract to pay. However, many courts will not find or enforce an implied contract to pay for an idea if the idea was not novel (and in some jurisdictions, concrete).

C. The contract-implied-in-law theory: A contract implied in law (or "quasi-contract") is not based upon the intentions of the parties but on a court's finding of unjust enrichment—that the defendant received a benefit for which equity and justice require him to pay. Most jurisdictions will not find that the defendant was unjustly enriched by receipt and use of a plaintiff's idea unless the idea was novel and concrete.

D. The confidential relationship theory: Some courts have found a right to recover for an idea if, when the plaintiff revealed her idea to the defendant, the parties were in a confidential relationship in which the plaintiff reposed trust and confidence in the defendant's good faith. The confidential nature of the relationship imposes a duty on the defendant to refrain from taking advantage of the plaintiff's disclosure. Again, some courts have added the requirement that the idea disclosed by the plaintiff be novel (and in some jurisdictions, concrete).

E. The property theory: Some courts and commentators have suggested that a plaintiff may have a right to recover for a novel, concrete idea on the same general basis as a person could recover for the unauthorized taking of an item of personal property, or for infringement of a copyright. This is an extreme theory and has rarely if ever been relied on as a sole basis of recovery.

II. THE NOVELTY AND CONCRETENESS REQUIREMENTS

A. The novelty requirement: Three views of the novelty requirement can be identified in the case law: (1) the idea must be original to the plaintiff (that is, the plaintiff must have conceived of the idea himself); (2) the idea must be innovative and creative in nature; or (3) the idea must be both original to the plaintiff and innovative in nature. In some cases, courts may differ in their construction of the novelty requirement, depending on the plaintiff's theory of recovery.

B. The concreteness requirement: Three views of concreteness can be identified in the case law: (1) the idea must be reduced to tangible form; (2) the idea must be fully developed—in a detailed form ready for immediate use with little or no additional work on the user's part; or (3) the idea must be both reduced to tangible form and fully developed.

CHAPTER 5

COPYRIGHT LAW

I. THE PURPOSE AND NATURE OF COPYRIGHT LAW

A. The nature of copyright law: The ultimate purpose of copyright law is to stimulate creation and dissemination of as many works of authorship as possible, in order to benefit the public. Copyright law does this by giving creators of works of authorship *limited* rights in their works. Copyright protection is limited to an author's particular method of expressing an idea. Copyright never gives rights in the idea being expressed, or in facts or other elements of the public domain that the author may have incorporated into the work.

   1. Property right vs. personal right: U.S. copyright law traditionally has focused on granting authors *economic rights* in their works. U.S. authors have relied on other areas of law, such as the law of defamation, unfair competition, privacy law and contract, to protect their *personal interests* in being identified as the author and in protecting their reputation as an author. By contrast, many countries have fashioned their copyright (or "authors' right") laws to extend such personal rights, along with economic rights. After ratifying the Berne Convention, Congress amended the U.S. Copyright Act to provide personal rights ("moral rights") in connection with a narrow category of subject matter denominated "works of visual art."

   2. Rights in the intangible: The common law of personal property protects rights in tangible embodiments of works of authorship, such as manuscripts and canvases. Copyright, by contrast, protects the *intangible expression itself.* A transfer of the physical embodiment of a work of authorship does not transfer the copyright. A separate writing is required to transfer copyright.

3. **Federal vs. state law:** Prior to the effective date of the Copyright Act of 1976 (January 1, 1978), the United States had a dual system of copyright. Unpublished works of authorship were protected by state common-law copyright. Once a work was published, common-law copyright ended. Federal statutory copyright was available to works published with proper notice of copyright. In the Copyright Act of 1976, Congress made federal statutory copyright available upon the fixation of a work in tangible form, regardless of publication, and provided that the federal copyright law would preempt state copyright protection for works of authorship fixed in tangible form.

II. THE SUBJECT MATTER OF COPYRIGHT

A. **The statutory definition:** The 1976 Act (§102(a)) provides that copyright subsists "in original works of authorship fixed in any tangible medium of expression, now known or later developed, from which they can be perceived, reproduced, or otherwise communicated, either directly or with the aid of a machine or device."

B. **The originality requirement:** A work of authorship must be *original* in order to qualify for copyright protection. This means that: (1) the author must have engaged in his own intellectual endeavor, rather than merely copying from a preexisting source; and (2) the work must demonstrate a minimal amount of creativity. *Feist Publications, Inc. v. Rural Telephone Service Co., Inc.*, 499 U.S. 340 (1991). Under this rule, *de minimis* "works" such as words, short phrases, slogans, and the like, are not protected. Because facts are "discovered" rather than "created," they are not original and thus not proper subject matter for copyright. Only the author's original means of expressing the facts can be protected. An author's exercise of judgment in selecting and arranging facts or other uncopyrightable elements in a work may constitute original expression.

   1. **Scènes à faire:** An author may not obtain copyright in "scènes à faire": incidents of action, characters, settings, or other elements that are indispensable, or at least standard, stock devices in the treatment of a given topic.

C. **The fixation requirement:** Federal copyright attaches to the intangible work of authorship, not the physical manifestation of it, but the work only qualifies for federal copyright protection once it has been fixed in a tangible form. Fixation may take many forms. The Copyright Act of 1976 (§101) provides that a work is fixed in a tangible medium of expression "when its embodiment in a copy or phonorecord, by or under the authority of the author, is sufficiently permanent or stable to permit it to be perceived, reproduced, or otherwise communicated for a period of more than transitory duration."

   1. **Copies and phonorecords:** All copyrightable works of authorship are fixed either in copies or phonorecords. "Phonorecords" are "material objects in which sounds, other than those accompanying a motion picture or other audiovisual work, are fixed . . . ." §101. All other material objects in which works of authorship are fixed are called "copies."

D. The idea/expression dichotomy: Copyright protection never gives rights in ideas, procedures, processes, systems, methods of operation, concepts, or principles (collectively called "ideas"). Moreover, when use or expression of these things *necessitates copying the plaintiff's expression,* the expression will not be protected — the expression will be deemed to "merge" with the underlying idea and become part of the unprotectable idea itself. *Baker v. Selden,* 101 U.S. (11 Otto) 99 (1879). In addition, courts may find merger when the subject matter of a work is so narrow and straightforward that there are only a *limited number* of ways to express it. To provide otherwise might enable a person to obtain a *de facto* monopoly in the subject matter, or idea, by obtaining copyright in all the alternative forms of expressing it.

    1. Thin copyright: An alternative way some courts deal with situations in which there are relatively few ways to express an idea is to recognize copyright protection in the plaintiff's work, but refuse to find infringement unless the defendant's copying is nearly exact. This is called "thin copyright." Typically, to infringe a thin copyright, the defendant's work must be "virtually identical" to the plaintiff's copyrighted expression, or "bodily appropriate" the plaintiff's expression.

    2. Blank forms: Courts deny copyright protection to blank forms that are designed for recording information and do not in themselves convey information.

E. Categories of protectable works of authorship: The 1976 Act provides that "works of authorship" include the following categories: (1) literary works; (2) musical works, including any accompanying words; (3) dramatic works, including any accompanying music; (4) pantomimes and choreographic works; (5) pictorial, graphic, and sculptural works; (6) motion pictures and other audiovisual works; (7) sound recordings; and (8) architectural works. 17 U.S.C. §102. This list is not meant to be exclusive, but the 1976 Act does not necessarily extend copyright to all subject matter that Congress is authorized to protect under the Constitution's Patents and Copyrights Clause.

    1. The literary works category — the copyrightability of computer programs: The 1976 Act, as amended, expressly protects computer programs, which §101 defines as "a set of statements or instructions to be used directly or indirectly in a computer in order to bring about a certain result." Copyright protection extends both to programs in source code and programs in object code and to both application and operating system programs. Likewise, copyright extends to programs regardless of the medium in which they are encoded, such as disks, flash drives, or chips.

        a. Copyright in the structure of programs: Computer programs are considered "literary works" for purposes of copyright, and their authors are entitled to copyright protection not only in their literal expression (source or object code) but also in nonliteral elements of expression, such as the program's structure or organization. In *Computer Associates International, Inc. v. Altai, Inc., 982 F.2d 693 (2d Cir. 1992),* the Second Circuit adopted the "abstraction-filtration-comparison" test for determining which (if any) elements of a program's structure are copyrightable. This test has been widely adopted.

            i. The abstraction, filtration, comparison test: In the abstraction phase, the program is broken down into its structural components, repeatedly, at increasing levels of abstraction or generality. In the filtration phase, the court identifies those components at each level of abstraction that (1) constitute an idea; (2) are required in order for the program to perform its functions efficiently; (3) are required by factors external to the program itself (and thus constitute scènes à faire); or (4) were taken from the public domain. These components are uncopyrightable and must be removed from consideration, or "filtered out." In the comparison phase, the court evaluates the remaining structural components, which constitute copyrightable expression.

  ii. **Selection and arrangement expression:** The Second Circuit has clarified that a programmer's original selection and arrangement of uncopyrightable elements may be protected under the *Altai* abstraction-filtration-comparison test, because even though uncopyrightable elements are filtered out at one level of abstraction, they may be considered to be copyrightable expression in the aggregate with other elements at a higher level of abstraction. However, a number of circuits have held that when the plaintiff is relying on selection and arrangement expression, it must demonstrate "bodily appropriation of expression" or "virtual identicality" of expression in the defendant's alleged infringing program. *Softel, Inc. v. Dragon Medical and Scientific Communications, Inc.,* 118 F.3d 955 (2d Cir. 1997), *cert. denied,* 523 U.S. 1020 (1998).

 b. **Copyright in the user interface:** A program's user interface is comprised of the visual and aural elements through which the program communicates with the user. Aspects of a screen display may be protected if they are sufficiently original and do not merge with the underlying idea. In *Lotus Development Corp. v. Borland International, Inc.,* 49 F.3d 807 (1st Cir. 1995), *aff'd,* 516 U.S. 233 (1996),[1] the First Circuit held that the menu command hierarchy of a program did not constitute copyrightable expression, but rather, constituted an uncopyrightable *method of operation* in its entirety. The *Lotus* court reasoned that even if the method of operation contained expressive elements, those elements would be uncopyrightable because they were part of the method of operation. The Tenth Circuit has subsequently disagreed that expressive elements *incorporated into* a method of operation are uncopyrightable. *Mitel, Inc. v. Iqtel, Inc.,* 124 F.3d 1366 (10th Cir. 1997).

 2. **The pictorial, graphic, and sculptural works category—Copyright in the design of useful articles:** A useful article is "an article having an intrinsic function that is not merely to portray the appearance of the article or to convey information." §101. Pictorial, graphic, or sculptural features embodied in useful articles may be copyrighted if they are *physically or conceptually separable* from the utilitarian aspects of the useful article. Physical separability exists if the design feature could be physically removed from the useful article and still be recognizable as a pictorial, graphic or sculptural work.

---

[1] The Supreme Court split 4–4 in reviewing the *Lotus* decision, which had the effect of affirming the First Circuit's decision, but the affirmation is not precedential.

a. **Evaluating conceptual separability:** The prevailing test for conceptual separability focuses on the design process. If the designer was *significantly influenced by utilitarian considerations,* then the pictorial, graphic, or sculptural design features are "inextricably intertwined" with the utilitarian function of the article and are not conceptually separable. If the design features were not significantly influenced by the utilitarian function of the article, but reflect the designer's purely aesthetic choices, then the design features are conceptually separable, and can be protected. *Brandir International, Inc. v. Cascade Pacific Lumber Co.,* 834 F.2d 1142 (2d Cir. 1987). While the Second and Seventh Circuits have adopted the "design process" standard described above, the Fifth Circuit has adopted a "likelihood of marketability" standard, at least in the case of costumes or clothing. Under this standard, conceptual separability will be found if there is a substantial likelihood that even if the article had no utilitarian use, it would still be marketable to some significant segment of the community simply because of its aesthetic qualities.

b. **Copyright in technical drawings:** Technical drawings and blueprints are protected by copyright. However, unauthorized use of copyrighted drawings or plans to build the useful article depicted in them generally does not in itself constitute infringement of the plans.

3. **The architectural works category:** Copyright Act §101, as amended by the Architectural Works Copyright Protection Act (AWCPA), defines an architectural work as the design of a building, as embodied in any tangible medium of expression, including a building, architectural plans, or drawings. The work includes the overall form as well as the arrangement and composition of spaces and elements in the design, but does not include individual standard features. The legislative history indicates that, in enacting the AWPCA, Congress intended to prohibit unauthorized copying of the two-dimensional architectural plans, unauthorized use of the plans to build a three-dimensional building, and unauthorized direct copying of the building. However, only those original architectural design elements that are *not dictated by functional considerations* will be protected "expression" within the work.

a. **The design of a "building":** The AWCPA defines a protectable "architectural work" as "the design of a building." "Buildings" are humanly habitable structures that are intended to be both permanent and stationary, such as houses, office buildings and other structures designed for human occupancy. Stores built inside an enclosed shopping mall are not "buildings" for this purpose.

b. **Pre–AWCPA works:** The AWCPA applies only to architectural works created on or after December 1, 1990, or that were unconstructed and embodied in unpublished plans or drawings on that date. *Architectural works that do not qualify for protection under AWCPA can only be protected as pictorial, graphic, or sculptural works.* The plans are treated as graphic works, and the buildings are treated as useful articles.

4. **The sound recordings category:** Sound recordings are "works that result from the fixation of a series of musical, spoken, or other sounds," but do not include

the sounds accompanying a motion picture or other audiovisual work. §101. The sound recording copyright is separate from any copyright that may exist in the work that is the subject of the recording, such as a musical composition or a literary work. Domestic sound recordings fixed before 1972 are not protected by federal copyright. Forms of state protection may be available for them, however.

5. **Copyright for fictitious characters:** Under the more widely accepted rule, fictitious characters are entitled to separate copyright protection, apart from the work in which they appeared, if the author very distinctly delineated them. When the character has a visual aspect as well as personality characteristics described by word and story line, courts have been more willing to find copyright protection. (The less widely applied standard that would be applied only in the case of characters without a visual aspect, if then, is the "story being told" standard: The character will be separately protected only if he or she constitutes the story being told, and is not just a vehicle for telling the story.)

6. **Compilations:** Compilations are works formed by collecting and assembling preexisting materials or data. Compilations include collective works (such as periodical issues, anthologies, or encyclopedias) that compile a number of separate, independently copyrightable works. Compilations that are *not* collective works include directories, catalogs, or automated databases that compile materials, such as facts, that are not separately copyrightable.

   a. **The protectable expression in compilations:** The copyrightable expression in a compilation is that expression contributed by the compilation author—usually the selection, coordination and arrangement of materials, along with any original explanatory matter. Compilations, like other categories of copyrightable subject matter, must be original. To be original, the compiler's selection and arrangement must entail a minimum threshold of creativity: If the act of compiling was merely rote, obvious, or clerical in nature, with no meaningful exercise of judgment or intellect, the originality requirement will not be satisfied. *Feist Publications, Inc. v. Rural Telephone Service Co., Inc.,* 499 U.S. 340 (1991).

7. **Derivative works:** Derivative works are works based upon one or more preexisting works, such as translations, musical arrangements, dramatizations, fictionalizations, motion picture versions, art reproductions, abridgments, etc. Derivative works are within the subject matter of copyright, but copyright protection extends only to the original material contributed by the derivative author, not to the preexisting material that the derivative author incorporated into the new work. In order to constitute a separately copyrightable derivative work, an adaptation must constitute a substantial, not merely trivial, variation from the preexisting work on which it is based. The Ninth Circuit has held, in addition, that a derivative work may not be copyrighted if doing so will affect copyright protection in the underlying work. This may occur if the derivative work copyright will enable the recipient to interfere with the ability of the person holding copyright in the preexisting work to license additional derivative works. *Entertainment Research Group, Inc. v. Genesis Creative Group, Inc.,* 122 F.3d 1211 (9th Cir. 1997), *cert. denied,* 523 U.S. 1021 (1998).

8. Government works as copyrightable subject matter: Copyright is not available for any work of the U.S. government. Works of the U.S. government are works "prepared by an officer or employee of the U.S. government as part of that person's official duties." §101. Government agencies that arrange for independent contractors to create works for the U.S. government may require independent contractors to waive their right to copyright in some cases, when it is in the public's interest that they do so.

    a. State government works: The Copyright Act does not prohibit state and local governmental entities from claiming copyright in works of authorship created by their officials or employees. However, case law indicates that judicial opinions, statutes, city ordinances, and other government laws and regulations must be accessible to the public because of due process considerations. This is generally understood to mean that these works, which have the force and effect of law, may be subject to copying by the public. When a governmental entity adopts a model code that was drafted by non-governmental entities, the model code loses copyright protection in its capacity as the law of the adopting governmental entity.

III. THE RIGHTS AFFORDED BY COPYRIGHT LAW

A. The exclusive rights of copyright: The *owner of copyright* in a work has the exclusive right to do or authorize the following: (1) reproduce the copyrighted work; (2) prepare derivative works based upon the copyrighted work; (3) distribute copies or phonorecords of the copyrighted work to the public; (4) publicly perform the work (this right applies in the case of all the types of copyrightable works except pictorial, graphic and sculptural works, architectural works, and sound recordings); (5) publicly display the work (this right applies in the case of all the types of copyrightable works except architectural works and sound recordings); and (6) in the case of sound recordings, to perform the copyrighted work publicly by means of digital audio transmission. 17 U.S.C. §106.

B. Moral rights in works of visual art: In the case of works of visual art, the *artist* has the right: (1) to claim authorship in the work; (2) to prevent use of her name as the author of works she did not create; (3) to prevent use of her name as the author of her own work if the work has been distorted, mutilated, or otherwise modified so that the use would be prejudicial to her honor or reputation; (4) to prevent any intentional distortion, mutilation, or other modification of her work that would be prejudicial to her name or reputation; and (5) to prevent the intentional or grossly negligent destruction of the work if the work is of recognized stature. 17 U.S.C. §106A.

IV. THE COPYRIGHTED WORK

To demonstrate that a defendant infringed any of the exclusive economic rights, it must appear that; (1) the defendant's work was *copied* from the plaintiff's; and (2) that the works are substantially similar in their *expression*, so that the copying amounts to an *unlawful appropriation*. *Arnstein v. Porter,* 154 F.2d 464 (2d Cir. 1946).

A. Copying: Copying may be demonstrated by direct evidence or by circumstantial evidence that: (1) the defendant had *access* to the plaintiff's work and the defendant's work is sufficiently *similar* to the plaintiff's to infer copying; or (2) the defendant's work is strikingly similar to the plaintiff's work, so that it is unlikely that it would have been independently created. In determining similarity for this purpose, all similarities — both in copyrightable and uncopyrightable elements of the works — may be considered, and expert witness testimony may be used.

B. Unlawful appropriation: To ascertain whether the defendant's copying amounted to an unlawful appropriation, one must determine whether the defendant's work is substantially similar to the copyrightable expression in the plaintiff's work. This evaluation usually is made from the standpoint of the average member of the intended audience for the copyrighted work. Under the *Arnstein* "audience" test, the evaluation is a *subjective* one, based on the *overall impression* of the average member of the intended audience. Similarities in uncopyrightable elements cannot support a finding of unlawful appropriation/substantial similarity, although similarities in the selection and arrangement of uncopyrightable elements can. The fact that the defendant's allegedly infringing work contains expression that the copyright owner's lacks, or varies from the copyright owner's in some aspects, does not in itself excuse the defendant from liability. (A defendant may not excuse himself by showing how much he *didn't* copy.)

1. **The Ninth Circuit's approach:** The Ninth Circuit has adopted a two-part "extrinsic/intrinsic" test to determine whether a defendant's copying amounts to an unlawful appropriation. The extrinsic test constitutes an *objective* evaluation of the similarities of expression, through use of dissection and expert witnesses. The intrinsic test constitutes a *subjective* evaluation, based on the overall impression of the average member of the intended audience, without analytic dissection or expert testimony, as in the *Arnstein* audience test The Ninth Circuit has held that a copyright infringement plaintiff must demonstrate substantial similarity under *both* the extrinsic and the intrinsic tests in order to prevail. *Shaw v. Lindheim*, 919 F.2d 1353 (9th Cir. 1990).

2. **Other approaches:** Jurisdictions that normally apply the audience test have used other standards for assessing infringement when the work at issue includes numerous uncopyrightable elements. In such cases, the audience test's subjective "total look and feel" approach may lead the fact finder to find substantial similarity and unlawful appropriation based on similarities of uncopyrightable elements. To avoid such overprotection of copyrighted works, courts have devised the *"more discerning"* standard and the *"abstraction, filtration, and comparison"* standard, which introduce an objective evaluation, such as that in the Ninth Circuit's extrinsic test, to the unlawful appropriation determination. When the plaintiff is relying on "selection and arrangement" expression in a "thin copyright" situation, courts may impose a "virtual identicality" or "a bodily appropriation of copyrighted expression" standard, instead of the normal "substantial similarity" of copyrightable expression standard.

C. Literal vs. nonliteral similarity: There are two types of substantial similarity that may lead to a finding of infringement: (1) literal similarity; and (2) nonliteral similarity (similarity in the works' underlying structure or arrangement). In the case of *literal similarity*, the *amount* of copying necessary to find infringement depends on how important the copied material is. The more important the material, the less must be copied. In the case of nonliteral similarity, the main problem is distinguishing uncopyrightable idea (which may be copied) from copyrightable expression of idea. As a general matter, the more *detail* that is copied, the more likely it is that copyrightable expression, rather than just the underlying idea, has been taken. Judge Hand's "abstractions" test is often used in drawing the line between idea and expression in this context. See *Nichols v. Universal Pictures Corp.*, 45 F.2d 119 (2d Cir. 1930), *cert. denied*, 282 U.S. 902 (1931).

V. THE EXCLUSIVE RIGHT TO REPRODUCE THE WORK

All classes of copyrightable subject matter enjoy the exclusive right to reproduce the work.

A. **The meaning of "reproduction":** The right of reproduction is the right to reproduce the work in material copies or phonorecords. To infringe, a defendant must fix all or part of the copyrighted work in a material object in a manner that is sufficiently permanent or stable to permit the work to be perceived, reproduced, or otherwise communicated for a period of more than transitory duration.

1. **RAM copies:** Courts have held that bringing a work into the random access memory (RAM) of a computer constitutes a reproduction for purposes of the Copyright Act, because the work can be perceived in RAM for a period of more than transitory duration. *MAI Systems Corp. v. Peak Computer, Inc.*, 991 F.2d 511 (9th Cir. 1993). However, the Court of Appeals for the Second Circuit has held that temporary "buffer" copies lasting no more than 1.2 seconds do not constitute copies because they do not last for more than a transitory duration. *Cartoon Network, LP v. CSC Holdings, Inc.*, 536 F.3d 121 (2d Cir. 2008). A number of courts have exonerated Internet Service Providers from reproduction right infringement when their computerized systems automatically make RAM or other temporary duplicates of works posted or transmitted by Internet users. These courts have reasoned that although copyright infringement is a form of strict liability, there must be some element of volition or causation on the defendant's part. Thus, an Internet Service Provider that provides the automatic means for users to post or transmit (and thereby reproduce) materials, but does not otherwise participate in making a reproduction, lacks the necessary volition/causation and should not be liable as a direct infringer. *CoStar Group, Inc. v. Loopnet, Inc.*, 373 F.3d 544 (4th Cir. 2004).

B. **Limitations on the exclusive right to reproduce — sound recordings:** The exclusive right to reproduce sound recordings extends only to mechanical reproduction of sounds fixed in the plaintiff's copyrighted recording. Simply mimicking the plaintiff's copyrighted sounds in an independent recording does not constitute infringement. The Court of Appeals for the Sixth Circuit has held that mechanical reproduction *alone* is enough to demonstrate infringement of the reproduction and/or adaptation right in a sound recording — it is not necessary to demonstrate that the defendant's work is substantially similar to the plaintiff's copyrighted expression. *Bridgeport*

Music, Inc. v. Dimension Films, 410 F.3d 792 (6th Cir. 2005). However, it is not clear whether other circuits will follow this precedent.

C. **Exception to the exclusive right to reproduce—computer programs:** Under Copyright Act §117, the lawful *owner* of a copy of a copyrighted computer program may reproduce the program, if the copying is an essential step in utilizing the program in a computer or is for archival purposes only. Section 117 also provides that the *owner or lessee* of a computer may temporarily copy a computer program if the computer is lawfully programmed with it, and copying is necessary and solely for purposes of maintaining or repairing the computer.

   1. **Ownership of copies:** The restriction of §117 to "owners" of copies of software disqualifies rightful possessors who obtained their rights under a license agreement, rather than through a transfer of title. The Federal Circuit has held that licensees may be deemed "owners," and thus entitled to the §117 exemptions, if the transaction giving them lawful possession *resembles* a transfer of title. Relevant considerations in determining whether this is the case include: (1) whether the possessor obtained its rights in the software through a single payment; (2) whether the rightful possession is perpetual; and (3) whether the rightful use of the software under the license is heavily encumbered by restrictions that are inconsistent with the status of an owner. *DSC Communications Corp. v. Pulse Communications, Inc.*, 170 F.3d 1354 (Fed. Cir.), *cert. denied*, 528 U.S. 923 (1999).

D. **Exception to the exclusive right to reproduce—compulsory licenses to record nondramatic musical works:** Once a musical composition has been recorded and distributed to the U.S. public in phonorecords under the copyright owner's authorization, Copyright Act §115 permits others to make their own recording of the musical composition (make a "cover") and distribute the recording to the public. However, the prerequisites spelled out in §115 must be satisfied. Among other things, the compulsory licensee's primary purpose must be to make phonorecords to be distributed to the public for private use, and the licensee must serve proper notice of her intention to take a compulsory license on the copyright owner. The compulsory licensee must pay royalties as set forth in §115.

E. **Other exceptions to the exclusive right to reproduce:** The Copyright Act contains a host of other narrowly drawn exceptions to the right of reproduction, including: (1) broadcasters' ephemeral recordings of programs containing performances or displays of copyrighted works (Copyright Act §112); (2) reproduction, distribution, and display of useful objects portrayed in copyrighted pictorial, graphic, and sculptural works (§113); (3) reproduction, distribution, and display of pictorial representations of useful articles incorporating copyrighted design features for purposes of advertising or sale of the useful articles, news reporting, etc. (§113); (4) reproduction, distribution, and public display of pictorial representations of copyrighted buildings visible from a public place (§120); (5) authorization for public libraries and archives to reproduce works under certain circumstances (§108); and (6) authorization to make and distribute previously published nondramatic literary works in specialized formats for persons with disabilities (§121).

VI. THE EXCLUSIVE RIGHT TO PREPARE DERIVATIVE WORKS

A. **The right to make derivative works:** The right to make derivative works is also known as the right to *adapt* the copyrighted work. As defined in Copyright Act §101, a derivative work is "a work based upon one or more preexisting works, such as a translation, musical arrangement, dramatization, fictionalization, motion picture version, sound recording, art reproduction, abridgement, condensation, or any other form in which a work may be recast, transformed, or adapted." In most (but not all) cases in which the right to adapt is infringed, either the right to reproduce or the right to publicly perform will be infringed as well.

   1. **Relevant considerations in determining whether a defendant's acts constitute "adaptation":** Some courts have suggested that a defendant's changes must constitute a "substantial variation" from the original before an *infringement* of the adaptation right can be found. (Another way to say this is that the defendant's alleged infringing work must be one that would have *qualified for a derivative work copyright* if it had been authorized.) However, other courts have rejected such a requirement. Courts may undertake to assess the *economic impact* of the defendant's acts on potential markets for the plaintiff's work in deciding whether the defendant's acts constitute actionable adaptation.

B. **The adaptation right and computer program enhancements:** The Ninth Circuit has held that even though a defendant need not reproduce a copyrighted work in order to infringe the owner's adaptation right, the defendant's work must *incorporate the underlying work in a concrete or permanent form. Lewis Galoob Toys, Inc. v. Nintendo of America, Inc.*, 964 F.2d 965 (9th Cir. 1992), *cert. denied*, 507 U.S. 985 (1993). However, in the digital context, an "exact, down to the last detail description of an audiovisual display" in code will constitute the necessary "incorporation" of the audiovisual display, just as sheet music, which describes in precise detail the way a copyrighted melody should sound, constitutes incorporation of the melody in a concrete and permanent form. *Micro Star v. Formgen, Inc.*, 154 F.3d 1107 (9th Cir. 1998).

C. **Limitations on the exclusive right to make derivative works—sound recordings:** The right to adapt a sound recording, like the right to reproduce it, is infringed only if the defendant mechanically recaptures or "lifts" sounds from the copyrighted sound recording, then alters or mixes them with other sounds. Copyright Act §114.

D. **Limitations on the exclusive right to make derivative works—computer programs:** The owner of an authorized copy of a computer program may make an adaptation of the program, if it is done as an essential step in utilizing the program in a computer or is done for archival purposes. However, the altered program may not be transferred to someone else unless the copyright owner consents, and the altered copies must be destroyed as soon as the owner no longer has a lawful right to possess the original program. Copyright Act §117.

E. **Limitations on the exclusive right to make derivative works—architectural works:** The owner of a building embodying a copyrighted architectural work may make or authorize alterations to the building. Copyright Act §120.

VII. THE EXCLUSIVE RIGHT TO DISTRIBUTE TO THE PUBLIC

A. **The right of distribution:** Copyright includes the exclusive right to distribute copies or phonorecords of the work to the public by sale or other transfer of ownership, or by rental, lease, or lending. Traditionally, to violate the exclusive right to distribute a copyrighted work, a person had to make an unauthorized *physical transfer* of a material copy or phonorecord to a member of the public. However, recent case law suggests that it is not always necessary to demonstrate physical transfer of a material copy. Transmission of an electronic (digital) copy is likely to suffice. Likewise, some precedent indicates that posting a copyrighted work on a web site, where it is readily available for download, or holding an unlawful copy of a work, indexed and available in a public library collection, can be an infringing distribution of the work to the public. See *Hotaling v. Church of Jesus Christ of Latter-Day Saints*, 118 F.3d 199 (4th Cir. 1997). Courts have differed over whether making a music file "available" for peer-to-peer file sharing is sufficient, in itself, to constitute distribution to the public. The Ninth Circuit has held that providing an HTML link to a file residing on another web site does not constitute distribution of that file. One must first have the file in his own possession (in this case, on his own computer hard drive) before he can distribute it to others. *Perfect 10, Inc. v. Amazon.com, Inc.*, 487 F.3d 701 (9th Cir. 2007).

B. **The doctrine of first sale:** The doctrine of first sale (17 U.S.C. 109(a)) is an important limitation on the distribution right. It provides that once the copyright owner authorizes transfer of title to a copy or phonorecord of the copyrighted work, the transferee and his successors in interest are entitled to retransfer or otherwise dispose of that copy or phonorecord without returning to the copyright owner for authorization. However, the doctrine of first sale only applies to *lawful* copies and phonorecords. A person who acquires a pirated copy of the work will infringe the copyright by reselling or otherwise redistributing it to the public. Moreover, the doctrine of first sale does not authorize the owner of a lawful copy to reproduce it or to distribute the unauthorized reproductions.

   1. **Exception to the doctrine of first sale for record and computer program rentals:** Owners of copyright in computer programs, in sound recordings of music, and in the musical compositions that are recorded in sound recordings, may prevent purchasers of program copies and phonorecords from renting out the phonorecords and program copies commercially, or may charge a royalty for granting them the privilege to do so. §109(b).

   2. **Droit de suite:** The *droit de suite* doctrine gives the author of a work of fine art the opportunity to share in its appreciation in value when it is resold by subsequent transferees. The U.S. Congress has not adopted the *droit de suite* as an exception to the doctrine of first sale, but the state of California has enacted a statute in the nature of the *droit de suite*.

   3. **Imports:** Copyright Act §602 provides that unauthorized importation of copies or phonorecords of a work into the United States infringes the copyright owner's exclusive right of distribution to the public. However, the Supreme Court has

held that the doctrine of first sale is applicable to the importation right. Thus, if a copyright owner manufactured goods incorporating the copyrighted work *in the United States* and exported them, it could not, absent an enforceable contractual restriction, prevent foreign purchasers from bringing the goods back into the United States to resell in competition with it. While the Supreme Court has not definitively ruled whether the doctrine of first sale likewise applies to copies and phonorecords manufactured by or under the authority of the U.S. copyright owner abroad, the Ninth Circuit has ruled that it does not. Under this interpretation, the U.S. copyright owner can manufacture and sell its copyrighted works abroad and use U.S. copyright law to prevent resale of those copies in the United States. *Omega, S.A. v. Costco Wholesale Corp.*, 541 F.3d 982 (9th Cir. 2008). In 2012 the U.S. Supreme Court granted certiorari in another case to review this issue. *Kirtsaeng v. John Wiley & Sons*, __ U.S. __, 80 U.S.L.W. 3365 (April 16, 2012).

4. **The doctrine of first sale on the Internet:** Because Internet transmissions generally entail *reproducing* the sender's copy and sending the reproduction, the doctrine of first sale will seldom apply to permit purchasers of digital works to transfer them to others via the Internet.

VIII. THE EXCLUSIVE RIGHT TO PERFORM PUBLICLY

A. **The meaning of "performance":** To perform a work is "to recite, render, play, dance, or act it, either directly or by means of any device or process or, in the case of a motion picture or other audiovisual work, to show its images in any sequence or to make the sounds accompanying it audible." Copyright Act §101. The initial rendition and any further act by which that rendition is transmitted or communicated or made to recur is a performance.

B. **When a performance is "public":** Copyright Act §101 spells out four ways in which a performance may be "public": (1) if the performance occurs at a *place open to the public*; (2) if the performance occurs at any place where a *substantial number of persons* outside the normal circle of a family and its social acquaintances is gathered; (3) if the performance is *transmitted or otherwise communicated* to a place described in (1) or (2) above; or (4) if the performance is *transmitted or otherwise communicated to the public* by means of any device, regardless of whether the public receives it in the same or separate places or receives it at the same or different times.

C. **Exception to the exclusive right of public performance — nonprofit performances of nondramatic literary or musical works:** It does not constitute infringement to publicly perform a nondramatic literary or musical work if the performance is direct (not transmitted), there is no purpose of direct or indirect commercial advantage, the performers, promoters and organizers are not paid specifically for the performance, and there is no direct or indirect admission charge (or, if there is such a charge, the proceeds, after deducting costs of the performance, are used exclusively for charitable purposes). §110(4). Other exceptions to the exclusive right of public performance also apply to the exclusive right of public display, and are discussed in the next section.

D. **The right to perform sound recordings publicly by means of a digital audio transmission:** The general right of public performance is not accorded to sound recordings. However, sound recording copyright owners have "the right to perform the copyrighted work publicly by means of a digital audio transmission." §106(6). This is a more limited public performance right than the general public performance right enjoyed by other categories of copyrightable subject matter. It does not extend to FCC-regulated over-the-air radio or television broadcasts to the public (though it does apply to Internet "webcasts"). Nor does it apply to digital transmissions of *audiovisual* works such as music videos, or to forms of digital performances that do not constitute transmissions, such as playing sound recordings on a compact disc player. There are numerous further limitations on the digital audio transmission performance right, including compulsory licenses to permit digital performances by third parties, under specified circumstances.

E. **Rights in unfixed musical performances:** Pursuant to the United States' TRIPs Agreement obligations, Congress enacted anti-bootlegging provisions giving "neighboring rights" in live musical performances. 17 U.S.C. §1101. These provisions prohibit unauthorized broadcasts of live musical performances, unauthorized fixations of such performances, and reproduction, distribution, offers to distribute, and trafficking in unauthorized fixations. Violators are subject to civil copyright infringement remedies.

IX. THE EXCLUSIVE RIGHT TO DISPLAY THE COPYRIGHTED WORK PUBLICLY

A. **What constitutes a public display:** To *display* a work is to show a copy of it, either directly or by means of a film, slide, television image, or any other device or process or, in the case of a motion picture or other audiovisual work, to show individual images nonsequentially. §101. A computer operator who stores an image as electronic information and then serves that information directly to Internet users displays that information. However, it does not constitute a display merely to link to or frame electronic information that resides on a different computer. A display is *public* under the same circumstances in which a performance is public.

B. **Important exception to the exclusive right of public display — owners of lawfully made copies:** The owner of a lawfully made copy of a work may display that copy publicly either directly or by the projection of no more than one image at a time, to viewers present at the place where the copy is located. Copyright Act §109(c). This exception limits the economic value of the public display right primarily to transmissions of displays via broadcast and Internet.

C. **Exception to the exclusive rights of public performance and display — transmissions received on home-style receivers:** Under Copyright Act §110(5), performance or display of a copyrighted work *by transmission* to a place open to the public or where the public is gathered, on a single receiving apparatus of a kind commonly used in private homes, will not infringe unless a direct charge is made to see or hear the transmission. Congress has amended this §110(5) exception to give commercial establishments *greater leeway to perform nondramatic musical works* by public reception of radio and television transmissions to the general public. Under the amendment, stores that are smaller than 2,000 square feet and restaurants and bars that are smaller than 3,750 square feet may play radio and television transmissions of nondramatic musical works, regardless of the type of receiver or number of speakers they use. Establishments that are larger than the specified square foot limitations are also exempt from liability if they use no more than 6 speakers or 4 televisions with screens smaller than 55 inches. (There are further limitations on the placement of the speakers and televisions.) A World Trade Organization dispute resolution panel has held the amendment described above to be in violation of the United States' international treaty obligations.

D. **Other exceptions to the exclusive rights of public performance and display:** Additional exceptions to the exclusive rights of public performance and public display permit such things as: (1) performances and displays of works by instructors or pupils in the course of face-to-face teaching activities in a classroom or similar place devoted to instruction (Copyright Act §110 (1)); (2) performance and display of certain works by transmission in the systematic instructional activities of a government body or nonprofit educational institution (§110(2)); (3) certain performances and displays of works in the course of religious services (§110(3)); and (4) a variety of forms of retransmission of transmitted broadcast signals. The Copyright Act also provides for compulsory licenses to enable cable systems and satellite companies to make secondary transmissions of broadcast signals. In addition, there is a compulsory license to enable public broadcasting entities to make public performances and displays of certain kinds of works.

X. MORAL RIGHTS

A. **The nature of moral rights:** Many countries recognize rights that are *personal* to authors, apart from the economic rights discussed thus far. These personal rights are known as moral rights and are based on the view that a work of authorship is an extension of the author's personality or self, and should be protected as such. Generally, moral rights include the *right of attribution* and the *right of integrity*. The Berne Convention requires member countries to protect these rights.

B. **The Visual Artists' Rights Act of 1990:** Congress enacted the Visual Artists' Rights Act of 1990 ("VARA") to comply with the Berne Convention requirement. The Act, however, is very limited in scope, because it only provides moral rights in *works of visual art*. Works of visual art include paintings, drawings, prints, or sculptures that exist in a single copy or in a limited edition of 200 or fewer signed, numbered copies. Still photographs are also included, if produced for exhibition purposes only and existing in a single, signed copy or in a limited edition of 200 or fewer signed, numbered copies. Works made for hire or that do not qualify for copyright are excluded. 17 U.S.C. §101. Authors of qualifying works of visual art are given the rights of attribution and integrity in their works. 17 U.S.C. §106A. These rights *attach to the single or limited edition copies described above*. They do not attach to the intangible work of authorship, as manifested in mass-produced or any other copies beyond the single and limited edition copies described above.

1. **The right of attribution:** The right of attribution gives the artist the right to be identified as the author of a work, the right to prevent attribution to her of works that she did not create, and the right to prevent use of her name in connection with a work that has been modified in a way that will injure her honor or reputation.

2. **The right of integrity:** The right of integrity gives the artist the right to prevent any intentional distortion, mutilation, or other modification of her work that would be prejudicial to her honor or reputation as an artist and, in the case of works of "recognized stature," the right to prevent intentional or grossly negligent destruction of the work.

3. **Ownership, transfer, and duration of the rights:** The moral rights are granted to the artist and retained by the artist even after she transfers the copyright in the work to someone else. The artist may not assign her moral rights, but may expressly waive them in writing in a particular instance. In the case of works created on or after the effective date of VARA (June 1, 1991), the rights of attribution and integrity last for the life of the author, or in the case of joint authors, for as long as any author survives. In the case of works created earlier than the effective date, the moral rights will endure as long as the economic rights in the work, assuming that the author retained title to the work June 1, 1991. If the author did not retain title on June 1, 1991, the work carries no moral rights.

4. **Exception to moral rights:** The owner of a building into which a work of visual art is incorporated may, *under limited circumstances*, remove the work from the building even though removal will destroy, distort, mutilate, or otherwise modify the work Copyright Act §113(d).

C. **Other sources of protection for moral rights:** Other, more indirect methods of protecting moral rights interests may be available in the case of works other than works of visual art. For example, the author may assert the copyright right of adaptation to prevent mutilation of the work, if he retains copyright. In addition, unfair competition laws may sometimes be used to prohibit false designations of the origin or false representations about the work. In addition, state contract and defamation law, and specialized *state* moral rights statutes may assist an author.

XI. DIRECT AND INDIRECT INFRINGEMENT

A. **Direct infringement:** Anyone who makes an unauthorized reproduction, adaptation, distribution to the public, public performance or public display may be liable for direct infringement to the *owner of the copyright* in the work. Lack of intent to infringe or lack of knowledge of the copyright will not avoid liability, but may affect the remedy available to the plaintiff. Anyone who violates the moral rights of attribution or integrity in a qualifying work of visual art is liable to the *author* of the work.

B. **Contributory infringement liability:** One who knowingly induces, causes, or materially contributes to the infringing conduct of another is liable for contributory infringement. Generally, two elements must be demonstrated: (1) the defendant must know or have reason to know of the other person's infringement; and (2) the defendant must actively participate by inducing, materially contributing to, or furthering the other person's directly infringing activity.

1. **The Sony rule:** In *Sony Corp. of America v. Universal City Studios, Inc.*, 464 U.S. 417 (1984), the Supreme Court held that a person will not be liable for manufacturing or selling products that may be used to infringe but are also capable of substantial noninfringing uses, merely because he has constructive knowledge

that some purchasers may use the products to infringe. The Ninth Circuit has subsequently held that if the provider *learns of specific acts of infringement through use of its products or services*, it then incurs a duty to act to stop further infringement. *A & M Records, Inc. v Napster, Inc.*, 239 F.3d 1004 (9th Cir. 2001). Failure to act will constitute contributory infringement with respect to any direct infringement that occurs thereafter. However, to incur this duty to act, the provider must have the actual knowledge of infringement *at a time in which he is in a position to stop it*. If the provider no longer has any substantial interaction with the direct infringer when he learns of the infringement, he will have no duty to act to stop the infringement.

2. **The Grokster "inducement" cause of action:** The Supreme Court held, in *Metro-Goldwyn-Mayer Studios, Inc. v. Grokster*, 545 U.S. 913 (2005), that the *Sony* rule does not apply to shelter the provider of products or services used to infringe (even if the products or services are capable of substantial, noninfringing uses) if the defendant distributed the product or service with the *clear object of promoting its use to infringe* copyright, as shown by clear expression or other affirmative steps taken to foster infringement. Relevant evidence of bad intent in *Grokster* included: (1) the defendants' attempts to capture an audience known to be seeking new means to infringe; (2) the defendants' failure to develop filtering tools or other mechanisms to diminish infringing use of the product; and (3) the defendants' adoption of a business model that was more profitable if users infringed. The Court stressed that neither (2) nor (3), on its own, would suffice to demonstrate the requisite intent, but that the three forms of evidence, in combination, could suffice.

C. **Vicarious infringement liability:** Vicarious liability may be found whenever the defendant has (1) the right and ability to control or supervise the direct infringer; and (2) a direct financial interest in the infringement. It is not necessary that the defendant know of or participate in the direct infringement.

D. **Infringement on the Internet:** Due to special concerns about copyright infringement on the Internet, and the possibility of Internet service providers being held liable for their users' infringement, Congress enacted Copyright Act §512, which provides a series of safe harbors from infringement liability for Internet service providers.

XII. THE FAIR USE AND OTHER DEFENSES TO INFRINGEMENT

A. **The nature of the fair use defense:** The fair use defense is available once a *prima facie* showing of copyright infringement or violation of the moral rights in a work of visual art has been made. It is founded on notions of equity and common sense, and must be applied on a case-by-case basis to identify and permit unauthorized uses of copyrighted works that further the purposes of copyright law without significantly undercutting authors' economic incentive to create. Examples of uses that may be found fair (listed in Copyright Act §107) include uses "for purposes such as criticism, comment, news reporting, teaching (including multiple copies for classroom use), scholarship or research."

B. The four factors: Copyright Act §107 provides four factors that courts should consider in determining whether a defendant's use was fair: (1) "The purpose and character of the use, including whether such use is of a commercial nature or is for nonprofit educational purposes"; (2) "the nature of the copyrighted work"; (3) "the amount and substantiality of the portion used in relation to the copyrighted work as a whole"; and (4) "the effect of the use upon the potential market for or value of the copyrighted work." Courts must consider all four of the factors. No one factor is dispositive, though the Supreme Court has indicated that the fourth factor (the effect of the use on the plaintiff's potential market) is the most important. *Harper & Row, Publishers, Inc. v. Nation Enterprises*, 471 U.S. 539 (1985). Courts have sometimes augmented these four factors with additional considerations.

C. Special considerations in parody cases: A parody based on a copyrighted work is more likely to be excused as a fair use if the parody is at least in part aimed at the copyrighted work itself. If it is, the defendant generally may copy to the extent necessary to "conjure up" the copyrighted work in the audience's mind, so that the audience will understand that the work is being parodied. This may involve taking the "heart" of the plaintiff's work. The amount the parodist can copy beyond what is necessary to conjure up the work may depend on whether his sole purpose was to parody the copyrighted work, or whether he was trying to address additional issues. *Campbell v. Acuff-Rose Music, Inc.*, 510 U.S. 569 (1994).

D. Reverse engineering object code: The copying of object code that takes place in the course of reverse engineering (decompiling) a computer program may be excused as a fair use when reverse engineering is the only means of gaining access to unprotected ideas and functional elements embodied in the object code, and the defendant has a legitimate interest in gaining such access. (This rule is sometimes referred to as the *Sega* rule. *Sega Enterprises v. Accolade, Inc.*, 977 F.2d 1510 (9th Cir. 1992).)

E. Copyright misuse: The copyright misuse defense is an equitable defense that renders a copyright unenforceable if the copyright owner has engaged in misconduct in licensing or enforcing the copyright, thereby broadening the scope of his monopoly right beyond what Congress intended. Under the misuse doctrine, the owner's copyright will be unenforceable until the misuse ends and its effects have dissipated. The misuse doctrine may apply even in the absence of an antitrust violation.

XIII. ANTICIRCUMVENTION AND DIGITAL RIGHTS MANAGEMENT PROVISIONS

A. Anticircumvention provisions: The Digital Millennium Copyright Act ("DMCA") makes it illegal to *circumvent* a technological measure that effectively controls *access* to a work protected under the Copyright Act. It also makes it illegal to manufacture or traffic in devices or services to defeat technological protection measures (both measures to *control access* to the work and measures to *control exercise of the exclusive rights of the copyright owner*, once access is gained). However, in the case of manufacturing or trafficking, the devices or services must be: (1) primarily designed or produced for the purpose of circumventing; (2) have only limited commercially significant purposes or uses other than to circumvent; or (3) be marketed for use in circumventing. 17 U.S.C. § 1201.

1. **Circumvention:** To circumvent a technological measure is to descramble a scrambled work, decrypt an encrypted work, or otherwise avoid, bypass, remove, deactivate, or impair a technological measure without the authority of the copyright owner.

2. **Technological measure:** A technological measure effectively controls *access* to a work if, in the ordinary course of its operation, it requires the application of information or a process or treatment, with the authority of the copyright owner, to gain access to the work.

3. **Unauthorized use of passwords:** Courts have disagreed over whether unauthorized use of a password that was properly issued to a different person constitutes circumvention of a technological measure that controls access to a copyrighted work.

4. **Relationship of anticircumvention violation to infringement of copyright:** The Circuits appear to differ over the relationship between copyright infringement and violation of the anticircumvention provisions. The Second Circuit has suggested that the DMCA targets circumvention and does not concern itself with what is done with copyrighted material after circumvention has occurred. *Universal City Studios, Inc. v. Corley*, 273 F.3d 429 (2d Cir. 2001). Thus, it is essentially irrelevant whether the circumvention results or can result in copyright infringement. The Federal Circuit, by contrast, has held that the anticircumvention provisions were not intended to provide a new property right (a new "right of access") to copyright owners, but only to provide a new means of protecting existing rights created under the Copyright Act. Thus, §1201 prevents trafficking in access control circumvention devices or services (and access control circumvention itself) only if the use of the device (or the circumvention) will infringe or facilitate infringement of copyright. *Chamberlain Group, Inc. v. Skylink Technologies, Inc.*, 381 F.3d 1178 (Fed. Cir. 2004), *cert. denied*, 544 U.S. 923 (2005).

5. **Exceptions:** There are some narrowly drawn, specific exceptions to DMCA liability to accommodate reverse engineering of software to achieve interoperability, law enforcement activities, good-faith encryption research, and security testing of computer systems or networks.

B. **Copyright management information:** Copyright management information includes information that identifies the work, or its creators or copyright owner; terms or conditions for use of the work; and any identifying numbers or symbols. The Digital Millennium Copyright Act prohibits persons from intentionally removing or altering copyright management information, or knowingly distributing copies or phonorecords with illegally modified copyright management information. 17 U.S.C. §1202.

XIV. OWNERSHIP OF COPYRIGHT

A. **Initial owner of copyright:** The author of a work is the initial owner of the copyright in it and may either exploit the work herself or transfer some or all of the rights to others. Unless the work is a work for hire, the author is the person who conceives of the copyrightable expression and fixes it or causes it to be fixed in a tangible form.

1. **Ownership of copyright in joint works:** The authors of a joint work are co-owners of a single copyright in the work. A joint work is "a work prepared by two or more authors with the intention that their contributions be merged into inseparable or interdependent parts of a unitary whole." Copyright Act §101. To create a joint work (as opposed, for example, to two separate works—an original work and a derivative work based on it), each author must have intended to contribute a part to a unitary whole at the time she created her portion. Each joint author must also have contributed copyrightable expression, not just ideas or facts.

   a. **Determining which contributors are joint authors:** The Ninth Circuit requires that a party have *decision-making authority* over the work before he will be deemed a joint author. *Almuhammed v. Lee*, 202 F.3d 1227 (9th Cir. 2000). The Second and Seventh Circuits have focused on whether the participants *intended* for an individual to be a joint author. Evidence that the individual had decision-making authority is relevant to that determination, along with other circumstantial evidence of the parties' intent, such as how they represent authorship to others, whether they share royalties, etc. *Erickson v. Trinity Theatre, Inc.*, 13 F.3d 1061 (7th Cir.1994).

2. **Works for hire:** If a work is "made for hire" within the meaning of the Copyright Act, the employer or other person who ordered and financed the work is deemed the author for copyright purposes and is the initial owner of the copyright. There are two ways in which a work may be found to be a work for hire. First, it is a work for hire if it was *prepared by an employee within the scope of his employment*. Common-law agency principles should be used to determine whether someone is an employee for this purpose. If the hiring party has the right to control the manner and means by which the worker accomplishes the work, then the worker probably is an employee. *Community for Creative Non-Violence v. Reid*, 490 U.S. 730 (1989). Second, works *created by independent contractors* (rather than employees) may be works for hire if: (1) the work *fits into one of nine categories of works* enumerated in Copyright Act §101; and (2) the parties have expressly agreed in a *written, signed instrument* that the work will be considered a work made for hire.

3. **Ownership of copyright in collective works:** In the absence of an express assignment of copyright, the author of each separate contribution in a collective work retains copyright in that contribution. The author of the collection owns copyright in the expression he or she contributed—usually the selection and arrangement of the individually copyrightable contributions and any explanatory material. Copyright Act §201(c) provides that in the absence of a writing to the contrary, the author of the collective work will have the following privileges with regard to the individual works he has collected: the privilege to reproduce and distribute the individual contributions as part of the collective work; the privilege to reproduce the individual contributions as part of later revisions of the same collective work; and the privilege to reproduce the individual contributions in a later work of the same series.

B. **Divisibility of ownership:** Copyright ownership is divisible. The copyright owner may transfer some or all of her *exclusive* rights. Any person who receives an *exclusive* *right* under the copyright is considered a copyright owner and has the right to sue to enforce the right she owns against others. A person who has only a *non-exclusive right* is a licensee and has no standing to sue for infringement.

C. **Transfer of copyright:** All transfers of *exclusive* rights must be in writing and signed by the transferor, unless the transfer is by operation of law. Transfers of *non-exclusive rights* (licenses) need not be in writing. The Copyright Act provides that assignments, licenses, and other documents pertaining to copyright may be recorded in the Copyright Office. Proper recordation of a document serves as constructive notice of the contents of the document to others.

D. **Implied licenses**: Nonexclusive licenses may be implied in fact. The Court of Appeals for the Ninth Circuit has held that an implied license may be found if: (1) a person (the licensee) requests the creation of a work; (2) the creator (the licensor) makes that particular work and delivers it to the licensee who requested it; and (3) the licensor intends that the licensee-requestor copy and distribute his work (or, in the case of computer programs, use, retain, and modify the programs). *Asset Marketing Systems, Inc. v. Gagnon*, 542 F.3d 748 (9th Cir. 2008), *cert. denied*, 129 S. Ct. 2442 (2009).

XV. NOTICE OF COPYRIGHT

A. **The Copyright Act of 1909:** Prior to January 1, 1978, the United States had a dual system of copyright protection. Common-law copyright protected works prior to publication. When the work was published, common-law protection ceased. Upon publication, federal statutory copyright protection began if all the authorized published copies carried proper notice of copyright. Failure to include notice on even a few published copies, or failure to give notice in the proper form or location, generally lead to forfeiture of all copyright in the work.

   1. **Publication under the 1909 Act:** The fact that a work had been made public or commercially exploited did not necessarily mean that it had been "published," for purposes of copyright protection. As a general matter, publication required physically distributing tangible copies of the work to members of the public without restriction. Courts sometimes distinguished between investive and divestive publications. In the case of divestive publications, they found that a "limited publication"—a distribution of copies to a selected group of people for a limited purpose—would not divest the owner of common-law copyright.

B. **The Copyright Act of 1976:** When Congress enacted the Copyright Act of 1976 (which became effective January 1, 1978), it did away with the dual system of copyright, providing that federal statutory copyright *commences upon fixation* of a work in tangible form. Congress preempted state copyright protection in fixed works. The 1976 Act provided that notice of copyright must be placed on all visually perceptible copies that were publicly distributed, and that notice of copyright in sound recordings must be placed on all publicly distributed phonorecords.

   1. **Savings provisions:** Copyright Act §405 provides that if authorized copies or phonorecords were publicly distributed without copyright notice, the copyright in the work is invalid unless one of three conditions was satisfied: (1) only a relatively small number of copies or phonorecords was distributed to the public without

notice; (2) the work was registered with the Copyright Office within five years of the public distribution without notice and the owner made reasonable efforts to add notice to all of the copies distributed to the public in the United States after the omission was discovered; or (3) notice was omitted in violation of an express, written agreement conditioning authorization to publish on provision of notice.

C. **The Berne Convention amendments:** When the United States joined the Berne Convention, it had to eliminate notice requirements in order to comply with the Berne Convention prohibition against subjecting enjoyment of copyright to "any formality." The Berne Convention Implementation Act amended the Copyright Act of 1976 to provide that compliance with the notice provisions would be voluntary, rather than mandatory, for copies and phonorecords distributed to the public *after March 1, 1989.* However, the Berne Convention Implementation Act did not restore copyrights that had already been lost due to lack of notice under either the 1909 or the 1976 Copyright Act.

   1. **Foreign copyright restoration:** As a general matter, the status of copyright in a work is determined pursuant to the notice provisions that were applicable at the time that copies or phonorecords were distributed without notice. If copyright was forfeited under those provisions, it remains forfeited. However, Congress enacted an important *exception to this rule* in the Uruguay Round Agreements Act. As amended, Copyright Act §104A restores (or, in the case of sound recordings fixed prior to February, 1972, creates) copyright in works originating in foreign countries belonging to the Berne Convention or the World Trade Organization that have fallen into the U.S. public domain for reasons other than the normal expiration of their term of protection. The Act restored (or created) copyright in qualifying foreign works automatically, and the restored copyright will endure for the remainder of the term the work would have enjoyed had copyright not previously been denied or forfeited under U.S. law. The restored copyrights are enforceable against persons having notice of the owner's intent to enforce. However, the Uruguay Round Agreements Act limits the circumstances in which restored copyrights can be enforced against "reliance parties."

XVI. DEPOSIT AND REGISTRATION

A. **Deposit requirements:** The owner of copyright or the publication rights in a published work must deposit two copies or phonorecords of the best edition of the work with the Copyright Office within three months of publication. Failure to comply with the deposit requirements is punishable by fine, but not by forfeiture of copyright. (The Copyright Office may make exceptions to the deposit requirement *via* regulation.)

B. **Registration requirements:** A copyright owner may register copyright in a work (published or unpublished) at any time during the copyright. If a work is registered before or within five years after first publication, the certificate of registration will constitute *prima facie* evidence of the validity of the copyright and the facts stated in the certificate. In the case of works whose "country of origin" is the United States, the owner of copyright *must* register her copyright or show that she attempted to register and was refused, before she can bring suit for infringement. Regardless of a work's country of origin, failure to register before infringement began (in the case of unpublished works) or within three months after first publication will result in a denial of statutory damages and attorney fees. (The author of a work of visual art is not required to register the work in order to enjoy or enforce her subsection 106A moral rights in it.)

1. **A work's country of origin:** A work's country of origin is the United States if it was first published in the United States, was simultaneously published in the United States and another country, or in the case of unpublished works, was created entirely by U.S. authors.

XVII. THE DURATION OF COPYRIGHT PROTECTION

A. **Commencement of federal copyright:** Under the Copyright Act of 1909, federal copyright in most cases commenced upon publication of the work with proper notice of copyright. Under the Copyright Act of 1976 (which became effective on January 1, 1978), federal copyright commences upon *creation* of the work. A work is "created" when it is first fixed in a copy or phonorecord.

B. **Duration of copyright for works created on or after January 1, 1978:** For works created on or after January 1, 1978, the duration of copyright is the life of the author plus 70 years. For works of joint authorship, the copyright endures for the life of the last of the joint authors to die plus 70 years. In the case of anonymous and pseudonymous works, and works made for hire, the duration of copyright is 95 years following first publication or 120 years following creation of the work, whichever period expires first. 17 U.S.C. §302.

C. **Duration of the copyright for works created but not published before January 1, 1978:** Works that were created but unpublished on January 1, 1978 (and thus were protected by state common-law copyright) became protected by federal copyright on that date. The copyright will last for the life of the author plus 70 years or until December 31, 2002, whichever is longer. If the work was published on or before December 31, 2002, the copyright will not expire before December 31, 2047. 17 U.S.C. §303.

D. **Duration of the copyright for works already protected by federal copyright on January 1, 1978:** Under the Copyright Act of 1909, federal copyright consisted of a term of 28 years. The copyright could be renewed at the end of that (first) term for a second term of 28 years, giving a total of 56 years of copyright protection. If the copyright was not renewed at the end of the first 28-year term, it expired. The 1976 Act retained the two-term arrangement for copyright for works that were protected by federal copyright at the time the 1976 Act became effective, but provided that the second term would be extended an additional 19 years (to a total of 47 years). The Sonny Bono Copyright Term Extension Act, enacted in 1998, further extended the second term of pre-1976 Act copyrights that were still in existence on its effective date (October 27, 1998). The Sonny Bono Act extended the Second Term an additional 20 years (to a total of 67 years). Thus, copyrights that *came into existence* before the effective date of the 1976 Act and *continued to exist* on that date enjoyed an initial term of 28 years and a second term of 47 years, for a total of 75 years. If they continued to exist on October 27, 1998, they enjoy a second term of 67 years, for a total term of 95 years. 17 U.S.C. §304.

E. **Duration of moral rights in works of visual art:** In the case of works of visual art created on or after the Visual Artists' Rights Act's effective date (June 1, 1991), the artist's moral rights of attribution and integrity will endure for the life of the author (or, in the case of joints works, the life of the last author to die). For those works of visual art created before the Act's effective date, but to which the author retained title on June 1, 1991, the rights will last as long as the economic rights of copyright. 17 U.S.C. §106.

F. **Rule for calculating the terms:** Under the 1976 Act, all terms of copyright run to the end of the calendar year in which they are due to expire. 17 U.S.C. §305.

XVIII. RENEWALS OF PRE-1976 ACT FEDERAL COPYRIGHTS

A. **Ownership of renewal right:** The Copyright Act of 1976 retained the two-term system for federal copyrights already in existence on January 1, 1978, so that federal copyrights in their first term on that date still had to be renewed in order to extend beyond the initial 28-year term. Like the 1909 Act, the 1976 Act specifies that the *author* of the copyrighted work owns the right to renew copyright in the work at the end of the first term (thus taking title in the renewal term of up to 67 years), if she is still living. If the author is not living at that time, her renewal rights pass to her *surviving spouse and children*, if there are any. If there is neither a surviving spouse nor children, the renewal right passes to the *author's executor*, who takes the right as the personal representative of the author's legatees under her will. If there is no executor, then the renewal right passes to the *author's next of kin*. The time to renew is the last (28th) year of the first term. Upon proper renewal, the person who is entitled to renew *takes the renewal term free of assignments and licenses executed in connection with the first term.* 17 U.S.C. §304.

B. **Transferability of expectancy of renewal right:** Any of the persons enumerated in subsection A, *supra*, may convey their expectancy of renewal to a third party, if they clearly indicate their intent to do so in writing. However, the most that any of them can convey to the third party is what they have — merely a contingent future interest. If the conveyor does *not* in fact qualify to renew at the time to renew, the third party/transferee takes no rights in the renewal term.

C. **Exceptions to the rule that the author and his statutory successors have the right to renew:** The person owning the copyright at the time to renew (rather than the author or his statutory successors) is entitled to renew if: (1) the work is a periodical, encyclopedia or other composite work and the copyright originally was secured by the proprietor rather than the author; (2) the work originally was copyrighted by an employer for whom the work was created for hire; or (3) the work was a posthumous one (one for which no copyright assignment or other contract for exploitation had been made during the author's life). 17 U.S.C. §304.

D. **The process of renewal:** Prior to the Copyright Amendments Act of 1992, renewal term claimants had to *file an application* to renew with the Copyright Office during the last year of the first term of the copyright. Failure to make a proper filing cast the work into the public domain at the end of the first term. Congress amended Copyright

Act §304 in 1992 to eliminate the filing requirement and provide that *renewal would be automatic for all remaining first-term copyrights.* The 1992 amendment nonetheless sought to encourage authors and their successors to continue filing for renewal on a voluntary basis: It provided that registration resulting from a properly filed application to renew would constitute *prima facie* evidence of the validity of the copyright during its renewal and extended term and of the facts stated in the certificate of registration. In addition, if a person who is entitled to renew registers the renewal term by filing an application, the renewal interest will *vest in that person as of the date of application.* By contrast, if the renewal occurs automatically, without filing, *the interest will vest in the person entitled to renew at the end of the first term.*

E. **Renewals and derivative works:** When a copyright owner grants a license to base a derivative work on the copyrighted work during its first term of copyright, and the licensee has obtained no rights in the renewal term, reproducing, adapting, publicly distributing, publicly performing, or publicly displaying the derivative work made pursuant to the license will constitute an infringement of the second-term copyright in the underlying work. *Stewart v. Abend*, 495 U.S. 207 (1990). However, 1992 amendments to Copyright Act §304 provide that if an author fails to file for renewal, merely relying on the automatic renewal provisions to obtain a second term, derivative works made under first-term licenses can continue to be exploited.

XIX. TERMINATION OF TRANSFERS OF COPYRIGHT

A. **Transfers executed on or after January 1, 1978:** All assignments and licenses of copyright executed by the author *after January 1, 1978*, are subject to termination under §203 of the Copyright Act of 1976 unless the work was a work for hire or the transfer was by will. It does not matter when the work that was the subject of the assignment or license was created.

1. **Persons entitled to terminate:** In the case of transfers by a single author, the author may terminate. If the author is dead, persons who have succeeded to more than one-half of the author's termination interest may terminate in the author's place. The persons succeeding to the author's termination interest are the author's surviving widow or widower and children (grandchildren stand in the place of deceased children). If the author leaves both a surviving spouse and surviving children or grandchildren, then the surviving spouse owns one-half of the author's interest and the surviving children or grandchildren share the other one-half. If there is no surviving spouse, children, or grandchildren, the author's executor, administrator, or trustee will own the author's entire termination interest.

   a. **Joint authors:** In the case of transfers by more than one author of a joint work, termination may be accomplished by a majority of the authors who made the transfer. If any of the original transferring authors is dead, his or her termination interest may be exercised as a unit by the statutory successors described above.

2. **Time for termination and notice:** An assignment or license may be terminated at any point during a 5-year period of time that begins in the 36th year after the

assignment or license was executed. (If the grant includes publication rights, the 5-year window of time begins in the 36th year after publication or the 41st year after the assignment or license was executed, whichever is sooner.) To terminate, the author or his successors must give notice to the assignee/licensee or her successor in writing two to ten years before the date on which the grant is to be terminated. The author's right to terminate may not be waived or relinquished by agreement.

3. **Effect of termination and further grants:** On the date that notice of termination is given, the terminated rights vest in the terminating parties. On the termination date, the rights revert to the persons in whom they have vested. If those persons have subsequently died, the rights pass to their next of kin or legatees. Further grants and agreements to grant the terminated rights may be made only after the effective date of the termination (unless the grantee will be the party whose rights are being terminated).

4. **Derivative works:** A derivative work prepared before termination of the assignment or license that authorized it may continue to be exploited after the termination.

B. **Transfers executed prior to January 1, 1978:** Copyright Act §304 applies to *all assignments and licenses of rights in the renewal (second) copyright term* executed before January 1, 1978, by either the author or the persons designated to take the author's renewal rights if he is dead at renewal time. It does not matter whether the grant of rights in the renewal term was made during the first or the second term of the copyright, as long as it was made *before January 1, 1978*, and gives rights during the renewal term. Assignments and licenses of works made for hire may not be terminated and dispositions by will may not be terminated.

1. **Persons entitled to terminate:** The persons entitled to terminate differ according to whether the *author* made the grant or his *statutory successors to renewal rights* made the grant. Grants by the author must be terminated by the author. If the author is dead, then the same persons are entitled to terminate as in the case of post-1978 transfers, and in the same fashion. In the case of grants by persons other than the author, all the persons who made the grant who are still surviving must join in the termination.

2. **Time for termination and notice:** Under Copyright Act *§304(c)*, an assignment or license may be terminated at any point during the five-year period of time beginning at the *later* of the following two dates: (1) the end of the 56th year of the copyright; or (2) January 1, 1978. Section *304(d)* provides that if the copyright is still in its renewal term on the effective date of the Sonny Bono Act (October 27, 1998), but the termination right set forth in §304(c) has *expired without being exercised*, then the author or his successors will have a *new opportunity* to terminate during a 5-year period commencing at the end of 75 years from the date the copyright was originally secured. In either case, written notice must be served on the assignee/licensee or his successors two to ten years prior to the date of termination.

3. **Effect of termination:** As in the case of §203, the terminated rights vest in all the persons entitled to terminate as soon as the notice of termination is filed. As with terminations under §203, no regrant or agreement to make a regrant can be made until the termination is effective, unless the grantee will be the party holding the rights to be terminated.

4. **Other provisions:** Authors and their successors may not waive or contract away their termination rights. Persons who have made derivative works pursuant to assignments or licenses that have since been terminated may continue to exploit the derivative works.

XX. REMEDIES FOR INFRINGEMENT

A. **Injunctions and disposal of infringing articles:** Preliminary and permanent injunctions may be awarded against copyright infringement and violation of the artist's moral rights in works of visual art. The Copyright Act also provides for the impounding and eventual destruction of infringing copies and phonorecords and/or articles used to make them.

B. **Damages and/or profits:** The copyright owner, or author of a work of visual art, is entitled to recover the actual damages that she suffered as a result of the infringement or violation, plus any of the defendant's profits attributable to the wrongdoing that were not taken into account in determining actual damages. However, there can be no double recovery. With regard to the defendant's profits, the plaintiff bears the burden of proving the defendant's gross revenues. The burden then shifts to the defendant to prove what, if any, amounts should be deducted as expenses or costs of producing the infringing work and what, if any, portion of his profits is attributable to factors other than his infringement.

1. **Statutory damages:** The copyright owner/author may elect to recover an award of statutory damages, instead of actual damages and profits. The court may award damages of not less than $750 or more than $30,000, as it considers just. If the plaintiff proves that the defendant willfully infringed or violated her rights, the court may, in its discretion, *increase the award* of statutory damages up to $150,000. If the defendant proves that she was not aware and had no reason to believe that her acts constituted infringement, the court may, in its discretion, *reduce the award* of statutory damages to not less than $200. Statutory damages are not available to copyright owners who did not register their works within the time frame set forth in the 1976 Copyright Act. 17 U.S.C. §504(c).

C. **Costs and attorney fees:** Courts may, in their discretion, award costs against either party to an infringement suit, though generally costs are only awarded against a party who acted in bad faith. Attorney fees are routinely awarded to the prevailing party, regardless of whether it is plaintiff or defendant.

XXI. INTERNATIONAL COPYRIGHT TREATIES

A. **The Berne Convention:** The Berne Convention, to which the United States adheres, is based on the doctrine of national treatment. In addition, the Berne Convention establishes minimum levels of substantive copyright protection that member nations must afford. Among other things, the Berne Convention requires members to protect a wide range of works (although sound recordings and the design of useful articles are not mandated), and to do so without imposing formalities as a prerequisite. The Berne Convention also prescribes a liberal term of protection, and specifies that member nations must protect a range of rights, including the right of reproduction, the right of translation, the right of adaptation, the right of public performance, the right of public recitation, the right of broadcasting, and the film right. The Berne also provides that member nations must protect the moral rights of attribution and integrity. Works first published in a Berne Convention member, or simultaneously in a member and non-member, and works created by nationals of Berne Convention members, must be protected.

B. The Universal Copyright Convention: The Universal Copyright Convention (U.C.C.), to which the United States also adheres, is likewise based on the doctrine of national treatment. It protects "literary, scientific and artistic works" of nationals of member nations and of non-nationals who first publish in a member nation. "Literary, scientific and artistic works" has been interpreted to include most of the works protected under U.S. copyright law except photographic works, works of applied art, and sound recordings. The U.C.C. imposes fewer substantive requirements than the Berne Convention does. The U.C.C. prescribes shorter minimum terms of protection, and only specifically provides that the rights of reproduction, public performance, and broadcasting must be protected. The U.C.C. permits members to impose notice requirements and other formalities, and does not require that moral rights be protected.

C. The TRIPs Agreement: The Agreement on Trade-Related Aspects of Intellectual Property Rights (TRIPs) is based on national treatment and requires World Trade Organization (WTO) members to comply with the provisions of the Berne Convention (with the exception of protecting moral rights). In addition, TRIPs specifies that computer programs and compilations must be protected as literary works, and that members must protect performers against unauthorized broadcast or fixation of their live performances, protect producers of sound recordings against unauthorized reproduction, and protect broadcasters or the owners of copyright in broadcast subject matter against unauthorized fixation, reproduction, and rebroadcasting. TRIPs also requires members to provide copyright owners with rights to prevent commercial rentals of sound recordings, computer programs, and cinematographic works.

D. The World Intellectual Property Organization (WIPO) Copyright Treaty: Ratified by the United States in 1998, the WIPO Copyright Treaty upgrades the Berne Convention by providing a general right of distribution for all works of authorship, and a specific right of communication to the public by online transmission. The WIPO treaty also requires that member nations provide protection against circumvention of effective technological measures used by copyright owners to protect their copyrighted works. In addition, members must prevent persons from tampering with rights management information, or knowingly trafficking in copies or phonorecords of works with altered or deleted rights management information.

CHAPTER 6

TRADEMARK LAW

I. THE NATURE OF TRADEMARK LAW

A. **The purpose of trademarks:** Trademark law ensures that consumers can rely on marks to identify the source of goods or services (and thus exercise their purchasing preferences) by prohibiting competitors from using marks in a way that confuses consumers about the source, sponsorship, or affiliation of goods or services. This makes a more efficient, competitive, and productive marketplace.

B. **The relationship of state and federal law:** Trademark law developed as one of a number of related doctrines comprising the *common law of unfair competition.* Congress enacted the Lanham Act in 1946, which draws on the common law trademark doctrine and builds on it. Lanham Act §43(a) provides federal relief for 1gement of unregistered indications of origin. The Lanham Act also provides ans of *registering marks*, through which traditional common-law rights can be iced.

   lministrative issues: The P.T.O. handles registration of marks on the Lanham t's Principal Register. In-house administrative appeals from examiners' istration decisions go to the Trademark Trial and Appeal Board. From there, atisfied parties can seek review on the record in the Court of Appeals for the eral Circuit, or seek *de novo* review in a U.S. District Court.

OF MARKS

   _. **Trademarks:** A trademark is a word, name, symbol or device, or any combination thereof, that is used to distinguish the goods of one person from goods manufactured or sold by others, and to indicate the source of the goods. 15 U.S.C. §1127.

B. **Service marks:** Service marks are the same as trademarks except that they identify and distinguish *services* rather than products. To register a service mark on the Lanham Act Principal Register, an applicant must provide a *service that is sufficiently distinguishable* from the sale of goods. This will not be the case if the service is normally expected and routinely rendered in furtherance of the sale of goods. 15 U.S.C. §1127.

C. **Certification marks:** Certification marks are words, names, symbols, or devices used by one person to certify that the goods or services of others have certain qualities or characteristics. Since consumers rely on certification marks for information about the products or services that bear them, the Lanham Act imposes restrictions on certification marks registered on the Principal Register. First, while the certification mark owner may use the mark to advertise or promote the certification program, or the goods or services of others that meet its certification standards, it *may not use the mark in connection with its own goods or services.* Second, the owner must *police use of the mark* and prohibit others from using it for purposes other than certifying and from falsely certifying the existence of characteristics that their products or services lack. Third, the owner may *not discriminatorily refuse to certify goods* or services that satisfy its stated, objective standards for certification. 15 U.S.C. §§1064, 1127.

D. Collective marks: Collective marks fall into two categories. First, *collective membership marks* indicate membership in an organization. Neither the organization nor its members use the mark to identify and distinguish goods or services. Second, *collective trademarks and service marks* are trademarks or service marks adopted by a collective organization, such as a co-op, for use by its members in selling their individual goods or services, and distinguishing their goods or services from those of non-members. 15 U.S.C. §1127.

III. DISTINCTIVENESS

A. Marks must be distinctive: Before a word, name, symbol, or device can be recognized and protected as a mark it must be *distinctive*—consumers must understand that it indicates source. Marks are often categorized according to their distinctiveness. Highest in the distinctiveness hierarchy are arbitrary, fanciful, and suggestive marks, which are deemed *inherently distinctive.* Inherently distinctive marks are the most highly protected and the easiest to acquire. Lower in the hierarchy are common, descriptive, and surname marks, which are not viewed as inherently distinctive, and can only be protected *upon acquiring distinctiveness* (or "secondary meaning") through use in the marketplace. These "secondary meaning" marks are not as highly protected, and claimants may have to use them for a significant period of time before acquiring ownership. At the bottom of the hierarchy are generic "marks," which are *incapable of becoming distinctive* and cannot be the subject of ownership rights. *Abercrombie & Fitch Co. v. Hunting World, Inc.,* 537 F.2d 4 (2d Cir. 1976).

1. Arbitrary or fanciful marks: Fanciful marks are marks that are coined or made up, and have no meaning other than their trademark meaning. Arbitrary marks are those that have a meaning, but in no way describe the particular product or service they identify.

2. Suggestive marks: Suggestive marks are marks that *indirectly describe* the product or service they identify. Two tests have been used to determine whether a particular mark is suggestive or merely descriptive. The first, called the *"degree of imagination" test,* holds that the more imagination the consumer must use to get a description of the product or service, the more likely the mark is suggestive. The second test looks to see if the mark is one that *competitors are likely to need* in order to describe their own products or services. If not really needed, the mark is more likely to be deemed suggestive.

3. Descriptive marks: The descriptive, or "secondary meaning," mark category includes: (1) marks that *appear to describe the product or service* they identify; (2) marks that appear to describe the *geographical location* from which the goods or services emanate; (3) marks that are primarily merely a *surname*; and (4) other marks that are *commonly used* in connection with the relevant type of goods or services. In determining whether marks fall into the "descriptive" category, one must consider what consumers encountering the mark are likely to think. If they are likely to think that the mark describes the product or its geographic origin, it is descriptive regardless of whether it does in fact provide accurate information. Highly laudatory and very common marks are often included in this "descriptive" category. These marks are not considered inherently distinctive, and cannot be the subject of ownership rights unless they have attained secondary meaning—that is, unless consumers have, through significant exposure to their use in the marketplace, come to understand them as indications of origin.

a. **Descriptive and deceptively misdescriptive marks:** A mark is considered to be descriptive or deceptively misdescriptive if: (1) it appears to provide information about the good or service it identifies; and (2) consumers are likely to believe that its description is correct. The mark is descriptive if it correctly describes the good or service, and deceptively misdescriptive if it does not. Either way, the mark can be protected under common law and registered on the Lanham Act Principal Register upon a showing that it has acquired secondary meaning. 15 U.S.C. §1052 (e)-(f).

b. **Geographically descriptive and deceptively misdescriptive marks:** A mark is considered to be *geographically descriptive* or *deceptively misdescriptive* if: (1) it conveys to a meaningful segment of the purchasing public primarily or immediately a geographical connotation; and (2) those persons are likely to think that the goods or services in fact come from that place (make a "goods-place association"). The second condition may turn on the nature of the claimant's goods or services, and whether the indicated place is known to produce those kinds of goods or services, or at least would be a likely point of origin. Geographically deceptively misdescriptive marks cannot be registered unless they attained secondary meaning prior to December 8, 1993. 15 U.S.C. §1052(e)-(f). The Federal Circuit has held that marks may not be deemed geographically deceptively misdescriptive unless the misdescribed geographical origin would be material to consumers' purchase decision. *In re California Innovations, Inc.*, 329 F.3d 1334 (Fed. Cir. 2003).

c. **Evaluating whether a mark falls into the descriptive/secondary meaning category:** Marks must always *be evaluated in light of the particular good or service that they identify.* In determining whether a mark is descriptive or inherently distinctive, it is essential to consider the overall commercial impression the mark would make on the average prospective customer. If the mark is a *composite mark*, one must consider the impression that the mark makes *as a whole* and not break it down into its constituent elements. *Misspelled* words must be treated as though they are properly spelled, as long as the phonetic identity between the misspelled word and the descriptive word is clear. *Foreign words* are generally translated into English and then evaluated to determine if they are descriptive of the product or service.

d. **Surname marks:** A mark is primarily merely a surname if its *overall impact* on the consuming public is a surname meaning and nothing more. If the mark has *no meaning* to the public, surname or otherwise, then it is not primarily merely a surname. If the mark has *both a surname meaning and some other reasonably well-known meaning in the language*, then it generally will not be deemed primarily merely a surname.

4. **Secondary meaning:** Secondary meaning is attained when, due to exposure to the mark in the marketplace, the relevant consuming public understands the mark not in its primary, common, descriptive, or surname sense, but in its trademark sense — as an indication of the source of the product or service. The Lanham Act provides that proof of substantially exclusive and continuous use of a descriptive/surname mark for five years in connection with the product or service may be deemed *prima facie* evidence that the mark has attained secondary meaning.

5. **Abstract designs and other nonverbal marks:** Many marks, such as abstract designs and packaging shapes, cannot readily be characterized as arbitrary, fanciful, suggestive, or descriptive. As a general rule, common, basic designs, such as circles, squares, or stripes, are viewed as *merely capable of becoming distinctive*, so that secondary meaning must be demonstrated. Design or symbol marks that are *striking or unusual* are more likely to be found inherently distinctive.

6. **Generic marks:** A generic "mark" is a word or symbol that the public associates with all products of a particular type or genus. Thus, a generic name or representation of a good or service cannot serve as a valid mark for that good or service. The standard for determining whether an alleged mark is or has become generic is whether its *primary significance to consumers* is an indication of the class or genus of product or service, or an indication of origin. *Murphy Door Bed Co., Inc. v. Interior Sleep Systems, Inc.*, 874 F.2d 95 (2d Cir. 1989).

   a. **Determining the relevant "genus":** When a producer introduces a product that differs from an established product class in a significant, functional characteristic, and uses the common descriptive name of that characteristic as the name of the product, the new product becomes its own genus, and the term denoting the genus becomes generic if there is no commonly used alternative that effectively communicates the same information. *A.J. Canfield Co. v. Honickman*, 808 F.2d 291 (3d Cir. 1986).

   b. **Descriptive marks as generic:** There is a difference of opinion among the circuit courts over whether a highly descriptive word like "tasty" or "best" should be treated as generic, and thus denied protection as a matter of law, even though it is not the common name for the type or genus of product or service.

IV. THE CONTENT OF MARKS

A. **As used, the mark must create a separate impression:** To qualify as a mark, a word, name, symbol, or device must be used in a way that creates a separate commercial impression on the viewer or listener, apart from the other material used with it, and its impact on the consumer must be primarily to identify or distinguish the goods or services, and not merely to serve as decoration or to serve some other function.

B. **Words, numbers, designs, etc. as marks:** Recognizable words and combinations of words (slogans), arbitrary combinations of letters, combinations of letters and numbers, and numbers alone may serve as marks. Drawings and other forms of art or design, scents, and sounds may serve as marks as well. A mark may be comprised of two or more of these various elements. Such composite marks must be evaluated as a whole for distinctiveness.

C. **Trade dress:** Trade dress may be protected and registered as a mark if it identifies and distinguishes the claimant's product or service. Under the modern view, color alone, such as the pink color of residential insulation, may be protected as a mark if secondary meaning is demonstrated. *Qualitex Co. v. Jacobson Products Co., Inc.,* 514 U.S. 159 (1995). Trade dress typically falls into one of two categories: product packaging and product feature. A third, hybrid form of trade dress consists of the overall image of a business. In order for *any* form of trade dress to be protected, it must be non-functional and distinctive.

1. **The distinctiveness requirement for trade dress:** In *Wal-Mart Stores, Inc. v. Samara Bros.*, 529 U.S. 205 (2000), the Supreme Court distinguished between product packaging and product feature trade dress, and held that *product feature trade dress can never be inherently distinctive.* The claimant of trade dress rights in product features must always demonstrate secondary meaning. *Product packaging trade dress can be inherently distinctive*, as long as the combination of elements as a whole is not descriptive of the product, commonplace for that type of product, or a trivial variation on a combination that is commonplace.

2. **The non-functionality requirement for trade dress:** Trade dress must be nonfunctional. In a §43(a) suit for infringement of trade dress, the plaintiff bears the burden of proving non-functionality. If product features are encompassed in the claims of a utility patent, this adds great weight to the statutory presumption that the product features are functional, and the trade dress claimant must carry the heavy burden of showing that the features are not functional, for instance, by showing that they are merely an ornamental, incidental, or arbitrary aspect of the product.

   a. **A two-part test for functionality:** In *TrafFix Devices, Inc. v. Marketing Displays, Inc.*, 532 U.S. 23 (2001), the U.S. Supreme Court set forth a two-part test for functionality in the case of product features (which presumably would also apply to other forms of trade dress). First, the court must apply the *Inwood Laboratories* test: Is the feature essential to the use or purpose of the article, or does it affect the cost or quality of the article? If the answer is yes, the product feature is functional and cannot be the subject of trade dress protection. If the answer is no, then the court must then apply the *Qualitex* standard: Would the exclusive use of the feature "put competitors at a significant, non-reputation-related disadvantage? If so, there is "aesthetic functionality," and the feature may not be protected. Only if the product feature is *nonfunctional under both tests* can it be protected as trade dress. The circuit courts of appeals have disagreed over whether it is appropriate to consider the availability of alternative product features in applying the *Inwood Laboratories* test. Compare *Eppendorf-Netheler-Hinz GMBH v. Ritter GMBH*, 289 F.3d 351 (5th Cir.), *cert. denied*, 537 U.S. 1071 (2002), with *Valu Engineering, Inc. v. Rexnord Corp.*, 278 F.3d 1268 (Fed. Cir. 2002).

V. OTHER LIMITATIONS ON THE REGISTRATION AND PROTECTION OF MARKS

A. **Scandalous or immoral marks:** Marks that are scandalous or immoral will not be enforced or registered. 15 U.S.C. §1052(a). Marks are scandalous or immoral if they give offense to the conscience or moral feelings or are shocking to the sense of decency or propriety. Generally, marks found scandalous or immoral involve vulgar language or imagery.

B. Matter that may disparage another: Under Lanham Act §2(a), a mark may not be registered or protected if it consists of matter that may *disparage persons*, living or dead, institutions, beliefs, or national symbols, or bring them into contempt or disrepute. In deciding whether a mark disparages a group of people, the issue of disparagement should be evaluated from the standpoint of a substantial component of the persons who allegedly are disparaged, not from the standpoint of the general public.

C. Matter that may falsely suggest a connection with persons, living or dead, institutions, beliefs, or national symbols: Lanham Act §2(a) provides that matter that falsely suggests a connection with persons, living or dead, institutions, beliefs, or national symbols may not be registered. In *ex parte* proceedings, the Trademark Trial and Appeal Board applies the following four-part test to determine whether an applicant's mark "falsely suggests a connection" with a person:

1. The mark is the same as, or a close approximation of, the name or identity previously used by the other person;

2. The mark would be recognized as such, in that it points uniquely and unmistakably to that person;

3. The person is not connected to the goods sold by the applicant; and

4. The fame or reputation of the person is such that consumers of applicant's goods will presume a connection between her and the applicant's goods.

It is not necessary to demonstrate that consumers will be misled to think that the identified person is the source of the marked goods, or sponsors or is otherwise affiliated with them. The key is that the mark evokes the person's identity in connection with the good or service.

D. Deceptive marks: Deceptive marks will not be enforced at common law or registered. A mark is deceptive if it: (1) falsely indicates that the product or service has a characteristic; (2) prospective purchasers are likely to believe that the misdescription correctly describes the product or service; and (3) the misrepresented characteristic would be a *material factor to a reasonable consumer* in deciding whether or not to purchase the product or service. *In re Budge Manufacturing Co., Inc.*, 857 F.2d 773 (Fed. Cir. 1988).

1. **Deceptive vs. "deceptively misdescriptive" marks:** Deceptive marks (that cannot be registered or protected under §2(a)) and deceptively misdescriptive marks (that can be registered or protected with a showing of secondary meaning under §2(e) and (f)) can be distinguished on the basis of materiality. If the misrepresented characteristic would be *material* to consumers in making their purchasing decision, the mark is deceptive. If it would not, then the mark is deceptively misdescriptive.

2. **"Deceptively misdescriptive" marks vs. "geographically deceptively misdescriptive" marks:** While Lanham Act §§2(e) and (f) permit deceptively

misdescriptive marks to be registered and protected with a showing of secondary meaning, they do not permit "primarily geographically deceptively misdescriptive" marks to be registered, unless they obtained secondary meaning prior to December 8, 1993. The Court of Appeals for the Federal Circuit has held that a geographic mark will not be *either* deceptive *or* primarily geographically deceptively misdescriptive, for purposes of Lanham Act §§2(a) or (e) and (f), *unless* the misdescribed geographical origin would be material to consumers in making their purchase decision. *In re California Innovations, Inc.*, 329 F.3d 1334 (Fed. Cir. 2003).

E. **Marks in prior use:** Lanham Act §2(d) prohibits registration of any mark that, when used in connection with the applicant's goods or services, is confusingly similar to a mark or trade name (business name) that *another person began using before the applicant and has not abandoned.* This rule reflects the common law doctrine that in cases of conflict, the first in time has priority over subsequent mark users (discussed below). However, the Lanham Act provides that an applicant's mark can be registered if the P.T.O. determines that *both* the earlier mark or trade name and the applicant's mark can be used *concurrently* without causing a likelihood of consumer confusion—for example, if each party restricts his use to a portion of the country that is remote from the other.

VI. ACQUIRING OWNERSHIP OF MARKS

A. **Use of the mark in trade:** To acquire ownership rights in a mark at common law one must be the *first* to *use it in trade* (and make continuous use in trade thereafter). To use the mark in trade is to use it in a way that allows consumers to rely on it for its ultimate purpose—to identify the user's goods or services and distinguish them from other producers' goods or services. *Blue Bell, Inc. v. Farah Manufacturing Co., Inc.*, 508 F.2d 1260 (5th Cir. 1975). The use must be "in the ordinary course of trade"—not merely a token use made for the purpose of reserving the mark. 15 U.S.C. §1127.

1. **Means of determining if use is sufficient:** Jurisdictions have varied in the *quantity of use* they will require of a mark claimant before recognizing ownership rights and priority over other claimants. Some courts have held that a mark claimant need only make a single use, as long as the use is systematic and ongoing thereafter. Others have held that the *unregistered* claimant's use must be sufficient to notify competitors of his claim. Still other jurisdictions have held that a mark claimant must achieve sufficient market penetration to pose a meaningful risk of consumer confusion if a competitor commences use of a similar mark. Some apply a four-factor test to evaluate whether the claimant's market penetration was sufficient to warrant recognition of rights: (1) the volume of sales of the trademarked product; (2) the growth trends (both positive and negative) in the area; (3) the number of persons actually purchasing the product in relation to the potential number of customers; and (4) the amount of product advertising in the area.

2. **Affixation:** In order to use a mark in trade and obtain ownership rights in it, one must also satisfy the *affixation requirement.* In the case of *goods*, the mark will be deemed "affixed" if it is: (1) placed on the goods themselves; (2) placed on their containers; or (3) placed on tags or labels attached to the goods or containers.

Under federal law, the affixation requirement may also be satisfied by prominently featuring the mark in a conspicuous display associated with the goods. If the nature of the goods makes all the above impracticable, use on documents associated with the goods or their sale may suffice. In the case of *services*, use or display of the mark in connection with the sale or advertising of the services is sufficient, as long as the mark is used in direct, explicit reference to the services rendered. 15 U.S.C. §1127.

B. **Use in the case of descriptive marks:** In order to obtain ownership rights in descriptive, geographically descriptive, surname, or other marks that are not inherently distinctive, one must demonstrate that he or she was the *first user to obtain secondary meaning in the mark.*

C. **Use in commerce:** To assert rights in a mark under the Lanham Act, a claimant must demonstrate that it has used the mark in interstate commerce, or in a manner that affects interstate commerce. 15 U.S.C. §1127.

　　1. **Services offered abroad:** The common-law doctrine of territoriality requires that one claiming U.S. rights in a service mark must render the services in the United States. However, the Fourth Circuit has held that a party may qualify for Lanham Act protection if it uses its service mark to advertise its services in the United States but only renders its services abroad, as long as it renders the services in *"foreign trade"* (that is, trade between subjects of the United States and subjects of a foreign nation). This will qualify as use in commerce for *service* marks. *International Bancorp, LLC v. Societe des Bains de Mer et du Cercle des Estrangers a Monaco*, 329 F.3d 359 (4th Cir. 2003), *cert. denied*, 540 U.S. 1106 (2004).

D. **Protection of foreign "well-known" marks:** The Paris Convention and TRIPs Agreement require the U.S. to protect marks owned by nationals of other member nations if the marks are "well-known" in the U.S. However, the circuit courts have split over whether the Lanham Act implements this requirement, thus enabling a foreign mark owner who does not use its well-known mark in the U.S. to bring Lanham Act infringement claims against domestic entities using confusingly similar marks.

VII. FEDERAL REGISTRATION OF MARKS

A. **The significance of registration on the Lanham Act Principal Register:** Ownership of marks is automatic under the common law as soon as the mark is first used in trade (or, in the case of marks that are not inherently distinctive, as soon as the claimant obtains secondary meaning). No registration or other administrative process is necessary to acquire ownership rights. However, federal law provides that mark owners may register their marks on the Lanham Act Principal Register. Registration provides additional rights beyond those that would be available under the common law.

B. **Advantages of registration on the Principal Register:** Only persons who have obtained ownership rights in marks by using them in trade and commerce may obtain federal registration. Registration on the Principal Register provides: (1) a right to assistance from U.S. Customs in preventing infringing goods from entering the country; (2) presumptions of mark ownership and validity and, after five years of registration, preclusion of certain challenges or defenses to the mark; (3) rights in the mark in a greater geographical area than often would be possible under the common law; and (4) immunity to dilution claims brought pursuant to state law.

C. **Registration:** There are two alternative routes a person may follow in applying to register. 15 U.S.C. §1051. First, a person who has already satisfied the use in trade and use in commerce requirements may file application papers with the Patent and Trademark Office. The P.T.O. will examine the application and publish it for opposition. If there is no successful opposition, the P.T.O. will then register the mark and issue a certificate of registration. Second, a person may file application papers with the P.T.O. alleging a *bona fide* intention to use the mark in trade and interstate commerce. The P.T.O. will make an initial examination of the application and publish it for opposition. If there is no successful opposition, the applicant will have up to three years to make the necessary use in trade and commerce and file a statement of use with the P.T.O. After the statement of use is filed, the mark can be registered and a certificate of registration can be issued. Under both routes to registration, the certificate of registration provides *prima facie* evidence of the validity of the registered mark, the registration of the mark, and the registrant's ownership of the mark and exclusive right to use it in connection with the goods or services specified in the certificate. 15 U.S.C. §1115.

   1. **Constructive use:** Once the registration process is completed, Lanham Act §7(c) (15 U.S.C. §1057(c)) provides the registrant with "constructive use" throughout the country, commencing from his application filing date. This permits the registrant to assert priority (rights as the first user) over persons who make their first use of the mark after the registrant's application filing date.

D. **The Supplemental Register:** Marks that are *capable of* distinguishing an applicant's goods or services but are not registerable on the Principal Register due to lack of distinctiveness may be registered on the Supplemental Register. The primary benefit of registration on the Supplemental Register is that it may assist the registrant in obtaining registration of the mark abroad.

VIII. CANCELLATION OF REGISTRATION

A. **During the first five years of registration:** During the first five years of a mark's registration, a person who believes himself injured by the registration may file a *petition to cancel* the registration on any ground that would have precluded registration in the first place.

B. **After five years of registration:** If the mark has been registered for over five years, the Lanham Act *narrows the available grounds for cancellation*. The three important grounds for cancellation that are precluded after five years of registration are: (1) that the mark is not inherently distinctive and lacks secondary meaning; (2) that the mark is confusingly similar to a mark that someone else used prior to the registrant and continues to use; and (3) that the mark is dilutive of a senior user's mark. 15 U.S.C. §1064.

IX. GEOGRAPHIC BOUNDARIES

A. **Geographic rights at common law:** Under the common law, the first person to use a mark (or in the case of a mark that is not inherently distinctive, the first to obtain secondary meaning in the mark) is the owner of it. However, if a second person later uses (or acquires secondary meaning in) a confusingly similar mark in good faith in a remote geographic area, the second person will have superior rights in the mark *in that remote area*, by virtue of the *remote, good faith user defense. United Drug Co. v. Rectanus Co.*, 248 U.S. 90 (1918).

   1. **Remote geographical area:** For purposes of determining whether the second party's use is "remote" from the first person's, the first person's geographic area is deemed to include not just the area in which it sells goods or services through use of the mark, but also those areas in which its mark has a presence by virtue of advertising or general reputation.

   2. **Good faith:** Under the majority rule, a remote user acts in "good faith" if it has no notice that another person has made an earlier, similar use that is ongoing in the United States.

   3. **The zone of natural expansion:** Under the common law zone of natural expansion doctrine, a senior user of a mark may assert seniority not just in his market, as defined above, but also in his "zone of natural expansion." He may prohibit a later user from using a confusingly similar mark in that zone even though the later user was the first actually to use the mark or have a presence there. The senior user's zone of natural expansion is that geographic area into which, at the time the other user entered, the senior user logically and foreseeably would eventually expand, given the nature of the senior user's business and the history of its prior expansion. This doctrine is rarely applied today.

B. **The Lanham Act:** Federal registration of a mark on the Lanham Act Principal Register expands the registrant's geographic rights in a mark beyond those she would enjoy at common law by giving *constructive notice* of her use of the mark, and/or *constructive use*.

   1. **Constructive notice:** Lanham Act §22 (15 U.S.C. §1072) provides that registration of a mark creates constructive notice of the registrant's use. Anyone who begins using a confusingly similar mark after the registration date is thus charged with notice of the registrant's prior use and *cannot claim to have begun his own use in good faith*. This deprives the subsequent user of the remote, good-faith use defense, and prevents him from obtaining superior rights in his remote geographic area. The practical result is that registration gives the registrant superior rights not only in her actual market area (as defined above) but also in all other areas of the country where the mark was not in use at the time of her registration.

   2. **Constructive use:** In the case of marks registered on applications filed on or after November 16, 1989, Lanham Act §7(c) (15 U.S.C. §1057(c)) provides that registration gives rise to constructive use by the registrant, throughout the country, as of its application date. This "constructive use" means that the registrant will be treated as though he used the mark in connection with the registered goods

or services *in every part of the country on his application* date. This gives him priority over every person who commences use anywhere in the country after the application date (except, of course, for persons who *applied* to register even earlier, and thus have an even earlier constructive use date).

C. A likelihood of consumer confusion: Under the majority rule, even if a mark owner has superior rights in a mark in a particular geographic area by virtue of federal registration, he will not be entitled to *enjoin another's use* in that area unless the defendant's use is likely to cause consumer confusion about the source, affiliation, or sponsorship of the parties' goods or services. This will only be likely if the registrant is also using the mark in the same area or has concrete plans to begin using it there in the near future. *Dawn Donut Co., Inc. v. Hart's Food Stores, Inc.*, 267 F.2d 358 (2d Cir. 1959). A minority of courts have rejected this legal presumption of no likelihood of confusion in the absence of use in the same geographical area (sometimes called the "*Dawn Donut* rule") as outdated. They have ruled that the geographic proximity of the parties should be just one factor in their multifactor test for likelihood of confusion.

X. INFRINGEMENT OF MARKS

A. The injury to be protected against: Trademark protection addresses two major concerns. First, it promotes the public's interest in being able accurately to ascertain the source of goods and services in the marketplace. Second, it protects a trademark owner's business good will against the lost sales and damage to reputation that may occur if others are permitted to use its mark in a manner that is likely to confuse consumers about the source of the parties' goods or services.

B. The infringement determination: To demonstrate infringement, the plaintiff mark owner must demonstrate that the defendant (1) used a mark "in commerce," in connection with the sale or advertising of goods or services, in a manner that (2) caused a likelihood that an appreciable number of consumers would be confused about the source, sponsorship, or affiliation of the parties' goods or services.

1. **Actionable use:** Under the language of Lanham Act §§32(1)(a) and 43(a) (15 U.S.C. §§1114(1)(a), 1125(a)), the defendant must make a "use in commerce" of the allegedly infringing mark, that is in connection with the sale or advertising of goods or services. This generally means that the defendant must closely associate the mark with goods or services that it is advertising or offering for sale (make a "trademark use"), so that consumers are likely to rely on the use for information about the source of the defendant's goods or services. Generally speaking, courts have held that trademark law is not meant to prevent all forms of free riding on a mark owner's business good will. Thus, a finding of free riding, or of predatory intent, in itself, will not be sufficient to impose infringement liability.

   a. **Actionable use in the Internet context:** In the Internet context courts have reached a host of conflicting decisions concerning what constitutes an actionable use of a trademark. For example, in cybersquatting cases, some courts have found that registering a domain name that incorporates a person's mark, with the intent to sell the registration to the mark owner, gave rise to infringement liability (even though the defendant did not use the mark to identify the source of any goods or services it was advertising or offering for sale). Likewise, in metatagging and contextual advertising cases, some courts have held that hidden uses of marks in metatags or to trigger contextual advertising was actionable, even though the defendants did not use the marks to identify the source of any goods or services they were offering for sale, or even expose consumers to the marks. Finally, in cases in which the defendant adopted a domain name that was confusingly similar to the plaintiff's mark, some courts have found the requisite "use in commerce" "in connection with the sale or advertising of goods or services" even though the defendant did not sell or advertise any goods or services on his web site. These courts found that the Lanham Act's "use" requirement was satisfied because: (1) the non-commercial site operator *linked* to other sites that sold goods or services; (2) the non-commercial site operator engaged in acts that *affected the plaintiff's sale of goods or services*; or (3) the non-commercial site operator (whose site criticized the mark owner or its product, or disagreed with its political, social, or religious stands) provided an "*information service*" within the meaning of the Lanham Act, which the domain name identified. However, a number of other courts have rejected arguments that these kinds of actions constitute the requisite Lanham Act "use."

b. Extraterritorial use: Generally, U.S. trademark law extends rights only to prevent infringing acts that take place in the United States. However, in some cases infringing uses made abroad may be actionable in the U.S. Relevant considerations include: (1) whether the defendant is a U.S. citizen; (2) whether the defendant's actions had a substantial effect on U.S. commerce; and (3) whether relief would create a conflict with foreign law.

2. The likelihood of confusion requirement: In addition to demonstrating an actionable "use" of the mark, infringement plaintiffs must prove that the use caused a likelihood of consumer confusion about the source, sponsorship, or affiliation of the goods. Courts have set forth a number of factors to consider in determining whether a defendant's mark is likely to confuse consumers. They include: (1) the similarity of the marks (in sight, sound, and/or meaning); (2) the similarity of the parties' products or services; (3) the similarity of marketing channels; (4) the similarity of purchasers; (5) the sophistication of prospective purchasers and the cost of the goods or services; (6) evidence of actual confusion; (7) the manner of presenting the mark; (8) the strength of the plaintiff's mark; (9) the defendant's intent; and (10) the plaintiff's interest in entering the defendant's market with the mark. In determining the likelihood of confusion, the court will not assume that consumers would have the opportunity to make a side-by-side comparison of the marks. A defendant's disclaimers of affiliation with the plaintiff are unlikely to avoid a finding of likely confusion unless the court is convinced that the disclaimers will be effective.

a. Post-sale confusion: The traditional focus of trademark law has been the likelihood of purchaser confusion *at the point of sale*. Some courts, however, have held that a likelihood of post-sale confusion may suffice to impose infringement liability.

    b. Initial interest (pre-sale) confusion: Some courts have based a finding of infringement on evidence of initial consumer confusion that is dissipated prior to the actual purchase. This doctrine has been particularly controversial in the Internet context.

    c. Reverse confusion: Most trademark infringement cases involve a *subsequent* user of a mark who causes purchasers to think that his goods or services come from the *prior* user. However, infringement can also be found when the subsequent user causes purchasers to think that the prior user's goods or services come from it (the subsequent user). This latter situation is called "reverse confusion."

C. Trademark parodies: In many cases the trademark infringement cause of action will not provide relief against a trademark parody because a successful parody depends on consumers realizing that the marks are not the same. If the parody is successful, consumers will not be confused. Moreover, the First Amendment protects parodies that *do not constitute commercial speech*. In such cases (as in all cases involving non-commercial speech) the court must balance the trademark interests against the First Amendment interests at stake. *Rogers v. Grimaldi*, 875 F.2d 994 (2d Cir. 1989).

D. Collateral use of marks: Trademark law does not give mark owners absolute rights in their marks. Generally, unauthorized uses of a mark that *do not create a likelihood of confusion* will not infringe.

    1. Resale of goods lawfully bearing a mark: The trademark doctrine of exhaustion (also known as the doctrine of first sale) provides that once a mark owner sells or authorizes goods to be sold bearing its mark, it cannot prevent subsequent owners from *reselling the goods with the mark*, even if the goods have been used or changed. However, subsequent owners' use of the mark must be truthful, and not misleading, and must not lead to a likelihood of confusion about the immediate source or nature of the goods. *Champion Spark Plug Co. v. Sanders*, 331 U.S. 125 (1947).

    2. Gray market goods: Gray market goods are goods that are manufactured abroad for sale in foreign markets, that the foreign manufacturer properly, legally marks with a trademark that is registered in the United States. After these goods are released in foreign markets, parties buy them and import them into the United States for resale in competition with the U.S. owner of the same mark. As a general matter, the import and sale of gray market goods will not constitute infringement of the U.S. registrant's mark if the imported goods are *the same* as those sold by the U.S. registrant (do not materially differ) and the *U.S. registrant and the foreign manufacturer are the same or related entities. Weil Ceramics and Glass, Inc. v. Dash*, 878 F.2d 659 (3d Cir.), *cert. denied*, 493 U.S. 853 (1989). However, if the gray goods are materially different from the goods sold domestically by the U.S. mark registrant, they will infringe, even if the U.S. mark registrant is related to the foreign manufacturer. (The reason for this is that consumers who rely on the mark to indicate that the goods are consistent with those they purchased in the past will be misled.) *Lever Bros. Co. v. United States*, 877 F.2d 101 (D.C. Cir.

1989). If the U.S. registrant and the foreign manufacturer are not related entities the gray goods will infringe, even if identical. *A. Bourjois & Co., Inc. v. Katzel,* 260 U.S. 689 (1923).

3. **Competitors' use of marks for comparison purposes:** A mark owner's competitors may use its mark in selling their own goods and services—for example, in comparative advertising or to inform consumers that their goods are compatible with the mark owners' goods—as long as their use is truthful and does not create a likelihood of consumer confusion about the source, sponsorship, or affiliation of their goods or services. *Smith v. Chanel, Inc.,* 402 F.2d 562 (9th Cir. 1968).

E. **Trademark counterfeiting:** Trademark counterfeiting entails *intentional, knowing use of a spurious mark that is identical to* (or substantially indistinguishable from) a registered mark, on the *same kind of goods or services* for which the mark is registered. 15 U.S.C. §1127. United States trademark law provides special civil remedies against counterfeiting, and criminal sanctions against persons who intentionally traffic or attempt to traffic in goods through use of marks they know to be counterfeit.

F. **Contributory infringement:** A defendant will be held liable for contributory infringement if: (1) he intentionally suggests, directly or by implication, that another person infringe the plaintiff's trademark, and the other does so infringe; or (2) he sells goods to another knowing or having reason to know that the buyer will use the goods in a direct infringement of the plaintiff's trademark. *Inwood Laboratories, Inc. v. Ives Laboratories, Inc.,* 456 U.S. 844 (1982). The Seventh Circuit has held that parties can be liable for contributory infringement if they assist the direct infringer, knowing or having reason to know that she or he is infringing. However, the defendant has no duty to seek out infringement by others, or to take precautions against it. *Hard Rock Café Licensing Corp. v. Concession Services, Inc.,* 955 F.2d 1143 (7th Cir. 1992).

G. **Vicarious liability:** A person may be vicariously liable for another person's infringement if he is the infringer's employer, if he and the infringer have an apparent or actual partnership, have authority to bind one another in transactions with third parties, or exercise joint ownership or control over the infringing product.

XI. TRADEMARK DILUTION

A. **The nature of the dilution cause of action:** Dilution statutes provide rights in highly distinctive, famous marks that are much broader than the rights available to mark owners under the trademark infringement cause of action. Liability for dilution may arise even though the defendant's use of its mark causes no likelihood of confusion, and even though the parties do not compete. (Often, the parties use their marks in connection with very different products or services.) About half the states have dilution statutes. These state jurisdictions have differed over whether the plaintiff's mark must be nationally famous or whether locally famous marks are protected from dilution. They have also differed over whether marks must be famous with the general public or whether "niche" fame is sufficient. The state dilution statutes create two causes of action for dilution: blurring dilution and tarnishment dilution.

1. **Blurring dilution:** Blurring dilution occurs when the defendant's use of a similar mark whittles away or "dilutes" the strong, immediate association consumers have between the famous mark and the plaintiff.

2. **Tarnishment dilution:** Tarnishment dilution occurs when the defendant's use of a similar mark casts the plaintiff's famous mark or trade name in a bad light and thus "tarnishes" the luster of the plaintiff's commercial image or reputation.

3. **First Amendment limitations:** The First Amendment may limit application of the state dilution cause of action when the defendant has used its mark outside of the context of commercial speech (speech that does no more than propose a commercial transaction).

B. **The Lanham Act §43(c) cause of action for dilution:** Congress enacted a federal dilution cause of action in 1995, and extensively revised it in 2006. As revised, Lanham Act §43(c) (15 U.S.C. §1125(c)) enables the owner of a *famous* mark that is *distinctive* (either inherently or through acquisition of secondary meaning) to enjoin a defendant's *use in commerce* of a similar mark or trade name that is *likely to cause dilution by blurring or tarnishment*, if the defendant first used its diluting mark in commerce *after* the plaintiff's mark became famous. Relief is available regardless of the presence or absence of actual or likely confusion, competition between the parties, or any actual economic injury. However, relief is limited to an injunction unless the plaintiff can demonstrate that the defendant used its diluting mark in commerce after the Trademark Dilution Revision Act of 2006 was enacted, and that the defendant's acts were willful.

1. **Fame:** The revised federal dilution cause of action is available only for *famous* marks that are widely recognized by the general U.S. consuming public as a designation of source of their owner's goods or services. In deciding whether a mark enjoys the requisite fame, courts must consider all relevant factors, including: (1) the duration, extent, and geographic reach of advertising and publicity of the mark; (2) the amount, volume, and geographic extent of sales of goods or services offered under the mark; (3) the extent of actual recognition of the mark; and (4) whether the mark is registered. 15 U.S.C. §1125(c).

2. **Dilution by blurring:** Under revised Lanham Act §43(c), dilution by blurring is "the association arising from the similarity between a mark or trade name and a famous mark that impairs the distinctiveness of the famous mark." In deciding whether a defendant's mark blurs a plaintiff's, courts should consider all relevant factors, including: (1) the degree of similarity between the mark or trade name and the famous mark; (2) the degree of inherent or acquired distinctiveness of the famous mark; (3) the extent to which the owner of the famous mark is engaging in substantially exclusive use of the mark; (4) the degree of recognition of the famous mark; (5) whether the user of the mark or trade name intended to create an association with the famous mark; and (6) any actual association between the mark or trade name and the famous mark.

3. **Dilution by tarnishment:** The revised §43(c) provides that dilution by tarnishment is "association arising from the similarity between a mark or trade name and a famous mark that harms the reputation of the famous mark."

4. **Exclusions:** As revised, §43(c) provides several *express exclusions* from the dilution cause of action. First, it excludes "any fair use" of a famous mark "other than as a designation of source for [the user's] own goods or services," including nominative fair use, descriptive fair use, use of a mark in comparative advertising, and use of a mark in identifying, parodying, criticizing or commenting about the mark owner or its goods or services. Second, §43(c) excludes uses of marks in news reporting and commentary. Finally, §43(c) excludes "any noncommercial use" of a famous mark. Courts have construed this last provision to confine the federal dilution cause of action to uses of marks in *commercial speech*, as that concept has been defined in the Supreme Court's First Amendment jurisprudence. The Supreme Court has defined core "commercial speech" as "speech that does no more than propose a commercial transaction." *Bolger v. Youngs Drug Products Corp.*, 463 U.S. 60, 66 (1983).

5. **Registration preempts state dilution claims:** Federal registration is a complete bar to dilution claims brought pursuant to state law.

6. **Dilution claims and trade dress:** The federal dilution causes of action apply to all forms of marks, including trade dress. The Lanham Act specifies that when unregistered trade dress is claimed to be diluted, the plaintiff bears the burden of proving that the trade dress is nonfunctional. If the trade dress incorporates marks that are registered, the claimant must prove that the unregistered portion of the trade dress, taken as a whole, is famous separate and apart from any fame of the registered marks. 15 U.S.C. §1125(c).

XII. DEFENSES TO INFRINGEMENT AND DILUTION CLAIMS

A. **The fair use defense:** Use of a mark that has the capacity to describe a defendant's product, or its geographic origin, or that constitutes the defendant's name, in its strictly descriptive capacity, is protected by the fair use defense. In determining whether a defendant's use is a protected fair use, a court will consider the manner in which the defendant used the mark, whether the defendant acted in good faith, and the extent to which the defendant's use is likely to confuse consumers. If it appears that the defendant used the descriptive, geographically descriptive, or surname word or symbol in good faith strictly for the purpose of describing his own product, the court will allow the use even if it causes some likelihood of consumer confusion. 15 U.S.C. §1115(b)(4).

B. **Nominative fair use:** The Court of Appeals for the Ninth Circuit has developed a doctrine of "nominative fair use" that is to be applied when a defendant has used the plaintiff's mark to describe or refer to the plaintiff's product. The doctrine applies in both infringement and dilution cases, and substitutes a three-factor test in place of the usual multifactor likelihood of confusion analysis or dilution analysis. The defendant's use will be excused under this doctrine if: (1) the plaintiff's product is not readily identifiable without use of the mark; (2) the defendant has only used so much of the mark as is reasonably necessary to identify the plaintiff's product; and (3) the defendant has done nothing that would, in conjunction with use of the mark, suggest sponsorship or endorsement of its product by the plaintiff. *New Kids on the Block v. News America Publishing, Inc.*, 971 F.2d 302 (9th Cir. 1992).

1. **The Third Circuit's version of nominative fair use:** Under the Third Circuit's version of nominative fair use, an infringement plaintiff must first prove that the defendant's use causes a likelihood of confusion under a "modified version" of the traditional multi-factor test that ignores the strength of the plaintiff's mark and the similarity of the marks, and emphasizes the degree of consumer care, length of time the defendant has used the mark without evidence of actual confusion, defendant's intent in adopting the mark, and evidence of actual confusion. If the plaintiff is able to prove a likelihood of confusion, the burden then shifts to the defendant to demonstrate fairness under a three-pronged test: (1) Is the use of the plaintiff's mark necessary to describe both the plaintiff's product or service and the defendant's product or service? (2) Does the defendant use only so much of the plaintiff's mark as is necessary? And (3) does the defendant's conduct or language reflect the true and accurate relationship between plaintiff and defendant's products or services? *Century 21 Real Estate Corp. v. LendingTree*, Inc., 425 F.3d 211 (3d Cir. 2005).

C. **Abandonment:** Under the Lanham Act, a plaintiff may be found to have *abandoned* its mark in two ways. First, when the registrant has discontinued use of the mark throughout the country in connection with the particular good or service, and has no intent to resume use in the reasonably foreseeable future, it will be deemed to have abandoned it. As amended, the Lanham Act provides that *nonuse for three consecutive years* is *prima facie* evidence of no intent to resume use. Second, a plaintiff may abandon its mark through acts or omissions that cause the mark to lose its significance as a mark. Such acts and omissions include: assigning the mark "in gross" (apart from the business good will that the mark symbolizes); and licensing others to use the mark without adequately supervising their use to ensure consistency. 15 U.S.C. §1127.

D. **Challenges to the validity of the mark and to the plaintiff's ownership rights:** If the plaintiff has registered the mark on the Lanham Act Principal Register, the registration will serve as *prima facie* evidence of the validity of the mark and the registrant's claim to it. This shifts the burden to the defendant to disprove these matters as a defense to the infringement claim. 15 U.S.C. §1115(a). At least until a registered mark attains incontestability status, the defendant may challenge the plaintiff's mark for failing to comply with *any requirement of common law or the Lanham Act*. If the defendant successfully challenges the validity of the plaintiff's mark, it cannot be liable for infringing it.

E. **Federal registration incontestability status:** A person whose mark has been registered for five years and is in continuous use may obtain "incontestability" status by filing an affidavit to that effect, along with other information. Incontestability status eliminates two important grounds for challenging or defending against the mark: (1) that the mark is not inherently distinctive and lacks secondary meaning; and (2) that the challenger/ defendant used the mark before the registrant (but this challenge/defense can still be asserted in connection with the geographical area the challenger/defender occupied prior to the registrant's registration and has continuously occupied since). 15 U.S.C. §1065.

XIII. TRADEMARK CYBERSQUATTING

A. **The Anticybersquatting Consumer Protection Act:** The Anticybersquatting Act amended Lanham Act §43 by adding a new subsection (d), that prohibits the registration, trafficking in, or use of a domain name that is identical or confusingly similar to, or dilutive of, another person's mark. There are two important limitations to the cause of action. First, the mark must have been distinctive (i.e., enjoyed trademark status) at the time the domain name was registered (or, if the claim is that the domain name dilutes, the mark must have been famous at the time the domain name was registered). Second, the plaintiff must demonstrate that the defendant acted with *a bad-faith intent to profit from the business good will of the mark*. 15 U.S.C. §1125(d). Courts have explained that Congress's purpose in enacting the Anticybersquatting Act was to prohibit registration of mark-encompassing domain names for the purpose of commercial exploitation.

1. **Factors to consider in determining whether the defendant registered the domain name with a bad-faith intent to profit:** Subsection (d) provides courts with a non-exclusive list of nine factors to consider in deciding whether a defendant acted with the requisite bad faith intent to profit from the business good will of the mark. These include:

    1. whether the domain name registrant has trademark or other intellectual property rights in the name;

    2. whether the domain name is the same as the registrant's own legal name or established nickname;

    3. the domain name registrant's prior use of the name, if any, in connection with the bona fide offering of goods or services;

    4. the domain name registrant's bona fide noncommercial or fair use of the mark in a web site that is accessible under the domain name;

    5. whether, in registering or using the domain name, the registrant intended to divert consumers away from the trademark owner's web site to a web site that could harm the good will of the mark by creating a likelihood of confusion as to the source, sponsorship, affiliation, or endorsement of the site (regardless of whether the defendant acted for purposes of commercial gain or in order to tarnish or disparage the mark);

    6. whether the domain name registrant, while failing to use the name itself in the bona fide offering of goods or services, offered to sell the domain name to the mark owner or to a third party for financial gain;

    7. whether the domain name registrant intentionally provided material and misleading false contact information in her application for the domain name registration application, or failed to maintain accurate contact information, and has engaged in a pattern of such conduct;

    8. whether the domain name registrant acquired multiple domain names that he or she knows to be identical, confusingly similar, or dilutive of, others' marks; and

    9. the extent to which the mark at issue is distinctive and/or famous within the meaning of Lanham Act §43(c).

The first four factors, if found, suggest a lack of bad-faith intent to profit. The second four factors, if found, suggest the presence of bad-faith intent to profit. The final factor might go either way.

2. **In rem jurisdiction:** The Anticybersquatting Act provides *in rem* jurisdiction, permitting the mark owner to file an action against the domain name itself. To qualify, the mark owner must demonstrate that he exercised diligence in trying to locate or obtain personal jurisdiction over the domain name registrant, and was unsuccessful. The relief available in *in rem* actions is limited to an injunction ordering the forfeiture, cancellation, or transfer of the domain name registration. The Court of Appeals for the Fourth Circuit has held that this *in rem* jurisdiction is applicable in the case of §43(a) and §43(c) claims against domain names, as well as §43(d) claims. *Harrods Ltd. v. Sixty Internet Domain Names*, 302 F.3d 214 (4th Cir. 2002). However, courts have held that *in rem* claims must be filed in the judicial district where the domain name registrar, registry, or other authority is located.

3. **Remedies and limitation of liability:** Courts in anticybersquatting cases may order the forfeiture, cancellation, or transfer of a domain name to the owner of the mark. In addition to regular trademark infringement remedies, the Anticybersquatting Act also provides for statutory damages, ranging from $1,000 to $100,000 per domain name. The Act limits domain name registrars' liability if they suspend, cancel, or transfer domain names pursuant to a court order or in the implementation of a reasonable policy prohibiting cybersquatting.

B. **The Uniform Dispute Resolution Policy as an administrative alternative to a cybersquatting suit:** The Internet Corporation for Assigned Names and Numbers' (ICANN's) Uniform Dispute Resolution Policy (UDRP) provides for quicker, less expensive "administrative" relief from cybersquatting. Under the policy, the aggrieved trademark owner must convince a panel of experts that: (1) the registered domain name is identical or confusingly similar to a trademark or service mark in which the complainant has rights; (2) the registrant has no rights or legitimate interests in the domain name; and (3) the domain name has been registered and is being used in bad faith. Factors for determining bad faith are somewhat similar to the factors to determine bad-faith intent to profit under the Anticybersquatter Act. If a dispute resolution panel finds the requisite bad faith, it can order cancellation of the domain name registration or transfer of the registration to the complainant. Either party to a UDRP proceeding can submit the dispute to a court for independent resolution. A disappointed trademark owner can bring suit against the alleged cybersquatter under Lanham Act §§32 or 43(a), (c) or (d). 15 U.S.C. §§1114, 1125(a), (c), (d). A disappointed domain name registrant can bring suit under Lanham Act §§32(2)(D)(v). That section permits the domain name registrant to establish that its registration and use of the domain name are *lawful*—that they do not violate *any* of the mark owner's Lanham Act rights. If the domain name registrant succeeds in making this showing, the court may grant injunctive relief to reactivate the domain name or transfer its registration back to the plaintiff.

XIV. REMEDIES FOR LANHAM ACT VIOLATIONS

A. **Injunctions:** To get a permanent injunction, the plaintiff must demonstrate that: (1) it has suffered an irreparable injury; (2) the remedies available at law, such as monetary damages, are inadequate to compensate for that injury; (3) considering the balance of hardships between the plaintiff and defendant, a remedy in equity is warranted; and (4) the public interest would not be disserved by a permanent injunction. Preliminary injunctions may be available, as well. Plaintiffs in §43(c) dilution cases may *only* receive injunctive relief unless they are able to demonstrate (1) that the defendant first used its mark after the effective date of the Trademark Dilution Revision Act of 2006; and (2) that the defendant's acts were willful.

B. Monetary recovery: The Lanham Act authorizes two measures of monetary recovery. First, the plaintiff may recover *actual damages* for injury to business reputation and lost sales. The Lanham Act authorizes courts to increase the actual damages the plaintiff is able to prove up to three times, if necessary, in order adequately to compensate the plaintiff. Second, the plaintiff may recover the amount of the *defendant's profits*, if the defendant has been unjustly enriched, the plaintiff has sustained damages from the infringement, or an accounting is necessary to deter a willful infringer from infringing again. 15 U.S.C. §1117. Courts sometimes permit plaintiffs to recover *both* the actual damages they can prove and the defendant's profits, as long as they do not thereby recover twice for the same sales to consumers. To recover the defendant's profits, the plaintiff must prove only the amount of the defendant's gross sales in connection with the infringing mark. The burden then shifts to the defendant to prove whatever amounts he contends should be deducted in determining the final award. Plaintiffs alleging violation of the Lanham Act's §43(d) anticybersquatting provisions may elect to recover an award of statutory damages in lieu of actual damages and profits. 15 U.S.C. §1117(d).

C. Attorney fees: In *exceptional cases* the Lanham Act authorizes a court to award reasonable attorney fees. This usually is not provided under common law.

D. Special remedies for use of counterfeit marks: Federal law provides special, enhanced civil remedies and criminal penalties for certain use of counterfeit marks. 15 U.S.C. §§ 1116, 1117(c).

XV. INTERNATIONAL TRADEMARK TREATIES

A. The Paris Convention: The Paris Convention undertakes to ensure that each of its member countries grants protection to the nationals of other member countries against unfair competition in commercial and industrial matters, including mark infringement. It bases its protection on the concept of *national treatment*. Each member nation must provide as strong protection to nationals of other member nations as it would to its own.

1. Registration of marks: The Paris Convention provides that a national of a member nation may register his trademark in any other member nation through *two alternative routes*: (1) by satisfying all the nation's registration requirements on the same basis as domestic applicants; or (2) by registering its mark in its home country and relying on that registration in its application to register abroad ("*telle quelle*" registration). In the case of *telle quelle* registration, registration in the foreign applicant's home country entitles the applicant to registration in the other member country, even if the applicant's mark otherwise would not qualify. However, a country may refuse *telle quelle* registration to a mark that is confusingly similar to a mark already owned by another in that nation, to a mark that has no distinctive character, or to a mark that is deceptive or contrary to morality or public order.

2. Effect of the telle quelle provision in the United States: The Paris Convention's *telle quelle* provision dictates that the United States treat foreign applications more favorably than it treats domestic applications, because most countries register marks without a showing of use, and marks registered in those countries must be registered in the United States. However, any advantage that foreign registrants might obtain in registering unused marks on the Principle Register is minimized by: (1) the availability of the U.S. intent-to-use registration process, (2) the difficulty of demonstrating a likelihood of confusion in the absence of use, and (3) Lanham Act provisions providing for cancellation of the registration of abandoned marks.

3. **Filing priority:** The Paris Convention provides that once a mark owner applies to register her mark in member nation A, she obtains filing priority (the benefit of her application date in nation A) in other member nations if she files to register there during the next six months. This means that in the United States, foreign applicants may obtain the benefit of constructive use dating back to their foreign application dates (as long as they applied in the United States within six months of filing in another Paris Convention member nation).

B. **The Trademark Law Treaty:** The Trademark Law Treaty simplifies international filings by harmonizing the member countries' trademark registration standards and procedures.

C. **The Madrid Protocol:** The Madrid Protocol provides an international system for centrally filing trademark applications in its over 80 member nations. A person owning a trademark registration or application in his home country can file one Madrid application that designates any number of other member countries in which the owner wishes to register. The applicant's home Trademark Office forwards the Madrid application to the International Bureau of the World Intellectual Property Organization, which processes it, provides an international registration, publishes the mark, and forwards the application to each of the countries the applicant has designated for territorial extension of the international registration. Each designated country then has 18 months to evaluate the application based on its domestic laws and either extend the international registration or refuse extension. Registrations under the Madrid Protocol have the same scope as the registrant's domestic registration, and are dependent on the validity of the domestic registration for the first five years.

D. **The Agreement on Trade-Related Aspects of Intellectual Property Rights:** The WTO TRIPs Agreement builds upon the Paris Convention and augments international trademark protection by defining the subject matter of trademark protection, and imposing procedural and substantive standards for protection.

CHAPTER 7

UNFAIR COMPETITION

I. THE NATURE OF THE LAW OF UNFAIR COMPETITION

A. **An umbrella term:** The law of unfair competition provides redress for various forms of improper marketplace behavior by businesses. While the law of unfair competition originated in common law, Congress has provided a federal cause of action in Lanham

Act §43(a) that tracks the common law unfair competition doctrines of passing off, false advertising, and commercial disparagement. 15 U.S.C. §1125(a).

II. PASSING OFF

A. **The nature of the "passing off" cause of action:** Passing off occurs when the defendant directly or indirectly makes a false representation that is likely to mislead consumers about the source, sponsorship or affiliation of goods, services, or businesses. Indirect misrepresentation includes use of a mark, trade dress, or trade name (business name) that is confusingly similar to the plaintiff's. Under modern law, neither a showing of intent to confuse consumers nor actual consumer confusion is necessary to recover, at least in the case of passing off claims involving use of confusingly similar marks, trade dress, or trade names. The law of trademarks, covered in Chapter 6, is derived directly from the common law of passing off. Rules regarding distinctiveness, functionality, ownership, priority, common-law geographic rights, and infringement, discussed in that previous chapter, apply equally to claims of unregistered mark infringement, trade name infringement, and trade dress infringement, regardless of whether the claim is brought pursuant to Lanham Act §43(a) or state law.

B. **Lanham Act §43(a):** Lanham Act §43(a) prohibits use of "false designations of origin" in connection with goods or services that are "likely to cause confusion, to cause mistake, or to deceive as to the affiliation, connection, or association of [the maker] with another person, or as to the origin, sponsorship, or approval of his or her goods, services, or commercial activities." 15 U.S.C. §1125(a). This provides a federal cause of action for passing off claims involving infringement of unregistered marks, trade dress, and trade names. Because Congress relied on its Commerce Clause powers to enact §43(a), plaintiffs must establish federal jurisdiction by showing that the prohibited activities they complain of took place in or affected commerce. Plaintiffs in §43(a) cases enjoy the same generous remedies that are available for infringement of registered marks. Moreover, the courts, in construing §43(a), look to Lanham Act registration provisions for guidance in determining eligibility for protection, *Two Pesos, Inc. v. Taco Cabana, Inc.*, 505 U.S. 763 (1992), and to case law defining the likelihood of confusion determination in registered mark infringement cases.

C. **Trade names:** In modern usage, a trade name is the name of a company, partnership, or other business and its good will. Even though the Lanham Act differentiates trade names from marks, permitting registration only of the latter, both the common law of passing off and Lanham Act §43(a) protect trade names on the same general basis that they protect unregistered marks.

D. **Use of the passing off claim to fill the gaps left by other intellectual property doctrines:** Because the passing off cause of action (particularly under Lanham Act §43(a)) is very flexible, it is often used to protect interests that fall within the general subject matter of copyright, the right of publicity, and other areas of intellectual property. However, the Supreme Court's opinion in *Dastar Corp. v. Twentieth Century Fox Film Corp.*, 539 U.S. 23 (2003), has set some limits on this practice, prohibiting construction of the Lanham Act in ways that undermine restrictions that Congress has placed on copyright and patent protection.

III. FALSE ADVERTISING

A. **The common law false advertising cause of action:** The common law false advertising cause of action is available to redress a defendant's misrepresentations about the nature or characteristics of *its own goods or services*. In addition to proving a misrepresentation, a false advertising plaintiff must demonstrate that the defendant's misrepresentation was *likely to deceive or mislead prospective purchasers*. Statements that are not literally false, but are misleading or constitute "half-truths," may suffice to support liability. However, the misrepresentation must concern a factor that is *material*, or likely to influence consumers' purchasing decisions. Though it is not necessary under modern law to prove that the defendant *intended* to deceive consumers, evidence of an intent to deceive may be relevant to support a finding that he succeeded in doing so. Traditionally, courts required plaintiffs to demonstrate that they lost customers as a result of the misrepresentation (which often is difficult or impossible to do), but the modern trend is away from strict application of this requirement.

B. **State statutes:** Many states have enacted statutes prohibiting false advertising, and many of them provide a civil cause of action for false advertising to both competitors and consumers.

C. **Lanham Act §43(a):** Lanham Act §43(a), 15 U.S.C. §1125(a), prohibits use of a "false or misleading description of fact, or false or misleading representation of fact" in commercial advertising or promotion that "misrepresents the nature, characteristics, qualities, or geographic origin of . . . goods, services, or commercial activities." The elements of the §43(a) false advertising cause of action for an injunction are:

1. a defendant's false or misleading statement of fact in advertising about its own product;

2. the statement actually deceived or had the capacity to deceive a substantial segment of the audience;

3. the deception was material, in that it was likely to influence the purchasing decision;

4. the defendant caused its goods to enter interstate commerce; and

5. the plaintiff has been or is likely to be injured as a result.

Because the Lanham Act §43(a) false advertising cause of action is limited to "commercial advertising or promotion," it is limited to false representations in commercial speech (speech that does no more than propose a commercial transaction). Courts have also found that "commercial advertising or promotion" entails speech that is intended to influence consumer purchase decisions and that is widely disseminated.

1. **The injury requirement:** To enjoin false advertising, the §43(a) plaintiff need only demonstrate that she is *likely to be damaged* as a result of the defendant's false representations. She can do this by demonstrating (1) that the plaintiff and defendant compete, directly or indirectly, in the same market; and (2) that there is a logical causal connection between the alleged false advertising and the plaintiff's

sales position. *Johnson & Johnson v. Carter-Wallace, Inc.*, 631 F.2d 186 (2d Cir. 1980). Injury will be presumed for purposes of injunctive relief when a defendant falsely compares its product with the plaintiff's product by name.

   a. **Injury for purposes of monetary relief:** To obtain money damages for false advertising, the §43(a) plaintiff must demonstrate *actual consumer reliance* on the false advertisement and a resulting *measurable economic impact* on the plaintiff's business. However, the impact may take a form other than lost customers.

2. **Other requirements:** The defendant's representation must be *material*, but it need not be false in the literal sense. Representations that are literally true but misleading, due to innuendo, omission, or ambiguity, may be deemed "*implicitly false*" and give rise to liability. In the case of implicitly false representations, the plaintiff must prove that consumers in fact understood the advertisement to convey the alleged false message. The §43(a) plaintiff need not demonstrate that the plaintiff's misrepresentation was intentional. However, proof of deceptive intent may shift the burden to the defendant to prove an absence of consumer deception.

IV. COMMERCIAL DISPARAGEMENT

   A. **The common law commercial disparagement cause of action:** The disparagement cause of action imposes liability for a defendant's false or deceptive representation about the quality or characteristics of *a plaintiff's goods or services*. While the elements differ somewhat, depending on the jurisdiction, three common elements are:

   1. a false or misleading representation about the plaintiff's goods or services;

   2. an intent to harm on the defendant's part; and

   3. specific economic loss, or "special damages" to the plaintiff.

   The defendant's statement may be any manner of communication, as long as it directly or indirectly communicates a false and disparaging message to consumers, and does not constitute mere puffing. While some jurisdictions will base liability on a false statement of *opinion*, most require a false statement of fact. A false statement of fact purports to give specific facts, or at least implies that the maker has specific facts to back up his assertion. While jurisdictions differ, the Restatement (Second), of Torts suggests that the defendant must have had knowledge that his statement was false or have acted in reckless disregard of its truth or falsity.

   1. **The special damages requirement:** To obtain damages relief under the common law, the plaintiff must demonstrate actual monetary loss resulting from the defendant's disparaging statement, and this requirement generally has been interpreted to mean that the plaintiff must demonstrate an *actual, specific loss of customers*. Jurisdictions differ over whether special damages must be demonstrated in the case of suits seeking only injunctive relief.

   B. **State statutory provisions:** The Uniform Deceptive Trade Practices Act provides injunctive relief against false or misleading statements of fact that disparage the goods, services, or business of another, if the plaintiff demonstrates that it is " likely to be damaged" by the statements. The Act specifies that proof of monetary damage and intent to deceive will not be required.

C. **The Lanham Act §43(a) disparagement cause of action:** Lanham Act §43(a) extends to disparaging misrepresentations about a plaintiff's goods or services. While this cause of action is similar to the common-law disparagement claim, it is more liberal. The elements include:

1. a defendant's false or misleading statement of fact in commercial advertising or promotion about the plaintiff's product, services, or commercial activities;

2. the statement actually deceived or had the capacity to deceive a substantial segment of the audience;

3. the deception was material to the purchasing decision;

4. the defendant caused its goods or services to enter interstate commerce; and

5. the plaintiff has been or is likely to be injured as a result.

Intent or knowledge on the defendant's part is not required. The plaintiff need not plead or prove special damages, at least in order to obtain an injunction.

D. **First Amendment considerations in disparagement actions:** Under the rule in *New York Times v. Sullivan*, 376 U.S. 254 (1964), developed in libel cases, *plaintiffs who are public figures* must show with convincing clarity that the defendant's libelous statement was made with *actual malice* — with knowledge that the statement was false or with reckless disregard of whether it was false or not — before they will be permitted to recover. The Court of Appeals for the Third Circuit has held that the *New York Times* rule will not apply in a commercial disparagement suit when the alleged disparaging statements constitute *commercial speech*. (The court defined commercial speech as "expression related to the economic interests of the speaker and its audience, generally in the form of a commercial advertisement for the sale of goods and services." See *U.S. Healthcare, Inc. v. Blue Cross of Greater Philadelphia*, 898 F.2d 914 (3d Cir.), *cert. denied*, 498 U.S. 816 (1990).) The Lanham Act §43(a) causes of action for false advertising and disparagement are expressly limited to statements made in commercial speech, Therefore, under the Third Circuit's rule, the *New York Times* rule will not apply in federal disparagement causes of action. The Third Circuit also suggested that a corporation engaged in commercial speech might not constitute a public figure, for purposes of the *New York Times* rule.

V. MISAPPROPRIATION

A. **The nature of the misappropriation cause of action:** To state a cause of action for misappropriation, the plaintiff must demonstrate three things: (1) the plaintiff has made a substantial investment of time, money, skill, or effort to create an intangible trade value in which the court can justify finding a property right; (2) the defendant has appropriated the intangible trade value in a manner that constitutes "reaping where he has not sown" or "taking a free ride"; and (3) the plaintiff has suffered competitive injury as a result. In a few cases, courts have dispensed with the requirement that the plaintiff demonstrate competitive injury (or any injury at all) upon determining that the public interest would be promoted by granting relief.

B. Limitations on the misappropriation cause of action: Because of the potential breadth of the misappropriation claim, courts are cautious in applying it, and generally will seek to avoid applying it in a way that will undermine the limitations imposed on other, more narrow, causes of action. The Court of Appeals for the Second Circuit has relied on federal preemption grounds to severely limit the misappropriation cause of action. *National Basketball Assn. v. Motorola, Inc.*, 105 F.3d 841 (2d Cir. 1997). For more information regarding preemption, see Chapter 9.

VI. INTERNATIONAL TREATIES REGARDING PROTECTION AGAINST UNFAIR COMPETITION

A. The Paris Convention: The Paris Convention for the Protection of Industrial Property requires member nations to provide protection against passing off, false advertising, and commercial disparagement types of activities. While it does not require members to maintain a system of registration for trade names, they must provide basic protection against infringement of trade names. By virtue of the Paris Convention's national treatment provision, member nations must provide essentially as great unfair competition protection for the nationals of other member countries as for their own nationals.

B. The TRIPs Agreement: The TRIPs Agreement incorporates the Paris Convention provisions on unfair competition, making them binding on all World Trade Organization members.

CHAPTER 8

THE RIGHT OF PUBLICITY

I. THE NATURE AND PURPOSE OF THE RIGHT OF PUBLICITY

A. The nature of the right of publicity: The right of publicity cause of action recognizes that an individual has a right to control others' use of his identity for commercial purposes. While some states continue to view the right of publicity cause of action as one branch of the right of privacy, the publicity and privacy causes of action generally vindicate separate interests. While privacy vindicates the personal interest in avoiding unwanted intrusions, the right of publicity primarily vindicates an economic interest in the ability to commercially exploit one's identity. Some states have found a right of publicity in the common law, but others have enacted statutes that undertake to create and regulate the right.

II. THE SCOPE OF THE RIGHT OF PUBLICITY

A. **Commercial invocation of the plaintiff's identity:** In order to recover for a violation of the right of publicity, the plaintiff must clearly demonstrate that the defendant has *invoked the plaintiff's identity* in the public mind. A defendant's use of the plaintiff's nickname, a cartoon image of the plaintiff, a phrase associated with the plaintiff, an impersonator, or other devices may suffice to identify the plaintiff to the public and give rise to a cause of action. *White v. Samsung Electronics America, Inc.*, 971 F.2d 1395 (9th Cir. 1992), *cert. denied*, 508 U.S. 951 (1993). A use of the plaintiff's identity may be deemed commercial for purposes of a right of publicity cause of action even if it would not qualify as "commercial speech," as that concept has been developed under the First Amendment.

B. **First Amendment concerns:** Unauthorized use of the plaintiff's identity in contexts such as news reporting and entertainment may be deemed "commercial," but frequently will be fully protected speech under the First Amendment. The Supreme Court has held that in cases where "fully-protected" speech is involved, the individual's personal interest and the state's interest in providing the publicity cause of action must be balanced against First Amendment interests to determine whether the use exceeds the bounds of First Amendment privilege. *Zacchini v. Scripps-Howard Broadcasting Co.*, 433 U.S. 562 (1977)

   1. **Differing standards for evaluating the balance:** When a defendant makes an unauthorized use of a plaintiff's identity for commercial purposes, but the use does not constitute commercial speech (as that concept is understood under First Amendment law), the court is likely to consider the extent to which the defendant's use of the plaintiff's identity is *transformative*—whether the work contains significant creative, expressive elements beyond the mere celebrity likeness or imitation. The more transformative the work, the more likely the First Amendment interests in a free marketplace of ideas and individual self-expression outweigh the plaintiff's and states' interest in protecting the plaintiff's economic publicity interest. Some courts evaluate the balance between privacy and First Amendment interests by considering whether the defendant used the plaintiff's identity in a work *related to* the plaintiff, or by considering whether the defendant's *predominate purpose* was commercial or expressive.

C. **Descendability of the right of publicity:** Jurisdictions differ about whether and how long a person's right of publicity endures after his death.

D. **Applicability of the doctrine of first sale:** The doctrine of first sale is applicable in connection with the right of publicity.

E. **Remedies for violation of the right:** Defendants may be enjoined from violating a plaintiff's right of publicity. Monetary damages generally consist of the fair market value of the defendant's use of the plaintiff's identity. Injury to the plaintiff's reputation that may lead to loss of future publicity revenues may be compensated. Some jurisdictions have permitted the plaintiff to recover the defendant's profit attributable to unauthorized use of the plaintiff's identity, as long as it does not lead to double recovery. Punitive damages may be granted in extreme cases.

Chapter 9

THE RELATIONSHIP BETWEEN FEDERAL AND STATE LAW

I. THE SUPREMACY CLAUSE

A. **Federal law prevails over conflicting state law:** The U.S. Constitution's Supremacy Clause provides that state causes of action are preempted if they stand as an obstacle to the accomplishment and execution of Congress's purposes and objectives in enacting a federal statue.

B. **The Sears and Compco cases:** In *Sears, Roebuck & Co. v. Stiffel Co.*, 376 U.S. 225 (1964), and *Compco Corp. v. Day-Brite Lighting, Inc.*, 376 U.S. 234 (1964), the Supreme Court held that state unfair competition causes of action that would prohibit the defendants from copying the unpatentable appearance of articles of commerce were preempted. The Court reasoned that, in enacting the patent laws, Congress attempted to balance two competing interests: (1) providing an incentive to invent by giving property rights in inventions and designs; and (2) fostering free competition by allowing freedom to copy others' inventive ideas and designs and build on them. Congress determined that the proper balance was to give limited monopoly rights in inventions and designs meeting the high standards of patentability and to relegate those inventions and designs not qualifying for a patent to the public domain, free for others to copy. The state unfair competition causes of action, by prohibiting the copying of the latter types of inventions and designs, interfered with Congress's purpose, and thus was preempted.

C. **The Goldstein case:** In *Goldstein v. California*, 412 U.S. 546 (1973), the Supreme Court found that in omitting sound recordings from copyright protection (as the Copyright Act did at that time), Congress did not specifically intend to leave them in the public domain. Thus, the states were free to protect sound recordings from copying. The Court stressed that the state law at issue only prohibited lifting recorded sounds: It placed no restraint on the use of ideas or concepts found in the sound recording.

D. **The Kewanee and Aronson cases:** In *Kewanee Oil Co. v. Bicron Corp.*, 416 U.S. 470 (1974), the Supreme Court applied a threefold purpose test in the place of the balancing language of the earlier *Sears* and *Compco* decisions. The Court described the purposes of Congress in enacting the patent laws as: (1) to provide an incentive to invent; (2) to promote public disclosure of inventions, so as to inform the public; and (3) to ensure that information already in the public domain would remain there. The Court found that a state trade secret cause of action did not interfere unduly with accomplishment of these purposes and that whatever interference there might be was counterbalanced by the states' interest in exercising their traditional police powers to prohibit commercially unethical behavior and invasions of privacy through trade secret doctrine. The Court later applied the same threefold purpose test in upholding the application of state contract law to enforce a contract to pay for an unpatentable idea in *Aronson v. Quick Point Pencil Co.*, 440 U.S. 257 (1979). In *Aronson*, the Court stressed that the state contract cause of action gave no monopoly rights in the idea.

E. **The Bonito Boats case:** In *Bonito Boats, Inc. v. Thunder Craft Boats, Inc.*, 489 U.S. 141 (1989), the Supreme Court found that the Patent Act preempted a state statute that prohibited the use of a direct "plug molding" process to duplicate unpatented boat hulls. The Court returned to its original "balancing" concept in *Sears* and *Compco*, but also purported to reaffirm its threefold purpose test, as well. The Court stressed that the plug molding statute removed ideas from the public domain and gave patent-like protection to the design ideas of boats. Moreover, the state was not pursuing any traditional police power goal apart from encouraging invention, which is a key purpose of the patent law.

F. **Where do we stand now?** One way the cases discussed above can be reconciled is as follows: In enacting the patent laws, Congress intended that ideas not meeting the high standards for patentability would remain in the public domain, free for the public to use. However, a state law that prohibits or restricts copying may be tolerated if: (1) the protection is limited in scope, so that the level of interference with Congress's purpose can be characterized as slight; (2) ideas that are already in the public domain are not withdrawn; and (3) the state law is intended to promote a legitimate state police power goal outside the sphere of Congress's concern when it enacted the patent laws.

II. COPYRIGHT ACT §301

A. **A uniform system of copyright:** In enacting the Copyright Act of 1976, Congress *intended to unify* copyright protection in fixed works of authorship and *federalize it*. Thus, it enacted §301, which expressly preempts state causes of action that duplicate federal copyright protection in fixed works. 17 U.S.C. §301. To be preempted under §301, a state cause of action must protect matter that is *"within the subject matter of copyright"* as set forth in §§102 and 103 of the Copyright Act. In addition, the state cause of action must *provide rights that are "equivalent" to the economic rights specified in §106* of the Copyright Act. More recently, in the Visual Artists' Rights Act of 1990, Congress amended §301 to add that state causes of action giving rights equivalent to the moral rights of attribution and integrity in works of visual art, as defined in Copyright Act §101, would also be preempted.

B. **Subject matter of copyright:** Questions have arisen whether ideas, procedures, processes, systems, methods of operation, concepts, principles, and discoveries (facts) that are described in or incorporated into works of authorship are within the "subject matter of copyright" as set forth in §102, so that state causes of action protecting them may be preempted. There is case precedent and legislative history to support arguments on both sides of the issue, but the majority of judicial opinions have held that the ideas, procedures, processes, etc., in works of authorship *are within the subject matter of copyright* for purposes of §301.

C. **Equivalent rights:** To be preempted, the state cause of action must provide rights that are equivalent to the exclusive rights of copyright (e.g., the rights to reproduce, adapt, publicly distribute, publicly perform, or publicly display a work of authorship) or are equivalent to the moral rights of attribution and integrity in works of visual art. The meaning of "equivalent" has been the subject of some disagreement in the courts, but *most courts have adopted what may be called an "extra elements" test* *for equivalency.* Under this test the court looks to see if the mere act of reproduction, adaptation, public distribution, public performance, public display, misattribution, or violation of integrity will in itself give rise to the state cause of action, or whether some additional element, that is not required for copyright infringement, must also be alleged. If no other element must be alleged, then the state cause of action is "equivalent" to copyright. If other elements are required, many courts will look to *see if the additional element causes the state cause of action to be "qualitatively different" from copyright.* If not, preemption may still be found. The tests for qualitative difference include: (1) determining whether the element indicates a state purpose that differs from the purpose of copyright; (2) determining whether the extra element goes to the *nature*, or merely to the *scope* of the state-created right; and (3) determining whether the "essence" of the state claim is one for copyright infringement or violation of an author's rights of attribution or integrity in a work of visual art.

D. Express exceptions to §301 preemption: Copyright Act §301 expressly provides that states may protect unfixed works, and it preserves local landmark, historic preservation, zoning, and building laws and codes relating to architectural works. In addition, §301 permits states to continue protecting (until Feb. 15, 2067) sound recordings fixed prior to Feb. 15, 1972.

EXAM TIPS

EXAM TIPS

SUMMARY OF CONTENTS

Exam Tips on
INTELLECTUAL PROPERTY GENERALLY

Public Policy

☛ Legislative bodies and courts frequently consider the public policies underlying the provision of intellectual property rights in drafting and construing the laws in this field. Especially when you encounter an exam question on an issue for which the law is unsettled, it is useful to consider whether a particular construction of the law would further or hinder accomplishment of the underlying public policies and discuss this consideration in your exam answer.

Multiple Forms of Protection

☛ Sometimes more than one area of intellectual property law may be relevant to resolve the problems raised in an exam question. For example, trade secret law, copyright law, and patent law all prohibit unauthorized copying of computer software under some circumstances. Thus, it might be appropriate to discuss all three legal doctrines in answering a question concerning software.

☞ However, it is important to read the call of the exam question carefully and to evaluate the facts to ensure that discussion of all of these doctrines is warranted. For example, patent law provides protection only when the creator of the software applied for a patent within a particular time frame and ultimately was granted a patent. If the facts make no mention of an application or a patent, then discussing patent law may exceed the scope of the question. Likewise, if the question asks only for an evaluation of copyright infringement, discussion of patents is not relevant. Because many professors do not read discussions that go beyond the scope of the question, and you are likely to have time and/or page limitations in answering the exam questions, discussion of patent law may be counterproductive.

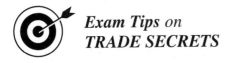

Exam Tips on
TRADE SECRETS

Trade Secret Status

☛ Trade secret exam questions often require that you evaluate whether information qualifies as a trade secret. To provide a thorough evaluation, state the Uniform Trade Secrets Act definition, and then think about the following six factors:

(1) how widely the information is known outside the claimant's business;

(2) how widely the information is known within the claimant's company;

(3) whether the claimant has taken reasonable measures to ensure that the information remains secret;

(4) how difficult it would be for others *properly* to acquire or duplicate the information;

(5) whether the information gives the claimant a commercial, competitive advantage over others who do not know it; and

(6) how much effort or money the claimant expended in developing or acquiring the information..

One way to organize your discussion effectively is to recognize that the six factors essentially ask two basic questions:

(1) Is the information secret? (factors 1, 2, 3, and 4); and

(2) Does the information have competitive value? (factors 5 and 6).

Be sure to consider each question.

Ownership Issues

☛ If the exam question involves an employer-employee situation, there may be an ownership issue. If the employee created the trade secret, apply the standards discussed *in Chapter 2 of the Capsule Summary, supra* pp. 66, to evaluate whether the employer owns the trade secret and thus has rights to assert against the employee. Also remember that even if the employer is not the owner of the employee-made trade secret and thus has no right to prevent the employee's use or disclosure, it may have a shop right, which permits it to continue to use the trade secret itself without liability to the employee.

Public Policy

☛ Trade secret law serves two basic purposes. First, it provides an incentive to businesses to develop and use innovative business know-how, which ultimately benefits the public. Second, it promotes the state's traditional police power interest in preventing dishonesty and immorality in commercial conduct. At the same time, strong enforcement of trade secret interests may be detrimental because it can interfere with marketplace competition and the ability of employees to move from one job to another and build their careers in their chosen fields. Courts are influenced by these potentially conflicting interests in deciding whether the facts in a given case give rise to liability for trade secret misappropriation.

☞ In resolving a close case, it may be useful to evaluate how the interests enumerated above would be promoted or hindered by the recognition of trade secret rights. For example, if the alleged trade secret is not highly innovative, then there is not as great an interest in providing trade secret rights as an incentive to create. Likewise, if the defendant's acts were not strongly objectionable from a moral standpoint, the police power interest in assuring a moral marketplace will not be undermined if the court declines to find a cause of action. On the other hand, if the information is highly innovative, or the defendant's actions involve "dirty tricks" or a blatant betrayal of the plaintiff's trust, the court is more likely to find enforceable trade secret rights. Finally, if recognition and enforcement of trade secret rights would interfere with the free movement of an employee, a court is less likely to find a cause of action.

Exam Tips *on* PATENTS

Understanding Novelty

☞ Because the Leahy-Smith America Invents Act (which transforms the U.S. Patent system from a "first to invent" to a "first to file" system) applies only prospectively to applications and patents granted on applications filed on or after March 16, 2013, it is important to pay attention to the date set forth in a problem with novelty or non-obviousness implications. If the facts give you an application or patent with an effective filing date *prior to the March 16, 2013 date*, you should apply the traditional rules of the "first to file" system.

    ☞ Under that system, the novelty provisions (Patent Act §§102(a), (e), and (g)) exist primarily to channel patents to first inventors, and to prevent latecomers from removing inventions from the public domain. Remember that to demonstrate that an invention lacks novelty (that the invention is "anticipated"), you must be able to identify an earlier invention or disclosure (an earlier "reference") that, prior to the applicant's *invention* date (1) *included all of the same elements arranged in the same way*; and (2) falls within the conditions of §§102(a), (e), or (g). An earlier invention or disclosure that lacked a claimed element or combined the claimed elements in a different way may be relevant to demonstrate that the invention at issue is obvious, but is not relevant to demonstrate that it lacks novelty. The standard for finding that an invention lacks novelty parallels the standard for literal infringement. It has been said that "that which infringes if later, anticipates if earlier." In other words, if A's invention would literally infringe a patent on B's invention (because it literally falls within the language of B's claims), then it would anticipate B's invention (render it non-novel) if it were shown to have preceded it.

    ☞ If the facts of a problem give you an effective filing date that is *on or after March 16, 2013*, apply the new, amended §102 (a) and (b) provisions to identify prior art and determine novelty. In determining novelty, focus on prior art in existence *before the application date*. Disqualifying disclosures may include disclosures made by the applicant itself. Bear in mind, however, that under the exceptions in §102(b), prior art disclosures made by the applicant's inventor herself (or those deriving the information from the inventor) are omitted from the prior art if made within a year prior to the filing date. Likewise, disclosures made by independent parties are omitted from the prior art if they occurred *after* a disclosure by the applicant's inventor or those deriving from her. Disclosures in pending patent applications (subsequently published and/or granted) and resulting patents *filed before your applicant's filing date* are applicable prior art for judging your applicant's invention novelty, *unless* (1) they were filed by someone who derived the disclosed information from your applicant's inventor; (2) were filed after your applicant's inventor (or someone deriving from her) disclosed; or (3) were filed by someone subject to the same joint research agreement as your applicant.

Understanding Non-obviousness

☞ The non-obviousness requirement exists primarily to restrict patents to true "inventions"—those inventions that are worth the "public embarrassment of granting a monopoly." The inventiveness, or obviousness, of an invention is determined from the perspective of a person of ordinary skill in the art, *in light of* earlier inventions and publications. It is important to remember that in evaluating the obviousness of an invention, you can consider two or more prior inventions or publications ("references") together. However, you must demonstrate that each prior invention or publication is: (1) "pertinent" to the invention at issue; and (2) falls within the scope of Patent Act §§102(a), (e), (f), or (g) (if the applicant/patentee's effective filing date was *before* March 16, 2013), or Patent Act §102(a) and (b) (if the applicant/patentee's effective filing date was *on or after* March 16, 2013). If the applicant/patentee's effective filing date was *before* March 16, 2013, evaluate obviousness as of the applicant's *invention* date. If the applicant/patentee's effective filing date was *on or after* March 16, 2013, evaluate the obviousness of the applicant's invention as of its *filing* date.

Distinguish Pre–Leahy-Smith §102(a) and (b) When Dealing with Applications/Patents Filed Prior to March 16, 2013

☞ Students often are confused by the superficial similarities in the statutory language of pre–Leahy-Smith Patent Act §§102(a) and (b). It is important to remember that these two provisions serve very different purposes and have a different focus. Subsection (a) is meant to ensure that the patent applicant's invention is novel, as discussed above. It focuses on events that occurred prior to the applicant's invention date. Subsection (b), in contrast, is meant to ensure that inventors file their patent applications in a timely manner—within a year after the invention enters into the public domain by one of the four described means (the invention is on sale or the subject of public use in the United States or the invention is the subject of a patent or a printed publication anywhere in the world). The focus thus is on events that occurred more than a year before the applicant's application date. The applicant's own actions may be relevant for purposes of §102(b), but will not be relevant for purposes of §102(a).

Distinguish Pre–Leahy-Smith §103 Obviousness and §102(b) Obviousness When Dealing with Applications/Patents Filed Prior to March 16, 2013

☞ Under pre–Leahy-Smith §103, one evaluates whether the applicant's invention is worthy of a patent. It is not worthy if it was obvious at the time it was invented. Under pre–Leahy-Smith §102(b), one evaluates whether the applicant (whose invention may have been worthy of a patent at the time it was made) has *forfeited* his or her right to a patent by failing to file the application within the specified time frame. Essentially, the courts have recognized that, even though A's invention was not obvious at the time it was made (and thus was worthy of a patent under §103), it may later become obvious, due to the subsequent public use or sale of a different invention in the United States, or a subsequent patent or printed publication. At that point, §102(b) requires that A file for a patent within one year. If A fails to do this, he loses his right to a patent.

Timelines Can Be Useful

☞ Dates can be important in analyzing the validity of a patent, and it is important to keep them straight. It is often useful to sketch a rough timeline to help you evaluate the facts in an exam question and determine their impact on the validity of a patent. For example, here is a sample timeline that you might draw to assist in determining the answer to Short-Answer, Question 13.

Keep the Various Forms of Infringement Straight

☞ Patent Act §271, which defines the various forms of infringement, is a patchwork: In addition to several broad definitions of infringement (for example, §§271(a), (b), and (c)), it contains several relatively narrow provisions in which Congress prohibited specific practices that were not covered by the existing infringement provisions (for example, §§271(f) and (g)). When facing an exam question that asks whether a party has infringed a patent, it is important to systematically *consider all* of the various §271 provisions. If the professor allows you to review statutory language, turn to §271 and quickly review each provision to ensure that you remember the scope and limitations of each provision and consider whether it provides a means of holding the party liable under the facts of the question.

Fitting Designs and Plants into the Novelty and Non-obviousness Scheme

☞ Congress enacted the utility patent provisions first, and the courts developed the novelty and non-obviousness standards in connection with industry, science, and engineering-related inventions. When Congress later provided for design and plant patents, it stated that the existing standards of novelty and non-obviousness should be extended to this new subject matter. However, the fit is sometimes awkward. If you are faced with an exam question that requires you to evaluate the novelty or non-obviousness requirements in connection with an ornamental design or plant, it may be useful to think about the underlying purposes of the novelty and non-obvious requirements in determining how they should apply.

Exam Tips on
RIGHTS IN UNDEVELOPED IDEAS

Look Out for Preemption

☞ The causes of action discussed in this chapter are state causes of action and cover subject matter that may also be subject to federal intellectual property rights. Thus, there may be a significant question of federal preemption. Preemption is covered in Chapter 9 of the Capsule Summary. Whenever you encounter an exam question that asks about a cause of action under undeveloped idea law, consider whether the question also gives rise to arguments that the cause of action is preempted by federal law, and if so, discuss those arguments in your analysis.

Overlap with Trade Secret Law

☞ Many deserving idea law cases could be resolved under a trade secret claim, especially since few jurisdictions now employ the Restatement of Torts §757, comment *b* requirement that the alleged trade secret be "continuously used" in the plaintiff's business. Under the more modern approach, which is reflected in the Uniform Trade Secrets Act, "one-shot" information may qualify for trade secret protection as long as the plaintiff can demonstrate that it is substantially secret and that he derives a competitive benefit from the fact that others do not know it. Accordingly, when you encounter an exam question involving a plaintiff's attempt to recover against another's unauthorized use of his ideas, consider the relevance of both an undeveloped idea and a trade secret claim.

Exam Tips on
COPYRIGHT LAW

Remember the Policies and Ultimate Purpose Underlying Copyright

☞ Copyright law can be vague and conceptually challenging, particularly when it is necessary to distinguish idea from expression, apply the originality standard, apply the "conceptual separability" test, or evaluate the fair use defense. It is often helpful, in the course of discussing such issues in an exam, to step back and consider how real courts might address them. Courts (who experience the same uncertainty and frustration with the law that you do) routinely consider the *underlying purposes of copyright* and try to determine *what interpretation of the precedent will best effectuate those purposes*, given the facts at hand. While the interest in protecting authors' "natural rights" in their creations sometimes surfaces in the judicial discussions, as a general matter, courts concern themselves with enriching the general public by adopting policies that will encourage the creation of as many diverse works of authorship as possible, while retaining as much public access to existing works as feasible. This entails a balancing act: The key is to find a resolution to the case that (if applied on a widespread basis) will not undercut authors' incentive to create, but will not give authors greater control over others' use of their works than is necessary to provide that incentive. It is also essential that the basic building blocks of expression — such as ideas, systems, methods of operation, facts, "functional" product features, and common stock devices — remain in the public domain to ensure a continued flow of expressive works in the future for the public benefit. In explaining why you would resolve an exam question in a certain way, it may be helpful to explain how your resolution would promote these goals.

The Idea/Expression Dichotomy

☛ As the likes of Judge Learned Hand have acknowledged, there is no way to devise a concrete or universal black-letter rule for distinguishing idea from expression for purposes of copyright protection. Discussing and applying Judge Hand's "abstractions" test can be a useful vehicle in addressing the question in exams, but the abstractions test gives you only a framework for making what ultimately will be an arbitrary decision based on a gut instinct: You will have to decide, as a matter of policy, where it makes the most sense to draw the line between idea and expression under the particular facts of the case, and in light of the policies underlying copyright and the distinction between copyright and patent protection. Be prepared to defend your choice in those terms.

☞ Also, don't forget that the abstractions test itself has been used in different ways. As originally conceived by Judge Hand in *Nichols v. Universal Pictures Corp.*, 42 F.2d 119 (2d Cir. 1930), it was meant to draw a line between copyrightable expression and uncopyrightable idea, in itself. In the *Altai* "abstraction-filtration-comparison" test, often used in connection with computer software and other utilitarian works, the abstraction test is merely a means to lay out a work in preparation for a process that identifies and filters out individual uncopyrightable elements at each level of abstraction. (*Computer Associates International, Inc. v. Altai, Inc.*, 982 F.2d 693 (2d Cir. 1992.)

The Originality Standard

☛ The originality standard of copyright law is generally a very low standard — much easier to meet than the novelty or non-obviousness standards of patent law. Under the *Feist* decision, originality requires only that the work not be copied and entail some minimal exercise of intellectual judgment, even if very modest. Only decisions that are "obvious" or "expected," such as the decision to order a list of telephone subscribers alphabetically by last name, are likely to fail the test. (In such cases, it is questionable whether the alleged author really exercised any independent judgment at all.) However, courts have adopted a somewhat different standard of originality (the "substantial variation" standard) in the case of derivative works. In evaluating originality in derivative works, it may be useful to consider the policy concerns that have led courts to adopt the "substantial variation" standard: the concern that derivative work copyrights may be used to bring harassing infringement claims against subsequent authors who make derivative works from the same underlying work, and the concern that derivative work copyrights may be used to interfere with exploitation of the copyright in the original work on which the derivative is based.

Overlap with Other Doctrines

☞ Courts have had considerable difficulty applying copyright to certain kinds of subject matter, such as computer programs and the design of useful articles. Assuming that it is consistent with the call of the exam question, it is always a good idea to discuss alternative ways in which this subject matter can be protected. Aspects of computer programs may be protected under trade secret law and utility patents, and aspects of the user interface might be the subject of trade dress rights. The design of useful articles may be protectable under a design patent or under trade dress law (although the Supreme Court has cut back recently on trade dress protection for product features). Notwithstanding these alternatives, producers of software and designers of useful articles have often complained that U.S. law does not provide adequate protection. There has been considerable discussion, in Congress and in the legal literature, of devising *sui generis* protection—legal protection tailored specifically for computer programs or useful articles—that borrows aspects from both patent and copyright law. If no form of existing protection seems to fit the subject of the exam question, it might be useful to discuss whether *sui generis* legislation would be appropriate, or whether public policy is better served by leaving the matter unprotected (or underprotected).

The Varying Infringement Standards

☞ As discussed in the outline, courts have used a range of standards for evaluating infringement claims, without always explaining when the different standards should be employed. A court's decision to use one standard over another frequently turns on concern about overprotection or underprotection. When the subject matter has a large number of uncopyrightable elements, application of an "overall subjective impression of the average lay observer" standard may lead to overprotection, because the fact finder may rely on similarities of uncopyrightable elements to find an unlawful appropriation. Thus, in such cases, courts may adopt a "more discerning" standard, an "abstraction, filtration, comparison" standard, or a "virtual identicality" or "bodily appropriation of copyrightable expression" standard (at least for selection and arrangement expression), all of which make it less likely that overprotection will occur. When there are fewer uncopyrightable elements (or the work is within the creative "core" of copyright protection—works of art, music, fiction, etc.), courts are more likely to favor the traditional "overall subjective response of the average lay observer" standard. In such cases, adoption of a higher standard may lead to underprotection. If the uncopyrightable elements of the work are identified and/or filtered out, the finder of fact may overlook protectable selection and arrangement expression in evaluating whether unlawful appropriation has occurred.

Infringement on the Internet

☞ Unauthorized transactions over the Internet may implicate a number of the copyright owner's rights simultaneously. Using a work in a computer almost always involves reproducing it, and there may be multiple reproductions made in the course of transmitting the work from one place to another. Moreover, when a work is transmitted, there may be a distribution to the public, and either a public display or public performance, depending on the type of work being transmitted and the destination of the transmission. Thus, a single transaction may implicate most of the exclusive rights of the copyright owner.

☛ The doctrine of first sale is unlikely to shelter alleged distributions to the public over the Internet, because the computer does not transmit a sender's lawful copy, but a reproduction of that copy. The fair use defense may be particularly problematic on the Internet, as well. Click-wrap licensing and electronic rights clearinghouses are likely to reduce the transaction costs of obtaining licenses to use copyrighted works in the digital world, and some courts have already indicated that the ready availability of licensing on reasonable terms will weigh against finding that an unauthorized use is fair.

Calculating duration

☛ While the provisions governing the duration of copyrights may seem daunting, you can keep them straight by simply asking which of three categories the work at issue falls into:

(1) works created after January 1, 1978;

(2) works created before January 1, 1978 that were already published with notice and covered by federal copyright on January 1, 1978; and

(3) works that were created before January 1, 1978 and had not been published as of January 1, 1978 (and thus were protected by state common law copyright).

☛ Works falling into the first category are governed by Copyright Act §302. Look to see whether the work is a work for hire, or an anonymous or pseudonymous work to determine whether to apply the life-plus-70 term or the 95/120-year term.

☛ Works falling into the second category are governed by Copyright Act §304. The first term is 28 years. Check to see when the first term ends to ascertain whether a filing had to be made to renew or if renewal was automatic. (A renewal filing had to be made for all copyrights commencing before January 1, 1964. Automatic renewal began in 1992.) Assuming there is a second term (because a filing was made or no filing was necessary), calculate when the second term would end if it lasted 47 years. If it would end after October 27, 1998, then add another 20 years to the end.

☛ Works falling into the third category are governed by §303. Calculate what the term would be under §302 and compare that to the year 2002 (or if the work was published prior to December 31, 2002, the year 2047) and take the later date.

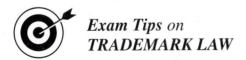

Exam Tips *on*
TRADEMARK LAW

Think About the Underlying Policies

☛ In the course of analyzing the fact situations in trademark problems, it is useful to *keep the policy concerns underlying trademark protection in mind*, as those policy concerns will often color courts' perception of the facts and influence the courts' analysis and reasoning. Overall, the purpose of trademark protection is to promote competition, but this goal is a complex one and involves a careful balance. On one hand, *strong protection of trademarks promotes competition* by ensuring that consumers can effectively distinguish the goods of one competitor from those of another and exercise their preferences. When consumers are able to exercise their preferences and reward quality with repeat business, businesses are encouraged to strive for better quality and innovative product characteristics, giving consumers more options in the marketplace.

☞ On the other hand, *overprotection of marks may impair competition* by depriving competitors of the ability effectively to describe their products to consumers, and by depriving them of access to functional and decorative elements that they legitimately need to compete effectively. It may also undermine the First Amendment interests in free speech and commentary and the free flow of useful product-related information to consumers. When these interests are at stake, they may outweigh the interest in avoiding consumer confusion and lead courts to permit an unauthorized use of a word, name, symbol, or device, even though consumers may understand it as indicating source in the plaintiff.

Remember That the Substantive Rules Are Similar for Both Registered and Common-Law Marks

☞ While class discussions, casebooks and commentaries on trademark law tend to focus on the Lanham Act registration provisions at some length, it is important to remember that *for the most part* the substantive rules governing whether a mark can be registered under the Lanham Act are similar to the common-law rules governing whether a mark can be protected. Moreover, the standards for infringement, abandonment, and many other such issues are essentially the same, regardless of whether an indication of origin is registered, and whether common-law rights are being pursued under Lanham Act §43(a) or state unfair competition law. The Lanham Act registration provisions simply build on the common law by providing some extra benefits to registrants as an incentive to register. Congress wanted to encourage businesses to register their marks for a variety of reasons, including to facilitate nationwide use of marks and to provide a centralized, public record of mark claims.

Use Lanham Act §2 as a Checklist

☞ In evaluating whether a mark is valid or qualifies for registration or for protection under the common law, it is useful to run through the provisions of Lanham Act §2 (literally, if it is an open book exam, or mentally, if not) to make sure that you have remembered all the possible challenges that might be made to the mark.

A Wide Range of Things May Be Protected as Indications of Origin

☞ Remember that a wide range of things may be protected as marks ("any word, name, symbol, or device") or as trade dress (including the overall appearance or ambiance of a product or place of business—even including a particular *method of marketing a product or service*). Moreover, on a single package, a number of different elements may qualify for protection as marks besides the brand name, including graphics, color combinations and designs, slogans, and made-up ingredient names. In addition, the overall combination of these various packaging elements may qualify as trade dress, so that a competitor's packaging may infringe if it creates an overall impression that is similar to the plaintiff's and likely to confuse consumers. When you encounter an exam problem, read the question carefully to determine what elements are at issue, and if the question does not specify otherwise, consider all the possibilities for protection.

Evaluate the Distinctiveness of Alleged Indications of Origin

☞ In many instances, the first issue to consider in a trademark question is whether the mark or trade dress at issue is distinctive. There can be no rights in an indication of origin unless it is either (1) inherently distinctive; or (2) capable of becoming distinctive and has acquired secondary meaning. If the alleged indication of origin is a word mark or a non-abstract illustration, then it is useful to consider the *Abercrombie & Fitch* hierarchy of distinctiveness—(1) arbitrary or fanciful, (2) suggestive, (3) descriptive, and (4) generic—remembering that arbitrary, fanciful, and suggestive indications are inherently distinctive; descriptive indications are capable of becoming distinctive on a showing of secondary meaning; and generic indications can never be distinctive, and thus cannot be protected. When the indication of origin at issue is an *abstract design, a combination of packaging features, or other such nonverbal matter*, it may be easier simply to categorize it as (1) inherently distinctive; (2) merely capable of becoming distinctive; or (3) generic. In these cases, a crucial consideration in distinguishing between inherently distinctive indications and those merely capable of becoming distinctive is whether the indication is commonly used, so that consumers are unlikely initially to perceive it as an indication that the good or service comes from a particular source, and competitors are likely legitimately to need it in their own marketing process.

Special Considerations for Product Feature Trade Dress

☞ Whenever you encounter an exam question involving rights in a feature or combination of features of a product, remember the concerns about trademark protection undermining patents. The Supreme Court has held that product feature (as opposed to product packaging) trade dress can never be deemed inherently distinctive and must always be demonstrated to have secondary meaning. *Wal-Mart Stores, Inc. v. Samara Brothers, Inc.*, 529 U.S. 205 (2000). Also remember to evaluate whether the product feature is functional. If it is, it cannot be protected even if it has acquired secondary meaning.

Timelines Can Be Useful

☞ Whenever an exam question raises an issue of priority, a timeline can be useful to sort out the facts and keep them straight in your mind. For example, here is a timeline to assist in evaluating the facts in Short-Answer Question 71.

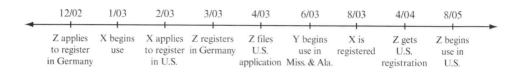

12/02	1/03	2/03	3/03	4/03	6/03	8/03	4/04	8/05
Z applies to register in Germany	X begins use	X applies to register in U.S.	Z registers in Germany	Z files U.S. application	Y begins use in Miss. & Ala.	X is registered	Z gets U.S. registration	Z begins use in U.S.

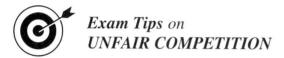

Exam Tips *on*
UNFAIR COMPETITION

Watch Out for Possible Preemption

☞ Whenever you encounter a problem involving a state cause of action to vindicate intellectual property interests, consider whether the cause of action is vulnerable to a preemption challenge. The law regarding preemption is covered in Chapter 9 of the Capsule Summary.

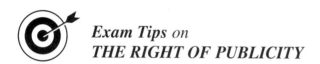

Exam Tips *on*
THE RIGHT OF PUBLICITY

Bear in Mind That There Is Significant Overlap

☞ The right of publicity often overlaps with other causes of action and may be brought as an alternative to those causes of action. For example, unauthorized use of a celebrity's identity in connection with the sale of goods or services may suggest to consumers that the celebrity endorses the goods or services, or is otherwise affiliated with their producer. Therefore, the celebrity may have a cause of action for trademark infringement or passing off, in addition to a cause of action for violation of the right of publicity. Likewise, a famous celebrity plaintiff might allege a cause of action for dilution, to the extent that aspects of his identity are already famous marks for goods or services. (A good example of this might be Paul Newman's image, which he uses as a mark to sell his own line of grocery items. If a defendant uses Newman's image on its own products, this may dilute Newman's mark.)

    ☞ The cause of action for violation of publicity rights may also overlap with the broad, amorphous cause of action for misappropriation. (See Chapter 7 of the Capsule Summary.) Moreover, if the defendant has appropriated the plaintiff's identity by reproducing or disseminating a work of authorship with which she is associated, or her performance of a work of authorship (so that the plaintiff is brought to the public mind) there may be overlap with a cause of action for copyright infringement. Especially in the case of overlap with copyright infringement, be on the lookout for possible arguments that the state publicity cause of action is preempted by federal copyright law.

Exam Tips on
**THE RELATIONSHIP BETWEEN FEDERAL
AND STATE LAW**

Preemption May Be a Hidden Issue

☞ Be alert for potential preemption issues whenever an exam question sets forth a state cause of action. Be on *high alert* if the question concerns a misappropriation cause of action, or a "property theory" idea claim. Recognize that even when a state cause of action (such as a breach of contract claim, passing off, or trade secret claim) normally is not preempted, *a particular claim may be*, if the plaintiff is essentially alleging a copyright interest, but is trying to disguise it as something else. Courts will look to the essence of what the plaintiff is seeking, given the facts of the particular case, and the court may examine the state law to determine if the state actually would impose the "extra element" that normally distinguishes the cause of action from a copyright claim.

Shrink-wrap and Click-wrap Licenses

☞ One question that a professor might ask is whether use of state law to enforce the terms of mass market (shrink-wrap or click-wrap) licenses is preempted. There has been considerable scholarly debate over this issue and several important court opinions. As a general matter, state breach of contract claims are not preempted under *Copyright Act §301*, even when the alleged breach consisted of an unauthorized reproduction, adaptation, public distribution, performance, or display of a copyrighted work. This is because *plaintiffs in contract cases must allege and prove the "extra element" of a bargained-for exchange*, which is not necessary in copyright infringement actions. Courts have generally found that this extra element renders the contract claim "qualitatively different" from copyright infringement. However, one might argue that, *as a practical matter, there is no meaningful "bargained-for exchange" in the case of shrink-wrap or click-wrap licenses* that restrict what purchasers may do with their copies. *All persons* wishing to purchase and use the works must consent to the terms of the license. Since all users are bound to the same terms, the "contract rights" created by the license look and feel much like a general property right, such as copyright gives. The Seventh Circuit has nonetheless rejected a §301 preemption challenge to enforcement of a shrink-wrap license. In *ProCD, Inc. v. Zeidenberg*, 86 F.3d 1447 (7th Cir. 1996), the Seventh Circuit equated shrink-wrap licenses with negotiated contracts, reasoning that "[a] copyright is a right against the world. Contracts, by contrast, generally affect only their parties; strangers may do as they please, so contracts do not create 'exclusive rights [that are equivalent to the rights provided by copyright law].'" *Id.* at 1454.

☞ As is demonstrated by *Aronson v. Quick Point Pencil Co.*, 440 U.S. 257 (1979), courts have not found *Supremacy Clause* preemption of contracts creating rights in intangible creations, in part because enforcement of contract restrictions does not give the plaintiff monopoly rights in the subject matter of the contract. The contract is only enforceable against other parties to the contract, not against the general public. However, in the case of shrink-wrap licenses, the rights created are uniformly created against *all purchasers* so that state enforcement provides a strong, broad, monopoly-like interest in the author. Indeed, these privately created, broad-based "property-like" rights threaten to compete with copyright law. Because shrink-wrap licenses can prohibit uses that the copyright law expressly permits (such as fair uses and uses expressly permitted by the other statutory exceptions to infringement liability set forth in Copyright Act §§108-121), authors' widespread reliance on shrink-wrap licenses may frustrate Congress's attempt to balance the competing interests of authors and the general public in drafting the Copyright Act. The Court of Appeals for the Fifth Circuit has held a state statute authorizing enforcement of specified shrink-wrap provisions to be preempted under a Supremacy Clause preemption analysis. *Vault Corp. v. Quaid Software Ltd.*, 847 F.2d 255 (5th Cir. 1988).

SHORT-ANSWER
QUESTIONS
AND
ANSWERS

SHORT-ANSWER QUESTIONS

CHAPTER 1

INTRODUCTORY ISSUES

1. How might intellectual property laws accommodate the potential conflict between the goals of providing an incentive to create, and ensuring the freest possible public and competitor access to the new products, services, and expressive works that are created? _____

CHAPTER 2

THE LAW OF TRADE SECRETS

2. Wong was formerly a laboratory scientist with Acme Co. When he first took employment with Acme, he signed a non-disclosure agreement in which he agreed not to use or disclose Acme's trade secrets without Acme's authorization. Wong lawfully knows the Acme Co. trade secret method for manufacturing ethanol because Acme revealed it to him to use in the course of his duties.

After leaving the Acme Co., Wong accepts a job with Bennet Co., which produces ethanol in competition with Acme. Wong will be the Director of Bennet's Research and Development Department. Acme wants to enjoin Wong from taking the job on the ground that his taking the job will "threaten" misappropriation, within the meaning of the Uniform Trade Secrets Act. How likely is Acme to succeed? _____

3. Assume that in each of the situations described below, Alice, who is employed by the Ace Company, gives Ace Company Brown Company's trade secret information. Ace and Brown are competitors.

   a. Alice meets Joe Blow, whom she knows to be one of Brown Co.'s chief chemical engineers, at a national chemical engineers' conference and offers to buy him drinks at a nearby bar. Alice does not hide the fact that she works for Ace. (In fact, early in the conversation, Blow laughingly remarks that Brown Co. warned him not to socialize with competitors' employees at conferences.) After several drinks, Alice manipulates the conversation, employing flattery to lead Blow to divulge more than he should about the secret chemical processes Brown Co. uses in producing its products. When Alice provides this trade secret information to Ace, she explains how she got it. Ace later uses the information to improve its own manufacturing process. Should Ace be found liable for trade secret misappropriation? _____

b. Alice buys Brown Co.'s product and takes it to the Ace Company's state-of-the-art laboratory. She uses the laboratory's highly sophisticated equipment to ascertain the components of the product and the relative amounts of each component, thus discovering Brown's trade secret product formula. When Alice provides this trade secret information to Ace, she explains how she got it. Ace later uses the information to produce a competing product. Should Ace be found liable for trade secret misappropriation? _____

c. Prior to joining Ace's research and development department, Alice interviewed for a job with Brown Co. During the course of the interview, the supervisor of Brown's research and development department tried very hard to convince Alice to join the Brown team. The supervisor told her that she would be on the "cutting edge" of the industry working for Brown. Alice then asked, "Can you give me an example?" The supervisor responded, "Well, this is strictly confidential, you understand, but Brown is developing a revolutionary new product, which will be introduced to the market next year." Alice asked for details and the supervisor provided them. After taking her job with Ace, Alice provided the Brown trade secret information to Ace and explained the circumstances in which she received it. Ace began immediately to develop its own version of the product and got it onto the market at nearly the same time as Brown. Should Ace be liable for trade secret misappropriation? _____

4. Acme Corp. creates and markets software that enables the user to more efficiently manage and track business inventory. Acme only provides the software to the public in object code form (machine-readable code that is not capable of being read by humans). It keeps the source code (which can be read by humans) locked away. X, a graduate student in computer science, purchases a copy of the software through Amazon.com. The software, which is encoded on a disk, arrives by mail. The packaging contains a shrink-wrap license that provides that the purchaser is the owner of the disk, but a mere licensee of the software encoded on the disk, and sets forth a number of things that the purchaser (as licensee) is prohibited from doing in connection with the software. Among other things, the purchaser/licensee is prohibited from reverse engineering the software, and publishing or otherwise communicating the results of any reverse engineering.

X proceeds to reverse engineer the software in order to study the underlying mathematical algorithms. He then posts the algorithms (but none of the code) on his web site, along with his commentary on the methodology Acme used. Y, a competitor of Acme, finds the algorithms on X's web site, downloads them, and uses them in devising his own software for tracking and managing business inventory.

Please evaluate what, if any rights Acme has against either X or Y for trade secret misappropriation. _____

5. MegaLabs Corp. operates a large number of medical laboratories throughout the United States to which doctors send their patients for various medical tests. (These laboratories take various kinds of specimens from patients, analyze and perform tests on the specimens, and report their findings back to the referring doctor for assistance in diagnosing and treating patients' medical problems.) Mega-Labs also operates its own Research and Development Division, which employs over 100 scientists who devote their time to developing and perfecting new testing methods and improved methods of interpreting test data.

In 2005, MegaLabs entered into a written joint research agreement with University, in which each party agreed to share information and resources and to collaborate in developing, among other things, a more effective method of testing patient blood samples for AIDS. (Hereafter, the "AIDS Project.") The agreement provided that any new laboratory tests developed as a result of the joint research agreement would be owned and exploited by MegaLabs, but that MegaLabs would pay a stated portion of its profits to University.

Appleton is a PhD in biochemistry who began work as a research scientist for MegaLabs in 1999. At the time he was employed he signed the following "Employment and Nondisclosure Agreement":

> Neither during the period of employment nor at any time thereafter will Appleton disclose to anyone any confidential information or trade secrets concerning the business affairs of MegaLabs, including but not limited to information relating to the experimental and research work of MegaLabs, its methods, processes, tools, machinery, formulae, drawings or appliances imparted or divulged to, gained or developed by or otherwise discovered by Appleton during his employment with MegaLabs.

In early 2006, Appleton was assigned primary responsibility for a project to develop a more efficient method of testing for parasites in human intestines. (This was another project covered by the MegaLabs/University joint research agreement.) In the course of his work he visited some laboratories at University to consult with Professor Bee on the parasite project. While there he encountered one of his old professors (Professor Cohen) who was presently working on the joint MegaLabs/University AIDS project. The two went to lunch and in the course of conversation, Prof. Cohen described one of his experiments to discover the AIDS virus in blood samples that had failed. After his meeting with Cohen, Appleton thought about Cohen's experiment and realized that if it was altered somewhat, it might work. In his spare time, he set up his own experiment (based on Cohen's but altered in the way he had envisioned) and succeeded in identifying the AIDS virus in a blood sample.

Appleton told his MegaLabs Supervisor about his experiment, and the Supervisor arranged for him to spend more time refining his experiment and testing the new method. For six months Appleton split his time 50-50 between the parasite project and his work on the new AIDS test. Then Appleton left MegaLabs and, in partnership with several other persons, set up a new medical laboratory that would compete with MegaLabs's individual patient testing laboratories. He took his notes on the new AIDS test experiment with him and continued to work on it in his spare time. MegaLabs, meanwhile, assigned McGee to continue work on the AIDS test and later filed an application for patent, naming Appleton and McGee as the inventors, and naming itself as the assignee of the rights in the invention. At all relevant times, both Cohen's original experiment and Appleton's and McGee's later work on the AIDS test were kept in confidence, shared only among the persons working on the projects.

The patent subsequently issued and Appleton, upon learning of it, sued MegaLabs, seeking a declaratory judgment that he is the rightful owner of the invention. Please evaluate this claim. _____

CHAPTER 3

PATENTS

6. Dr. Feelgood discovers that taking an antihistamine every other day is effective for treating high blood pressure in men over 50 years of age. Is this discovery patentable subject matter? _____

7. While doing research on the arctic tundra, Jim discovered a new plant that had never before been known or recorded. The plant's leaves produce a beautiful natural red dye. Can Jim obtain a utility patent for the plant? Why or why not? Can Jim obtain a plant patent? Why or why not? _____

8. In the course of research at Topeka State University, Professors Brown and Jones jointly devised a new form of widget that gave advantages over previously known widgets and reduced the new widget to actual practice. This occurred in November 2007. The professors made no attempt to commercialize the widget or to apply for a patent. Instead, they undertook to write a paper for publication that would fully describe the widget and the scientific principles underlying it. They worked diligently on the paper until it was completed in November 2008.

Prior to August 2008, the professors did not discuss their new widget with others. However, in August, Professor Brown sent a draft of the paper to Professor Smith, an expert in the field at Minneapolis State University, for his preliminary comments. Professor Smith read the paper and replied that the widget was an important breakthrough, congratulated Brown and Jones, and stated that he had no suggestions for improvement. In November 2008, Professors Brown and Jones sent their completed paper to a scientific journal, which accepted it and ultimately published it in January 2009.

In October 2008, Ginger Greer created a new widget design that had all the same elements as the widget invented by Professors Brown and Jones arranged in the same way. If she applies for a patent, should her invention be deemed "novel" under Patent Act §102? _____

9. Same facts as in Question 8, but instead of writing a paper, Professors Brown and Jones decide to file a patent application, and do so in January 2008. It turns out that Dr. Gupta had invented the same widget in India in April 2007, and had filed a U.S. patent application in September of the same year disclosing it. Will Dr. Gupta's earlier invention prevent Professors Brown and Jones from getting a patent? _____

10. Martinez invented a new form of widget in New Jersey in January 2014. In February 2015, Martinez published a paper in the *United States Journal of Engineering* that fully disclosed his new widget.

In August, 2014, Levine invented a widget that had all the same elements as the Martinez widget, arranged in the same way. In December 2014, Levine attended a trade show in Tokyo, Japan. At the trade show he demonstrated the widget to attendees, and gave embodiments of the widget to the three persons who organized the trade show and had invited him to attend.

Levine files an application with the U.S. P.T.O. to patent his widget in November 2015. Based on these facts, should the P.T.O. reject the application for lack of novelty?

Suppose that instead of Levine, Martinez filed for a U.S. patent in November 2015. Should the P.T.O. reject Martinez's application for lack of novelty? _____

11. In April 2010, Chu (an employee of Soft, Inc., which is located in Florida) conceived of a new kind of computer program to be used by banks in administering the reinvestment of certificates of deposit for bank customers. In a memo to Jefferson (also an employee of Soft, Inc.), dated May 16, 2010, Chu described the new program at some length, and directed Jefferson to make a prototype. Without further consultation, Jefferson went to work. He completed the coding in January 2011. Chu and Jefferson have both assigned all their inventions in advance to Soft, Inc., and both are under a duty of confidentiality to Soft, Inc.

In late November, 2010, Soft, Inc. placed advertisements in several banking trade journals announcing and promoting the new program, providing general information about what it could accomplish, stating the price, and comparing the price to that charged by competitors. Soft, Inc. began to accept and fill orders for the new program in February, 2011. It filed for a U.S. patent (as Chu's assignee) in December 2011.

Assuming that a patent issues, what, if any, objections might be raised to its validity? Would the objections be likely to succeed? _____

12. X invents a new scanner for an anti-shoplifting security system in December 2001 in New York. He does not apply for a patent, but immediately goes to work to create a commercial embodiment of the scanner and an accompanying mechanism which will be used to mark merchandise tags. X intends to sell the scanner and marking mechanism together as a package, since the scanner will be of little use without the compatible marking mechanism. X works continuously on getting the security system to the market, and ultimately places it on the market in December, 2003.

In April 2003, Y invents an anti-shoplifting security scanner that, while not identical to X's scanner, would be obvious to the person of ordinary skill in the art in light of X's scanner. If Y applies for a patent before the date that X places his scanner on the market, will Y be able to get a patent?

What if all the events above occurred *after* the Leahy-Smith America Invents Act became effective? _____

13. In August 2001, Dr. Science invented a novel and non-obvious method of synthetically producing a medically useful compound formerly only extracted from tree bark. He did not immediately file a patent application, but instead worked on related projects. In September 2002, Dr. Kato published an article in a Japanese scientific journal that, while not describing Dr. Science's method as such, rendered it obvious to a person with ordinary skill in the art when considered in combination with an earlier method of synthesizing chemical compounds that was well-known in the United States.

Dr. Science applied for a U.S. patent in November 2003. Should the application be granted? What if Dr. Science applied in November 2002? What if Dr. Kato had published his article in November 2000?

Add 15 years to each date in the problem above, so that the Leahy-Smith America Invents Act applies. How would your answers differ? _____

14. In 2010, X Co. purchased one of Y Co.'s patented machines (which was in the final year of its patent), analyzed its constituent parts, and began to manufacture the parts. X Co. placed the parts into boxes, to create "kits" for making Y's machine. Each box contained all the parts necessary to make the machine, along with instructions for assembly. The parts in the box were unassembled. X Co. did not advertise or sell any of the kits until the day after Y Co.'s patent expired. Is Y Co. likely to have a cause of action for patent infringement against X Co.? _____

15. X Co. did all the things described in Question 14, but in addition, before Y Co.'s patent expired, X Co. sold some of the kits in Canada to Canadian purchasers, who then assembled the machines. Would this render X Co. liable to Y Co. for patent infringement? _____

16. On January 1, 1996, Ace Co. applied for a patent on its new widget. The patent was granted two years later, on January 1, 1998. Lee had purchased Ace Co.'s patented widgets in the past, but felt that Ace Co. was abusing its patent by charging too much for them. In March 2015, Lee proposed to Bell Co. that Bell Co. manufacture two widgets with the same specifications as Ace Co.'s patented widget. The parties agreed on a price, signed a contract, and Bell Co. began work. Bell Co. completed making and testing the widgets as specified in December 2015, and delivered them to Lee in the second week of January. Lee immediately put the widgets to work in his business. Does Ace Co. have a cause of action for patent infringement against Lee? _____

17. On January 1, 1996, Acme Co. applied for a design patent on its new lamp base design. A patent was granted a year later, on January 1, 1997. Acme proceeded to manufacture lamps incorporating the new design at its New Jersey factory, and also at its factory in Mexico City, Mexico. In July 2013, Montes purchased a number of the lamps produced by Acme's factory in Mexico City and imported them into the United States without Acme's permission. Does Acme have a cause of action against Montes for design patent infringement? _____

18. Alice was in the wholesale flower business on the east coast. One day she discovered that one of her "fufu" plants had mutated: its bloom had a pleasant "spicy vanilla" scent. Prior flowers of this species had been odorless except on very rare occasions when the mutation had appeared before briefly in the wild. Recognizing the value of this mutation, Alice took cuttings of the plant and grew additional fufu plants with the spicy scent. She applied for a plant patent, which was granted in May 1999. She began to produce the new patented variety of fufu plant in large quantities for the market.

In January 2008, Bill bought one of Alice's patented fufu plants. Liking the spicy scent, Bill took seeds from the plant and planted them in his window boxes.

In July 2008, Cliff, a San Francisco flower wholesaler, noticed that one of his own fufu plants had mutated so that the flower had a pleasant spicy vanilla scent. In fact, Cliff's mutated plant was exactly like Alice's patented plant. Cliff took cuttings from his fufu plant and produced large numbers of the mutated variety and began to sell them. Is either Bill or Cliff liable to Alice for infringement of her plant patent? _____

19. The Power Company has a "combination patent" on a new kind of washing machine. The patent is now in its fifteenth year. Wong, a retiree, goes to the local junkyard and buys two of the patented washing machines, which are old and beat up. When he gets them home, he takes them apart. He then begins to assemble a new machine, using parts he has salvaged from the two old machines. He finds, however, that one key part—the agitator—is missing: neither of the agitators in the two old machines is usable. Thus, Wong goes to Yee, a machinist friend, and asks him to make a new replacement agitator. Yee knows that the agitator is specially made and adapted for use in the Power Co.'s patented washing machine and that it has no other substantial use. However, he agrees to make one for Wong, and delivers it the next week. Wong pays Yee for this work, incorporates the new agitator into the machine, and washes his laundry. Is Yee liable to the Power Co. for contributory infringement of its patent? _____

20. Liu and Gonzales are unrelated inventors who live and work in the United States. On January 15, 2010, Liu conceived of a new widget design. He then set the project aside until March 3, 2010, while he attended to other business. Starting March 3, he worked continuously on the project. On December 11, 2010, he built a working model of the widget. He filed a U.S. patent application on December 19, 2010. Gonzales conceived of an identical widget on March 15, 2010. She never built a working model, but filed a U.S. patent application disclosing and claiming the widget on April 4, 2010. Please explain which party is entitled to a patent and explain why. _____

21. In January 2010, Western Pacific Co. applied for U.S., European, and Japanese patents for its novel, non-obvious, and useful locomotive engine. Between September 2011 and February 2012, Zoom Corp. (which is headquartered and has its factory in upstate New York) produced twenty locomotive engines that had all the same elements as claimed in Western Pacific's pending patent application. It immediately sold ten of the engines to an English purchaser. The following month Zoom transferred the remaining ten engines to its wholly owned subsidiary in Mexico. In April 2012, Western Pacific's patent issued. In June 2012, the president of Zoom called a prospective purchaser in Pakistan from his office in New York and offered to sell the Pakistani Zoom's remaining ten engines. The offer was accepted two weeks later, and the engines were shipped from Mexico to Pakistan. Payment was made in Pakistan, upon delivery. Please explain what, if any, rights Western Pacific has against Zoom Corp. under U.S. patent law. _____

CHAPTER 4

THE LAW OF UNDEVELOPED IDEAS

22. Mary, a homemaker, decided that it would be useful to have a shopping center built on a series of vacant lots near her home. She believed that the surrounding neighborhoods would generate a great deal of business for such a shopping center. Accordingly, she made an appointment to see Cindy, a wheeler-dealer on the local real estate development scene, who had developed other shopping centers. At the meeting Mary told Cindy her idea, and then told her that if she acted on the idea and built a shopping center in the place Mary suggested, Mary expected to be paid a commission. Cindy told Mary that

she wasn't interested, but two years later Cindy acquired the lots Mary had told her about and commenced building a shopping center. Is Mary likely to have a cause of action for compensation from Cindy? _____

23. Tom, the owner of a small ceramic tile business, met Jerry, a business consultant, at a cocktail party. Upon learning Jerry's profession, Tom began to discuss his business. He mentioned that he had hired a consultant to help devise a better way to keep track of his inventory, but that the consultant's suggestions had not been helpful. Tom then asked Jerry if he knew of a more efficient means of tracking his inventory. Jerry responded: "Just between the two of us, I do." Jerry proceeded to tell Tom the details of a method. Jerry had learned about the particular method he described to Tom from a prior client, who had been using the method for a number of years. Tom implemented the inventory method that Jerry described and found it quite efficient. Later, upon learning that Tom had implemented the system, Jerry demanded compensation. Is he likely to prevail? _____

CHAPTER 5

COPYRIGHT LAW

24. Eileen published a book containing the Minnesota-style hot dish (casserole) recipes that she had created over the years. Wanda Sue made one of the recipes, but changed one of the key ingredients in the course of doing so. (She substituted grits for the canned cream of mushroom soup that the recipe called for.) Eileen would never authorize such a shocking substitution. Has Wanda Sue infringed Eileen's exclusive right of adaptation? Why or why not? _____

25. Arco, Inc., a designer and producer of heavy machinery, produces and sells a highly automated assembly-line production machine. The machine is operated through use of a series of four-digit numeric instructions, or "command codes." These command codes are used to access the computerized features of the machine and cause the machine to perform various production tasks. In creating the four-digit codes, Arco divided the production tasks to be represented by the codes into logically related categories and assigned a separate number to each category. It then reflected the category number in the first two digits of the four-digit command code for each production task. The last two digits in the command code reflect whether the particular task is a higher- or lower-level task, on a scale of 01-10.

Arco's machine was the first of its kind and is the standard in the industry. Most workers who operate such machinery were trained on and are accustomed to using the Arco four-digit command codes. Brown Co. has begun to produce competing machines and wants to adopt the Arco command codes for operation of its own machines, so that workers will not need to be retrained to use them. If it does, will it risk liability for copyright infringement? Please provide both sides of the argument. _____

26. What is the difference between a phonorecord and a sound recording? _____

27. X has created the form of a running deer from various materials, which he uses as a mount for deerskins in his taxidermy business. He mounts a deerskin on the form, and after adding glass eyes, etc., he is able to create a very realistic looking facsimile of a living deer. He sells these facsimiles to museums of natural history, to hunters (as a hunting trophy), and other public and private collectors.

X would like to market his running deer form to other taxidermists and claim copyright in the form to prevent others from copying it without his authorization. Would the "physical or conceptual separability" test be likely to prevent him from obtaining copyright? _____

28. Acme Corp. designs and manufactures high-quality, expensive, classically styled furniture. One chair, which Acme calls "The Philadelphian," is a standard wingback chair design and has been on the market for a number of years. In the course of designing and manufacturing The Philadelphian, Acme's designers created a set of drawings, annotated with manufacturing specifications, that Acme uses in mass-producing the chair. There were four copies of the annotated drawings at the Acme plant when X, a worker at Acme, got access to one of the copies and took it without authorization. X had decided to set up his own furniture business. He used the annotated drawing to produce his own chair for sale in competition with Acme. X did not use the same fabric to upholster his chair, and he called his chair "The Bostonian" in advertising and sales literature. Is Acme likely to have a cause of action against X for copyright infringement? _____

29. Arnie composed a nondramatic musical work (a song) and registered his copyright in it. The following year Bill, a famous singer, acquired a license to record Arnie's song. Bill recorded the song shortly thereafter and sold the recording to the public. He paid royalties to Arnie in accordance with the license agreement. The following year Charles, who had learned to mimic Bill's distinctive voice and singing style, also took a license to record Arnie's copyrighted song, and proceeded to make his own recording, mimicking Bill's recording so effectively that a casual listener could not tell the difference between Bill's recording and Charles's recording. Charles advertised his recording extensively and sold a number of copies to the public. Charles paid royalties to Arnie, but not to Bill. Based on these facts, is Bill likely to have a cause of action for copyright infringement against Charles? _____

30. In 1998, Alice wrote a short novel centered upon a romantic relationship between a man and woman. At the end of the novel these characters had a disagreement and parted. Satisfied with the work, Alice made plans to publish it. Before she was able to publish, however, she was killed in an automobile accident. In her will, Alice left all her property to her husband, Tom, and her son, Jerry, in equal shares. In going through Alice's effects, Tom found the short novel and read it. Dissatisfied with the ending, Tom added four additional chapters to the end. In the new chapters, the man and woman met again after three years, were reconciled, married, and lived happily ever after. Tom then published the novel in this form. Later, Tom licensed Dizzy, Inc. to make a movie based on the novel as published. What, if any, rights does Jerry have with regard to the movie license? _____

31. Alice purchased (over the Internet) an authorized digital colorized copy of an old cowboy movie entitled "Homes on the Range," that was popular in the early 1950s. Bill, an actor who was popular in the 1950s, starred in the movie. Alice also purchased an authorized digital copy of a more modern movie starring Brad, a very popular, current movie star. Through digital manipulation, Alice substituted Brad's head for Bill's in a 20-minute segment of "Homes on the Range," and posted the altered 20-minute segment on her web site. Alice sold advertising space on her web site, and charged advertisers a fee based on the number of persons visiting the site. Cliff Enterprises is the owner of copyright in "Homes on the Range." Cliff authorized the sale of the digital copy of the movie to Alice and received a royalty from the sale. Does Cliff Enterprises have a cause of action for copyright infringement against Alice? _____

32. ZBS Corp., a nationwide broadcasting company, produced and aired a very popular soap opera called "Law School Lovelorn." The show centered around the complex love lives of several glamorous law school students. The show had a considerable following. However, many of the show's fans were lawyers, who found it necessary at times to miss the show (which was aired during the day) in order to make court appearances and meet with clients. The Sensational Bar Journal decided to publish a weekly column that explained what had happened in the past week's episodes for the benefit of fans who had to miss them. The column generally consisted of about eight to ten paragraphs that described the events that had taken place in the particular week's episodes. The column did not quote dialog from the show, or provide photographs or other visual imagery from the show. Is ZBS, the owner of copyright in the show, likely to have a cause of action against Sensational Bar Journal for copyright infringement? _____

33. Goodreads, Ltd., a British bookseller, sets up a web page through which consumers around the world can order and pay for books. The books are then shipped to the consumer by regular mail. Among the books Goodreads, Ltd. sells is Myra Mistique's newest romance novel, *Sizzle*. Myra assigned the British copyright to U.K. Publishers, Ltd., and the American copyright to Old Glory Publishers, Inc., which is unrelated to U.K. Publishers, Ltd. The copies Goodreads, Ltd. sells over its web site were produced and originally sold by U.K. Publishers, Ltd. Old Glory Publishers, Inc., would like to prohibit Goodreads from making any further sales of the British-produced *Sizzle* to American purchasers. Would it have a cause of action for copyright infringement, on the theory that Goodreads is engaged in unauthorized importation of the book? _____

34. Artist created a highly inspiring painting of a forest with sun streaming through the trees. He sold the painting to Mr. and Mrs. Devout, who donated it to Church. Shortly thereafter, Church's pastor delivered a sermon about "The Wonders of God's Nature," and to inspire the congregation, projected the painting on an opaque projector, in a manner that created images of the painting on three different locations of the Church sanctuary walls — one in the front behind the pastor, and one on each side wall. Did this constitute infringement of Artist's copyright? _____

35. X downloaded Y's copyrighted photograph from the Internet into his computer's random access memory. He proceeded, with the assistance of some software, to alter the photographic image for his own amusement. He did not save the altered image to his hard drive or print it out. All of his work took place in the random access memory of his computer only. When he exited his computer, the original and altered images in his random access memory were destroyed. Assuming that X's actions were unauthorized, is it likely that he violated Y's exclusive right of adaptation? _____

36. DeBartolomeo, the owner of a small Italian restaurant, often brings his accordion to the restaurant and plays popular Italian tunes for the guests' enjoyment when he has a spare moment. Needless to say, he makes no separate charge for this music, and makes no recording or transmission of the performance. Assuming that some of the songs he plays are copyrighted, do his acts constitute infringement? _____

37. Compare and contrast the right of integrity granted to the author of a work of visual art under the Visual Artists' Rights Act with the exclusive right of adaptation in the same work. _____

38. Mary purchased a lawful copy of a copyrighted photograph and scanned it onto her computer's hard drive. She later posted the digitized photograph on an Internet bulletin board. Could her acts constitute a public display of the photograph? What if she had instead posted the lawful copy she bought on the cork bulletin board in her college dormitory? What if she kept the copy she bought in her room and instead printed a digitized copy and posted it on the dormitory bulletin board? _____

39. Architect designed and built a highly innovative office building, which quickly became a famous landmark in the city. Photographer made a photograph of the building from a nearby city park, and had it mass-produced as a post card, for sale to tourists in various local shops. Does Architect have a cause of action against Photographer for copyright infringement? _____

40. Elbert drafted a list of "The Ten Worst-Dressed Professors at Law School," in descending order of worst dress, and circulated it to the student body. Campus Newspaper obtained a copy of the list and published it without Elbert's permission. Is Newspaper likely to have infringed Elbert's copyright? _____

41. In 2005, Y, an architect, filed the plans for a house he had recently designed with the City Planner's Office, as required by local ordinance. Y built the house the following year. X admired the house, stole the plans from the City Planner's files, and built his own house from the plans without Y's permission. Is X likely to be liable for copyright infringement? _____

42. Patty purchased a new computer game on a CD-ROM. Pursuant to the instructions accompanying the game, she e-mailed the game's producer and registered her purchase. The producer then issued Patty a "personal password" that she must use to activate the game each time she wants to use it. The game cannot be used without the password. Patty later lent the game to her friend Fred, and told him her password so that he could use the game while she was away on vacation. If Fred used the password to play the game, did this violate the producer's rights? If so, on what basis? _____

43. Dr. Heckel and Dr. Jeckel, research scientists and professors, worked together on a research project. In the course of their research, they collaborated to write a paper describing the project and its results to date. Each of them wrote a substantial portion of the paper. Shortly thereafter, Heckel attended a conference. At the conference, Heckel presented the paper, but did not acknowledge Jeckel's role in writing it, suggesting instead that Heckel was the sole author.

Two years later, Heckel revised the paper, describing the latest developments in the project. He did this by himself and did not obtain Jeckel's permission to do so. Shortly thereafter,

Jeckel found and reproduced the revised paper and, without Heckel's permission, distributed copies of it to participants at a conference. Jeckel named both Heckel and Jeckel as the authors, and included copyright notice.

What are Heckel's and Jeckel's respective rights against one another under the Copyright Act? _____

44. In 1963, Able completed and published a novel with proper copyright notice. The novel was a moderate success. In 1969, Able executed a license to Brown, authorizing Brown to produce and publicly perform a play based on the novel. The license expressly stated that Able conveyed the exclusive right to base a play on the novel, and to publicly perform the play, "both in the original and renewal term" of the novel's copyright.

Brown produced the play pursuant to the license and it was a great success. It ran for a number of years on Broadway and was taken on tour in the United States and in Europe. In 1975, Brown executed a license to Cohen Productions, Inc., to make a movie based on the play. The movie was produced and distributed in 1979.

Able died in 1982, and was succeeded by her son, David. In 1991, David renewed the copyright in the novel. In 2012, Brown decided to stage a revival of his play on Broadway, and Cohen Productions, Inc. decided to make its movie available for purchase on videotape. David has consulted you about his rights, if any, with regard to Brown and Cohen's activities. Please advise him. _____

45. In 1969, Allen, a staff artist employed in the Promotions Department of Gemco Films, Inc., was assigned to design a poster promoting a recently released Gemco movie. The poster Allen designed consisted of the name of the movie, the names of the persons starring in the movie, and a watercolor sketch of one of the action scenes in the movie. Gemco printed a thousand copies of the poster and sent them to theaters featuring the movie, with a letter stating that the poster could be used to promote greater audience attendance. Notice of copyright was properly indicated on the poster and the copyright was registered in 1969. Allen died in 1984 and did not undertake to assign any rights in the poster to anyone. When will copyright protection in the poster end? _____

46. Brown was a staff artist at Ace Pictures, Inc. In that capacity, in 1982, he created paintings of various action scenes from Ace Pictures' upcoming motion picture release, which he incorporated into a poster to advertise the motion picture. Ace Pictures published the poster with proper copyright notice in 1984. Brown died in 2013. When will copyright in the poster expire? _____

47. On August 12, 1980, Allen, a freelance commercial artist and printer, entered into a contract with Brown, Inc., to produce a brochure for Brown to advertise various of Brown's products. Allen completed the work on October 25, 1980. However, Brown, Inc., only began to distribute the brochure (with proper copyright notice) to the public on February 5, 1982. Allen had a heart attack and died on November 1, 1985. When will the copyright in the brochure expire? _____

48. Joe Lee was a newspaper journalist in New York, who worked hard to support his wife and two children. In 1954, he began work on a novel during his spare time, and continued to work on it for the next six years on weekends and in the evenings after work. He and his wife were divorced in 1957. In 1960, Joe finished his novel and assigned it to a publisher

that published it with proper notice of copyright the same year. The publisher immediately registered the copyright. In 1972, Joe moved in with a girlfriend and lived with her for the rest of his life. He died in 1981, devising all of his real and personal property to his girlfriend. Assuming that his girlfriend filed renewal paperwork with the Copyright Office in a timely fashion, when will the copyright expire? _____

49. Mark created a play and obtained copyright in it in 1979. The play was publicly performed and published in 1984. In 1992, Mark executed a license to XBS to produce a movie based on the play. Mark died in 1994, survived by his wife Marla, his daughters Olivia and Patricia, and two children (Randy and Steve) of a deceased son. Mark's children and grandchildren disliked the movie that XBS produced pursuant to its license, believing that it distorted the moral lesson that Mark wanted to communicate in his play. They would like to terminate the license. Under what circumstances could they do that, and would the termination take care of their concerns? _____

50. Chang was a witness to the Hindenberg explosion on May 6, 1937, in New Jersey. He was deeply moved by the experience, and wrote extensively about it in his private diary. He died 13 years later, in November 1950. His niece inherited all of his personal property. In 1960, the niece donated all of Chang's books and private papers to Archive. In 2012, Johnson was doing research on a book about the Hindenberg explosion, and came upon Chang's diary in the Archive. He would like to quote lengthy excerpts from the diary in his book—more than would be likely to be allowed under the fair use doctrine. Does he need to worry about potential copyright infringement liability? Please explain your answer. _____

51. Buildings.com is a web site that permits subscribing real estate brokers to post photographs and descriptions of buildings that they are offering for sale in major U.S. cities. The system operates automatically: A subscriber wishing to post photographs and descriptions simply follows a step-by-step automated procedure to do so. The Buildings.com system retains posted materials on the web site for two weeks and then deletes them. If the subscribing broker wants to retain them on the web site for a longer period, she must repost them. The owner of the Buildings.com web site does not itself review or select the materials being posted on its site. Whenever a visitor to the web site logs on, he or she can download posted materials, either to view on-line or to print. One of Buildings.com's subscribing brokers posts infringing photographs on the web site. Without discussing the Copyright Act §512 safe harbor provisions, please explain whether Buildings.com should be liable for direct infringement of the copyright owner's reproduction rights. _____

52. X wrote a song and made a recording of it, which was sold to the general public. Y bought a lawful copy of X's recording and took a digital sample of it, without authorization. He then incorporated it into his own recording. The sample Y took consisted of three chords of background guitar. Y speeded them up and added reverberations, so that the sampled chords produced a very different sound on Y's recording than on X's recording. It is very unlikely that anyone listening to Y's recording would recognize the sampled material as coming from X's recording. Is X likely to have a cause of action for copyright infringement against Y? Please explain your answer. _____

53. Acme Corp. created and markets software that enables the user to more efficiently manage and track business inventory. Acme only provides the software to the public in

object code form (machine-readable code that is not capable of being read by humans). It keeps the source code (which can be read by humans) locked away. X, a graduate student in computer science, purchased a copy of the software through Amazon.com. The software, encoded on a disk, arrived by mail. The packaging contained a shrink-wrap license that provided that the purchaser would be the owner of the disk but a mere licensee of the software, and set forth a number of things that the purchaser was prohibited from doing. It then provided that the purchaser would manifest his/her agreement to these limitations by opening and using the software. The prohibitions included reverse engineering the software and publishing or otherwise communicating the results of any reverse engineering. X proceeded to reverse engineer the software in order to study the underlying mathematical algorithms. He then posted the algorithms (but none of the code) on his web site, along with his commentary on the methodology Acme used. Y, a competitor of Acme, found the algorithms on X's web site, downloaded them, and used them in devising his own software for tracking and managing business inventory.

(a) Please evaluate whether Acme has a cause of action against X for copyright infringement and explain your answer. _____

(b) Please evaluate whether Acme has a cause of action against Y for copyright infringement and explain your answer. _____

54. In 1947, Vik, a reporter for BigNews Magazine, researched and wrote an expose of government corruption. BigNews published the expose in 1948. In 1970, BigNews Magazine went out of business. In 1976, Vik filed to renew the copyright in the article. Vik died in 1989, leaving all his personal and real property by will to Friend, deliberately cutting off Son, who would otherwise have been his sole heir. In 2010, Publisher, Inc. published a book that reproduced large portions of Vik's article without authorization. Both Friend and Son want to bring an infringement action. Assuming that the year is 2012, what are their respective rights? _____

55. In 1930, Famous Poet wrote a colorful but shocking letter to his Mistress. The Mistress saved the letter. In 1988, she showed it to Emma, who worked as her nurse. Emma observed where the Mistress kept the letter, and later "borrowed" it long enough to make a photocopy. She did not seek or receive permission to make the copy. (Famous Poet had died in 1960.) Emma later sold the photocopy to Mary, a wealthy business woman, who collected memorabilia of famous persons. Mary died in 2003, leaving her entire estate to University. The University placed the photocopy of Famous Poet's letter in its Library's documents collection, where it was indexed and made available to researchers and other members of the University community and the public. Famous Poet's Widow discovered the letter in the Library index and has brought suit against Library for copyright infringement. There is nothing in the Library records to suggest that anyone ever checked out the letter. How would you evaluate the respective rights of the parties? Please explain your answer. _____

56. Acme, Inc., a multinational corporation, owns copyright worldwide in a sound recording. It produces phonorecords of the sound recording at its factory in Australia, and sells them all over the world, including in New Zealand and the U.S.A. DiscountCo purchases numerous phonorecords of the sound recording in New Zealand, ships them to the U.S.A. and sells them through its retail outlets in Florida, Georgia, Alabama and Mississippi.

Acme brings suit against DiscountCo for copyright infringement in the U.S.A. How would you evaluate the claim? Please explain your answer. _____

57. Trucking, Inc. designs, manufactures, and sells heavy-duty trucks and trailers for log-distance hauling. It is the leading seller of trucks, but has significant competition in the market for the trailers that are to be attached to its trucks. Trucking, Inc. developed a new type of high-tech trailer hitching device, which it now attaches to all the trucks it manufactures and sells. The hitching device contains software that controls the movement of the mechanisms necessary to hitch a trailer to the truck. This software cannot be activated unless encrypted software in the trailer's hitching mechanism sends a special code to the software in the truck hitching mechanism to make a secret "handshake." Only when the handshake routine is completed will the Trucking, Inc. truck hitching device release the mechanisms needed to hitch the trailer to the truck. This effectively requires persons buying Trucking, Inc. trucks to buy Trucking, Inc. trailers.

Long-Haul, Inc., a leading manufacturer and seller of trailers for long distance hauling, and a competitor of Trucking, Inc. in the market for trailers, develops software for its trailer hitching devices that avoids the Trucking, Inc. handshake routine, allowing owners of Trucking, Inc. trucks to activate the truck's hitching software and hitch trailers made by Long-Haul to their trucks. The Long-Haul software does not reproduce any copyrightable expression from the Trucking, Inc. software.

Is Trucking, Inc. likely to succeed in a lawsuit against Long-Haul? Please explain your answer. _____

58. Alex created an original comic strip that was carried by a number of daily newspapers around the country and enjoyed significant success. Alex licensed Betty to make and sell dolls based on the leading characters in the comic strip. Several years later, Alex licensed Charles to create and sell greeting cards featuring the comic strip characters. The depictions of the comic strip characters in Charles's cards are highly similar to the dolls that Betty is marketing. Betty, accordingly, has brought suit against Charles, alleging copyright infringement. How would you evaluate the respective rights of the parties? _____

59. Dave, a veteran of years of television and radio work, decided to go into business with his wife, Becky, to make a series of low-budget children's videos. Dave and Becky wrote the scripts, directed and acted in the videos, which introduced young children to such things as firefighting, construction work, the manufacture of cars, the postal service, etc. Dave and Becky did almost everything themselves except the camera work, for which they hired an employee. Generally they just acquired a license to incorporate pre-existing recorded music into their videos, but in commencing work on a video to introduce children to airplanes, Dave and Becky decided to include some original music. They contacted Janet, an old friend of theirs, who sang and played guitar, and asked her if she would write and sing a song about flying to be used in the video. Janet did so. Because the parties were old friends, they made no written contract. Dave and Becky told Janet that she would be paid a sum constituting 5 percent of net sales of the video, to be paid yearly, for the first 10,000 videos sold.

A year after the airplane videos went on sale, Janet arranged to give a series of children's concerts. In each concert, she sang the song about flying that she had written and performed for the video. In the background on stage, she projected scenes from the video. When Dave and Becky learned that Janet had been showing the video in her performance they demanded that she stop. However, Janet refused. Please evaluate the respective rights of the parties, given the available facts. _____

CHAPTER 6

TRADEMARK LAW

60. How might the P.T.O. evaluate an application to register "Mr. Justice" as a mark for study aids for law students? _____

61. How might the P.T.O. evaluate an application to register a stylized graphic representation of a fish as a mark for cat food? The cat food is comprised of horse meat, soy flour, water, and various preservatives and other chemical additives. The company has already registered the word mark "Yummies" for the cat food. _____

62. How might the P.T.O. evaluate an application to register the configuration of a clip, as shown below, that surrounds an ink pen and secures it to the inside of a person's shirt pocket? The evidence indicates that there are numerous alternative designs that would work just as well to clip a pen to the inside of a person's pocket. _____

63. How might the P.T.O. evaluate an application to register the words "Apple Sauce" as a mark for children's clothing? _____

64. How might the P.T.O. evaluate an application to register the words "Champs Elysees" as a mark for luxury automobiles manufactured in Birmingham, England? _____

65. How might the P.T.O. evaluate an application to register the following mark for chairs? _____

66. How might the P.T.O. evaluate an application to register the color gold for the gilded edges of the pages of a leather-bound diary? _____

67. How might the P.T.O. evaluate an application to register a mark for pickled onions comprised of the words "Super Pickled" superimposed over a cartoon caricature of a well-known former politician who was noted for heavy drinking? The applicant has used this mark continuously and exclusively for the past eight years. _____

68. In March 2005, Ace Corp. filed an "intent-to-use" application to register the mark "Alpine Splendor" for the new carbonated water beverage it intended to introduce to the market. The P.T.O. allowed the application in July 2005. In January 2006, Ace filed for an extension of time, which the P.T.O. granted as a matter of course. The following July, Ace filed for another extension, which the P.T.O. granted. In September 2006, Ace introduced the new carbonated beverage to the market bearing the "Alpine Splendor" mark, filed an affidavit of use with the P.T.O., and obtained registration. Brown Corp. began using the mark "Alpine Splendor" for a new bottled water product in January 2005. Assuming that the parties are both marketing their products in the same geographic location, which party has priority? _____

69. In 1998, X began manufacturing erasers (to fit on the end of pencils) at its Roanoke, Virginia factory. It marketed the erasers under the unregistered mark "Peccadillo" throughout the State of Virginia. In 2003, X expanded its sales of erasers under the Peccadillo mark to Tennessee. Shortly thereafter, in 2004, X sold his Roanoke factory and assigned the Peccadillo mark to Y. Since then, Y has continued to manufacture and sell erasers, under the Peccadillo mark, in Virginia and Tennessee, and has further expanded sales into parts of North and South Carolina.

Z Co., which manufactures various writing accessories in its Texas factory, began preparations to manufacture and sell pencil erasers. It filed an "intent-to-use" application to register the mark "Peck-a-dillo" for the erasers in April, 2000. It first sold erasers under the Peck-a-dillo mark in November, 2002, at which point it filed an affidavit of use and completed its registration of the mark. During the next five years, Z Co. confined its sales activities to Texas and other states west of the Mississippi River. However, in December, 2007, Z Co. completed a new factory to manufacture its erasers and launched a nationwide marketing campaign. Z Co. completed the paperwork necessary to attain incontestable status for its Peck-a-dillo mark, and then brought suit to enjoin Y's use of the Peccadillo mark under Lanham Act §32. What are the respective rights of the parties? _____

70. X Co. decided to adopt the mark "Heckofawallop" for the new fortified wine product it planned to put on the market. It introduced the new fortified wine product (with much advertising and fanfare) to the market in New York in January 2003, and filed an application to register the mark the following month (in February 2003). The registration was granted in August 2003.

Meanwhile, in June 2003, Y Co., a small Mississippi company, began marketing a malt liquor under the mark "Hellofawallop." It sold the malt liquor in Mississippi and parts of western Alabama, but did not register its mark and engaged in relatively little advertising.

X Co. now wants to expand sales of its fortified wine product nationwide under its "Heckofawallop" mark. What are X's and Y's respective rights?

_____

71. Assume that, in addition to the facts set forth in Question 70, Z Co., a German Company, decided to adopt the mark "Heckawallap" (a made-up word) for table wines. It applied to register the mark in Germany in December 2002, was granted registration the following March 2003, and applied the following month to register the mark in the United States pursuant to Lanham Act §44. It attached a certified copy of its German registration to its application and alleged a *bona fide* intent to use the mark in commerce. However, it had not used the "Heckawallap" mark at the time it applied to register in the United States, and did not do so at any time prior to its ultimate U.S. registration in April 2004. Z Co. began to use the mark for table wines in the United States in August 2005, selling its wines throughout the United States under the Heckawallap mark. Germany is a member of the Paris Convention. What are Z Co.'s rights as opposed to X Co. and Y Co.? _____

72. X Co. manufactures and sells widgets under the federally registered mark "Whiz," and has done so throughout the country for many years. Y Co. began selling widgets under the mark "Excelsior." Y then registered "Whiz.com" as a domain name and set up a web page under that domain name. The web page extolled the virtues of Excelsior widgets, and explained why Excelsior widgets were better than whiz widgets. The web site made it clear that whiz widgets were manufactured and sold by another company that was unrelated to Y Co. Visitors to the web page could place orders for Excelsior widgets by filling out an electronic form that was provided on the web page, and providing a credit card number. X Co. is unhappy about this. What is the best argument X can make that Y's actions constitute *trademark infringement*? Is X Co. likely to have *any other* cause of action against Y Co.? _____

73. X runs a flower shop in downtown San Francisco, with the trade name and mark "Flower Fracas." Y opened a flower shop in downtown Oakland (which is directly across the Bay from San Francisco) under the trade name and mark "Blossom Brawl." At the time he opened his shop, Y had no knowledge of X's preexisting business. X advertises in the San Francisco Chronicle, and does no business in Oakland. Y only advertises in the Oakland Tribune, and does no business in San Francisco. Would X likely have a cause of action for infringement against Y? _____

74. The Rojas Corp., a Mexican Company, owns the mark "Rojas," which it applies to the fine leather goods it produces. Carlos Martinez is the sole shareholder of the Rojas Corp. In 1997, Martinez created a corporation in Delaware, under Delaware law, which he named Segundo Corp. Martinez took ownership of all the Segundo Corp. shares. The Segundo Corp. entered into an agreement with the Rojas Corp. to become the exclusive distributor of Rojas leather goods in the United States. As a part of the transaction, Segundo Corp. paid Rojas Corp. $100,000 for the exclusive rights to the Rojas mark in the United States, which Rojas Corp. duly assigned over to Segundo. Segundo Corp. began buying leather goods from Rojas and reselling them in the United States under the Rojas mark. It registered the Rojas mark on the Lanham Act Principal Register.

The Rojas Corp. sells its goods, with the Rojas mark, in a number of other countries. Recently, Gregor Ivanov, an international businessman, bought a large shipment of Rojas

Corp.'s leather goods in Chile and shipped them to the United States for resale. The goods bear the Rojas mark, which was placed on them at the Rojas factory in Mexico. Segundo Corp., which was tipped off about the shipment, wishes to bring suit against Ivanov to prevent the importation of the leather goods into the United States, or to prevent their resale in the United States. Is it likely to succeed? _____

75. CalPacific sells sweet pickles, with no preservatives, in glass jars under the "Zip" mark. Because the pickles have no preservatives, they need to be kept refrigerated. CalPacific places a notice to that effect on its labels, always delivers wholesale shipments of the pickles in boxes bearing a warning to "refrigerate," and delivers the boxes in refrigerated trucks.

In the middle of summer, 2011, Albertini's, a large grocery store chain, ordered a shipment of 500 boxes of "Zip" pickles, and had them delivered to its Dallas warehouse, planning to divide the boxes up and send them to the 20 retail Albertini's stores in the Dallas area. Due to a mix-up in the paperwork, Albertini's employees let the boxes of Zip pickles stand on the floor of the hot warehouse (unrefrigerated) for several days before shipping them to the retail stores. Several consumers who subsequently bought the pickles from Albertini's stores wrote to CalPacific complaining that the Zip pickles "tasted disgusting." One of them claimed to have "felt sick" after eating eight of the pickles. Does CalPacific have a viable cause of action for trademark infringement against Albertini's? _____

76. Plaintiff is a European Corporation that operates a chain of high-end restaurants under the name "Bon Bon." The chain consists of five restaurants, located in Paris, London, Madrid, Milan, and Geneva. Plaintiff advertises its restaurants in a number of American magazines and travel guides, and estimates that approximately 5-7 percent of its customers are American tourists. The defendant, which has no relationship with the plaintiff, has just opened a high-end restaurant in New York under the name "Bon Bon." Plaintiff has brought suit to enjoin defendant's use of "Bon Bon" pursuant to Lanham Act §43(a). Assuming that the defendant's use creates a likelihood of consumer confusion about the affiliation of the New York restaurant, is plaintiff likely to succeed? Why or why not? _____

77. The hip musical group "Outtathisworld" wrote and recorded a song entitled "Home from the Star Wars," which has become a top hit. The owner of the "Star Wars" mark for movies, books, video games, and related merchandise has filed suit to enjoin the use, alleging trademark infringement and dilution claims. What is the appropriate standard for evaluating each of these claims? On what ground would the defendant be most likely to prevail? _____

78. Acme Muffler Company seeks to register the unusual, low-pitched "purring" sound that running cars make when equipped with an Acme muffler. The muffler has been on the market for approximately ten years, and is quite popular with drag racing enthusiasts and young men who like to "enhance" their cars. Should the P.T.O. register it? _____

79. John Mallenkrodt seeks to register the word "Mallenkrodt," enclosed in a red circle, as a mark for woven floor mats particularly designed and cut to fit in a Ford Taurus station wagon. Should the P.T.O. accept it for registration? _____

80. Novelties, Inc. has filed an intent-to-use application to register the word "Superior" for its new line of kitchen sponges. Should the P.T.O. allow the application?

_____

81. Law, Inc., applies to register the words "Mexican Law Summaries" and "Canadian Law Summaries" on the Principal Register as marks for books summarizing Mexican law and Canadian Law for American lawyers whose practice would be improved by a basic understanding of the law of these countries. This is a use-based application that demonstrates use for over 10 years and heavy advertising in journals and newspapers directed to lawyers. Should the P.T.O. register these marks? _____

CHAPTER 7

UNFAIR COMPETITION

82. Jacques, a French actor who acted in a supporting role in a French-made movie, learns that the American Company that has obtained the American rights in the movie is distributing the movie on videotape. The videotape credits state that Francois, rather than Jacques, acted in the supporting role. Jacques has asked that the mistake be rectified, but the American Company has refused. Please evaluate whether Jacques might have a cause of action against American Company under the Lanham Act, and explain your answer. _____

83. The Zenpok Corporation manufactures, sells, and services widgets nationwide under the registered mark "Superior." It advertises its widgets heavily, often including the name "Zenpok Corp." in the text of the advertisement. Zenpok also places its name, in small type, at the bottom of its widgets' label. John Jones incorporates a widget repair service under the name Zenpok-Jones, Inc., and begins conducting business under that trade name. Does Zenpok Corp. have a cause of action against Jones? _____

84. Twinkle, Inc., a manufacturer of perfume, advertised that its perfume scent would last for over 48 hours after application to the skin. In fact, no perfume scent will be noticeable more than 24 hours after application. Eau de Waft, Inc., also a manufacturer of perfume, wishes to sue Twinkle for false advertising. What, if any, problems is it likely to encounter? _____

85. Purchasers' Confederation, a nationwide consumer interest group, tests products and publishes the test results in its magazine, entitled "Purchasers' Reports." Purchasers' tested plaintiff's stereo speakers and later published an article falsely stating that individual instruments heard through the plaintiff's speakers "tended to wander about the room." Assuming that this statement is false and disparaging to plaintiff's stereo speakers, would plaintiff have a cause of action under Lanham Act §43(a)? _____

86. Joe and Schmoe own and operate competing carpet installation services. One day Joe tells a customer that he can install carpets "as fast as you can say jackrabbit." In fact, it would take Joe at least an hour to install carpet even in a single small room. Does Schmoe have a cause of action for false advertising against Joe under Lanham Act §43(a)? _____

87. Carla sets up a web site entitled "What's Up in the Entertainment World?" On it, she provides a list of currently popular movie stars, along with a photograph of each star. Next to each star's name and photograph, Carla places a link to another web site that posts a current magazine or newspaper story about the particular star. Her link takes users directly to the story on the other web site, bypassing the other web site's home page (this is known as a "deep link"). When viewers exercise one of the links they see the story in a "frame." The frame divides the viewer's computer screen into sections, one of which shows the story, another of which shows a banner advertisement sold by Carla to an advertiser, and the last of which provides a table of contents and links to other parts of Carla's web site.

Operators of the web sites to which Carla links include a number of entertainment magazines and newspapers, which provide current stories to persons visiting their web sites free of charge. Their hope is that visitors will decide to subscribe to their publications, and they provide the means to do so online. They are displeased with Carla's links, which bypass their subscription information, and would like to prohibit them. Would they have a cause of action for misappropriation? _____

CHAPTER 8

THE RIGHT OF PUBLICITY

88. The Acme Soap Company places a recognizable image of Demi Moore in a low-cut dress as back-ground on the label of its Acme Beauty Bar, without Moore's authorization. The Acme mark and other printed information is superimposed over the image. Moore's name is not used. Nor is any reference made to her in the printed material on the label. Does Moore have a cause of action for violation of her publicity rights? _____

89. The creators of the weekly comedy program "Friday Night Live" write and perform a skit that satirizes three prominent politicians. The actors performing the skit wear clothes similar to those customarily worn by the politicians, and affect voices, speaking mannerisms, and points of view that effectively bring the politicians to viewers' minds. The comedy show is produced and aired for profit on commercial television stations. (Most of the profits are made by selling advertisements.) Do the three politicians have a cause of action for violation of their publicity rights? _____

CHAPTER 9

THE RELATIONSHIP BETWEEN STATE AND FEDERAL LAW

Jeff Jones is a famous country-western singer (known affectionately to his fans as "JJ"), who is known for his deep, husky, gravelly voice, which he accompanies with a banjo. JJ has had a number of hits over the years, but he is probably best known for his rendition of "Lonely, Lonely Me." Although JJ did not compose this song and does not own copyright in it, the public associates the song with him.

General Products, Inc., which manufactures and sells a line of pickup trucks, wanted to hire JJ to sing in an advertisement for its trucks, but JJ refused to do so. Undaunted, General Products' advertising agency hired David Dursley, a "JJ sound-alike" to sing in the ad, and Bill Brown, a professional banjo player, to accompany him. The advertising agency obtained a license to perform "Lonely, Lonely Me" from the owner of copyright in that song, and instructed David and Bill to perform the song in a manner that sounded as much like JJ's famous rendition as possible. The resulting ad features video shots of a General Products truck traveling up a mountain and through a stream, far from civilization, with audio of David and Bill's performance in the background. The ad does not mention JJ's name or show his image, or say anything expressly to suggest that JJ is singing in the background. Nor does it show or say anything to suggest that he is not.
JJ brings suit to enjoin any further showing of the ad and for damages. Based on these facts, please answer the following questions.

90. JJ's complaint sets forth a state unfair competition (passing off) claim alleging that the public associates him with the song "Lonely, Lonely Me." He further alleges that by playing the song in its advertisement, General Products and its advertising agency falsely represent that JJ endorses or is affiliated with General Products' pickup trucks, leading to a likelihood of consumer confusion. General Products' answer to the complaint alleges that the complaint is preempted under Copyright Act §301 and the Supremacy Clause. How should the court rule on the preemption issue? _____

91. JJ's complaint also sets forth a Lanham Act §43(a) claim to the same effect as the state unfair competition claim set forth above. General Products answers that this claim is preempted under both Copyright Act §301 and the Supremacy Clause. How should the court rule on the preemption issue? _____

92. JJ's complaint also sets forth a state right of publicity claim alleging that by using a singer who imitated Boss's distinctive voice and singing style, and a banjo accompaniment that imitates JJ's distinctive playing style, General Products and its advertising agency made an unauthorized use of JJ's identity for commercial purposes. General Products answers that this claim is preempted under Copyright Act §301. How should the court rule on the preemption issue? _____

93. Finally, JJ's complaint alleges that he has developed an innovative method of playing the banjo with quick, jerky motions with a bamboo pick, which produces a particularly distinctive, unusual "twang." Through the years he has developed a strong public demand for this distinctive form of playing through his own investment of effort and talent. David's use of this unique method of playing constitutes an actionable misappropriation of JJ's innovation and resulting business good will. General Products' answer to the complaint again defends that this claim is preempted under both Copyright Act §301 and the Supremacy Clause. How should the court rule on the preemption issue? _____

SAMPLE ANSWERS TO SHORT-ANSWER QUESTIONS

1. Intellectual property laws generally try to tailor the property rights they convey, providing only those rights that are deemed necessary to induce creators to engage in the creative process. For example, most intellectual property rights are granted for a limited duration. When the term of the rights has expired, the public and competitors may have full access to the creation. Moreover, intellectual property rights often are limited in their scope so that some public uses of creations are permitted, even while the rights are in effect. In addition, some intellectual property doctrines are designed to encourage disclosure of the creations to the public so that the public may benefit from the knowledge underlying or conveyed by the creations, and use that knowledge for other, non-infringing purposes.

2. There is a strong public policy against interfering with the ability of employees to move to new employment within their field. This policy is likely to lead a court to find against Acme, under the facts of this case.

   Wong has a duty (both by virtue of his agency relationship with his employer and by virtue of the nondisclosure agreement he signed) not to use or disclose the trade secret formula without Acme's permission. However, he has not signed a covenant not to compete with Acme. (Even if he had, it is not clear that it would be enforceable because such agreements are disfavored by the law.) Moreover, there is nothing in the facts to suggest that Wong is about to disclose the secret in violation of this duty.

   Acme might argue that it has a right to enjoin Wong under the doctrine of inevitable disclosure. The theory is that in the position he has accepted, it is inevitable that Wong will use the secret information. However, this case can be distinguished from *Pepsico, Inc. v. Redmond, 54 F.3d 1262 (7th Cir. 1995),* which adopted and applied the doctrine of inevitable disclosure. Unlike the marketing strategies in *Pepsico,* the Acme secret formula can be readily "compartmentalized." Wong probably can avoid using it in the course of performing his new duties. Moreover, unlike in the *Pepsico* case, there are no facts here to suggest that either Wong or his new employer are untrustworthy or have schemed to acquire the secret formula. Finally, unlike in *Pepsico,* an injunction against Wong would probably have to be a long-term injunction, since the trade secret at issue — the formula — will not dissipate in value and importance in a matter of months.

   Under these circumstances the rather extreme remedy of enjoining Wong from taking the job is unwarranted, as a matter of policy. It would damage his career and would be contrary to the public interest in allowing him free movement. The risk of harm to Acme does not warrant this. Wong could be enjoined from disclosing or using the trade secret method while employed by Bennett Co. if there were grounds to believe that he plans to do so.

3. **(a)** A good argument exists that Ace is liable for trade secret misappropriation. Both the Restatement of Torts §757 and the Uniform Trade Secrets Act prohibit use or disclosure of trade secret information obtained through improper means. If Alice's means of obtaining the information were improper, then Ace will be liable for subsequent use of

the information because it clearly had notice that the information was secret and that Alice had obtained it through improper means.

In *E.I. DuPont DeNemours & Co. v. Christopher, 431 F.2d 1012 (5th Cir. 1970), cert. denied, 400 U.S. 424 (1971)*, the court held that "improper means" encompasses not only conduct that is independently illegal, but also conduct that is below generally accepted standards of commercial morality. The court suggested that when the plaintiff is taking reasonable measures to protect the information, the defendant has a duty not to take the information under circumstances that permit it to avoid making the same kind of investment as the plaintiff did in developing it. The court also suggested that it is below generally accepted standards of commercial morality to take advantage of a temporary vulnerability on the plaintiff's part that the plaintiff could not reasonably have avoided. Finally, it is certainly below generally accepted standards of commercial morality to deliberately induce another's breach of duty to his employer, as Alice did in this case when she intentionally got Blow drunk in order to question him. Alice could also be characterized as taking advantage of a temporary vulnerability, as in the *DuPont* case. (Indeed, Alice *created* the vulnerability — the engineer's drunkenness — and then capitalized on it.) Certainly Alice's actions allowed Brown Co. to obtain the information without making the kind of investment that Ace Co. made.

It appears that Brown Co. had warned its engineers not to socialize with competitors' employees at conferences, presumably to avoid the very mishap that occurred in this case. It thus had taken reasonable measures to protect the information. It would be unreasonable to require Brown Co. to take further measures, such as sending bodyguards with its engineers, or prohibiting the engineers from participating in what may be highly useful conferences.

An alternative approach would be to argue that Alice (and through Alice, Ace) received the trade secret information with notice that it was a trade secret and that it was being disclosed in breach of Blow's duty to Brown Co. Under both the Restatement of Torts and the Uniform Trade Secrets Act, this would impose a duty on Alice (and on Ace because it knew what Alice knew) not to disclose or use Brown Co.'s secret information without Brown's permission. As a Brown employee, Blow clearly had a duty not to disclose Brown's trade secrets. Alice was aware of the engineer's status and was likely to know, or at least have inquiry notice, that the information being divulged was trade secret. After all, Alice deliberately set out to obtain confidential information and knew enough about the business to ask the right questions.

(b) Ace should not be liable for trade secret misappropriation under these facts. The courts have made it clear that obtaining trade secret information through reverse engineering a competitor's finished, publicly available product does not constitute improper conduct.

(c) Ace may be liable. Alice was on notice of the trade secret status of the information (the supervisor notified her that it was "confidential") and asked to hear it. Under these circumstances, in many jurisdictions, she would be deemed impliedly to consent to the supervisor's terms that the information be kept in confidence. This would give rise to an implied contractual duty of confidence that Alice breached in revealing the information to Ace. Because Ace (presumably) had notice of the confidential status of the information, and that Alice was breaching her duty of confidence, Ace incurred its own duty to Brown, which it breached when it used the information to develop a competing product.

4. **Acme v. X:** The first issue is whether the program (and its algorithms) enjoy trade secret status. Clearly the program provides commercial, competitive value to Acme. X might argue, however, that the program is not substantially secret because Acme sold the program to the general public. This argument should be rejected because Acme only provided the program to the public in unreadable object code form, and it appears that Acme took precautions to keep the human-readable source code secure. Acme's actions are comparable to those of a company that makes a product through use of a secret formula and then sells the product to the general public. Assuming that the product does not itself reveal the formula, the act of selling the product does not destroy the trade secrecy of the process. In the present case it is possible for persons possessing the object code to reverse engineer it back into source code and thus learn the program's secrets, but this is a difficult, time-consuming task that only programming experts are able to accomplish with special decompilation programs. It has long been understood that the ability to reverse engineer a product's secret formula by subjecting the product to complex scientific experimentation using sophisticated, expensive laboratory equipment does not destroy the trade secret status of the formula. Likewise, the ability to reverse engineer a computer program's object code should not, in itself, destroy the trade secret status of the software and its algorithms.

However, even though the software algorithms are protectable trade secrets, X acquired them through reverse engineering of a lawfully purchased copy. This generally is considered "proper means" and does not constitute trade secret misappropriation. Acme will argue that the shrink-wrap license imposed an express contractual duty of confidentiality on X, which he breached by engaging in the reverse engineering and disclosure, in violation of the shrink-wrap prohibitions. Whether Acme could prevail with this argument depends on whether the shrink-wrap license is enforceable. There is mixed case authority on this point. X might challenge the shrink-wrap license under contract principles, arguing that the restrictions are attempts to change the terms of his purchase transaction after the transaction has been completed (X never learned of the restrictions until after he paid his money and Amazon.com sent the software), and thus are unsupported by consideration. He might also argue that enforcement of the terms would be unconscionable. On another track, Y might argue that enforcement of state contract law in this case is preempted by federal patent law (enforcing universal prohibitions against reverse engineering frustrates Congress's purpose in enacting the patent law, and relegating unpatented inventions to the public domains). Only if the shrink-wrap is enforceable could Acme prevail against X since X had no other relationship with Acme that would impose a duty of confidence to Acme.

Acme v. Y: Y could only be liable for misappropriation of the program trade secrets if X disclosed them in breach of a duty of confidentiality (successfully imposed by the shrink-wrap license) and Y had notice that the information was trade secret and was being disclosed in breach of a duty of confidence. There are insufficient facts to determine whether X had the requisite notice.

Even if it were found that X breached an enforceable duty of confidentiality and that Y had the requisite notice, Y might argue that the information was no longer a trade secret when he acquired and used it—rather, the earlier trade secret status was lost when X made the algorithms available to the general public on the web.

5. The rules for determining ownership of an invention (as between employer and employee) are the same, regardless of whether the invention is to be protected as a trade secret or patented.

Ownership under the common law: Under the common law, if the inventor (here, Appleton) was hired or directed especially to create inventions of the type involved, and the employer placed time and resources at the employee's disposal for that purpose, then an implied agreement will be found between the parties that any inventions developed by the employee in connection with this work will belong to the employer. If, on the other hand, the employee was not hired or directed to create inventions of the type involved, but nonetheless creates an invention during the course of employment, or the employer placed no special resources at the employee's disposal for development of the invention, the employee will be deemed the owner of the invention. However, if the employee used the employer's work time, facilities, or supplies to develop the trade secret, then the employer will likely have a shop right in it.

Here, Appleton was hired to make medical-testing-related inventions generally, but he was not hired or expressly assigned to work on the AIDS testing invention involved here. Whether MegaLabs gave him resources for that purpose, at least initially, is arguable. Appleton could argue that MegaLabs provided few resources in the beginning, and only authorized him to spend half his time on the project after he had made the basic invention and was testing it. This would suggest that Appleton should be deemed the owner. On the other hand, MegaLabs might argue that by virtue of the Joint Research Agreement, Cohen's failed experiment (which was itself a trade secret) belonged to it, and that in using the failed experiment as a starting point, Appleton used valuable MegaLabs trade secrets in producing his own test. (Indeed, MegaLabs might go further to argue that since Appleton "substantially derived" his test from Cohen's test, and MegaLabs owned Cohen's test, Appleton could not use or disclose his own test without misappropriating the Cohen test, in violation of MegaLabs' ownership rights.)

The effect of the nondisclosure agreement: If the court found ownership in Appleton, it would then be necessary to consider the effect of the employee nondisclosure agreement Appleton signed. As a general matter, an employee nondisclosure agreement only prohibits the employee from disclosing or using trade secrets that the common law or some other express contractual provision would allocate to the employer. However, the language of the purported "nondisclosure" agreement in this case is so broad that it might be construed to prohibit disclosure of trade secret information that the common law would otherwise allocate to Appleton. (The agreement provides that Appleton will not disclose any confidential information concerning the business affairs of MegaLabs "developed by" Appleton.) Broad construction of this contractual language would have the practical effect of a contractual advance assignment of all trade secrets created by Appleton to MegaLabs. This construction might be criticized as contrary to public policy, however. Courts generally prefer to construe employee nondisclosure, assignment, and non-competition agreements narrowly because all three may impair the employee's opportunities to move to new employment and/or set up independent, competing businesses. Thus, a court might prefer to adopt a narrower construction of the contractual language, so that it creates a contractual duty not to disclose or use confidential experimental and research information developed by Appleton *and to which the common law would assign ownership rights to MegaLabs.*

To recap, a liberal construction of the nondisclosure agreement language would possibly assign rights in the AIDS test to MegaLabs even though the common law would otherwise allocate ownership to Appleton. A narrower, more conservative construction of the agreement would find that the agreement only bound Appleton to avoid disclosing information that MegaLabs otherwise would own under the common law rule. In the latter case, Appleton would continue to own the AIDS invention (although MegaLabs might possess a shop right to practice the test since Appleton used its resources in developing the test).

A "joint invention" argument: Another approach might be to argue that the AIDS test was jointly invented by Appleton and Cohen (Cohen having contributed to the inventive concept) and thus, by virtue of the Joint Research Agreement, MegaLabs owns a half interest in the invention as Cohen's assignee.)**Final considerations: If MegaLabs were the owner.** If the court were to find either that the common law allocates ownership to MegaLabs or that the nondisclosure agreement assigns Appleton's common law rights to MegaLabs, Appleton would be prevented from disclosing or using the AIDS test at least as long as it remains a trade secret or confidential. (Note that the facts say that the AIDS test was retained in secrecy throughout, and it undoubtedly gave its owner a competitive advantage. Thus, it probably qualified as a trade secret.) However, once the patent application (or the final issued patent) was published by the Patent Office the secret would be generally disclosed to the public, and Appleton could argue that he is no longer bound to keep the test in confidence. He might, however, face a patent infringement suit if he tried to use the test.

6. The use of antihistamines to treat high blood pressure falls into the "process" (or "method") category of patentable subject matter. Patent Act §100(b) specifies that the term process "includes a new use of a known process, machine, manufacture, composition of matter, or material." While antihistamines are "known," the method of taking one tablet every other day to control blood pressure is a new use of the known material and is patentable as such.

7. Jim could not obtain a utility patent for the plant itself, because it is a natural phenomenon. Utility patents can be granted only for things that are "man-made." A genetically engineered plant can be deemed man-made because man has given it characteristics it would not have had in nature. However, this plant, though never before known, developed in nature.

   Jim could not obtain a plant patent for the plant because (so far as we know) he has not asexually reproduced it, and it is not novel (to be novel, it must not have existed in nature in a form capable of reproducing its novel characteristics). Moreover, the Plant Patent Act provides patents only for cultivated plants, not for plants found in an uncultivated state.

   Note that Jim might get a utility patent for a process of using the plant to produce the red dye or for an isolated and purified version of the chemical compound that dyes things red.

8. Since Ginger's application would be filed before the effective date of the Leahy-Smith America Invents Act (for present purposes, March 16, 2013), we must apply the law as it existed prior to that Act. Under that law, Ginger has two potential novelty problems. First, there is a possibility that the invention was "known" in the United States prior to Ginger's

invention date, under Patent Act §102(a). Professors Brown and Jones, the first inventors, kept their invention to themselves until August 2008, when they sent their draft article to Professor Smith. While there is relatively little case law to indicate what it takes to make an invention "known" within the meaning of §102(a), it appears that the invention must be (1) fully disclosed; and (2) the disclosure must be available to the public. Assuming that the draft paper "fully discloses" the new widget, one could argue that providing the draft to Professor Smith made it available to the public. There is nothing to suggest that Professor Smith was subject to any duty of confidentiality that would prohibit him from discussing the content of the paper with others. Because Smith is an expert in the field, one might reason that he is in a good position to further disseminate and possibly use the new widget, thus bringing the benefit of it to the public. (It is less likely that sending the draft to Professor Smith constituted a "printed publication" for purposes of §102(a): Generally, before finding a printed publication, courts require that a written disclosure be accessible to an interested American exercising reasonable diligence to find it. In this case, to constitute a printed publication, the paper would probably have to be posted and properly indexed in a library collection, or disseminated to a larger group of people in the field—perhaps at a conference. It is likely that the standard for finding that an invention is "known" is lower than the standard for finding that the invention is the subject of a "printed publication.")

If the disclosure to Professor Smith makes the new widget "known in the U.S." in August 2008, then Ginger's invention in October 2008 will be disqualified under §102(a). Note that the subsequent journal publication (in January 2009) would not affect the novelty of Ginger's invention because it occurred after her invention date. It would, however, serve as a "printed publication" that triggers the §102(b) statute of limitations, requiring Ginger to file a patent application within one year of the paper's publication date.

Ginger's second (and probably more serious) novelty problem arises under Patent Act §102(g), which prohibits a patent if the applicant's invention had already been made in the United States and not abandoned, suppressed, or concealed at the time of the applicant's invention. Here, Professors Brown and Jones clearly made the invention prior to Ginger, in the United States. The only issue is whether they had abandoned, suppressed, or concealed it. Case law suggests that to avoid a finding of abandonment, suppression, or concealment, the first inventor must work diligently to bring the benefit of his invention to the public. Here, it appears that Brown and Jones did this. Even though they decided not to pursue a patent or commercialize their invention, they worked diligently to produce and publish a paper that would fully disclose and make the benefit of the invention available to the public. Thus, they probably did not abandon, suppress, or conceal the invention, and §102(g) would bar Ginger from obtaining a patent.

9. Patent Act §102(e) provides that Brown and Jones's application for patent must be denied if their invention was disclosed in a U.S. patent application that was pending at the time of their invention and later published or granted. Accordingly, Dr. Gupta's earlier invention can disqualify Professors Brown and Jones under Patent Act §102(e) if his U.S. application is subsequently published or granted. Even though the publication or patent issuance may occur after Brown and Jones's invention date, the publication or granting of Dr. Gupta's application makes the information disclosed in it "prior art" as of Gupta's application date, which is prior to Brown and Jones's invention date.

Note that Dr. Gupta's earlier invention may prevent Brown and Jones from obtaining a patent under §102(g), as well, if Gupta is able to establish his earlier invention date in India in an interference proceeding. It is clear that he has not abandoned, suppressed, or concealed the invention.

10. Since the application would be filed after March 16, 2013, we apply Patent Act §102 *as amended* by the Leahy-Smith America Invents Act. Under the amended §102, Levine's application would not be deemed anticipated. It does not matter that Levine was not the first to invent the widget — it matters that he was the first to apply for a patent. Assuming that amended §102(b)(1)(A) applies to disclosures via public use, Levine's public use in Japan should not disqualify him from getting a patent, because that public use was made by Levine himself less than a year before his effective filing date. Under the amended §102, the geographic location of the public use is irrelevant. Martinez's disclosure in February 2015 will not disqualify Levine because Levine had already disclosed the invention to the public himself at that time, as provided by amended §102(b)((1)(B).

If Martinez had filed for a U.S. patent in November 2015 instead of Levine, he would not be entitled to a patent. Again, assuming that public use constitutes a disclosure for purposes of amended Patent Act §102(b)(1), Levine's December 2014 disclosure in Tokyo would serve as prior art to disqualify Martinez.

11. Since Soft's application will be filed prior to March 16, 2013, the Leahy-Smith America Invents Act amendments will not apply. One possible objection to a patent for the program would be that a patent is barred under Patent Act §102(b), which provides that a patent must be denied if the invention was on sale in the United States more than a year before the patent application was filed. In *Pfaff v. Wells Electronics, Inc., 525 U.S. 55 (1998),* the Supreme Court held that an invention will be on sale if it is "ready for patenting" and is the subject of a commercial offer for sale. It will be ready for patenting if it has been described in sufficient detail to enable a person with ordinary skill in the art to make it.

Under this standard it appears that the new program was "ready for patenting" more than a year before Soft's application date. Chu's memo, dated May 16, 2010, appears to have provided the enabling information, since Jefferson was able to create the program without further consultation.

The only other question is whether the program was the subject of a commercial offer for sale more than a year before the application date. It will have been only if the November 2010 advertisements constituted a commercial offer for sale. The Court of Appeals for the Federal Circuit has held that a commercial offer for sale must be one that would give a right to accept and form a binding contract under the Uniform Commercial Code. *Group One, Ltd. v. Hallmark Cards, Inc.*, 249 F.3d 1307 (Fed. Cir.), *cert. denied*, 534 U.S. 1127 (2002). Generally, advertisements do not rise to this level. Therefore, it is unlikely that §102(b) would apply to disqualify or invalidate the patent.

Neither the advertisements nor Chu's memo to Jefferson is likely to constitute a "printed publication" for purposes of the §102(b) statutory bar. The advertisements are not likely to be sufficiently detailed to enable a person of ordinary skill in the art to make the program. While the memo was enabling, it was not accessible to the public. The recipient was bound by a duty of confidentiality.

One other possible objection might be that the invention is a computer program or mathematical algorithm, which is an abstract idea, and thus not patentable subject matter. We would need further information to evaluate whether this particular program, as claimed, might be deemed "a particular application of an abstract idea" (rather than the abstract idea itself), and thus patentable.

12. The first part of this question calls for application of pre–Leahy-Smith America Invents Act law. The question is whether the P.T.O. should reject Y's scanner as obvious under Patent Act §103. The facts state that Y's scanner would be obvious to the person of ordinary skill in light of X's scanner. Therefore it is necessary to determine whether X's scanner would be deemed a part of the pertinent prior art as of Y's invention date, and therefore would be considered by the person of ordinary skill in making the obviousness determination. X's scanner would probably be deemed pertinent, since it is from the same field of endeavor. It will come into the prior art if it falls within the provisions of pre–Leahy-Smith Patent Act §§102(a), (e), (f), or (g). The best bet is subsection (g). X's scanner was invented in the United States prior to Y's invention date, and X has not abandoned, suppressed, or concealed it (since he has worked diligently to bring the benefit of his scanner to the public through marketing). Assuming that X's scanner is considered part of the prior art, then Y's application should be rejected pursuant to Patent Act §103 for obviousness.

   If all the events in the problem were to take place after the Leahy-Smith America Invents Act becomes effective, then the outcome would likely differ. The issue would be whether X's scanner would be part of the pertinent prior art as of Y's application date. Assuming that Y applies before X releases his scanner to market, then X's scanner probably will not be deemed a part of the prior art as set forth in amended Patent Act §102(a). There is nothing in the facts to suggest that X's scanner was patented, described in a printed publication, or in public use, on sale, or otherwise available to the public before the effective filing date of Y's application.

13. If Dr. Science applied in November 2003, his application should be denied. Under pre–Leahy Smith law, Dr. Kato's publication triggered the §102(b) statute of limitations because (in combination with the earlier prior-art method) it rendered Dr. Science's method obvious. Dr. Science had to file within a year of the article's publication, and he failed to do so.

   If Dr. Science applied in November 2002, then his patent should be allowed: He would have filed within a year of Dr. Kato's publication.

   If Dr. Kato had published his article in November 2000, then Dr. Science's application should be denied not only due to his failure to file within one year of the publication, but also because the article would have rendered his invention obvious at the time it was made. (Kato would be the prior inventor, and his publication would come into the prior art under Patent Act §102(a) in evaluating the obviousness of Dr. Science's method as of August 2001, pursuant to Patent Act §103.)

   If we added 15 years to each date in this problem, the Leahy-Smith America Invents Act amendments would apply. Obviousness would be determined as of Dr. Science's application date, which would be November 2018, or in the second part of the question, November 2017. Since Dr. Kato would publish his article in September, 2017, it would be part of the prior art on either application date. Since there is no basis for excepting Dr. Kato's printed publication disclosure from the prior art under amended Patent Act §102(b), it would be considered in evaluating the obviousness of Dr. Science's invention and would disqualify Dr. Science's application. If Dr. Kato had published his article in November 2015, it would likewise render Dr. Science's invention obvious and unpatentable.

14. The issue is whether X Co. directly infringed Y Co.'s patent within the meaning of Patent Act §271(a), which prohibits (among other things) making, using, offering to sell, and selling the patented invention in the United States during the patent term. Presumably, Y's patent is a "combination patent," meaning that the invention is in Y's unique combination of known elements, not in the individual elements themselves. According to the Supreme Court, to directly infringe such a patent, someone must combine the elements into an operable assembly (which constitutes a "making") or use, sell, offer to sell, or import the operable assembly. Merely making, using, or selling the individual parts of the patented machine, as X Co. does, in the United States, will not constitute infringement. Note that X Co. apparently did not test subassemblies of the patented machine's parts, which probably distinguishes this case from the Federal Circuit's decision in *Paper Converting Machine Co. v. Magna-Graphics Corp.*, 745 F.2d 11 (Fed. Cir. 1984).

    Since X Co. did not offer to sell or sell the kits to anyone during the patent term, it appears that nobody combined the parts into an operable assembly during the patent term, so that X Co. cannot be held liable for others' direct infringement through a contributory infringement or inducement claim. There can be no liability for contributory infringement or inducement to infringe unless the defendant's actions lead to a direct infringement by someone else.

15. Under these additional facts, X Co. would be probably liable under Patent Act §271(f), which prohibits persons (1) from supplying all or a substantial portion of the uncombined components of a patented invention from the United States in order to actively induce combination of the components outside the United States; and (2) from supplying from the United States an uncombined component of a U.S.-patented invention that is especially made or adapted for use in the invention, knowing that the component is so made or adapted and intending that it will be combined outside of the United States into the patented invention.

16. The term for Ace's patent lasts for a period of 20 years from Ace's application date. Thus, the patent endured through December 31, 2015. Under the facts in this problem, Bell Co. would be directly liable for patent infringement under Patent Act §271(a) because it made the patented invention in December 2015, before the patent expired. Since testing constitutes using the patented invention, Bell would be directly liable for using the invention, as well. (An argument might be made that Bell Co. sold the patented invention during the patent term, too, but we are given insufficient facts to determine exactly when the sale took place.)

    Lee took delivery only after the patent expired, so any use or subsequent sale he might have made will not directly infringe. However, Lee is likely to be liable for inducing Bell Co.'s direct infringement during the patent term, pursuant to Patent Act §271(b). It appears that Lee actively, intentionally solicited and assisted Bell's infringement by asking Bell to make the widget and agreeing to pay Bell for its work. Moreover, it appears from the facts that Lee had knowledge that Bell's actions would infringe the patent.

It is not a defense to patent infringement that the patentee charges too much for the patented invention.

17. The term for design patents is 14 years from the date the patent issued, as specified in Patent Act §173. Therefore Montes's importation occurred after the patent had expired (the patent only endured through December 31, 2010) and cannot constitute infringement. If the term had not expired, it appears, under the Federal Circuit's ruling in *Jazz Photo Corp. v. International Trade Commission*, 264 F.3d 1094 (Fed. Cir. 2001), *cert. denied*, 536 U.S. 950 (2002), that the importation would infringe. Even though the U.S. patentee made the first sale of the patented lamp bases, it did so outside of the United States so that the doctrine of exhaustion does not apply to them.

18. Bill would not be liable for plant patent infringement. A plant patent grants the holder the right to prevent others from asexually reproducing the patented plant or selling or using a plant produced asexually from the patented plant. Bill would not be liable because he reproduced the patented plant sexually (i.e., by seed) rather than asexually.

Cliff would not be liable because he did not asexually reproduce Alice's patented plant, but another plant that was unrelated to Alice's plant and its clones. A plant patent does not prohibit someone from discovering an independent mutation that is the same as the patented one and asexually reproducing it.

The fact that the same mutation had occurred before in nature would not invalidate Alice's patent on novelty grounds, as long as the mutated plant was unable naturally to reproduce and pass the distinctive characteristics that are the subject of the patent on to future generations. The statement that the mutation had appeared "briefly" before suggests that when the scent appeared in the wild it was not reproduced in subsequent generations.

19. Yee is not liable to the Power Co. for contributory infringement even if he sold a material component of the patented invention with the requisite knowledge. In order for Yee to be liable for contributory infringement, it must be shown that Wong, to whom he sold the material component, directly infringed the patent. However, merely taking apart two old washers and reassembling the parts—even when one of the key parts is replaced with a new one—constitutes permissible repair of an existing machine that was sold under Power Co.'s authorization, rather than the unauthorized reconstruction or "making" of a new machine, which would infringe the patent.

20. Under pre–Leahy-Smith America Invents Act law (which applies in this case), the patent goes to the first to invent, which is Liu. The first to reduce the invention to practice (Gonzales, who made a constructive reduction to practice in April 2010) is presumed to be the first to invent, but the first to conceive of the invention (Liu) can rebut that presumption and prevail if he was diligent in reducing the invention to practice from a time prior to Gonzales' conception date. Here, although Liu was not diligent in reducing to practice at first, the facts say that he worked continuously on the project starting on March 3, which is a couple of weeks prior to Gonzales's conception date. Liu gets the benefit of his resumption date. Thus, he was the first to conceive (effectively, March 3, 2010) and was diligent in reducing to practice from a time prior to Gonzales' conception date.

21. There are two separate sets of acts that should be considered. First, since Western applied for patents in both the United States and in Europe and Japan, its application was probably

published by the U.S. P.T.O. 18 months after its application date. It thus had provisional rights from that point until the patent issued in April 2012. Zoom's manufacture of 20 engines in New York occurred after the publication but before the patent issued. Thus, if Western gave Zoom actual notice of its published patent application and the claims that were published were substantially identical to the claims that ultimately issued, Western may be able to recover damages for the unauthorized manufacture, consisting of a reasonable royalty payment.

Second, after the patent issued, Zoom called a prospective purchaser in Pakistan from New York and offered to sell ten of the engines. Even if the provisional rights approach does not work, Western might recover if this call constituted an infringing "offer to sell" the patented invention, within the meaning of Patent Act §271(a). However, this claim may not succeed. While the offer occurred in the United States, the actual sale probably occurred outside of U.S. territory and thus did not itself infringe. There is some case authority (reasoning from the definition of "offer to sell" in Patent Act §271(i)) that in order to make an infringing offer to sell, the contemplated sale must also infringe. The sale in this case would not infringe because it probably occurred outside of the United States.

22. Mary is unlikely to recover. First, there is nothing in the facts to suggest that Cindy expressly or impliedly promised to pay Mary for the information if she used it. Moreover, even if she did, arguably there was no consideration to support such an agreement. Note that Mary disclosed her idea (performed her part of the alleged agreement) before Cindy had a chance to agree to pay. Mary had nothing left to give as consideration for Cindy's promise to pay. Mary should have gotten an agreement to pay before disclosing her idea.

Likewise, there is no basis for Mary to claim a right to compensation on an unjust enrichment (quasi-contract) theory. Her disclosure was entirely unsolicited. Those officiously conferring benefits on others are not entitled to demand compensation. Mary would have a much stronger claim if Cindy had solicited her idea disclosure.

Also, if the relevant jurisdiction imposes a concreteness requirement as a prerequisite to recovering for ideas, Mary might be disqualified on this ground as well. Case precedent suggests that the plaintiff's idea will not be deemed concrete unless it is reduced to some tangible form. Moreover, some cases indicate that the idea must be developed to the point that it is ready for implementation. Clearly Mary's idea, which was unsupported by any documentation, plans, or details, would not qualify.

23. Jerry has some chance of recovering, but not a great chance. He might argue that there was a contract implied in fact that Tom would pay for use of the idea. He could argue that the parties both expected and intended that there would be payment because Tom had paid a prior business consultant for similar kinds of information. Also, Jerry, as a professional business consultant, was accustomed to being paid for his business advice. Undoubtedly, the custom is for business owners to pay business consultants for advice about inventory methods. The fact that Jerry told Tom that the information was being revealed in confidence ("just between the two of us") further suggests that the parties were aware that Jerry was supplying valuable information at Tom's request, and that they intended payment. Of course, the setting in which Jerry gave the advice might undermine

Jerry's argument, suggesting that the parties were not engaged in a serious business transaction. Most professionals are accustomed to having social acquaintances ask for casual advice at cocktail parties. In most instances, those acquaintances do not anticipate receiving a bill for the advice.

Jerry might also argue that he is entitled to compensation under an unjust enrichment (contract implied in law) theory. Tom did solicit the information and receive a benefit from it. Under normal circumstances, a businessman would pay for a consultant's advice about inventory methods.

However, courts generally require that information be novel before they will imply a contract to pay for it, either in fact or in law. Here the chances are good that a court would not find the inventory method novel. First, it was not original to Jerry—he learned it from a prior client. Some courts also have required that the information be innovative. Though there are not enough facts to judge for sure, the fact that Jerry's client has been using the method for years may suggest that it is not new.

Sometimes when the plaintiff is a professional idea person, as Jerry is here, courts will skip the novelty and concreteness requirement, and treat the claim as a *quantum meruit* claim for the value of services solicited and rendered. While the inventory method may not have been original to Jerry (so that he has no property rights in it), he did perform a valuable service to Tom in bringing it to his attention. This approach probably represents Jerry's best opportunity for compensation.

24. Wanda Sue has not infringed. First, Eileen's recipe may not constitute copyrightable expression. Recipes generally consist of a list of ingredients, coupled with straightforward, highly utilitarian instructions for combining the ingredients. The language of the recipe may merge with the underlying idea that is being expressed because there are a limited number of ways effectively to express the ingredients and steps of the recipe. At most, the recipe is likely to enjoy a thin copyright that protects against "virtual identicality." (While Eileen's selection and arrangement of recipes within the book is likely to be protected, Wanda Sue did not copy selection and arrangement because she only used one recipe.)

    More importantly, *Baker v. Selden*, 101 U.S. 99 (1879), teaches that copyright never extends rights to the underlying idea or art that a literary work teaches. Here, even if Eileen enjoyed copyright in the recipe, Wanda Sue's use of the recipe to create the casserole (the underlying useful article the recipe explains) would not constitute infringement. To hold otherwise would permit copyright to be used to gain monopoly rights in things meant to be judged by the higher standards of the patent laws. The fact that Wanda Sue altered the recipe in the course of making it is irrelevant for purposes of a copyright infringement claim.

25. Brown can argue that the command codes are uncopyrightable methods of operation, under the authority of the First Circuit's opinion in *Lotus Development Corp. v. Borland International, Inc.*, 49 F.3d 807 (1st Cir. 1995), *aff'd*, 516 U.S. 233 (1996). The command codes do not describe the method of operating the machine, but constitute the actual means by which the machine is operated, like the "record" and "play" buttons on a VCR. That being the case, Brown could argue, it does not matter whether the codes contain expressive elements, such as the selection and arrangement of numbers, and the

assignment of particular numbers to categories of tasks and to represent levels of task complexity. These expressive elements should be excluded from copyright because they are part of a method of operation, as in *Lotus*.

Brown might also argue that the command codes are uncopyrightable for lack of originality. While some intellectual judgment may have gone into the decision to begin codes with a number representing the category in which the task falls, and to assign lower numbers to simple tasks and higher numbers to more complex tasks within a category, such decisions are "obvious" and "inevitable," like the decisions to list telephone subscribers alphabetically by last name in *Feist Publications, Inc. v. Rural Telephone Service Co., Inc.*, 499 U.S. 340 (1991). Moreover, as a matter of policy, the courts should not construe the copyright laws to provide a cause of action in this case because of the public's interest in a competitive marketplace. It appears that Arco's machines were the first of their kind in the marketplace, and have become the *de facto* standard. The work force is trained in the Arco codes. To change to another command code system would require users to make a considerable investment in retraining. The cost of a switch thus may serve as a barrier to competitors' entering the market for this type of machinery. If Arco is permitted to use the copyright laws to prohibit competitors from using similar command codes, this may seriously deprive the public of beneficial competition.

However, Brown cannot be sure of success. Not all jurisdictions have accepted the logic of the *Lotus* decision. Based on precedent from the Tenth Circuit, a court might apply the abstraction-filtration-comparison test and find that while the numeric sequences are part of a method of operation at a high level of abstraction, their individual expressive elements may still be protected at a lower level of abstraction. *Mitel, Inc. v. Iqtel, Inc.*, 124 F.3d 1366 (10th Cir. 1997). Moreover, while Arco cannot claim copyright in the *idea* of assigning particular numbers to represent categories of tasks or complexity, there are practically limitless combinations of numbers that can be assigned to a particular category or level of complexity, and there is no reason (from a copyright standpoint) why Brown must use the same numbers. With regard to Brown's policy argument, a court might reply that it would undercut copyright policy to penalize a copyright claimant for being the first in the market and creating a system that is so successful that it has become the standard in the field.

26. A sound recording is a category of copyrightable expression. According to Copyright Act §101, sound recordings are "works that result from the fixation of a series of musical, spoken, or other sounds, but not including the sounds accompanying a motion picture or other audiovisual work, regardless of the nature of the material objects, such as disks, tapes, or other phonorecords, in which they are embodied."

A phonorecord is the material object upon which a sound recording is fixed. Copyright Act §101 defines phonorecords as "material objects in which sounds, other than those accompanying a motion picture or other audiovisual work, are fixed by any method now known or later developed, and from which the sounds can be perceived, reproduced, or otherwise communicated, either directly or with the aid of a machine or device."

27. No. The physical and conceptual separability tests only apply to pictorial, graphic, or sculptural works that are embodied in a useful article. A useful article has an intrinsic utilitarian function that is not merely to portray the appearance of the article. The deer

form appears to have no utilitarian function other than to portray the appearance of a deer, and thus is not a useful article.

28. A chair is a useful article. Only design elements that are original, and physically or conceptually separable would be protected by copyright. Since Acme's chair is a "classic" wingback chair, it is not likely that it is any of these things. (The fabric in which the chair is upholstered might qualify if Acme created it or has acquired proprietary rights in it, but X did not copy the fabric.)

The two-dimensional annotated plans would be subject to copyright. However, the facts do not indicate that X copied the plans. Rather, he used the copy he stole to manufacture his competing chair. Using plans for a useful article to build the article itself does not infringe the copyright in the plans. See Copyright Act §113(b).

29. No. Bill's copyright in his sound recording cannot be infringed unless Charles mechanically reproduced sounds directly from Bill's recording, which he did not. An independent fixation of sounds will not infringe a sound recording copyright, no matter how similar. 17 U.S.C. §114(b).

30. Tom did not violate any of Jerry's rights in licensing Dizzy to make a movie. However, Jerry could demand that Tom share royalties payable under the license.

Tom and Jerry inherited equal shares in the copyright for Alice's original novel. The revised novel that Tom published was a derivative work to which Tom alone held copyright. However, Tom's derivative work copyright only gave him exclusive rights in the new material he added. Dizzy's movie undoubtedly uses expression from Alice's original novel, as well as the new material Tom added in his adaptation. Tom, as a co-owner of the copyright in Alice's original work, was entitled to license Dizzy to use material from the original, as well as from the derivative work. However, he must share the proceeds of the license that are attributable to use of the original work with Tom.

31. Cliff has a good cause of action. While Cliff authorized sale of a digital copy of "Homes on the Range" to Alice, the doctrine of first sale does not entitle Alice to reproduce or adapt the movie. Alice's altered 20-minute segment incorporates the copyrighted movie in a concrete or permanent form (on her computer hard drive), as required by *Lewis Galoob Toys, Inc. v. Nintendo of America, Inc.*, 964 F.2d 965 (9th Cir. 1992), *cert. denied*, 507 U.S. 985 (1993), and is substantially similar to the original movie. The only question is whether her alteration (replacing Bill's head with Brad's head) is a sufficient *change* to constitute an infringing adaptation. The case law is not clear about whether the change must constitute a "substantial variation" (such as is required to qualify for a derivative work copyright) in order to infringe. If the relevant jurisdiction did impose this requirement, then Alice might successfully argue that the change was not sufficient. Moreover, it is not clear whether Alice's acts interfered with any meaningful market opportunities Cliff Enterprises might have had.

Even if Alice's acts did not constitute an infringing adaptation, however, she clearly infringed Cliff's reproduction rights. She reproduced "Homes on the Range" when she uploaded the 20-minute segment to her web site, and she may reproduce it every time a visitor to the site downloads it to view it on his or her computer screen. (When a user downloads the segment, Alice's server creates and transmits a digital copy of it.) While an authorized sale of a digital copy of a movie may carry with it an implied license permitting the purchaser to reproduce the movie as necessary to *play it* for her own personal enjoyment, that implied license is unlikely to authorize reproduction for other purposes, such as adaptation, posting to a web site, and transmitting to downloaders.

Moreover, Alice's posting of the segment on her web site probably constitutes a distribution to the public because she is making copies available on her web site, and is transmitting copies to members of the public who visit the web site. It is important to note that the doctrine of first sale would not apply to shelter Alice's activities because the copies she is transmitting to web site visitors are not the same copy she purchased. They are new copies that she caused to be made by posting the altered segment on her web site.

Finally, Alice's posting of the segment on her web site arguably constitutes a public performance because she is essentially causing the performance to recur through a transmission "to the public," as provided in Copyright Act §101.

Even if Alice's acts in maintaining the 20-minute segment on her web site did not constitute direct infringement, her site visitors infringe by reproducing the segment without Cliff's authorization. Pursuant to *MAI Systems Corp. v. Peak Computer, Inc.*, 991 F.2d 511 (9th Cir. 1993), bringing a work into the random access memory of a computer constitutes a reproduction, and downloaders must bring the segment into their random access memories in order to view it. Alice could be indirectly liable for their direct infringement under either a contributory, a vicarious, or an inducement liability theory. First, under a contributory infringement theory, Alice has assisted the visitors to infringe (indeed, has made it possible for them to infringe by making the segment available on her web site) with actual knowledge that the visitors' downloading and reproduction of the movie segment is unauthorized by the copyright owner. Second, under a vicarious liability theory, Alice has the right to control the visitors' actions (she has the power to remove the infringing material from her web site, so that visitors cannot infringe by downloading it) and stands to gain a direct financial benefit from their infringement (under *Fonovisa, Inc. v. Cherry Auction, Inc.*, 76 F.3d 259 (9th Cir. 1996), the infringing material on her site constitutes a "draw" for visitors, and the more visitors she gets, the higher her advertising revenues). Finally, Alice might be liable for inducing the visitors' infringement under *Metro-Goldyn-Mayer Studios, Inc. v. Grokster*, 545 U.S. 913 (2005), by knowingly and intentionally placing the infringing segment on her web site and inviting visitors to reproduce it by downloading it.

Alice would not enjoy the benefit of the safe harbor provisions that Congress enacted in the Digital Millennium Copyright Act (codified at 17 U.S.C. §512) to protect Internet service providers from liability for their users' infringement. Alice is not a passive, automated provider of services that others use to initiate infringement. She is directly, knowingly initiating and participating in the infringement and gaining a financial benefit that is directly attributable to the infringement.

Moreover, Alice is unlikely to enjoy a fair use defense. Her purpose is commercial, and her use does not appear to be overly transformative: It does not appear that she added much expressive content in replacing Bill's head with Brad's. She was not undertaking to produce a parody or other commentary about the "Homes on the Range" movie that would enrich the public, but rather to capitalize on Brad's popularity and show off her technical skills in digital manipulation. In addition, there is no apparent reason why

Alice needed to use a substantial portion (20 minutes) of Cliff's movie to do this. She could have made her own film and manipulated it. Moreover, Alice's actions could be characterized as interfering with Cliff's potential market to make or license derivative works constituting digital remakes of the copyrighted cowboy movie (if a market for such rights can be found).

32. The Sensational Bar Journal's column is likely to infringe ZBS's rights. Even though the Journal did not take any direct quotes or any visual imagery, it engaged in nonliteral infringement. The various events, scenes, and characters in the "Law School Lovelorn" program are fictitious, and their conception, selection, and arrangement into program plots constitutes copyrightable expression. Journal's reproduction of this expression, even though paraphrased, is an unauthorized reproduction (as well as an adaptation and distribution to the public). There is little doubt that the column would be deemed "substantially similar" because it reproduces all the important developments in the plot.

33. Goodreads probably is liable for infringement. While the Supreme Court indicated (in *Quality King Distributors, Inc. v. L'Anza Research International, Inc.*, 523 U.S. 135 (1998)) that the doctrine of first sale limits the importation right, the doctrine only applies to first sales made by or under the authorization of the U.S. copyright owner (and under the Ninth Circuit's decision in *Omega, S.A. v. Costco Wholesale Corp.*, 541 F.3d 982 (9th Cir. 2008), the doctrine applies only to copies made within the geographical boundaries of the United States[1]). Since U.K. Publishers, Ltd. made and sold the copies at issue in the U.K., and is not related to or authorized by Old Glory (the U.S. copyright holder) there is no argument that the first sale doctrine should apply.

34. The pastor's acts would not be excused under Copyright Act §109(c) because he projected more than one image of the work. However, they probably would be excused under §110(3), which permits display of a work in the course of services at a place of worship or other religious assembly.

35. In *Lewis Galoob Toys, Inc. v. Nintendo of America, Inc.*, 964 F.2d 965 (9th Cir. 1992), *cert. denied*, 507 U.S. 985 (1993), the Court of Appeals for the Ninth Circuit held that to infringe the adaptation right a defendant must incorporate the plaintiff's work into the alleged derivative work in a permanent or concrete manner. The court emphasized that this requirement differed from the fixation requirement.

Here it is clear that the plaintiff's work is incorporated into the alleged derivative work because the defendant integrated his own additions into the original in RAM. The only question is whether the incorporation (which only took place in the defendant's RAM) is "permanent or concrete" as required in *Galoob*.

When X downloaded Y's photo he "fixed" it in his random access memory (under the reasoning in the *MAI* decision). Thus, presumably, the altered version in RAM is also "fixed." One might argue that if the altered photo is "fixed" it should be deemed "permanent and concrete" too. Thus, while the *Galoob* court suggested that "incorporation in a permanent or concrete form" was not the same requirement as "fixation," a court might

---

[1] The U.S. Supreme Court has recently agreed to address the issue of whether the doctrine of first sale applies to copyrighted goods manufactured by or under the authority of the U.S. copyright owner abroad. *Kirtssaeng v. John Wiley & Sons*, __ U.S. __, 80 U.S.L.W. 3365 (April 16, 2012).

find fixation in RAM to be sufficiently "permanent and concrete" to satisfy the *Galoob* standard, under the facts of this case.

36. DeBartolomeo's acts constitute a public performance of the copyrighted songs, because he renders them in a place open to the public. This public performance is not excluded under any of the §110 exceptions to liability. Section 110(4) does not apply because the restaurant is a commercial enterprise and the performance augments the guests' enjoyment of the restaurant and thus provides indirect commercial advantage to DeBartolomeo. Section 110(5) does not apply because it only extends to performances by transmission, not to live performances. The fair use defense would not likely apply because (1) DeBartolomeo's purpose is commercial; (2) the songs are "at the heart of copyright protection," rather than functional or factual; (3) DeBartolomeo performs the entire song; and (4) if such unauthorized performances were regularly undertaken, they would significantly interfere with the existing market for performance licenses for the musical compositions.

37. The artist's right of integrity enables her to prevent intentional distortions, mutilations, or other modifications of the work that would be prejudicial to her honor or reputation. The right cannot be transferred, and remains with the author even after she has assigned her copyright in the work of visual art. The right of adaptation is an economic right that permits the owner to make or authorize others to make changes to the work. Because the right of adaptation may be assigned, the owner of the adaptation right may differ from the owner of the right of integrity. In such cases, the copyright owner's right of adaptation may be restricted by the author's right of integrity, to the extent that the adaptation the copyright owner undertakes would be deemed prejudicial to the author's honor or reputation.

38. Mary's posting of the digitized copy on the Internet bulletin board is likely to constitute a public display of the photograph. Mary's act is a display because she showed a copy of the photograph, by means of a device. The display is public because it is transmitted "to the public, by means of any device or process, whether the members of the public capable of receiving the display receive it in the same place or in separate places and at the same time or at different times." 17 U.S.C. §101.

This public display on the Internet bulletin board is likely to infringe, because there is nothing in the facts to suggest that it was authorized. Copyright Act §109(c) will not exempt Mary's acts because (even though her original copy was a lawful one) the digitized copy she posted was not lawfully made. Moreover, even if the digital copy was lawfully made, the §109(c) exception to the public display right is limited to displays that are direct or are made by projection of no more than one image at a time to viewers present at the place where the copy is located. When Mary posted the photograph on the bulletin board she caused it to be transmitted to persons who were not in the same location as the digital copy.

If Mary posted her original copy on the college dormitory bulletin board her display would fall under the §109(c) exception to the copyright owner's right of public display, and would not infringe. However, if she posted the unauthorized digital copy, §109(c) would not apply to shelter her from liability because the digital copy was not a copy that was lawfully made.

39. Architect has no cause of action, due to Copyright Act §120, which provides that "[t]he copyright in an architectural work that has been constructed does not include the right to

prevent the making, distributing, or public display of pictures, paintings, photographs, or other pictorial representations of the work, if the building in which the work is embodied is located in or ordinarily visible from a public place."

40. It probably did infringe copyright. Composing the list (or database) of badly dressed professors required Elbert to exercise intellectual judgment and creativity in determining and applying the appropriate criteria, giving rise to selection and arrangement expression. While the copyright in such a list is likely to be thin, Newspaper engaged in a "bodily appropriation of expression," when it reproduced the list in its entirety, thereby meeting the higher than normal standard for infringement of works covered by thin copyright.

41. Because Y's work qualifies for protection under the Architectural Works Copyright Protection Act, it can be protected as a "work of architecture." A work of architecture is protected from copying regardless of the physical format from which it was copied. (Note that if pre-AWCPA law were applied, the plans would be protected as a graphic work, and it would likely not constitute infringement for X to build a building (a useful article) through use of the copyrighted plans.) Assuming that Y's work of architecture is original, X's unauthorized copying is likely to infringe Y's rights, since X's building seems to be an exact duplication of Y's design.

42. Fred may be liable under the anti-circumvention provisions enacted in the Digital Millennium Copyright Act. The Act prohibits the "circumvention of a technological measure that effectively controls access" to a copyrighted work. 17 U.S.C. §1201. By making the game inaccessible without a password, and restricting the password to Patty (as arguably was done in giving Patty a "personal" password), the producer implemented a technological measure that effectively controls access to the game, which is copyrightable subject matter, and probably is copyrighted. By using Patty's "personal" password, Fred arguably circumvented that measure, in violation of the Act. However, courts are divided over whether unauthorized use of a password constitutes circumvention. Some have held that to circumvent, one must bypass the technological measure, not just pass through it without permission. Other courts have held that passing through the technological measure without permission constitutes bypassing it, and thus circumventing it. If Fred is in a jurisdiction that adopts the latter line of reasoning, he will be liable. There is no fair use defense to liability for circumventing technological measures controlling access to works.

43. Heckel and Jeckel were probably joint authors of the original paper. Joint authorship requires that both authors contribute copyrightable expression with the intent that their portions be merged into inseparable or interdependent parts of a unitary whole. In this case, Heckel and Jeckel each wrote a substantial portion of the paper (which means that they each probably contributed copyrightable expression), and the size of each participant's contribution, coupled with the nature of the work (a single scholarly paper describing research they had jointly done) provides circumstantial evidence that the parties intended to merge their portions into a unitary, jointly owned whole. The only evidence suggesting otherwise is the fact that Heckel left Jeckel's name off the paper when he later presented it at a conference. Presumably, each of them had equal control over the creation and contents of the paper.

Assuming that Heckel and Jeckel were joint authors, both had the right to exploit the paper independently, subject only to the obligation to account to the other for any profits made through exploitation.

Heckel had the right to present (publicly perform) the paper, with or without Jeckel's knowledge or consent. The only issue is whether Heckel violated a right on Jeckel's part to have joint authorship attributed to him. While many countries recognize the moral right of attribution in connection with all copyrighted works, the United States only provides an express right of attribution for works of visual art. Thus, the Copyright Act would provide Jeckel no relief. He might consider avenues of legal relief outside of the Copyright Act.

Heckel had a right to revise (adapt) the paper with or without Jeckel's knowledge or consent. Because Heckel was the sole author of the revisions, he was the sole owner of copyright in the resulting derivative work (assuming that the revisions constituted a "substantial variation" from the original and thus qualified for copyright as an adaptation), and he had the exclusive right to reproduce it and distribute it to the public. Accordingly, unless Jeckel's acts can be justified as a fair use, they will infringe. A fair use defense seems unlikely because Jeckel's actions seem to undermine Heckel's interest in first publication and may fully satisfy demand for the paper. It should also be noted that Jeckel's use is not a "productive" one (he did not further enlarge on Heckel's work), and Jeckel copied the whole work. While Jeckel's purpose was for scholarship and was not commercial, this is unlikely to outweigh the other relevant factors mentioned above.

44. David's rights against Brown: Brown's license expired in 1991, with the first term of the novel's copyright. Even though Able's grant purported to give Brown rights in the second term of the novel's copyright (and would have done so if Able had lived to renew), the grant only created a contingent interest in Brown which expired when Able failed to live to renew the copyright. David, Able's son, had the right to renew and took the renewal term free from any grants Able made during the first term of the copyright. Thus, if Brown wants to continue to exploit the play, he must negotiate a new license with David. If he publicly performs the play in the United States during the second term without doing so, he will be liable to David for infringing the copyright in the novel. (If further facts were available, it might be possible to argue that B is liable for C's infringement, discussed below, on a contributory infringement theory.)

Presumably, Cohen's movie took copyrightable expression derived from the novel, as well as the copyrightable expression that Brown added in the course of creating the play based on the novel. However, the facts indicate that Cohen only obtained a license from Brown, not from Able or David. Brown had no authority to license Cohen to adapt the novel, and his license was not binding on Able or his successors. Thus, it appears that Cohen's creation and exploitation of the movie infringed the novel's copyright during the first term, and will continue to infringe during the second term.

45. Since the poster was already protected by federal copyright on January 1, 1978, when the Copyright Act of 1976 became effective, the length of protection is determined under Copyright Act §304, as amended. That section provides that copyrights in their first term of protection on January 1, 1978 enjoy 28 years of protection, beginning on the date of publication with proper notice, the same as under the Copyright Act of 1909. However, if the copyright is renewed, it will enjoy a second term of 67 years. Here, the first term of copyright terminated on December 31, 1997 (28 years after first publication). Under post-1976 Act amendments, the copyright was automatically renewed (in favor of the proprietor, since the poster was a work for hire). Thus, the protection will last through the year 2064. The date of Allen's death is irrelevant.

46. The poster is a work for hire, which was created after the effective date of the 1976 Act. Therefore its duration is governed by Copyright Act §302(c). It will endure 95 years from the date of first publication or 120 years from the date of creation, whichever expires first. Here the copyright will expire in 2079. The date of Brown's death is irrelevant.

47. Under Copyright Act §302(a), the copyright would expire on December 31, 2055. The work appears not to be a work for hire, since the facts suggest that Allen was not an "employee" of Brown, and there is no suggestion that the requirements for making an independent contractor's work a work for hire were satisfied. Thus, Brown is the "author" and initial owner of copyright, and the proper measure is 70 years from Allen's death.

48. The copyright term ended 28 years after first publication with notice. While that first term might have been renewed, it could only be renewed by the author or the next persons in line under §304—his two children. Even though author left all his personal property to the girlfriend, the law allocates his renewal rights to his children. Since the children did not renew, the second term is forfeited. (Note that automatic renewal was not yet in effect.)

49. The license could be terminated in the year 2029, but in order to do this, owners of a majority of the interest in the termination rights must give notice of intent to terminate between two to ten years prior to that date. (The children and grandchildren would have to convince Marla to join them in the termination.) Unfortunately, even if the license is terminated, XBS will be able to continue to exploit the movie without liability for infringement. Termination will only prevent XBS from making more movies based on the play.

50. Yes, he does. Since Chang never published his diary, it was protected under common law copyright. When the Copyright Act of 1976 became effective, that copyright became a federal copyright which will endure for Chang's life plus 70 years (the year 2020) or until the end of the year 2002, whichever is longer. 17 U.S.C. §303. Depositing the diary in Archive probably does not constitute a publication of it, nor does it transfer ownership of the copyright from niece. Johnson should contact niece for a license.

51. There is precedent for holding that Buildings.com's actions should not be found to constitute direct infringement. In *Costar Group, Inc. v. Loopnet, Inc.*, 373 F.3d 544 (4th Cir. 2004), the Fourth Circuit held that even though copyright is a strict liability statute, there must be some element of volition or causation, which is lacking when a defendant's automated system is merely used to make a copy by a third party. Passive ownership and management of an electronic Internet facility on which others post infringing materials thus would not lead to direct infringement liability on the system owner's part. The system owner must engage in the act that constitutes infringement to become a direct infringer. The court also suggested that an ISP does not "fix" a copy in its system for more than a transitory duration (and thus make a copy) when it provides the kind of Internet hosting service described in the problem.

52. There are two copyrights at issue here, both presumably owned by X. The first is the copyright in the musical composition. The facts indicate that Y only took three chords of background guitar. In order to demonstrate an infringing reproduction, X would have to show not only that Y copied from his work (which he clearly did) but also that the copying resulted in a substantial similarity of copyrightable expression (judged by the average lay listener's overall, subjective response). Given the very limited nature of the material taken, the changes, and the fact that listeners would not recognize the inclusion of X's material, it is likely that a court would find Y's copying *de minimis* and non-infringing.

However, the second copyright for the sound recording might be infringed by the mere act of digital sampling, even in the absence of a substantial similarity of copyrightable expression. In *Bridgeport Music, Inc. v. Dimension Films*, 410 F.3d 792 (6th Cir. 2005), the Sixth Circuit construed the language of Copyright Act §114(b) to impose liability upon the mechanical lifting of *any* of the copyrighted recorded sounds. This is a very liberal reading of the statutory language, and contrary to the United States' long history of requiring a showing of substantial similarity of copyrightable expression (at the very least) as a prerequisite to infringement liability in all categories of copyrightable works. It is not clear whether other Circuits will follow the *Bridgeport* lead. In other circuits, the analysis regarding infringement of the sound recording copyright may entail a determination of whether the parties' recordings are substantially similar. If so, as in the case of the musical composition copyright, Y is not likely to be found liable.

53. **(a)** *Acme v. X*. Acme might argue that in reverse engineering the object code, X was circumventing an access control measure, in violation of the DMCA anti-circumvention provisions. There is little precedent to indicate whether a court would read the DMCA provisions this broadly. However, since the question specifically asks about a cause of action for copyright infringement (as opposed to a cause of action for circumvention), copyright infringement will be the focus of this answer.

A copyright infringement cause of action is unlikely to be successful. X did reproduce the whole program in order to translate it from object to source code. However, this copying is likely to be excused as a fair use. Under fair use factor number 1, X made the copy for non-commercial purposes (for study and scholarship), and he did not avoid paying the customary price: he bought the copy he reverse engineered. Moreover, his ultimate creation (the posting of the algorithms, along with his critique of Acme's methodology) was transformative and beneficial to the public. Under factors 2 and 3 of the fair use analysis, the Acme program was a highly utilitarian work, with numerous public domain elements, and it was necessary for X to copy the entire work in order to obtain the mathematical algorithms, which are in the public domain. (Mathematical algorithms are most likely equivalent to the underlying idea of the program, or a system or method of operation, which would not constitute copyrightable subject matter.) Finally, under factor 4, X did not supplant demand for the Acme program by marketing an infringing substitute for it. In the *Sega* case, the Ninth Circuit held that "where disassembly is the only way to gain access to the ideas and functional elements embodied in a copyrighted computer program, and where there is a legitimate reason for seeking such access, disassembly is a fair use of the copyrighted work, as a matter of law." This rule of law would seem to fit X's actions in creating a copy in the course of reverse engineering and excuse it. (X's posting of the algorithm would not itself infringe, because the algorithm is not copyrightable expression.)

(b) *Acme v. Y*. Acme is unlikely to have a copyright cause of action against Y since Y only copied the Acme program mathematical algorithms, which are not likely to be deemed copyrightable expression. He appears otherwise to have independently created his program.

54. Neither Friend nor Son has any rights, because Vik's renewal was not effective. The article was most likely a work for hire, since Vik wrote it in his capacity as a reporter for BigNews. In that case, under §304, BigNews (the proprietor) had the right to renew, not Vik. Since there is nothing to suggest that BigNews or its successors in interest (if any) renewed, the article probably entered the public domain in 1977.

If Vik had had the right to renew, he would have owned the second term of the copyright, and would have been free to pass his interest by will to Friend. As long as the will was valid, Son would have no claim.

55. The letter was protected by common law copyright until January 1, 1978, when the copyright was converted to federal copyright. The new federal copyright will end 70 years from Famous Poet's death, and thus is still valid. The facts do not indicate who succeeded to Famous Poet's copyright interests, but assuming that it is his Widow, then Widow would have a cause of action against Emma for unauthorized reproduction (if the statute of limitations has not run). Perhaps Widow's best bet would be to allege that University has infringed her exclusive right to distribute copies of the work to the public. Because the photocopy of the letter was unauthorized and infringing, any further distribution of it will also infringe, regardless of whether University knew that the copy it distributed was unauthorized.

Distribution to the public traditionally has entailed physically handing a copy of the work to a member of the public. Here, there is no evidence to show that the Library ever loaned the photocopy to anyone. However, the Fourth Circuit has held, in *Hotaling v. Church of Jesus Christ of Latter-Day Saints*, 118 F.3d 199 (4th Cir. 1997), that when a library makes an infringing work available to the public, properly indexed in its collection, this constitutes an infringing distribution. This is because the library has taken all the steps necessary for distribution of the copy to the public, and any member of the public could obtain it, if he or she tried. This decision was undoubtedly influenced by cases finding that posting an infringing copy of a work on an Internet web site constitutes a distribution to the public.

56. This case raises the question of the extent to which the doctrine of first sale applies to parallel imports. In *Quality King Distributors, Inc. v. L'Anza Research International, Inc.*, 523 U.S. 135 (1998), the Supreme Court construed Copyright Act §§602 and 106 to provide that the doctrine of first sale applies when the U.S. copyright owner manufactures copyrighted goods in the United States for sale abroad, and permits foreign purchasers to bring the goods back into the U.S. for resale. In this case, the U.S. copyright owner (Acme) made the first sale of the sound recordings abroad, but did not manufacture the sound recordings in the United States. The *L'Anza* decision did not address this situation. Copyright Act §109(a) provides that the doctrine of first sale applies only to copies and phonorecords "lawfully made under this title." Some lower courts (including the Ninth Circuit) have construed this language to impose a geographical limitation on the doctrine of first sale—reasoning that "lawfully made under this title" means lawfully made within the United States where the Copyright Act applies. Under this construction, Acme could assert that the phonorecords purchased in New Zealand infringe its U.S. copyright under Copyright Act §602.

However, there are alternative ways to construe §109(a). A phonorecord may be "lawfully made under this title" if it is made by the U.S. copyright owner. (The key would be that the person holding rights "under this title" made the copies and authorized their sale.) This result would be consistent with the rationale (adopted by the Third Circuit) that applying the doctrine of first sale turns not on where the first sale was made but on who made it—any first sale made by or under the authority of the U.S. copyright owner triggers the doctrine of first sale, no matter where it was made. Why should the U.S. copyright owner be able to keep goods out of the country in one instance, but not the other? Construing the doctrine of first sale to apply only to goods that the U.S. copyright owner manufactures in the United States encourages U.S. copyright owners to do their manufacturing abroad, rather than domestically.

57. The issue here is whether Long-Haul (LH) can be found liable under the DMCA, 17 U.S.C. §1201(a)(2), for trafficking in a device that circumvents a technological measure that effectively controls access to a copyrighted work (the software in the Trucking, Inc. trailer hitching device). The literal language of §1201 suggests that it could. However, circuit court decisions addressing circumvention of software access measures in consumer goods have construed these provisions narrowly to prevent the plaintiffs from using the DMCA provisions in this way. In *Lexmark International, Inc. v. Static Control Components, Inc.*, 387 F.3d 522 (6th Cir. 2004), the court held that the handshake device did not "effectively control access" to the product software (and thus did not qualify as a protectable "access control device") because other forms of access (such as simply reading or reproducing the code) were available to users. That approach probably wouldn't work here, because Trucking Inc. encrypted its software, as well as controlled access to its functionality.

However, in *Chamberlain Group, Inc. v. Skylink Technologies, Inc.*, 381 F.3d 1178 (Fed. Cir. 2004), *cert. denied*, 544 U.S. 923 (2005), the Court of Appeals for the Federal Circuit held that the DMCA only prohibits forms of circumvention that constitute a threat to rights created under the copyright law: Thus, trafficking in a circumvention device will only violate §1201(a)(2) if use of the device will infringe or facilitate infringement of a copyright. Here, it appears that it will not. All LH's software does is permit the truck owner to access the functionality of the hitching software to hitch a trailer to the truck. It does not permit the user to reproduce, adapt, publicly distribute, perform or display the copyrighted software. Moreover, the *Chamberlain* court held that when a producer sells consumer goods to a purchaser without an express restriction, the purchaser should be deemed authorized to access the software in the consumer good for purposes of using aftermarket replacement parts or accessories. The facts do not suggest that the plaintiff sold its trucks subject to an express restriction against use of the trucks with competitors' trailers. Thus, in this case, two of the factors identified by the *Chamberlain* court as necessary to a §1201(a)(2) claim are missing: 1) a lack of the copyright owner's authorization to circumvent; and 2) a showing that use of LH's device will infringe or facilitate infringement of one of the §106 rights of the copyright owner.

It is not yet clear whether other Circuits will follow the Federal Circuit's lead on this issue. If they don't, then a reasonable argument could be made that the handshake routine is a technological measure that effectively controls access to a copyrighted work (the truck hitching software): It requires that information or a process be applied, with the authority of the copyright owner, to gain access to the software. LH's trailer software "circumvents" the measure because it "avoids, bypasses, or impairs" the technological measure without the authority of the copyright owner, and the trailer software "is primarily designed or produced for the purpose of circumventing a technological measure that effectively controls access to a" copyrighted work (the truck hitching software).

58. Normally dolls would constitute copyrightable subject matter — sculptural works. However, these dolls are derivative works, based on a preexisting copyrighted work — Alex's comic strip characters. The issue is whether the dolls would qualify for their own derivative work copyright. Before derivative works can be copyrighted as such, it must appear that they constitute a substantial variation from the underlying work on which they are based (here, the comic strip characters). Courts have expressed concern in cases such as this that unless the law requires a very significant variation, the first person to make a derivative work based on a particular preexisting work may be able to chill the making of subsequent derivative works by threatening harassing infringement claims. It is difficult to gain summary judgment in copyright cases, so the costs of litigation may be high. Since the unlawful appropriation evaluation is often subjective in nature, and it may be difficult to determine wither the defendant copied from the underlying work or from the first derivative work, the outcome of infringement litigation may be hard to predict. This may lead others to decide that the risks of making their own derivative works based on the same underlying work are too great, to the general detriment of the public. Requiring a substantial variation as a prerequisite for the derivative work copyright makes it harder for the first derivative work maker to obtain copyright, and ensures that the underlying work and the first (copyrighted) derivative work are sufficiently different that it will be easier to tell what was copied from the derivative work and what was copied from the original.

In this case there are insufficient facts to determine whether Betty's dolls constitute a substantial variation from the comic strip characters, and thus are copyrightable under the standard discussed above. Betty probably tried to make the dolls as much like the comic strip characters as possible in order to capitalize on the comic strip's popularity. Moreover, the case law indicates that a mere change of medium (and changes necessitated by the new medium) often are not sufficient to constitute a substantial variation. It might be noted, too, that the Ninth Circuit, applying a similar standard, found that three-dimensional costumes based on two-dimensional cartoon characters did not constitute a substantial variation from the original and thus did not qualify for a derivative work copyright.

In addition, the Ninth Circuit has held that copyright in a derivative work that was based on a copyrighted original should only be recognized when the derivative work copyright will not interfere with the exploitation of the original copyrighted work. Under this standard, it seems clear that Betty's ability to sue Charles for infringement will interfere with Alex's ability to exploit his own copyright by licensing adaptations.

If Betty fails to demonstrate the prerequisites for a derivative work copyright, then she cannot succeed in an infringement suit against Charles.

59. The rights of the parties depend on the status of the parties' work. If the video and song together constitute a single joint work, then Janet is a joint owner along with Dave and Becky, and has the right to exploit the whole thing, subject to a duty to account to the other co-owners of copyright for the profits she makes. If the video and song together

are not a single joint work, then Janet has no right to publicly perform the images from the video, and is infringing Dave and Becky's copyright. Of course, if Janet's song was a work for hire, then she has no rights in the song, either—making her performance of the song an infringement, as well.

It seems clear that Janet's song was not a work for hire because Janet is an independent contractor, not an employee. She worked for Dave and Becky for only a short time, performing only one task. Presumably a new contract would have been required to perform additional tasks. There is nothing to suggest that Dave and Becky paid employee benefits for Janet, and Janet's form of payment is somewhat contingent in nature—not the kind of payment arrangement generally made for regular employees. There is nothing to suggest that Dave and Becky provided the location or tools for Janet to write her song (though they may have provided the studio for her to record it), or controlled the hours she worked. Writing and recording songs is not a part of Dave and Becky's regular business. Thus, it does not appear that Dave and Becky controlled the manner or means of Janet's creation of the song, and that the song is not a work for hire. Moreover, even though a contribution to a motion picture created by an independent contractor can be a work for hire if the necessary written agreement is made, there is nothing in the facts to suggest that there was such a written agreement.

The chances are pretty good that the song-video combination is not a joint work, either. A joint work is "a work prepared by two or more authors with the intention that their contributions be merged into inseparable or interdependent parts of a unitary whole." (Copyright Act §101). According to the Ninth Circuit, to be a joint author, one must contribute copyrightable expression (which Janet clearly did), and have some final say regarding what comprises the finished work as a whole. Janet would not meet this second factor. According to the Seventh and Second Circuits, all the parties have to intend for each to be a joint author. Here, that is unlikely. Dave and Becky clearly are accustomed to being the only authors of the video, and did not expect that Janet would be an equal owner. They retained the final decision-making power regarding whether Janet's material would be included. Moreover, Janet's contribution was only a relatively small part of the whole video, which is circumstantial evidence that the parties did not intend equal partnership. The fact that Dave and Becky offered to pay Janet 5 percent of the net proceeds, for only the first 10,000 videos sold, also suggests that they did not intend for Janet to be the owner of a joint work. Finally, it does not appear that the parties intended for the song to be merged into the video as an inseparable part of a unitary whole. Janet clearly understood that the song could be separately performed.

Thus, it appears that Janet is the owner of the copyright in the song, and that Dave and Becky have an implied license to reproduce and perform the song in the video. Dave and Becky are the sole owners of copyright in the video images, and Janet infringes when she publicly performs them without a license.

60. "Mr. Justice" for legal study aids: The P.T.O might object that this is primarily merely a surname, within the meaning of Lanham Act §2(e). If it is, then it cannot be registered absent a showing of secondary meaning. Generally, if a word that is a surname also has another well-known meaning in the language, it will not be deemed "primarily merely a surname." Here, however, even though the word "Justice" alone has a well-known, non-surname meaning, we must evaluate the impact of the mark in its totality. The use of the

word "Mr." preceding the word "Justice" emphasizes the surname significance of the mark, and may render the mark as a whole primarily merely a surname.

In arguing against this result, the applicant should point out that to prospective customers (law students), "Mr. Justice" primarily evokes the image of a U.S. Supreme Court justice or state judge — what many law students aspire to become. If that is the case, the mark is suggestive rather than primarily merely a surname, and can be registered without a showing of secondary meaning. It is not descriptive because it requires the exercise of imagination to get a description of the product from the mark (if you use these study aids, you will be so successful that you will become a judge!).

61. The fish mark for cat food comprised of horse meat: This mark may be rejected as deceptive under Lanham Act §2(a). First, since many cat foods contain fish it is likely that consumers would understand the outline of the fish to indicate that this product contains fish. Because it does not, it is either primarily deceptively misdescriptive (Lanham Act §2(e), in which case it can only be registered upon a showing of secondary meaning) or deceptive (Lanham Act §2(a), in which case it cannot be registered at all). In deciding whether the mark is primarily deceptively misdescriptive or deceptive, the P.T.O. must determine whether the presence of fish in the product would be a material factor in consumers' purchasing decision. Given the persnickety tastes of cats, it is likely that the presence or absence of fish would be a material consideration for their owners, the prospective purchasers. The mark should be deemed deceptive and refused registration.

62. The configuration of the clip: The appearance of the clip is product feature trade dress. While the Supreme Court's decision in *Wal-Mart Stores, Inc. v. Samara Brothers, Inc.,* 529 U.S. 205 (2000), addressed protection of unregistered trade dress under Lanham Act §43(a), the *Wal-Mart* reasoning is applicable to *registration* of product configuration trade dress as well. Thus, the clip configuration could not be deemed inherently distinctive, and could only be registered on a showing of secondary meaning.

Moreover, an argument could be made that the clip configuration is unregisterable because it is functional, under the guidelines set forth in the Supreme Court's decision in *Traffix Devices, Inc. v. Marketing Displays, Inc.,* 532 U.S. 23 (2001). Under *TrafFix*, one must first apply the *Inwood Laboratories*, 456 U.S. 844 (1982), standard for functionality: Is the feature essential to the use or purpose of the article, or does it affect the cost or quality of the article? Here, the finding might depend on the jurisdiction.

For example, under the Fifth Circuit's construction of this standard in *Eppendorf-Netheler-Hinz GMBH v. Ritter GMBH,* 289 F.3d 351 (5th Cir. 2002), *cert. denied,* 537 U.S. 1071 (2002), the configuration might be deemed functional, because it plays a significant role beyond identifying source: The configuration enables the clip to encircle and hold a pen and to secure the pen to a person's pocket top or to the top of a notebook. The availability of alternative designs to perform the same function would not be relevant. The configuration is not an arbitrary, incidental or strictly ornamental element of the product, and therefore it is functional.

Under the Federal Circuit's construction in *Valu Engineering, Inc. v. Rexnord Corp.,* 278 F.3d 1268 (Fed. Cir. 2002), however, the configuration might not be functional. According to the Federal Circuit, product features are not functional merely because they perform a useful function in a product, other than to indicate source. Rather, product feature trade dress will only be deemed functional if competitors need to copy it in order to compete effectively, because the particular design gives an advantage over alternatives. Four kinds of evidence may be relevant to this inquiry: (1) Is there an expired utility patent that discloses the utilitarian advantage of the design? (2) Does the designer tout the design's utilitarian advantages through advertising? (3) Does the design result from a comparatively simple or cheap method of manufacturing? (4) Since the effect upon competition "is really the crux of the matter," are there other alternatives available to competitors to accomplish the same function? There is no evidence to suggest that competitors need to copy the clip configuration under the first three factors. Under the fourth factor, there are numerous alternative configurations that might work as well, which suggests that the configuration is non-functional under the Federal Circuit's construction of the *Inwood Laboratories* standard.

According to the *TrafFix* decision, even if a product feature is non-functional under the *Inwood Laboratories* standard, one must still apply the *Qualitex* "aesthetic functionality" standard: Would the exclusive use of the feature "put competitors at a significant non-reputation-related disadvantage?" This is a "competitive necessity" inquiry. The presence of numerous alternatives that would give comparable aesthetic satisfaction to consumers makes it likely that the clip configuration would be non-functional under the *Qualitex* standard.

63. "Apple Sauce" for children's clothing: Marks must be evaluated in connection with the particular goods or services they identify. While "apple sauce" may be generic for an item of food made of apples, it has no direct relationship to children's clothing, and thus its use is arbitrary. Arbitrary marks are inherently distinctive and can be registered without any showing of secondary meaning. (One might argue that the mark is suggestive of children because most children are fond of apple sauce, and eat a lot of it. Still, the mark would be inherently distinctive and could be registered without a showing of secondary meaning. There is no direct description of the product to support an argument that the mark is merely descriptive.)

64. The words "Champs Elysees" as a mark for luxury automobiles manufactured in Birmingham, England: The Champs Elysees is a world-famous avenue in Paris, lined with exclusive shops, restaurants, theaters, and parks. The words have a strong geographic connotation. Thus, the question arises whether use of the mark for automobiles made elsewhere than the Champs Elysees is primarily geographically deceptively misdescriptive (Lanham Act §2(e)) or deceptive (Lanham Act §2(a)). In either case, the mark cannot be registered.

Since the mark conveys primarily and immediately a geographic connotation to a significant segment of the consuming public, one must ask whether consumers are likely to think that the use of the mark is meant to indicate the geographic origin of the product. Here, most consumers probably *would not think* that the mark was meant to indicate that the cars were *manufactured* on the Champs Elysees because the Paris avenue is not an industrial or manufacturing area. Rather, consumers are likely to understand the mark as associating the car with the general qualities of the Champs Elysees—chic, expensive, attractive, and fashionable. This would render the mark suggestive or arbitrary, and inherently distinctive. There would be no bar to registration.

If, on the other hand, consumers would think that the mark indicates that the cars are manufactured on the Champs Elysees (unlikely), then, according to the Court of Appeals for the Federal Circuit, one would have to ask whether the physical place of manufacture would be *a material factor* in consumers' purchasing decision. The Federal Circuit has indicated that the mark will not be deemed either deceptive (under Lanham Act §2(a)) or geographically deceptively misdescriptive (under Lanham Act §§2(e) and (f)) if the misdescribed geographic origin *would not be a material factor.*

65. The illustrated mark for chairs: This is a composite mark, consisting of a simplistic drawing of a chair and hearth rug, and three renditions of the word "chairs." The overall impact of a mark must be considered in evaluating its distinctiveness. Even though a composite mark contains individual elements that may be deemed generic or merely descriptive of the product, the combination of elements nonetheless may be sufficiently striking and arbitrary to make the composite mark inherently distinctive. In such cases, recognition of rights in the composite mark gives the owner no rights in the individual generic or merely descriptive elements—only in their combined effect.

In the present case, the word "chairs" is the common generic name for the product, and could not be separately recognized or protected as a mark. Likewise, the drawing of a chair could be deemed generic or (more likely) merely descriptive of the product (although an argument could be made that the drawing is sufficiently whimsical that it is inherently distinctive—cartoon characterizations of products are often found inherently distinctive, if not too realistic). Even if all of the elements are generic or descriptive, however, the use of the drawing of the chair in combination with the hearth rug and the repetitive use of the word "chairs" at arbitrary locations could be deemed inherently distinctive and registered without a showing of secondary meaning.

66. The color gold for page gilding on a leather-bound diary: The Supreme Court has held that colors can be protected as marks. *Qualitex Co. v. Jacobson Products Co., Inc.*, 514 U.S. 159 (1995). However, color alone is never considered inherently distinctive. Therefore secondary meaning would have to be demonstrated in order to register. That would be hard to do, as gold gilding is very common—even standard—in fine, leather-bound books and diaries. Indeed, gold gilding might be argued to be generic, much as grape leaves are considered generic for wine and the color yellow-green is considered generic for lemon-lime sodas: Consumers may consider it a designation of the product itself (a fine, leather-bound book), rather than a designation of a particular producer.

Moreover, the color gold for gilded pages (a product feature) would likely be deemed unregisterable because it is functional. First, under the *Inwood Laboratories* test, 456 U.S. 844 (1982), one could argue that the color gold is not merely arbitrary, incidental, or ornamental. It plays the significant role in accomplishing the purpose of a fine, leather-bound diary, which is to give consumers not just paper to write on, but a fine, opulent, quality journal to display and treasure.

Even if the gold gilding were not deemed functional under the *Inwood Laboratories* standard, it would likely be found functional under the *Qualitex* "aesthetically functional" or "competitive necessity" standard. The color gold carries a special, traditional meaning of luxury and quality to consumers that no other color can emulate. There is no alternative color that would substitute for gold in the binding of a fine leather-bound diary.

67. "Super Pickled" superimposed over a cartoon caricature of a well-known politician who was noted for heavy drinking: This composite mark would need to be evaluated in its entirety. The presence of descriptive elements, in themselves, will not necessarily render the mark "descriptive" of the product (and thus unregisterable under Lanham Act §2(e) absent a showing of secondary meaning). While the words "Super Pickled" might be descriptive of pickled onions, the combination of words and drawing may not. Together they suggest a play on the word "pickled," which, in slang, means "drunk." If that is the meaning that consumers take from the composite mark, it might be suggestive of the product (pickled onions are often placed in cocktails), but not directly descriptive, and thus would be registerable without a showing of secondary meaning. (Even if the mark were deemed primarily descriptive, the applicant may be able to demonstrate secondary meaning, given its eight years of continuous use.)

The applicant might encounter protests under §2(a), however. By invoking the image of the well-known politician, the mark may "falsely suggest a connection" with the politician, or bring him into "contempt and disrepute." Here, the mark clearly invokes the politician's identity in consumers' minds. The only question would be whether the politician is in fact connected to the applicant's goods. If not it seems likely that consumers of applicant's goods will nonetheless make the connection. Section 2(a) can be used to prevent such violations. Moreover, the politician may be deemed to be disparaged by the disrespectful depiction.

68. Brown Corp. has priority because it began its use *before* Ace filed its intent-to-use application. Ace gets the benefit of constructive use as of its application date. Brown, having an earlier use date, prevails because its mark is inherently distinctive, and there is no need to demonstrate acquisition of secondary meaning.

69. The marks, though spelled somewhat differently, sound very similar, and are used for similar products. Their concurrent use in Virginia, Tennessee, and the Carolinas is likely to cause consumer confusion about the source, sponsorship, or affiliation of the parties' products. Z is likely to prevail against Y everywhere except in Virginia.

X was the first to use the mark. His assignment to Y included the good will represented by the mark because it included the factory, and Y continued to use the mark on similar goods. Thus, the assignment was effective to transfer any geographic or temporal rights X had in the mark to Y. However, X's rights would be limited to Virginia. This is because Z was the first to register, and his mark has now attained incontestable status. This effectively freezes the earlier user's area of priority to the area it occupied on Z's application date. Since X only used the mark in Virginia on that date, Y can only assert superior rights in that portion of its current territory.

70. X Co. has superior rights throughout the country. Even though it only initially used its mark in New York, far from Y Co., and it filed a use application rather than an intent-to-use application, X's registration in August 2003 gave it the benefit of nationwide constructive use of its mark as of its application date (February 2003). (See Lanham Act §7(c).) Thus, X Co. is officially senior in time to Y Co. in Mississippi and Alabama and should be able to enjoin Y Co. there if Y's use of the "Hellofawallop" mark creates a likelihood of consumer confusion. Following is a list of factors a court is likely to consider in determining the likelihood of confusion issue, along with an analysis of how each factor might weigh.

a. *Strength of the plaintiff's mark.* "Heckofawallop" is likely to be deemed suggestive of the product, which means that it is inherently distinctive, and thus relatively strong. While the mark is relatively new, the facts state that X introduced the new fortified wine bearing the mark "with much advertising and fanfare," suggesting that it may have acquired secondary meaning as well. Thus, a court is likely to find that the plaintiff's mark is a fairly strong one, which weighs in favor of a finding of confusion.

b. *Proximity of the goods.* While the goods (fortified wine and malt liquor) do not directly compete, they are related, and consumers thus may think that they come from the same source. This weighs in favor of a finding of confusion, though not as strongly as it would if the products were identical.

c. *Similarity of the marks.* The two marks are similar in sight, sound, and meaning. It should be noted that both words consist of five syllables with the same stress pattern. All of the syllables are the same except for the first one, and the first one is similar (the first syllable of each word begins with "He"). Both words provide the same basic mental image—a drink that hits the user hard—except that the defendant's mark may strike observers as slightly more profound (or profane). This similarity weighs in favor of a likelihood of confusion.

d. *Evidence of actual confusion.* There is none here. However, courts do not require that such evidence be provided. While the presence of such evidence would weigh in favor of a finding for the plaintiff, the lack of it does not necessarily favor the defendant, since actual confusion is not required in order to find infringement.

e. *Marketing channels used.* Here, both parties are likely to use similar marketing channels—retail liquor outlets—and sell to similar or the same customers. They may use similar channels of advertising, but we have no facts on that issue. Similar marketing channels weighs in favor of a finding of likely confusion.

f. *Type of goods and the degree of care likely to be exercised by the purchaser.* Neither of the goods is likely to be expensive or directed to sophisticated connoisseurs. Customers are likely not to exercise great care. This weighs in favor of a finding for plaintiff.

g. *Defendant's intent in selecting the mark.* Here, it appears that the defendant acted in good faith because it is unlikely that it knew of plaintiff's use at the time that it began its own use. While this will not stop a court from finding a likelihood of confusion, it may motivate the court to tailor the relief it grants as narrowly as possible to permit the defendant to protect its investment in developing good will under the mark.

h. *Likelihood of expansion of the product lines.* We have no facts to suggest that the parties actually plan to expand their lines, but consumers may anticipate that they would, since the products are related.

Given the above analysis, a court would be likely to find that the parties' concurrent use of their marks in Mississippi and Alabama is likely to cause consumer confusion about the source, sponsorship, or affiliation of the parties' goods, and award relief to X Co.

71. Pursuant to the Paris Convention (as implemented in Lanham Act §44(d)), a national of Germany who files an application to register a mark in Germany, and files an application to register the mark in the United States within six months of its German application, gets the benefit of the German application date. Thus, *Z will be treated as having applied to register its mark in the United States in December 2002, its German filing date.* The P.T.O. acted properly in registering Z's mark without a showing of actual use because Z's mark was registered in Germany, and Z alleged a *bona fide* intent to use the mark in commerce. See Lanham Act §§44(b), (c), and (e). Once Z's mark was registered, it obtained the benefit of *constructive use* dating back to its filing date. *Thus, Z's mark enjoys nationwide priority throughout the United States as of December 2002.* See Lanham Act §7(c). Z accordingly has priority over both X and Y, and can obtain relief against these parties if their concurrent use of the mark causes a likelihood of consumer confusion.

Applying the factors listed in the answer to Question 70, *supra*, it appears that Z could show a likelihood of confusion, once it begins using the mark throughout the United States on its table wines. Since "Heckawallap" is a made-up word, it is likely to be deemed fanciful, and thus strong. Z's product does not directly compete with fortified wine and malt liquor, but is a related product, that consumers might expect to come from the same producer. While Z's mark consists of only four syllables, the overall appearance and sound of the mark are highly similar to "Heckofawallop" and "Hellofawallop." The parties' marketing channels are likely to overlap because Z's wines are likely to be sold in retail liquor outlets. While consumers may pay closer attention to the label of a table wine than that of fortified wine or malt liquor, German table wines do not tend to be expensive, and the degree of care is unlikely to be as high, for example, as that paid to the label of an expensive French wine. Thus, while there is no evidence of actual confusion, and the defendants are likely to have acted in good faith, it seems quite possible that Z could make the necessary demonstration of a likelihood of confusion and thus enjoin or limit X and Y's use of their respective marks.

72. X Co. may have a cause of action for trademark infringement, based on an "initial interest confusion" theory. By incorporating X's mark into a domain name and using the domain name for a web site that advertises goods or services, Y uses the "whiz" mark "in connection with" the sale or advertisement of goods that Y is offering for sale. Moreover, that "use" is likely to confuse consumers, at least initially. Internet users often assume that a company will use its trademark in its domain name. Thus, persons wishing to visit X Co.'s web page, to purchase or learn about X's product, may input "whiz .com," or select "whiz.com" from a search result using X's mark as a search term. Y's use of X's mark in its own domain name will divert those potential customers to Y's web page. While the consumers will learn of their mistake once they read the material on Y's web page, Y will have obtained an opportunity to make its "pitch" to those web site visitors that Y otherwise would not have had, and possibly take sales from X. It is Y's use of X's mark in its domain name, which initially confuses consumers and causes them to *visit* Y's web site, that makes this diversion of sales and interference with X's business good will possible.

X Co. might also have a cause of action for *trademark dilution* under Lanham Act §43(c). To demonstrate dilution, X must show: (1) that its mark is famous; (2) that Y's use qualifies as a use in commerce; (3) that Y's use began after X's "Whiz" mark became famous; and (4) that Y's use "blurs" X's distinctive mark.

The following facts may assist X in establishing the requisite fame: (1) the Whiz mark is inherently distinctive; (2) X has used the mark for a long time; (3) X has used the mark throughout the country; and (4) X has registered the mark.

Use of a mark as a domain name for a *commercial* web site is clearly a "use in commerce," as required by Lanham Act §43(c). Moreover, it appears that Y's use began *after* X's mark became famous. Accordingly, the remaining question is whether Y's use blurs the distinctive quality of X's mark.

Under the newly revised Lanham Act §43(c), dilution by blurring occurs when the similarity of a famous mark and the defendant's mark causes consumers to associate them, and this association impairs the distinctiveness of the famous mark. Factors that are relevant to this determination include: the degree of similarity between the marks, the degree of the famous mark's inherent or acquired distinctiveness, the extent to which the owner's use of the mark is exclusive, the degree of the famous mark's recognition, whether the defendant intended to create an association with the famous mark, and evidence of actual association of the marks by consumers. Under this standard, X may be able to succeed in demonstrating that Y's actions create a likelihood of dilution by blurring. A number of the statutory factors seem to apply.

First, for all practical purposes, "whiz" and "whiz.com" are virtually identical. To most consumers, the ".com" top level domain just indicates a web presence. Thus, most consumers would assume that the "Whiz" mark would be represented as "whiz.com" on the Internet. Second, "Whiz" is inherently distinctive, and given its long use, probably enjoys wide public recognition. While we have no facts about who else uses "Whiz" as a mark, it probably is not commonly used. Clearly Y intended to cause consumers to associate the "whiz.com" domain name with the plaintiff's mark. One could certainly argue that the use of "whiz.com" as a domain name for a competing web site will dilute the effectiveness of the mark to sell X's products. (Of course, given the content of Y's web site, one could argue in response that Y's use is *reinforcing* of the public association of the mark with X as a source of widgets, rather than diminishing.)

Finally, X might bring an anti-cybersquatting action under Lanham Act §43(d). It appears that X's mark was distinctive at the time Y registered the "Whiz.com" domain name and set up its site, and arguably was "famous" (for purposes of §43(c)), as well. The key issue is whether Y acted with a *bad-faith intent to profit* from the business good will of the mark. Section 43(d) lists a number of factors to assist in making the bad-faith determination. Looking at these factors, it appears that the following groups of facts would support a finding of bad faith on Y's part. First, Y had no preexisting trademark or other legitimate intellectual property rights in the "Whiz" mark prior to the domain name registration, and "Whiz" was not Y's own legal name or nickname. Y had (so far as we know) never used the "Whiz" mark in connection with the *bona fide* offering of goods or services before. Second, Y's use was strictly commercial. While Y might argue that its use of the Whiz mark was a nominative fair use (because its web site compared Y's product with X's, and needed to refer to X's product by name) this argument is unlikely to prevail. While Y might be privileged to use X's mark on the web site, or even incorporate it into its domain name, it was not necessary to place it in the site's domain name in the "mark.com" form, with no differentiating matter. The Ninth Circuit has held that use *in this form* may conflict with the third element of the nominative use standard: Selection of the "mark.com" form constitutes an element that, in conjunction with the mark, suggests sponsorship or endorsement by the trademark holder. *Toyota Motor Sales, U.S.A., Inc. v. Tabari*, 610 F.3d 1171 (9th Cir. 2010). It seems clear that Y registered and used the domain name with the *intent to divert consumers* away from X for commercial gain, and to injure X's business by creating a likelihood of consumer confusion.

73. The first issue is whether "Blossom Brawl" is confusingly similar to "Flower Fracas." The two indications of origin do not sound or look alike, but they have similar meanings, both evoking the image of fighting or chaotic flowers. Both names also employ alliteration as a device to make their names more noticeable and memorable. Similarity of meaning may be sufficient to support a finding of likelihood of confusion, especially if other factors also favor such a finding. Here the parties are in the same business, presumably selling through similar channels of trade to similar consumers. Indeed, some of the consumers may overlap, as many people in Oakland commute to San Francisco to work, shop, or socialize, and thus might buy flowers in either location. While the parties do not advertise in the same newspaper, they both advertise in newspapers, and Oakland residents may subscribe to the San Francisco paper and vise versa. Flowers are not highly expensive items, so consumers might not exercise the same degree of care in ascertaining the source as they might if the items were more expensive. Finally, X's composite mark is inherently distinctive, and arguably a strong mark. While Y did not intentionally adopt a similar name, and there is no evidence of actual confusion, the combination of factors may weigh in favor of a finding of likelihood of confusion.

Since there is no indication in the facts that the parties had registered the names as marks, the common-law rule of geographic rights would apply. The common law provides that a junior user who adopts a confusingly similar mark in good faith in a geographic area that is remote from the senior user's geographic area will not infringe. Defendant in this case probably won't get the benefit of this "remote, good-faith user" defense, however, because his area of use probably was not geographically "remote" for this purpose. Given the close proximity of Oakland to San Francisco, and the likelihood that Oakland residents would encounter plaintiff's shop and its ads in the *San Francisco Chronicle*, a court could find that plaintiff had a "presence" in Oakland, so that it was the first user there.

74. The Segundo Corp. is unlikely to succeed in its suit, as long as the goods Ivanov imports are the *same* as those that Segundo sells in the United States. Though Ivanov's imported goods are gray market goods, they will not infringe Segundo's U.S. trademark rights because Segundo and the foreign manufacturer (Rojas) are *related entities*, subject to common ownership and control. Under these circumstances, they will be deemed effectively to be the same person. Under the doctrine of exhaustion, once a trademark owner places its mark on goods and releases them into the stream of commerce, he cannot prohibit their resale with the mark, as long as the use of the mark is truthful and not misleading.

If the goods Ivanov sells are a different grade or quality or have materially different characteristics than those sold by Segundo in the United States, then infringement may be found even though Segundo and the manufacturer are related. In that case, sale of Ivanov's goods is likely to mislead consumers, because consumers will assume that the mark on Ivanov's goods indicates that the goods have the same qualities and characteristics as Segundo's goods, when they do not.

75. CalPacific marked the pickles and sold them to Albertini's. The doctrine of first sale (or doctrine of exhaustion) allows Albertini's to resell the goods under the mark, as long

as the use of the mark is truthful and not misleading. Here, due to Albertini's failure to refrigerate the pickles, arguably its subsequent resale of them under the Zip mark was misleading and thus infringing. Consumers rely on the mark to indicate quality and the characteristics of goods. When they encounter a jar of pickles bearing the Zip mark, they expect that the pickles will have essentially the same quality and characteristics as prior (properly refrigerated) jars of pickles they bought in the past that bore the same mark. In this case Albertini's has changed the nature of the Zip pickles, so that consumers relying on the mark to indicate quality will be misled, and purchase goods that differ from the goods they meant to buy.

76. The issue is whether the plaintiff meets the "use in commerce" requirement and thus is entitled to protection under the Lanham Act. In *International Bancorp LLC v. Societe Des Bains De Mer Et Du Cercle Des Estrangers A Manaco*, 329 F.3d 359 (4th Cir. 2003), *cert. denied*, 540 U.S. 1106 (2004), the Fourth Circuit held that a foreign plaintiff could prevail under similar circumstances, even though it only offered its services abroad. The court noted that Lanham Act §45 provides that a mark is used "on services when it is used or displayed in the sale or advertising of services *and* the services are rendered in commerce." The plaintiff used the mark in the U.S. to advertise its services and it rendered its restaurant services "in commerce." "Commerce," for purposes of the Lanham Act, includes foreign trade (trade between subjects of the U.S. and subjects of a foreign nation), and the evidence indicated that the plaintiff's restaurant services were rendered in foreign trade because a number of U.S. citizens patronized the plaintiff's restaurants abroad. The *International Bancorp* case distinguished the Second Circuit's decision in *Buti v. Impressa Perosa, S.R.L.*, 139 F.3d 98 (2d Cir. 1998), *cert. denied*, 525 U.S. 826 (1998) (which found no use in commerce because the plaintiff's restaurant services were only rendered abroad), on the grounds that the *Buti* plaintiff conceded that its restaurant services were not a part of U.S.-Italy trade.

77. The defendant is most likely to prevail on the dilution claim because Lanham Act §43(c) expressly provides that the dilution cause of action does not extend to uses of marks in non-commercial speech. Some courts have held that titles of songs, movies, and books are not core commercial speech, as that concept has been defined by the Supreme Court, and thus that the federal dilution cause of action does not reach unauthorized uses of famous marks in titles.

In the case of infringement claims, the modern trend is to follow the Second Circuit's balancing of interests approach in the case of titles of expressive works. *Rogers v. Grimaldi*, 875 F.2d 994 (2d Cir. 1989). The *Rogers* approach balances the public's expressive, First Amendment interests against trademark interests in determining whether to find infringement liability. Under this approach, the unauthorized use of plaintiff's mark in defendant's title will not constitute actionable infringement unless the title has no artistic relevance to the underlying work whatsoever, or if it has some artistic relevance, unless the title explicitly misleads as to the source or the content of the work. While it is not clear what relationship the title has to the song in this case, there does not appear to be any explicit deception in the title.

78. The purring sound of the muffler: Marks can consist of any word, name, symbol or device. A sound may be a symbol or device that indicates source to consumers. Here, however, the purring sound would probably be considered to be a product feature, so that

the P.T.O. would want to consider evidence of secondary meaning and non-functionality. The fact that the muffler has been sold with the sound for 10 years, and is popular, would provide some evidence of secondary meaning. However, since consumers are not necessarily accustomed to relying on the sound of a muffler for information about its source, the P.T.O. might require additional evidence. (While Lanham Act §2(f) permits the P.T.O. to presume secondary meaning from the fact that the applicant has made continuous and exclusive use of the alleged mark for 5 years, it does not require it to do so.) The P.T.O. might also take into account the fact that consumers don't normally hear the sound that a muffler makes at the time they purchase it, and thus are more likely to rely on other indications of origin, such as a word mark or packaging, in making their purchase selection. Functionality would probably turn on whether the purring is a natural byproduct of the muffler's functional structure or whether the sound has been manipulated to communicate source, or so that it can be characterized as "arbitrary or incidental" with regard to the muffler's function.

79. "Mallenkrodt" enclosed in a red circle as a mark for woven floor mats: Composite marks are considered as a whole. The question for the P.T.O. would be whether this composite mark is primarily merely a surname. The red circle is so commonplace that it may not make enough of an impression on consumers to differentiate the applicant's mark from a plain word mark. If that is the case, then the P.T.O. must determine whether consumers would understand the word "Mallenkrodt" as a surname.

A word is considered "primarily merely a surname" if consumers are likely to infer a surname meaning, and that is the only well-known meaning the word has. With regard to the first question, the P.T.O. might look to telephone directory listings and do an Internet search to see how often the name shows up. If it is not a common name, consumers may not associate it with a surname meaning, so that the mark could be registered as inherently distinctive, with or without the red circle. On the other hand, if the public would recognize the word as a surname, and nothing else, and if its combination with the red circle would have the same meaning to consumers, then the P.T.O. would require a showing of secondary meaning.

80. The intent-to-use application to register "Superior" for sponges: The word "superior" is a very common, descriptive (laudatory) term that would require a showing of secondary meaning. Since the applicant merely intends to use the mark, it cannot have acquired any secondary meaning, and the application should not be allowed. The Federal Circuit has held that some marks are so highly descriptive and common that they should be deemed incapable of indicating source, as a matter of law. (They should, in effect, be treated as "generic.") In re *The Boston Beer Company Limited Partnership*, 198 F.3d 1370 (Fed. Cir. 1999). However, this is not the majority rule. Under the majority rule, a descriptive word that is not part of the common name of the product may be registered with a showing of secondary meaning, no matter how common the descriptive word. Thus, once the applicant makes its intended use and acquires secondary meaning, it might be able to register.

81. The words "Mexican Law Summary" and "Canadian Law Summary" for summaries of Mexican and Canadian law. The P.T.O. might object that these marks are generic — the common name of a type or genus of product. The standard for making this determination is whether the primary significance of the mark to consumers is the name of the product

or an indication of source. If it is the former, it is generic and cannot be registered, regardless of how long it has been used. Both of these marks are composite marks, which must be evaluated in their entirety. While the words "Law Summary" may be deemed generic, that does not automatically mean that the combination of the terms with a country name is. The P.T.O. might do a Google or Nexis search to see if it could find the phrases "Mexican Law Summary" and "Canadian Law Summary" used in a generic sense. It might check dictionaries to see if there are any listings for the full combinations of words. The burden would be on the P.T.O. to make a *prima facie* showing of genericness. At that point, the burden would shift to the applicant to overcome the *prima facie* showing.

A.J. Canfield Co. v. Honickman, 808 F.2d 291 (3d Cir. 1986), provides a different approach. In the *Canfield* case (involving the words "Chocolate Fudge Soda") the Third Circuit held that when a producer introduces a product that differs from an established product class in a significant, functional characteristic, and uses the common descriptive word for that characteristic as its name, that new product becomes its own genus, and the term denoting the genus becomes generic if there is no commonly used alternative that effectively communicates the same functional information. In such a case, we essentially assume that the primary significance of the alleged mark to the public will be the name of the product itself. Here, the P.T.O. might argue that "Law Summaries" is a class or genus of product, and that the applicant's products differ from that class or genus in a significant, functional characteristic (the summaries are of the law of a particular country). The producer uses the common descriptive word for that characteristic (Mexican, Canadian) as its name. Thus, each of the summaries becomes its own genus, and the term denoting that genus, along with the name denoting the root genus, is generic. There is no commonly used alternative that would effectively communicate the same functional information.

82. Jacques might allege a "reverse confusion" claim under Lanham Act §43(a). Under this claim, the American Company's actions have led consumers to think that the acting services in the movie come from Francois rather than Jacques. This injures Jacques by depriving him of the credit and good will that would otherwise accrue to him in the acting business, and that is necessary in order to get future acting roles. In effect, Jacques is trying to vindicate his moral right of attribution, which the United States is obligated to protect under international treaty, but which is not expressly protected under the Copyright Act. There have been findings for plaintiffs in Jacques's situation under Lanham Act §43(a) in the past. However, the Supreme Court's more recent decision in *Dastar Corp. v. Twentieth Century Fox Film Corp.*, 539 U.S. 23 (2003), casts doubt on Jacques's chances of success. In *Dastar*, the Court held that Lanham Act §43(a) could not be construed broadly to undercut limitations built into the Copyright Act. There the plaintiff alleged that the defendant's video took most of its material from the plaintiff's earlier video (which had fallen into the public domain), without crediting the plaintiff. The Supreme Court rejected the plaintiff's §43(a) claim on the ground that to allow it would frustrate Congress' purpose in relegating works whose copyright had expired to the public domain, and would undercut Congress's decision to limit the moral right of attribution set forth in the Copyright Act to original works of visual art (which excludes motion pictures).

Jacques could distinguish *Dastar* on a couple of grounds. First, his movie is not in the public domain, so finding that he has a cause of action will not undermine Congress's purpose of limiting the duration of protection for copyrighted works. However, construing §43(a) to extend to Jacques's situation might still be found to undermine Congress's intent in limiting the Copyright Act's moral right protection to works of visual art. Jacques could also argue that his claim is for *misattribution*, while *Dastar* involved essentially a *lack of attribution*. Misattribution directly deceives the public, and this may be more objectionable from the Lanham Act standpoint. However, the case law to date has not construed *Dastar* to be limited to "lack of attribution" claims.

83. Zenpok is a trade name—the name of a business. Trade names cannot be registered on the Lanham Act Principal Register, but they are indications of origin, and Zenpok Corp. could sue for infringement of its trade name under Lanham Act §43(a) or under state unfair competition (passing off) law. Here, Zenpok appears to be a fanciful name, which is inherently distinctive, and therefore strong. (It is possible that Zenpok is a surname, but because it is so rare, it is unlikely that its meaning would be perceived as "primarily merely a surname" by consumers.) The facts indicate that Zenpok Corp. was the first to use the trade name throughout the country. Therefore it would have priority over Jones and could enjoin Jones's use if Jones's use causes a likelihood of consumer confusion over the identity, source, sponsorship, or affiliation of Jones's business. The court would apply the same factors that are commonly applied to determine the likelihood of consumer confusion in trademark infringement cases.

Here, the plaintiff's name is strong because it is fanciful and probably has significant secondary meaning, by virtue of plaintiff's use of the trade name in advertising and on its labels. The parties both deal with widgets, and their marks are similar (the defendant merely duplicating plaintiff's name and adding his own surname to it). We do not have much information on marketing channels, actual confusion, or the degree of care likely to be exercised by purchasers, or Jones's intent. (Given that Zenpok is nationwide, and Jones is in the same business, he likely was familiar with the Zenpok trade name and may have adopted it for the purpose of suggesting a connection.) However, the first several factors are probably enough to support a finding of likelihood of confusion. Consumers encountering defendant's business are likely to think that it has a connection with the manufacturer of Zenpok widgets—perhaps that defendant is an authorized service provider.

If plaintiff prevails under Lanham Act §43(a), it will be entitled to the same Lanham Act damages that would be available for infringement of a registered trademark.

84. Under the common law, Eau de Waft must demonstrate that it lost customers as a result of Twinkle's false advertising. This might be difficult, since there are many manufacturers of perfume. Even if Eau can show that Twinkle customers would not have bought from Twinkle in the absence of the false advertising, it would be very difficult to prove that they would have bought from Eau rather than from one or more of the other manufacturers.

Eau's best chance is to sue under Lanham Act §43(a). Plaintiffs alleging false advertising under this provision need only show a likelihood of injury in order to enjoin further false advertising. Here, Eau may satisfy this requirement by showing that it competes with Twinkle in the same market and that there is a logical causal connection between Twinkle's false advertising and Eau's sales position—that it is logical to believe that Twinkle's false claims may have lured away Eau customers. (To win damages, Eau would probably still have to demonstrate lost customers.) Other alternatives include suit for an injunction under a state Uniform Deceptive Trade Practices Act or to complain to the F.T.C. in the hopes that the F.T.C. will institute an investigation of Twinkle's advertising practices.

85. No. Lanham Act §43(a) expressly limits false advertising and commercial disparagement claims to misrepresentations of fact made in "commercial advertising or promotion." This limits the cause of action to a defendant's commercial speech. A magazine article such as Purchasers' is not likely to constitute commercial speech, but rather fully protected First Amendment speech. Plaintiff might consider a common-law commercial disparagement claim. However, it might face difficulties satisfying the jurisdiction's requirements for demonstrating damages. Moreover, there is some precedent for finding the *New York Times* rule applicable in a product disparagement case that does not involve commercial speech. If it is applicable, then the plaintiff would have to demonstrate, with clear and convincing evidence, that the defendant acted with actual malice—with knowledge of falsity or reckless disregard for whether the article was false or not.

86. Schmoe has no cause of action for false advertising. First, Joe's statement merely amounts to trade puffery. No consumer would be likely to take his claim literally. They would just take it as a general claim of quick or efficient service. (In legal terms, Schmoe would not be able to demonstrate that Joe's statement "actually deceived or had the capacity to deceive a substantial segment of the audience.") Second, it is not clear that a statement to a single customer, even if a false statement of fact, would fall within §43(a). Some case law indicates that the false claims, which must be made in "advertising or promotion," must be widely disseminated.

87. These facts are somewhat similar to those of *International News Service v. Associated Press*, 248 U.S. 215 (1918), which gave rise to the misappropriation cause of action. The misappropriation factors might be evaluated in the following way.

First, the plaintiffs no doubt expended significant time, effort, and expertise to research and write and publish their stories, and the stories have a trade value. Much of the material is time sensitive, and only valuable for a limited time.

Second, by linking to the plaintiffs' sites, Carla is free-riding on the plaintiffs' efforts by incorporating the stories wholesale into her visitors' segmented screens while the stories are still "hot." She does not make the investment in research and writing that the plaintiffs make. Carla profits from providing the stories to her own web site visitors, because the stories attract more visitors, and this enhances her advertising revenues.

Third, the plaintiffs may be injured because, if it were not for Carla's site, Carla's visitors might visit plaintiffs' sites directly, and see the plaintiffs' home pages and the materials that enable visitors to sign up for subscriptions. When visitors read the plaintiffs' stories via Carla's deep links, they bypass the home page and other materials, and may be less likely to sign up for a subscription.

The plaintiffs' misappropriation claim might be preempted by federal law.

88. Moore is likely to have a cause of action for violation of her right of publicity. By using a recognizable image of her on its label, Acme is appropriating her identity to sell its soap. Use of her image alone is enough, as long as she is recognizable. Since the label of a product is classic commercial speech, Acme is unlikely to have a First Amendment defense.

89. The politicians are unlikely to have a cause of action. The comedy program will not be deemed commercial speech even though aired on commercial television stations and produced for profit. Rather, the show will be deemed fully protected First Amendment expression. Moreover, a satiric comedy skit is likely to be highly transformative, adding significant creative elements of expression, and not merely reproducing the identities of the politicians. The Restatement's "relatedness" standard would dictate a finding for the defendant, because the skit was "about" the identified politicians. Even the Missouri Court's "predominate purpose" standard would likely lead to a finding of First Amendment protection, as the skit appears to have been created "primarily" for expression purposes.

90. The state unfair competition claim may be preempted under Copyright Act §301, because it alleges that a public performance of the copyrighted song violates JJ's rights. The state cause of action claims rights in copyrightable subject matter (the musical composition) and arguably gives rights equivalent to one of the exclusive rights of copyright (control over public performance of the song). Even if JJ were to argue that the state cause of action requires the extra element of distinctiveness, or secondary meaning (that is, a showing that the public understands the use of the song to indicate JJ as a source), that "extra element" arguably would go only to the *scope* of the claim, not the nature of it.

JJ might argue that a further "extra element" in the state cause of action is a likelihood of consumer confusion. In other cases, courts have found that the passing-off cause of action's "likelihood of consumer confusion" element renders the claim "qualitatively different" from a copyright infringement claim, because it demonstrates that the cause of action furthers a state interest (avoiding consumer confusion about the source of goods or services) that differs from the purpose of copyright. However, in this case, a court might evaluate the overall "essence of the claim" and find that, in essence, JJ is just trying to assert a copyright-like interest in a musical composition. Thus, even though the passing off cause of action generally would not be preempted, it may be under the particular facts of this case.

Even if the court found that the passing off claim is not "equivalent" to one of the exclusive rights of copyright, due to the presence of extra elements that render the cause of action "qualitatively different," the court might nonetheless find the claim preempted under the Supremacy Clause. In enacting the Copyright Act of 1976, Congress intended to give composers and their successors in interest the exclusive right to publicly perform their musical compositions. This right enables the composer to exploit the market for his song and profit from his labors. If JJ is able to assert a state right in a manner that prevents others from publicly performing the song, this will interfere with the copyright owner's ability to license public performance of the song, undercutting the value of the right and composers' incentive to create. This would frustrate accomplishment of Congress's purpose in enacting copyright protection for musical compositions. The Court of Appeals for the Ninth Circuit has found that a claim similar to the one described here is preempted under the Supremacy Clause. *Sinatra v. Goodyear Tire & Rubber,* 435 F.2d 711 (9th Cir. 1970), *cert. denied,* 402 U.S. 906 (1971).

91. The Lanham Act §43(a) claim would not be preempted, because it is brought pursuant to *federal,* not state, law. The Supremacy Clause and Copyright Act §301 have no bearing on federal laws, whether they conflict with other federal laws or not. General Products should argue that §43(a) should not be construed to provide a cause of action under the facts of this case, because to do otherwise would create a conflict between the Copyright Act and the Lanham Act. See *Dastar Corp. v. Twentieth Century Fox Film Corp.*, 539 U.S. 23 (2003).

92. The state right of publicity claim is unlikely to be preempted under §301. Under Ninth Circuit precedent, the court would find that the claim concerned defendants' use of JJ's *distinctive voice and performing style, which is not copyrightable subject matter.*

93. The misappropriation claim concerning the method of playing a banjo with a bamboo pick is unlikely to be preempted under §301, because a method of playing an instrument is not copyrightable subject matter. (One might argue that the method is nonetheless part of copyrightable works of authorship—JJ's sound recordings—and thus should be considered copyrightable subject matter under the case law holding that facts and ideas expressed in works of authorship are within the subject matter of copyright. However, that line of cases arguably is distinguishable: JJ's sound recordings do not express the method, as such—only sounds resulting from the method.)

The misappropriation claim may be *preempted under the Supremacy Clause,* however. JJ's method of playing is a "process," which is patentable subject matter. Under the *Sears/ Compco* and *Bonito Boats* decisions (*Sears, Roebuck & Co. v. Stiffel Cos.*, 376 U.S. 225 (1964); *Compco Corp. v. Day-Brite Lighting, Inc.*, 376 U.S. 234 (1964); *Bonito Boats, Inc. v. Thunder Craft Boats, Inc.*, 489 U.S. 141 (1989)) General Products could argue that because the method is within the subject matter of patents, but is unpatented, Congress intended that it remain in the public domain, free to be copied. Removal of the process from the public domain through use of a state misappropriation claim would frustrate Congress's purpose in enacting the Patent Act. None of the special circumstances that the Supreme Court recognized in *Kewanee, Aronson,* or *Bonito Boats* seems to be applicable to excuse the cause of action from preemption. (*Kewanee Oil Co. v. Bicron Corp.*, 416 U.S. 470 (1974); *Aronson v. Quick Point Pencil Co.*, 440 U.S. 257 (1979)) A plaintiff's rights under the misappropriation cause of action are strong and comprehensive—much like the monopoly rights granted by a patent. Indeed, this misappropriation claim, if allowed, would permit JJ to *prevent all other musicians* from employing the method. Nor does it appear that the state would be promoting independent state interests in providing the misappropriation cause of action, apart from the interest in promoting invention. In addition, the cause of action would undermine Congress's intent to leave matter that has already entered the public domain in the public domain.

ESSAY EXAM
QUESTIONS
AND
ANSWERS

ESSAY EXAM QUESTIONS AND ANSWERS

The following are some sample essay exam questions dealing with multiple doctrines of intellectual property law. They will be useful for testing your knowledge and for practicing exam-taking. You should write out your answers fully in essay form and then check them against the sample answers. Note that while the sample answers demonstrate *a good way* to approach the questions, they are *not necessarily the only good way.*

Here are some suggestions about how to answer an essay exam question:

1. Remember that you are taking an *essay* examination. The complete essay examination answer must contain not only the "answer" to the question, but of greater importance, must also contain your **analysis:** the applicable **black-letter law**, and an **explanation** of how you have applied the black-letter law to the facts and reasoned to the answer. It is also important to *consider the policies* underlying the black-letter rules, and discuss them in the course of explaining how the black-letter rules should be applied to the particular facts at hand.

2. Begin by **reading the question** thoroughly.

3. Next, **reread the question;** read it as it is written; try to avoid giving it your own "spin."

4. As you read, spot **key issues** and the applicable principles and concepts they invoke.

5. **Analyze** the fact pattern and the key issues that you have spotted.

6. **Organize your thoughts** into an orderly, logical sequence.

7. **Work out a game plan** for your answer, including the sequence of those things that you are going to write about, the priority for writing, and the general amount of space and time to be allocated to each.

8. Make a brief **word-phrase outline** of your proposed answer.

9. Use *at least* 25 percent of the time allotted for answering the question to do all of the things outlined above **before you begin to write** the answer. An organized answer can be written quickly. If you are not organized when you begin your answer, time will be wasted adding issues, crossing out the part of your answer that is not relevant, and writing too much about minor issues. Your answer will also be disorganized and hard for the professor to follow.

10. Write your answer in **clear, professional, lawyer-like English prose**, using full and complete **legal terminology**. Remember: This is an essay examination in the English language, at the graduate level, in a learned profession. Use proper grammar and punctuation.

11. Be certain to include **full statements of black-letter law** on each of the key issues. However, *do not write a treatise on the general field* of law involved in the question, and do not feel compelled to write everything you know about the issue. Write only those rules of law that are directly relevant to resolving the specific issues raised by the facts and the call of the question. If an issue is not fairly raised by a question, do not discuss it.

12. **Do not merely rehash the facts.** A complete answer requires analysis, black-letter law, and a description of how that black-letter law applies to the specific facts set forth in the question, in light of any relevant policy considerations. Rehashing of the facts is not enough. Nor is it particularly productive.

13. **Use short, complete, simple sentences.** Avoid long, wandering, convoluted sentences that deal with several issues and subjects.

14. **Reason to a lawyer-like conclusion.** If you have time and space, add a wrap-up concluding sentence to your answer.

15. **Reread your answer** to make certain that you have made no unintended errors or omissions, and to ensure clarity and completeness of your answer.

16. **Use the full time allotted** for the question — no more and no less.

ESSAY EXAM QUESTIONS

QUESTION 1

Mary, a software engineer with experience in the insurance business, devised a new mathematical algorithm for calculating a customized amount that a customer should be charged for earthquake insurance. The algorithm draws from a number of existing databases containing information about the risk of earthquakes in each part of the United States, the estimated damage that would occur in an earthquake in each of those geographic areas, costs of construction materials and labor in each area, and a range of other geographic and projected financial data. It combines these data with information supplied by the customer concerning the style, age, and environment of the building to be insured, assigns a weighted value to each factor, and then calculates a recommended insurance premium that reflects the precise risk the insurer undertakes to cover.

With the assistance of an old friend who is a patent agent at a law firm, Mary immediately filed patent applications with the U.S. Patent and Trademark Office and the European Patent Office. The patent applications state a single claim for a "method of calculating customized earthquake insurance premiums." The claim describes a series of nine "steps" that the new algorithm takes in selecting the relevant data and calculating the premium.

Mary then began to look for venture capital funding to begin producing and selling a computer program implementing the algorithm. Four months later, having acquired some "seed money" for the venture, Mary formed a corporation, and hired 12 professional programmers to work on creating a commercial embodiment of the program. The programmers were hired under a range of circumstances: Most of them agreed to work for a low wage and no benefits in return for stock options in the new corporation. Some of them only agreed to work for three-month periods, which could be renewed on mutual agreement. Being somewhat new to the role of employer, Mary did not have the programmers sign any written, employment-related, or non-disclosure agreements.

Eight months later, Mary and the programmers completed an early, or "test" version of the program. At that point, Mary called persons she knew at a cross-section of insurance companies, and asked them to try the program free of charge and provide feedback to be used in perfecting the final version. Mary sent disks containing the program to those who agreed. She only distributed the test program in object code, keeping the source code in confidence. Mary did not require the recipients to sign any non-disclosure agreements or other express contractual undertakings.

Five months after that, Mary's new company completed a final version of the program, and began the next phase of launching it on the market. At this point, Mary decided that she should consult with your law firm for expert advice on the best way to protect her rights in the program. Her patent applications are still pending, but she is having some second thoughts about them. She is wondering whether she would be better off retaining the algorithm as a trade secret. After all, her customer pool will be such as to make it possible to negotiate individual licensing agreements with each purchaser, with prohibitions on reverse-engineering, unauthorized uses, etc.

The prospects for the program's success look good. The venture capitalists who examined Mary's proposal were convinced that Mary's product will be well received as a significant breakthrough by the insurance business. What will you advise her? Specifically, please evaluate the likelihood of Mary's obtaining a patent, based on the available information, and the feasibility of protecting the algorithm as a trade secret. What would the relative advantages and disadvantages be to each approach? If Mary decided on trade secret protection, what additional steps should she take to preserve trade secret status? Should Mary also be thinking about copyright? What, if anything, would copyright add to the protection Mary would obtain under patent or trade secret law? Would Mary be likely to encounter any problems with regard to copyright protection?

SAMPLE ANSWER TO QUESTION 1

Is Mary's invention patentable?

The key issue regarding patentability is whether Mary's claimed algorithm/business method constitutes patentable subject matter under the Supreme Court's recent decision in *Bilski v. Kappos*, 130 S. Ct. 3218 (2010), and related decisions from the Court of Appeals for the Federal Circuit. While a method, or "process" is patentable subject matter under Patent Act §101, "abstract ideas" and laws of nature are not patentable. The question is whether Mary's claimed algorithm/business method is an unpatentable abstract idea or law of nature.

The Supreme Court has held that a mathematical algorithm (a procedure for solving a given type of mathematical problem) is like a mathematical formula or abstract idea, and thus cannot be patented. However, incorporating a mathematical algorithm as a step in a process or as a component of a physical apparatus does not render the claimed process or apparatus unpatentable. It appears from the facts that Mary's single patent claim does not call for any physical apparatus — only the nine steps constituting the algorithm. Nor does the claim call for use of the algorithm as one of multiple steps. Rather, the claim is limited to the nine steps performed by the algorithm itself. While there is Federal Circuit precedent for holding that the algorithm itself may be patentable as a process under certain circumstances, that line of cases has been brought into question by the Supreme Court's subsequent decision in *Bilski.*

In *Bilski,* the Supreme Court rejected arguments that business methods are categorically outside the subject matter of patents. However, the court found that the claimed method in that case (a method for buyers and sellers of commodities to protect, or hedge, against the risk of price changes) constituted an unpatentable abstract idea. The following discussion will note the main considerations that the *Bilski* Court raised and apply them to Mary's claimed business method.

First, the *Bilski* Court held that while the "machine or transformation" test (which asks whether the claimed invention is tied to a particular machine or apparatus, or transforms a particular article into a different state or thing) is not the sole test of patentability, it is a useful tool in determining whether a claimed method constitutes an abstract idea. In this case, Mary's algorithm may not be deemed tied to a particular machine or apparatus. While we don't have the claim language before us, the facts state that Mary's claim "describes a series of nine steps that the new algorithm takes in selecting the relevant data and calculating the premium." It does not appear that Mary limits the claim to use of the algorithm to any particular machine or device. The fact that the algorithm might be performed by a computer is probably not enough to bring the claim within the machine part of the machine or transformation test. The question then arises whether Mary's claimed method transforms a particular article into a different state or thing. Mary's method does not transform physical matter to a different state or thing. It might be characterized as transforming data representing financial information and risk. However, that is more or less what the claimed method did in the *Bilski* case, and the Supreme Court found that that method constituted an unprotectable abstract idea. Thus, it is likely that the machine or transformation test is not met in this case.

The *Bilski* court also stressed that an abstract idea is one that, if patented, would "wholly preempt" use of a mathematical algorithm, and that merely limiting an abstract idea to a particular technological environment (field of use) is insufficient to transform an abstract idea into patentable subject matter. There is nothing in the facts to suggest that Mary's claim is limited in a way that would avoid wholly preempting use of the algorithm in the earthquake insurance businesses, or anywhere else. Again, this suggests that the claim is to an abstract idea.

Finally, The Court of Appeals for the Federal Circuit has held that methods that can be performed mentally, or that are the equivalent of human mental work, constitute unpatentable abstract ideas. It seems likely that Mary's claimed method of computing insurance rates is the equivalent of human mental work, and thus is an unprotectable abstract idea. The chances of her successfully patenting the claimed algorithm are not good.

If Mary's claim were found to state patentable subject matter, the only other question would be whether the claimed invention is novel, non-obvious, and sufficiently disclosed in the patent application. Here, the facts state that Mary's algorithm is "new" and that the venture capitalists who examined Mary's funding proposals were convinced that the invention would be well received as a significant breakthrough by the insurance business. This suggests that the invention is novel and non-obvious. So, based on the facts that are given, it is likely that Mary would be able to obtain a U.S. patent for her invention, *if* she could overcome the patentable subject matter hurdle.

Is protection as a trade secret feasible?

To be protectable as a trade secret, Mary's algorithm must be substantially secret and provide a commercial advantage over others who do not know or use it. Here, there is little doubt that the algorithm will provide a commercial advantage, since Mary's corporation will be able to sell the program that incorporates it, and it represents a significant advance over existing programs available to insurance firms.

The main question is whether the algorithm is secret. Mary has undoubtedly revealed the algorithm to the programmers she has hired, but a trade secret owner has leeway to reveal a secret to her employees or agents so that they can perform their duties. Even in the absence of express non-disclosure agreements, the programmers are bound by a common law duty not to use or disclose the secret in an unauthorized manner. Mary may also disclose the algorithm, if necessary, to the venture capitalists for the purpose of convincing them to provide funding. They, too, are likely to be bound by a duty of confidentiality, since they had notice that the information was being revealed in confidence, and agreed to review it, thus impliedly accepting a duty not to use or disclose the information without Mary's permission.

Mary provided copies of the early version of the program implementing the algorithm to a cross-section of insurance companies to test, without requiring them to sign non-disclosure agreements or other express contractual undertakings to maintain secrecy. However, there is case authority that distributing a trade secret in object code does not in itself destroy trade secret status, as long as the source code is kept in confidence, as was done in this case. The fact that the object code is capable of being decompiled will not destroy the trade secret status of the algorithm against persons who learn it through other means. Thus, assuming that Mary's jurisdiction follows that precedent, Mary's acts in distributing disks containing the program to testers should not disqualify the algorithm from trade secret protection.

Mary's main problem with trade secrecy is that her application will be published by the U.S. Patent Office 18 months after it is filed. (The European Patent Office will publish her application 18 months after filing, as well.) Under the facts, Mary filed her application about 18 months ago. Thus, it has already been, or will soon be, published. Once it is published, all the information in the application, including the claim and the specification describing the invention and how to practice it, will lose its trade secret status. If the applications have not already been published, and Mary wants to retain the information as a trade secret, she must move quickly to withdraw her applications.

Which form of protection is preferable?

A patent is probably preferable because it gives much stronger protection than trade secret law, allowing Mary to prohibit all unauthorized uses, regardless of how the defendant obtained the algorithm. While patents are often more costly to obtain, Mary may already have paid a significant portion of the expense of applying for a patent. However, in this case, given the patentable subject matter problem, it would be risky to continue to pursue patent protection, which would entail publishing information about the invention and destroying trade secrecy. The P.T.O. may reject the application. Even if it grants the patent, the patent may be subject to challenge and invalidation in subsequent (expensive) litigation.

Trade secret protection potentially can last longer than a patent (the period of time the information actually remains secret versus 20 years from application date). However, this advantage is unlikely to carry much weight in this case, since the art in computer science advances so rapidly: Mary's algorithm is likely to become obsolete within the next 18 years. Moreover, while Mary may successfully retain trade secret status through individually negotiated licensing agreements prohibiting reverse engineering and other unauthorized uses, there is still a risk that the trade secret will be lost, either because other firms independently create it and disclose it, or because the information leaks to the rest of the industry. Thus, proceeding with trade secret protection is also risky, though perhaps less risky than seeking and enforcing a patent.

What would copyright protection add?

Copyright would protect the particular expression that Mary and her programmers used to implement their algorithm and ideas. Thus, copyright protects the code used in the program, and original, expressive aspects of the program's structure, including the selection and arrangement of uncopyrightable elements. It may also extend to aspects of the program's user interface. It would be possible for a competitor to copy portions of the program Mary's corporation creates without infringing the business method/algorithm claim (if Mary were to succeed in patenting it) or misappropriating trade secrets. Thus, copyright protection adds to whatever existing protection Mary may have, and she should claim copyright in the program. This will not be difficult, since copyright arises automatically upon fixation of the program in tangible form. There is no conflict under the law in simultaneously claiming patent or trade secret protection and copyright protection, because the copyright law protects different aspects of the program. Mary should register the program with the Copyright Office and include notice of copyright on the copies she distributes to purchasers or licensees, in order to preserve her opportunity to claim all available infringement remedies.

Potential problems with regard to copyright protection:

Mary's corporation may run into difficulties in claiming sole ownership of the copyright in the new program. This is because the status of the programmers she hired is unclear. If they are "employees" within the meaning of Copyright Act §101, then the corporation has the sole ownership of the program by virtue of the work for hire doctrine. However, if they are not "employees," they may have ownership rights in the portions they created, or even qualify as joint authors. The facts suggest that Mary has not obtained any advance assignment of their interest in the copyright to her or to the corporation.

In determining whether a work is created by an "employee," and thus is a work for hire, the general law of agency applies, and the ultimate question is whether the hiring party (Mary, or her corporation) had the right to control the process of creating the program. Some of the key factors are discussed below, in light of the facts that are provided.

1. The skill required: Programming requires a high level of skill, which weighs in favor of independent contractor status.

2. The source of instrumentalities and tools and the location of the work: Here, presumably the corporation provided the computers, workplace, and other tools used by the programmers, which weighs in favor of employee status.

3. The duration of the relationship between the parties: Here, some of the programmers were only hired for a three-month stint, with the possibility of renewal on mutual consent. This may weigh slightly in favor of independent contractor status, especially since the parties seem to have contemplated that the programmers would only work on one project.

4. The method of payment and the provision of employee benefits: Here, most of the programmers were working without payment of benefits, which suggests independent contractor status.

5. The hired party's role in hiring and paying assistants: Here there is nothing to suggest that the programmers hired their own assistants, such as secretaries or other support staff, which weighs in favor of employee status.

6. Whether the work was part of the regular business of the hiring party, and whether the hiring party is in business: Here, the answer is yes, which weighs in favor of employee status.

It appears that the factors are about equally weighted, so it is hard to predict how a court would rule if one of the programmers were later to assert individual or joint authorship of the program. Mary would be well advised to negotiate for an express assignment, as well as for an agreement that the programmers' work product is a work for hire, when she enters into new employment agreements at the end of the programmers' existing terms of employment, and in hiring new programmers who will work on subsequent versions of the program.

QUESTION 2

In January 2009, Alvin, an avid skateboarder, conceived of a new style of skateboard that, rather than being flat on top, would sport an aerodynamically designed fin rising from the middle of the board. The board would be pointed in front rather than rounded, and would have platforms for the rider's feet on either side of the fin, as depicted below. The two front wheels would be placed closer together than the two back wheels.

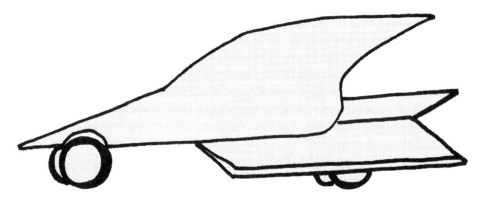

Alvin, who had taken some college courses in engineering, believed that this style of skateboard would provide a faster, more stable ride than other existing skateboard designs. Besides, the fin would look way cool and could be decorated with something awesome like painted orange flames, a skull and crossbones, or eagle wings. While the fin might take any of several shapes and be equally efficient aerodynamically, Alvin believed that the shape he selected was best because of the "retro" look it gave the skateboard.

Alvin believed that the skateboard should be constructed of fiberglass. He did not himself have the means to construct one. However, he made diagrams and drawings to scale that showed the precise shape of the fin and the body of the skateboard, the proper dimensions, the size and placement of the wheels, and all the other information that would be needed to construct a prototype.

In June 2009, Alvin sent letters of inquiry to five "invention services." Invention services are firms that serve as "middle men," representing independent inventors who are seeking to sell their inventive ideas to companies interested in marketing the inventions. Alvin's letters described his invention as "a breakthrough in skateboard design," but provided no further details. After receiving literature from the five services, Alvin selected one, Invention Brokers Inc. ("Brokers"), to represent him. He and Brokers executed an agreement in July 2009 in which Alvin agreed to provide Brokers with all the drawings and other information needed to make the skateboard, along with a general written description explaining how the skateboard worked and why it provided advantages over existing skateboard designs. In turn, Brokers promised to use its best efforts to market the new design to skateboard manufacturing companies, and to maintain the confidentiality of the new design.

Brokers received Alvin's information, and approached several manufacturers with Alvin's design during the following year. In each case, it obtained a confidentiality agreement from the manufacturer before disclosing details of the design. Ultimately, none of the manufacturers was interested in pursuing it. Then in August, 20010, Brokers contacted Cool Cat Surfboards, Inc., which was considering branching out into the skateboard business. Cool Cat was intrigued by Alvin's design and agreed to pay Alvin $75,000 for the design concept and to pay Brokers' commission. The same month, Alvin assigned all his rights in the design to Cool Cat and provided Cool Cat with his original drawings and diagrams.

In September, 2010, Diane, an employee of Cool Cat, made an unauthorized set of photocopies of Alvin's drawings and diagrams and took them home with her, without telling anyone about her actions. Shortly thereafter, she gave the photocopies to her boyfriend, Elton, who was an international businessman. Elton was aware that Diane had made the copies without permission. He sent them to a manufacturer in Hong Kong with an order for production of 10,000 skateboards. He directed that the skateboards be produced in a vibrant blue with the word "Elton" in large, bold crimson script running diagonally up the fin. The Hong Kong manufacturer completed the order in January 2011 and sent the skateboards, pursuant to Elton's direction, to a wholesaler in the European Union, who proceeded to sell all of them in France, Germany, and Great Britain during the next two months.

In December 2010, Cool Cat began manufacturing the skateboard Alvin had designed. It manufactured the skateboard in a bright yellow enamel paint, with black racing stripes, and two large blocky black "C's" marked prominently on the fin.

The same month (December 2010), Cool Cat filed an application for a utility patent in Alvin's design. The utility patent application claimed a skateboard with a fin rising from the middle of the board, a pointed front, platforms for the rider's feet on either side of the fin, and front wheels placed more closely together than the back wheels. Cool Cat began marketing the skateboard in the United States in March, 2011, under the "Cool Cat" trademark.

Meanwhile, Elton ordered 20,000 more of the "Elton" skateboards from the Hong Kong manufacturer. He sold them to Freewheelers, Inc., a U.S. sports distributor, in December, 2011. Freewheelers received the shipment of skateboards from Hong Kong in April 2012, and began selling them in its retail outlets in several states.

The P.T.O. granted a patent to Cool Cat in August 2012. Cool Cat did not apply for a patent in any country other than the United States.

Cool Cat has become aware of all the facts set forth above and has come to you for legal advice. Please identify and evaluate all the possible causes of action Cool Cat might consider bringing against Diane, Elton, Freewheelers, or any other persons arising out of these facts. In the case of each cause of action you discuss, state whether you would advise Cool Cat to pursue it, and explain your reasoning.

SAMPLE ANSWER TO QUESTION 2

A. Patent Infringement

Cool Cat obtained a utility patent in August 2012. It might explore a suit for direct infringement against Freewheelers and a possible suit for inducement of infringement against Diane and Elton. However, before exploring the specifics of these claims, it is useful to consider whether the patent might be vulnerable to an affirmative defense of patent invalidity, based on the available facts. The new rules regarding novelty and non-obviousness introduced by the Leahy-Smith America Invents Act will not apply to the Cool Cat patent, because the application for patent was filed before the effective date of those provisions.

1. Patent invalidity

To be patentable, an invention must be novel, non-obvious, and useful as of its invention date, and fully disclosed as provided in Patent Act §112. There is nothing in the facts to suggest that these requirements are not met. However, Patent Act §102(b) provides that an otherwise patentable invention may be disqualified for a patent if the inventor fails to file his application within a year after the invention is revealed in a printed publication anywhere in the world, or is on sale or in public use in the United States. The defendants might argue that the Cool Cat patent is invalid under §102(b), on the ground that the invention was on sale, in public use, or the subject of a printed publication prior to the critical date—December 2009. However, their arguments are unlikely to succeed.

The on-sale bar: Alvin contracted with Brokers to represent him in his attempt to sell his inventive concept, and Brokers undertook sales activities prior to the critical date of December 2009. In *Pfaff v. Wells Electronics, Inc. 525 U.S.55 (1998)*, the Supreme Court held that an invention could be deemed "on sale" for purposes of §102(b) even if it had not yet been reduced to actual practice, as long as the invention was "ready for patenting." Here, Alvin's skateboard could be deemed "ready for patenting" prior to the critical date because he had produced diagrams and drawings that were sufficient to enable a person with ordinary skill in the art to make a physical embodiment without undue experimentation.

However, Alvin's and Brokers' actions would not trigger the §102(b) statute of limitations because their actions did not constitute an offer to sell embodiments of the patented invention. Rather, they were only offering to assign rights in the inventive concept itself, in return for payment. Under the *Moleculon* case, an offer to sell or assign the inventive concept, as opposed to an offer to sell physical embodiments of the invention, will not put the invention "on sale" for purposes of §102(b).

"Printed publication" and "public use": Nor could Alvin's or Brokers' actions amount to a "printed publication" or "public use" within the meaning of §102(b). A "printed publication" requires a fixed description of the invention that is sufficient to enable a person of ordinary skill in the art to make or practice the invention without undue experimentation. While this requirement may be satisfied, it must also appear that the description was available to a person exercising reasonable diligence to find it. Here, Alvin's and Brokers' careful use of confidentiality restrictions make it unlikely that Alvin's drawings and diagrams could be deemed reasonably available to a person exercising reasonable diligence to find them.

A court would be unlikely to find a "public use" prior to the critical date for two reasons: First, the invention itself was not yet reduced to practice and thus could not be put to use; and second, even if Brokers' and the skateboard manufacturers' actions could be deemed a "use" of the patented skateboard, the confidentiality restrictions would likely prevent the use from being deemed "public."

2. Infringement

Direct infringement claims: Patent Act §271(a) provides that it will constitute infringement to make, use, offer to sell, sell, or import the patented invention in the United States during the term of the patent. Cool Cat's patent term began when the patent issued, in August 2012. [There is nothing in the facts to suggest that the patent application was published in the United States, triggering provisional rights against infringement prior to the issuance date. Since Cool

Cat only applied in the United States, the application would not be required to be published.] Thus, we can assume that the only actions that would constitute a direct infringement are those that occurred in the United States in or after August, 2012. If Freewheeling continued to sell the skateboards that it acquired through Elton in the United States on or after August, 2012, that would constitute an unauthorized "sale" of the patented invention pursuant to §271 and would constitute infringement. However, only sales that occurred on or after the patent issuance date would be deemed infringing, and subject to injunctive or monetary relief.

Inducement claims: Liability for inducement of patent infringement, under Patent Act §271(b), requires a showing that the defendant actively, intentionally solicited or assisted another to infringe, with knowledge that the induced actions will constitute infringement, or evidence of willful blindness to that fact. Here, Cool Cat might argue that Diane and Elton both induced or assisted Freewheelers' direct infringement. However, this might prove difficult because at the time that Diane and Elton engaged in the acts that induced or assisted Freewheelers' infringement, the Cool Cat patent had not yet issued. (In Diane's case, the application had not even been filed.) Nor do the facts suggest that Cool Cat notified them of its plan to obtain a patent. Thus, it would be difficult to demonstrate that either Diane or Elton had specific intent to cause infringement or knowledge that patent infringement was likely to occur as a result of their actions.

3. Conclusion

Thus, while Cool Cat's patent may be valid, its usefulness under the current facts is limited. It can be asserted to *prevent further infringing actions* by Elton and Freewheelers, and to collect damages from any of Freewheelers' sales of infringing skateboards made on or after the patent issuance date. However, the patent will provide no redress for the unauthorized manufacture of the skateboards in Hong Kong, the sales in the European Union, or the importation, sales, or offers to sell in the United States prior to August 2012.

B. Trade Secret Claims

The inventive concept underlying the skateboard might be deemed a trade secret prior to the skateboard's marketing in the United States, because it was substantially secret and gave Cool Cat a competitive advantage. Alvin and Brokers apparently took reasonable precautions to retain the concept as a secret, requiring all potential assignees to sign confidentiality agreements before receiving the particulars of the inventive design. There is nothing in the facts to suggest that Cool Cat was any less careful in this regard, or that the skateboard design was generally known in the industry or to the general public. Moreover, the new design probably gave Cool Cat a competitive advantage over other skateboard manufacturers/ sellers, who did not know or use it. Cool Cat's willingness to pay Alvin $75,000 for rights in the concept, the hot sales in the European Union, and the eagerness of Diane and Elton to take and implement the design concept suggest that the design presented an opportunity for profit. While one might question whether the skateboard design was "continuously used" in Cool Cat's business at the time Diane took it, the Uniform Trade Secrets Act has done away with this requirement, making it possible to claim trade secret status in information that the claimant has yet to put into ongoing use.

As Cool Cat's employee, Diane had a duty not to use or disclose the skateboard design without Cool Cat's permission. She clearly acted in breach of this duty when she made the unauthorized copies and handed them over to Elton. Elton likewise breached a duty to Cool Cat, because he probably had notice (at least inquiry notice) at the time he obtained the secret information that it was a trade secret and was being provided to him in breach of Diane's duty. Thus, his use and disclosure of the design would infringe Cool Cat's rights, as well.

However, Diane and Elton might not be subject to an injunction against further use of the trade secret information at this point. As a general matter, injunctions against trade secret misappropriation are granted only for the time that the information remains secret, or for a reasonable time thereafter (adding the time it would have taken the defendant to obtain and utilize the information once it entered the public domain). Here, the information clearly entered the public domain when the U.S. patent issued and Cool Cat began to market the skateboard itself. Thus, trade secret law might not provide much help in preventing Elton's future marketing of the skateboard design. Likewise, monetary remedies (which would likely take the form of defendants' profits in this case) would only be likely for Elton's use of the trade secret during the time it remained a secret in the United States.

C. Trade Dress Infringement

Cool Cat might claim rights in the mark "Cool Cat," the two large blocky black C's it placed on the fin of the skateboard it marketed, the bright yellow color with black racing stripes, or any combination of these things, as protectable indications of origin. However, the facts do not indicate that Elton copied any of these indications of origin. The only feature of the Cool Cat skateboards that Elton copied was the configuration of the skateboard itself. While it is possible for a producer to claim trade dress rights in the configuration of its product, and thus use Lanham Act §43(a) to prevent competitors from manufacturing knock-offs, Cool Cat would encounter two major problems in taking this approach under the current facts.

First, in *Wal-Mart Stores, Inc. v. Samara Bros., Inc.*, 529 U.S. 205 (2000), the Supreme Court held that product configuration trade dress cannot be deemed inherently distinctive. Secondary meaning must be demonstrated in all cases before trade dress protection can be afforded under §43(a). This means that the public must have been exposed to the configuration sufficiently to come to think of it as an indication that the skateboard comes from a particular source. Here, it is not clear that the Cool Cat skateboard configuration has had sufficient public exposure and publicity to attain that status. It is highly unlikely that it had in April 2012, when Freewheeling first began selling skateboards with the same configuration, because it had only been on the market for one month. Presumably, Cool Cat would only be entitled to §43(a) protection as of the date it acquired the necessary secondary meaning in the skateboard configuration.

Second, Elton and Freewheeling will argue that the skateboard configuration is unprotectable as trade dress because it is functional. In *TrafFix Devices, Inc. v. Marketing Displays, Inc.*, 532 U.S. 23 (2001), the Supreme Court provided that product feature trade dress must be found non-functional under both the *Inwood Laboratories* and the *Qualitex* standards before it can be protected. Under the *Inwood Laboratories* standard, the product configuration is functional if it "is essential to the use or purpose of the article, or if it affects the cost or quality of the article." Under the *Qualitex* standard, the configuration will be functional if exclusive rights would "put competitors at a significant non-reputation-related disadvantage."

It seems likely that the skateboard configuration would be found functional under the first (*Inwood Laboratories*) standard. The facts state that Alvin believed that his particular combination of product features would create a faster, more stable design. Thus, the configuration affects the quality of the skateboard and is directly related to accomplishment of its purpose. Moreover, Cool Cat's utility patent claimed all of the key features of the configuration. Under *TrafFix*, the inclusion of trade dress elements in utility patent claims constitutes strong evidence that the trade dress is functional. To overcome the strong presumption of functionality created by the presence of the features in the utility patent claims, defendants must show that the configuration is merely an ornamental, incidental, or arbitrary aspect of the skateboard. They would be unlikely to be able to do so in this case.

While the facts do suggest that the fin could be shaped in any of several ways and still be efficient aerodynamically, the fin does nonetheless serve a utilitarian function in the product: It adds to the aerodynamic quality of the skateboard. Thus, arguably it would still affect the "quality" of the skateboard, under the *Inwood Laboratories* standard, and thus be found functional. The Court of Appeals for the Federal Circuit has held that the availability of alternatives remains relevant in determining functionality under *TrafFix* and *Inwood Laboratories,* so perhaps a court following that circuit's opinion (as opposed to the Fifth Circuit's) would consider the particular shape of the fin to be non-functional under *Inwood Laboratories*. However, since the "retro" look is fashionable, the Federal Circuit could find functionality under *Qualitex*, because giving Cool Cat-exclusive rights in the retro design would put other skateboard designers at a significant, non-reputation-related disadvantage.

Accordingly, Cool Cat would have to overcome a functionality challenge and demonstrate secondary meaning before it could assert rights in the skateboard configuration under Lanham Act §43(a). And even assuming that it did, it would still have to demonstrate that the Elton/Freewheeling use caused a likelihood of consumer confusion about the source of the skateboards. This would include showing that the parties marketed the skateboard in the same geographic area, through similar channels, to similar consumers. Since the products and the fin shapes are identical, the similarity of the configuration itself would weigh in favor of a finding of infringement. The fact that each party clearly placed other identifying information on the fin of each skateboard it sold, on the other hand, would seem to weigh against a finding of likelihood of confusion.

D. Copyright Infringement

Cool Cat might have a cause of action against Diane for copyright infringement because of her unauthorized photocopying of the skateboard diagrams and drawings. The photocopying would infringe Cool Cat's reproduction rights in the graphic drawings. It might likewise claim that Elton is liable for contributory infringement, if it can demonstrate that he knew of the infringing activity and induced or assisted it. To the extent that Elton made further two-dimensional copies of the skateboard plans in the United States, he might be directly liable for those reproductions.

However, the skateboard itself is a useful article, and under current case law, it generally is not deemed an infringement to produce a useful article from copyrighted plans. So producing the skateboard itself from the plans would not infringe the reproduction or adaptation rights, nor would the subsequent importation or sale of the skateboards made from the plans. The only way that Cool Cat could demonstrate that the Elton skateboards themselves infringed Cool Cat's copyright would be to show that "sculptural" elements of the skateboard design are copyrightable under the "physical or conceptual separability test." Here, the design elements of the skateboard do not appear to be *physically* separable. They would be deemed *conceptually* separable under the Second Circuit's standard if the design elements reflect Alvin's artistic judgment exercised independently of functional influences. Here, Cool Cat may argue that the fin was so designed, since there were alternative ways that it could have been designed and still have functioned as well. However, it would probably fail because the facts do indicate that Alvin was influenced by aerodynamic concerns in designing the fin. Under the Second Circuit's decision in *Brandir International v. Cascade Pacific Lumber Co.*, 834 F.2d 1142 (2d Cir. 1987), all that is necessary to disqualify a useful article design from copyrightability is a showing that the design was significantly *influenced* by utilitarian concerns. It is not necessary that it be *dictated* by them. Also, even if the fin contour was deemed conceptually separable from the utility of the skateboard, it is not clear that it would be deemed "original," by itself. It is a very common, basic shape or design.

If Cool Cat could demonstrate that aspects of the skateboard design were copyrighted, then it could hold Elton and Freewheelers both liable for infringement. Elton distributed infringing skateboards to the public (by virtue of his sale to Freewheelers), and may have contributed to Freewheelers' infringement, as well. Freewheelers infringed the right of distribution to the public, and perhaps public display rights, as well. However, it is unlikely that Cool Cat can demonstrate that the skateboard's configuration, or the fin by itself, is copyrightable.

QUESTION 3

Dazzlesmile, Inc., holds a valid, enforceable U.S. patent on a new kind of battery-run, disposable electric toothbrush. Dazzlesmile sells its invention in various forms (including toothbrushes whose plastic handles are shaped and colored like rocket ships and racing cars) to appeal to children. The handles hold batteries, and extend to form a shaft with a flat, circular brush attached to the end with three tiny screws. A button on the handle activates the power, which rotates the brush at the end of the shaft and cleans the user's teeth.

Dazzlesmile sells its toothbrushes for $10.00 each to U.S. retailers. It intends that purchasers use the toothbrush until the bristles on the brush wear down, and then throw the toothbrush away. It does not market replacement brushes or offer the service of replacing the brush on toothbrushes whose brush has worn down. It advertises and promotes the toothbrushes as "disposable," and on the packaging of each toothbrush, it expressly states that the toothbrush "should be thrown away once the brush bristles have worn down."

In August 2011, Dazzlesmile shipped a large quantity of its patented toothbrushes shaped like rocket ships and race cars to Rojo, Inc., a Brazilian importer, in Rio de Janeiro for sale to Brazilian and other South American consumers. It charged Rojo $6.00 per toothbrush. The package of each toothbrush stated the following (in reasonably conspicuous lettering) in Spanish, Portuguese, and English: "Not for import or resale in the United States."

Rojo resold half of the toothbrushes to Martinez, a Chilean businessman, who resold them to CheepCo Discounters, a large American discount retailer. CheepCo imported the toothbrushes back to the United States and sold them in its stores for $8.00 each.

Rojo resold the other half of the toothbrushes to Blanco, Inc., which resold them to Argentinean consumers. Azul, Inc., advertised to Argentinean consumers that it would pay 50 cents for each discarded Dazzlesmile toothbrush delivered to it. After collecting a large quantity of the discarded toothbrushes, Azul sterilized them, and replaced the worn brush with a new brush that it manufactured itself, and replaced the batteries in each toothbrush. Azul then packaged the refurbished toothbrushes in its own new packaging and sold them to MegaMiddleMan, Inc., which in turn sold them to CheepCo Discounters. CheepCo imported the refurbished toothbrushes into the United States and sold them in its large discount outlets for $3.00 each.

Dazzlesmile would like to sue CheepCo for patent and/or copyright infringement. What is your assessment of each possible cause of action? Please discuss all the issues fairly raised by the facts, even if your disposal of one of them would resolve the case.

SAMPLE ANSWER TO QUESTION 3

1. Patent infringement claim

There are several issues raised by these facts. First, absent the restrictive statement on the labels, would it be infringement for CheepCo to import the new toothbrushes back into the United States for resale? Second, even if new toothbrushes could be imported, could the "refurbished" toothbrushes also be imported? Finally, what, if any, difference does the restrictive statement make?

Parallel imports: Parallel imports are patented goods that were originally made (or authorized to be made) by the U.S. patentee and sold abroad in foreign markets. Until recently, case precedent allowed persons to import such patented goods that they purchased abroad. Essentially, courts applied the doctrine of exhaustion (or the doctrine of first sale) to all goods sold by or under the authority of the U.S. patentee, regardless of whether those goods were first sold domestically or abroad. (This doctrine is known as the doctrine of international exhaustion.) Thus, once the U.S. patentee sold the goods without restriction anywhere in the world, the purchaser and/or its successors in interest could resell the goods, in any country they wished, without infringing the U.S. patent.

However, in *Jazz Photo Corp. v. International Trade Commission*, 264 F.3d 1094 (Fed. Cir. 2001), *cert. denied*, 536 U.S. 950 (2002), the Court of Appeals for the Federal Circuit held that the doctrine of exhaustion applies only to the patentee's *domestic* sales. (This doctrine is known as the doctrine of territorial exhaustion.) Thus, under this decision, none of the toothbrushes could be imported into the United States, even in the absence of the restrictive statement on the labels, because the U.S. patentee originally sold them abroad, rather than domestically.

The refurbishment: Even if the new toothbrushes could be imported under *Jazz Photo*, the question arises whether the refurbished ones could be. The answer would turn on whether the refurbishment constituted permissible repair or infringing reconstruction. The refurbishment would constitute reconstruction if it amounted to making a new article after the old one was spent. In *Sandvik Aktiebolag v. E.J. Co.*, 121 F.3d 669 (Fed. Cir. 1997), *cert. denied*, 523 U.S. 1040 (1998), the Federal Circuit listed four factors to consider in making this determination: (1) the nature of the defendant's actions; (2) the nature of the device and how it is designed (namely, whether one of the components of the patented combination has a shorter useful life than the whole); (3) whether a market has developed to manufacture or service the part at issue; and (4) objective evidence of the patentee's intent.

In this case, Azul replaced the brush and batteries, which clearly have a shorter useful life than the plastic handle and motor. Moreover, Azul's actions appear to be fairly simple and straightforward: In replacing the brush, presumably all it did was unscrew the screws holding the first brush to the shaft and screw the new brush in its place. Both these factors seem to weigh in favor of permissible repair. However, the third and forth factors may weigh in favor of infringing reconstruction: There are no facts suggesting the existence of a market to refurbish used disposable toothbrushes. Moreover, the patentee made it clear that it intended that the brushes be discarded after use, and not refurbished. In *Hewlett-Packard Co. v. Repeat-O-Type Stencil Manufacturing Corp., Inc.*, 123 F.3d 1445 (Fed. Cir.), *cert. denied*, 523 U.S. 1022 (1997), the Federal Circuit refused to permit a patentee's express statements that its product should be discarded determine the outcome of the case. Under this precedent, and given all the evidence, a reasonably good argument could be made that Azul was engaged in permissible repair, which would not infringe in itself if it occurred in the United States, or if the importation of the refurbished brushes was otherwise legal under the laws governing parallel imports. However, even if the refurbishment is legal, the import of the goods is illegal and the legality of the refurbishment in itself cannot change that outcome.

The restrictive provision: Even if it were not patent infringement for CheepCo to import toothbrushes that the U.S. patentee sold abroad without restriction, it must be determined whether the statement on the toothbrush packaging prohibiting import or resale in the United States would be enforceable against subsequent purchasers. Similar questions arise in connection with shrink-wrap and click-wrap ("mass market") licenses for software. Courts have differed over whether such provisions are enforceable, questioning whether there is adequate consent to the restrictions, whether the restrictions constitute contracts of adhesion or are unenforceable as against public policy, and whether state enforcement of such provisions might be preempted by federal law. Here, given the product and the circumstances, and the fact that alternative toothbrushes are readily available, it seems unlikely that the restriction against import would be deemed anticompetitive. As long as purchasers had clear notice of the restriction, it may be deemed enforceable. It appears that the initial packaging made the restriction reasonably clear.

In *Mallinckrodt, Inc. v. Medipart, Inc.*, 976 F.2d 700 (Fed. Cir. 1992), the Federal Circuit upheld a patentee's restriction on the label of a medical product that prohibited reuse of the product. Indeed, the court found that persons reusing the product in violation of the restriction could be liable both for breach of contract and for patent infringement. This would be strong precedent for finding that Martinez' and Cheepco's importation in violation of the restriction constitutes patent infringement. However, it is possible that the authority of the *Mallinckrodt* decision has been undermined by the Supreme Court's more recent decision in *Quanta Computer, Inc. v. LG Electronics, Inc.*, 533 U.S. 617 (2008), which endorsed a strong doctrine of first sale as against the Federal Circuit's tendency to restrict it.

If the restriction were found enforceable, Cheepco would be bound by the restriction on the toothbrushes it purchased from Martinez, and would be liable for importing the toothbrushes into the United States in violation of the restriction, even if parallel imports were otherwise legal. However, the refurbished toothbrushes that CheepCo bought via Azul did not bear the restrictive legend, as they were repackaged in Azul's own packaging. Generally, restrictive legends of this sort will only be binding on those with notice of them. The question would be whether CheepCo had notice from other sources.

2. Copyright infringement claim

Design separable from utility: The toothbrush handles, decorated to look like rocket ships and racing cars, are likely to be copyrightable. While a toothbrush (and its handle) is a useful article, the sculpted surface features on the handle could be deemed conceptually separable from the utility of the toothbrush. The handle would perform its function just as well without as with the sculpted surface. Thus, one could say that the sculpted surface represents the designer's unfettered artistic judgment, and was not significantly influenced by functional considerations. This would be consistent with the Second Circuit's decision in *Keiselstein-Cord v. Accessories by Pearl, Inc.*, 632 F.2d 989 (2d Cir. 1980), where the court held that the decorative sculpting on the surface of a belt buckle was conceptually separable from the functional purpose of the buckle.

Parallel imports: Under the Supreme Court's decision in *Quality King Distributors, Inc. v. L'Anza Research International, Inc.*, 523 U.S. 135 (1998), the parallel imports would not infringe Dazzlesmile's copyright, because the toothbrushes were made in the United States under the U.S. copyright owner's authority. It would not matter that they were first sold abroad—the doctrine of first sale would attach.

The refurbishment: Dazzlesmile might argue that the refurbished toothbrushes constitute adaptations of its copyrighted handles, which are not subject to the doctrine of first sale. However, Azul did not change the handles themselves. Indeed, the appearance of the toothbrush as a whole was unchanged, as all Azul did was replace the old brush with a new one that looked similar. Thus, even the Ninth Circuit's liberal interpretation of the adaptation right in *Mirage Editions, Inc. v. Albuquerque A.R.T. Co.*, 856 F.2d 1341 (9th Cir 1988), *cert. denied*, 489 U.S. 1018 (1989), might be distinguished. The only argument that might support a finding of infringing adaptation would be that the defendant has taken toothbrushes sold in one market (the new toothbrush market) and moved them to a different market (the refurbished toothbrush market), thereby interfering with Dazzlesmile's opportunities to exploit the new market for the copyrighted handles. This seems a stretch, however.

The restriction: As for the restriction on the label, copyright law has not been as liberal with restrictive labels as the Federal Circuit has in patent law. Even if the label was found to create a binding contractual restriction on the initial purchaser, and even if that restriction were found to be binding on subsequent purchasers who were not in privity of contract with the original parties to the sales contract, a subsequent importer would likely be liable only for breach of contract, rather than for copyright infringement. There is authority that breach of a contractual restriction through acts that would not otherwise constitute copyright infringement (like importing goods subject to the doctrine of first sale) will not constitute copyright infringement.

QUESTION 4

Both the Dipsy City Post Newspaper Co. and its rival, the Dipsy City Tribune Newspaper Co., maintain web pages on the Internet on which they post international, national, and local news stories. Members of the public are permitted to visit the web sites and read the stories free of charge. The newspaper companies maintain the web sites in order to promote subscriptions to their respective newspapers by showcasing their news reporting.

X maintains a web page that lists the "top 10" news items of the day. X "links" each listing of a "top 10" news item to a relevant news story on the Dipsy City Post's or Dipsy City Tribune's web site. Thus, due to X's actions, visitors to X's web site can click their mouse on a "top 10" news item from the list and read a news story concerning that item from either the Post's or the

Tribune's web site, framed with material from X's site, including X's paid advertisements. The link to the newspaper sites is a "deep" one, so that visitors who use X's link are taken directly to the news story, bypassing the identifying information that each newspaper company puts on the home page of its web site (including subscription information). X does not expressly notify link users of the identity of the site to which they are linked. As noted earlier, when visitors to X's web site exercise a link to a Post or Tribune news story, and see the story on their computer screen, the news story is "framed" along the top, bottom, and sides of the computer screen with advertisements. The advertisements are placed in the frame by X. X sells the advertising space to a number of entities doing business on the Internet.

Neither the Post nor the Tribune has authorized X to establish the links to its news stories. You should assume that in establishing the links, X does not reproduce the Post's or the Tribune's news stories, or any other material on the newspapers' web sites. Given these facts, please answer the following questions.

a. Has X infringed the Post's or the Tribune's rights of adaptation in the copyrighted news stories to which X has established links? Why or why not?

b. Is there any other cause of action available to the Post and the Tribune against X, other than copyright infringement? Please describe any possible causes of action and explain why they would or would not be likely to succeed.

SAMPLE ANSWER TO QUESTION 4

A. A Cause of Action for Infringing the Adaptation Right

Even though facts are uncopyrightable, news articles containing their authors' original expression of the facts are copyrightable subject matter. The newspaper plaintiffs are likely to own copyrights in at least some of the articles by virtue of the work for hire doctrine, or by assignment from the individual authors.

It is not necessary to demonstrate a reproduction in order to demonstrate an infringement of the adaptation right. The Ninth Circuit made it clear, in the *Mirage* case, that one may infringe the adaptation right by recasting or transforming a preexisting, authorized copy of the plaintiff's work. In *Mirage Editions, Inc. v. Albuquerque A.R.T. Co.*, 856 F.2d 1341 (9th Cir. 1988), *cert. denied*, 489 U.S. 1018 (1989), the court held that merely cutting authorized reproductions of works of art from books and mounting the works on tiles infringed the adaptation right in the works. The Ninth Circuit rejected the argument that the defendant's action was equivalent to merely changing the frame on a picture (which is generally understood not to constitute an adaptation). However, in the *Lee* case, the Seventh Circuit found that a similar process of mounting works on tiles was an insufficient change to constitute an adaptation as defined in Copyright Act §101.

In *Lewis Galoob Toys, Inc. v. Nintendo of America, Inc.*, 964 F.2d 965 (9th Cir. 1992), *cert. denied*, 507 U.S. 985 (1993), the Ninth Circuit held that the defendant must *incorporate* a portion of the copyrighted work into the alleged adaptation in some *concrete or permanent form*. In *Galoob*, the defendant sold a device that permitted users to intercept data bytes flowing from a copyrighted video game cartridge to a central processing unit and substitute other bytes, thus changing the "rules" under which the copyrighted video game was played. This had the effect of altering the screen display when the game was played, but the court held that it did not constitute an infringing adaptation of the copyrighted game. The court reasoned that users did not reproduce the copyrighted game, or incorporate it into a new work in a permanent or concrete way. The device only worked in conjunction with a copyrighted game, and did not replace it or supplant the market for it. Any alterations ceased to exist as soon as the game was complete or the game console was turned off.

Under this precedent, X might argue that it (and persons exercising its link) did not infringe the newspapers' adaptation right. Assuming that X made no infringing reproductions, as specified in the facts, then the facts in this case are somewhat like those in *Galoob*. Due to X's actions, when users exercise a link on X's web site, X's frame is superimposed around the newspaper's copyrighted article on the user's computer. Even if this would otherwise constitute an infringing adaptation under *Mirage* (the articles are placed into a new context, much like the art in *Mirage* after the defendant pasted it on tiles), the combination of frame and article is only temporary (unlike in *Mirage*), and will vanish once the user moves on to other material on the Internet or turns off his or her computer. Thus, the article is not incorporated into a new framed version in any concrete or permanent way, either by X or by visitors to X's web site.

The plaintiffs might respond that users' incorporation of the article and frame is "permanent," by analogizing to the Ninth Circuit's reasoning in *MAI Systems Corp. v. Peak Computer, Inc.*, 991 F.2d 511 (9th Cir. 1993). In that case, the Ninth Circuit found that bringing a work into a computer's RAM was "permanent," (and thus a "reproduction") even though the reproduction would be extinguished as soon as the user moved to another document or turned off his or her computer. It was "permanent" because it enabled the work to be perceived for more than a transitory duration. In the same manner, when users combine plaintiffs' articles and X's frame in their RAMs and on their screens, the combination is capable of being perceived for more than a transitory period. Arguably, if bringing a work (or combination of works) into RAM is permanent enough to constitute a reproduction, it ought to be permanent enough to constitute an adaptation under *Galoob*. While the newspapers may have impliedly authorized Internet users to make RAM reproductions of their articles (by virtue of posting them on their web sites and making them freely available for download), there is nothing to suggest that they have implicitly authorized viewers to make adaptations of the articles.

If visitors to X's web site infringe the newspapers' adaptation right, then X may be held liable for their infringement under a contributory infringement theory. (X knew of the visitors' infringing conduct, and induced and materially assisted it.) X might also be liable under a vicarious liability theory: X was in a position to control his visitors' actions because he controlled the link, and X stood to gain direct financial benefit from users' infringement (since presumably the availability of the links drew visitors to X's web site, and X was able to charge his advertising clients according to the number of visitors to his site).

B. Other Possible Causes of Action

X might also be liable under Lanham Act §43(a), under a reverse passing off theory. Under the facts, X arguably is passing off the plaintiff newspapers' articles as his own product. Visitors to X's web site who exercise the links may believe that they are accessing X's own articles, due to the fact that X does not tell them they are linking to another web site, and the deep link bypasses identifying information on the newspapers' home page. However, if X's actions do not confuse visitors into thinking that the articles come from X, then his failure to credit the proper source may not in itself constitute a §43(a) violation. To constitute passing off under §43(a), X's action must cause a likelihood of consumer confusion about the source, sponsorship, or affiliation of the parties' goods or services. Merely failing to provide information about the source, in itself, is not actionable. If the newspapers enjoyed a moral right of attribution in their articles, then X would be in violation of that right. However, no such right is recognized, as such, in newspaper articles in the United States. The Supreme Court, in *Dastar Corp. v. Twentieth Century Fox Film Corp.*, 539 U.S. 23 (2003), made it clear that Lanham Act §43(a) should not be construed to provide moral rights in works of authorship.

The plaintiffs might also try a state cause of action for "hot news" misappropriation. The facts in this case are somewhat like those in *International News Service v. Associated Press*, 248 U.S. 215 (1918). The newspapers have invested time, effort, and money to create the stories, and the stories have an economic value. X, in establishing links, can be characterized as reaping where he has not sown, or free-riding, because he did not have to invest the labor, skill, or effort the newspapers did in order to reap the benefit of the stories. Finally, arguably the newspapers are injured, because X's actions may make it unnecessary for Internet users to visit the papers' home pages to obtain the news, and thus may deprive the newspapers of the opportunity to enjoy the advertising and promotional benefits of providing subscription information to visitors. X's actions may also interfere with their opportunity to sell advertising in frames of their own devising.

Copyright Act §301 preempts state causes of action that give rights equivalent to the exclusive rights of copyright in copyrightable subject matter. The Court of Appeals for the Second Circuit has held, in *National Basketball Assn. v. Motorola, Inc.*, 105 F.3d 841 (2d Cir. 1997), that state misappropriation claims are generally preempted under §301 whenever the plaintiff asserts that the defendant misappropriated material that is within the subject matter of copyright. The court reasoned that the rights provided under the misappropriation cause of action in such cases are generally equivalent to the exclusive rights of copyright. Newspaper articles clearly are copyrightable subject matter, so X might argue that the plaintiffs' misappropriation claim is preempted in this case.

However, the *National Basketball* court and succeeding Second Circuit decisions have found that Congress intended an exception to the general rule of preemption when a misappropriation claim has facts highly similar to those in the *International News Service* case. The newspapers may argue that this exception applies, and thus avoid preemption.

QUESTION 5

Smith invented a new kind of widget and filed an application for a U.S. patent on April 20, 2000. The patent was granted for the new widget on January 3, 2002.

In February 2009, the CEO and various other employees of Jones Co. met with representatives of the Taiwan government at the Jones Co. corporate headquarters in Indianapolis, Indiana. At this meeting, the Jones Co. CEO offered to sell the Taiwanese government 30 widgets that would literally fall within the claims of the Smith patent. The widgets would be manufactured by a Jones Co. subsidiary in South Africa, and shipped from there to Taiwan. The shipment would be delivered in February 2011. The Taiwanese government representatives agreed to a purchase price of $4,000,000.

Assume the applicable law is the same as in 2011.

   a. Smith has learned of all this, and wants to bring a suit for patent infringement. Assume that his patent is valid. Is he likely to have a cause of action? If so, against whom?

b. Instead of agreeing to deliver the widgets to the Taiwanese government in February 2011, assume that the parties agreed that Jones Co. would deliver the widgets in May 2020. Would this make any difference in your analysis?

c. Instead of the dates set forth above, assume that the described meeting occurred in April 2001, with delivery to take place in Taiwan in February 2004. Would this make any difference in your analysis?

SAMPLE ANSWER TO QUESTION 5

A. Patent Infringement

Patent Act §271(a) grants the patentee the right to prohibit others from making, using, selling, offering to sell, or importing the patented invention in the United States during the patent term. Absent evidence of term extensions, it appears that the patent in this case will be valid until April 20, 2020. The widgets have not been made at the time of the agreement. Since they are to be made in South Africa and shipped directly to Taiwan, there is no instance of making, using, selling, or importing the patented invention in the United States during the patent term.

The only argument for patent infringement under §271(a) is that Jones Co. "offered to sell" the patented invention in the United States during the patent term. Patent Act §271(i) provides that an "offer to sell" is one in which the sale will occur before the expiration of the patent term. The sale arranged in this case will occur during this time frame. However, there is uncertainty in the law about *whether the offered sale must take place in the United States,* or whether an offer to sell abroad will infringe, as long as the offer itself was made in the United States. Some district courts have held that there can be no liability for offering to sell unless the contemplated sale would itself infringe. Since a sale outside U.S. territory will not infringe, an offer to sell outside U.S. territory also will not infringe (even if the offer itself took place in the United States). This is consistent with the Court of Appeals for the Federal Circuit's opinion in *Transocean Offshore Deepwater Drilling, Inc. v. Maersk Contractors U.S.A., Inc.,* 617 F.3d 1296 (Fed. Cir. 2010), which held that an offer made in Norway by a U.S. company to a U.S. company to sell the patented invention within the United States (to be delivered and used within the United States) constitutes an infringing offer to sell within the United States under §271(a). The court reasoned that the focus should not be on the location of the offer, but on the location of the future sale that would occur pursuant to the offer.

Under this line of reasoning, the Jones Co. would not be liable for an infringing offer to sell the patented invention.

B. Delivery in May 2020

Assuming that the sale occurred on delivery, a delivery date of May 2020, would occur *after the patent expired.* Jones Co. would not be liable for offering to sell the widgets by virtue of the provisions of Patent Act §271(i), discussed above.

C. Meeting in April 2001 with delivery in February 2004

If the offer took place in April 2001, it took place *before the patent term commenced,* and would not infringe. Even if Smith had provisional rights under his patent, those rights would not commence until his patent application was published, which is likely to have been in October 2001 (18 months after the application was filed), several months after the offer was made. Apart from provisional rights, patents provide no retroactive protection against infringement.

QUESTION 6

In 2008, Bella Bennett, a business efficiency consultant whose hobby was metal sculpture, conceived of and developed a new type of multifunction tool that performed the functions of a wire cutter, pliers, and adjustable wrench, all in one. Bella decided to call the new tool a "plirench." Shortly after making her invention, Bella applied to the U.S. Patent and Trademark Office for a utility patent for the plirench.

The following year, while her patent application was still pending, Bella entered into negotiations with Andrew Anston, President of Anston Tool, Inc. (a tool-manufacturing enterprise) concerning an exclusive license to manufacture the plirench. Andrew was extremely interested in entering into an agreement with Bella, and in order to convince her that Anston Tool was the best company to license, he told her that Anston had a secret process for molding metal objects that was very efficient and inexpensive. Using this secret process, he told Bella, Anston would be able to make the plirench a commercial success. Bella asked him what the secret process was, and Andrew proceeded to tell her.

Of the 35 firms in the tool manufacturing business, six (including Anston Tool) used this particular metal molding process. Four of them—Anston, Duffy Co., Essex Co., and Foley Co.—had developed the process independently. The other two (Gall Co. and Gilson Co.) were licensees of the Essex Co. All of them took reasonable measures to keep the process secret.

As a result of their negotiations, Andrew (acting on behalf of Anston Tool) and Bella entered into an exclusive license agreement for manufacture of the plirench. Their written agreement acknowledged that Bella had applied for a patent for the plirench and provided that she would use her best efforts to obtain a patent. Until the patent was granted, and thereafter, Anston Tool would pay Bella royalties of 50 cents for each plirench that it manufactured and sold. The agreement further provided that if Bella was unsuccessful in obtaining a patent, Anston's royalties would be reduced to 25 cents per plirench effective on the date of the P.T.O.'s rejection. The agreement further provided that Anston would pay either the 50-cent or the 25-cent royalty to Bella for as long as it manufactured the plirench, and that as long as Anston manufactured the plirench, Bella would not license any other company to do so.

Anston Tool began immediately to manufacture and sell the plirench, and to pay royalties to Bella. The following year (2010), despite Bella's best efforts, the P.T.O. denied a patent for the plirench on the grounds that it was neither novel nor non-obvious.

In 2011, two competitors of Anston Tool began manufacturing and selling the plirench, without consulting with either Bella or Anston Tool.

Also in 2011, Bella made a new invention: scissors with a built-in scotch tape dispenser on the handle. She called the new invention "tassers." In the course of negotiating with Tod Taber of the Taber Household Tool Co., regarding a license to manufacture "tassers," Bella asked Tod: "By the way, do you use the special metal molding process?" Tod asked: "What process is that?" Bella proceeded to describe the Anston Tool Company's secret process to

Tod. When she had finished, Tod said: "I've been in the business 20 years and I've never heard of that process. How did you learn about it?" Bella replied that she had learned about it from Andrew Anston when negotiating her license agreement with Anston Tool. Tod immediately implemented the new molding process, which saved his company considerable money.

In 2012, Anston Tool was still profitably engaged in manufacturing and selling the plirench, but felt that it was at a disadvantage vis-à-vis its two competitors in the plirench business, who paid no royalties to Bella. Under the circumstances, Anston Tool decided its agreement to pay royalties to Bella was void and unenforceable, and it notified Bella of its intention to continue manufacturing the plirench without paying her any further royalties.

Bella brought suit against Anston Tool Co. for breach of the licensing agreement. Anston responded that the license agreement was unenforceable and filed a counterclaim against Bella, alleging trade secret rights in its metal molding process and seeking damages resulting from Bella's wrongful disclosure of the trade secret to Tod Taber. Anston also sued Tod Taber and Taber Household Tool Co. for damages for misappropriation of its trade secret.

Please evaluate the strength of each claim.

SAMPLE ANSWER TO QUESTION 6

Bella v. Anston Tool for Breach of License Agreement

The main issue in determining the enforceability of the license is whether state enforcement of a contract to pay indefinitely for use of an unpatentable invention would unduly frustrate Congress's purposes in enacting the patent laws. If so, then the state contract cause of action is preempted and the license is unenforceable. In *Sears, Roebuck & Co. v. Stiffel Co.*, 376 U.S. 225 (1964), and *Compco Corp. v. Day-Brite Lighting, Inc.*, 376 U.S. 234 (1964), the Supreme Court said that in enacting the patent laws, Congress attempted to accommodate two conflicting interests: (1) providing an incentive to invent by granting property rights in inventions, and (2) promoting free competition by keeping ideas freely available to the public. To do this it drew a line: All those ideas meeting the high standards of federal patent law would qualify for patents, which would give exclusive rights for a limited period of time. Those ideas not meeting these standards would be left in the public domain, free for all to use. Based on these cases, Anston may argue that since the plirench is not patentable it must be freely available to all, including Anston, without the obligation of paying. Anston will probably lose, however. The facts of this case are very similar to those in *Aronson v. Quick Point Pencil Co.*, 440 U.S. 257 (1979), in which the Supreme Court found that enforcement of a contract to pay for use of an unpatentable idea/invention was not preempted. The Court reasoned that state enforcement of such contracts poses little real interference with the availability of ideas in the public domain. Only the immediate parties to the contract are bound. Third parties remain free to use the idea. Indeed, enforcement of contracts is consistent with the three purposes of Congress set out in *Kewanee Oil Co. v. Bicron*, 416 U.S. 470 (1974): (1) enforcement provides further incentive to invent; (2) it promotes public disclosure of ideas (without an enforceable license contract providing for royalties, it is less likely that inventors will make their ideas known and available to manufacturers); and (3) assuming that the idea was not already in the public domain prior to the contract, enforcement of the contract will not withdraw the idea from the public domain. (Of course, the P.T.O.'s finding that the plirench was neither novel nor non-obvious is evidence that it was already in the public domain. However, the Supreme Court has not clarified the meaning of "public domain" in this context. It is possible that evidence that the plirench was not generally known or available on the market may be sufficient to show that it was not "in the public domain.") While the Supreme Court, in *Bonito Boats, Inc. v. Thunder Craft Inc.*, 489 U.S. 141 (1989), reinforced the *Sears* and *Compco* reasoning, it also appeared to uphold *Kewanee* and *Aronson* as well.

The other issue with respect to the license is whether state law will enforce an express contract to pay for an idea such as the plirench. Some states require that the idea be novel and concrete before they will enforce such a contract. However, even if the state in this case imposes such a requirement, it may be met. The plirench was a completed invention in physical form, and thus was concrete. While the Patent Office did not find it novel under the standards of §102 of the Patent Act, the idea law standard may be lower. The idea of the plirench was original to Bella (she did not copy it from another source) and apparently it was novel enough to be valuable not only to Anston, which has marketed it successfully to the public, but also to two of Anston's competitors. It does not appear to have been widely known by others prior to Bella's invention, or specifically known to Anston.

Thus, Anston probably will not be excused from performing its license agreement, even if it was not an advantageous one.

Anston Tool v. Bella for Trade Secret Misappropriation

In analyzing Anston Tool's case against Bella, two questions must be addressed. First, was Anston's process a protectable trade secret; and second, if it was, did Bella violate a duty in disclosing it to Tabor?

Trade secret: To prevail, Anston Tool must demonstrate that its process was a secret that gave it a commercial advantage over its competitors. It probably can do this. First, *the process was substantially secret.* Only four companies had managed to develop it themselves (so it must not have been obvious), and only six (out of 35) knew of it. The Restatement specifies that absolute secrecy is unnecessary. The relatively small percentage of firms that knew of the secret process in this case probably is acceptable, since the facts say that all six of the firms took reasonable measures to keep it secret. Thus, it would be difficult for others to acquire knowledge of the secret process. Tod, who had been in the business 20 years, had never heard of it. Second, *it appears that the process gave users a competitive advantage over manufacturers who did not know or use it.* Andrew told Bella that the process was very efficient and inexpensive to use and that he believed that it would help in making the plirench a commercial success. Tod obviously recognized its value, since he implemented it immediately upon learning of it. The facts state that the process saved Tod's company considerable money. While the facts do not indicate precisely what efforts Anston Tool made to keep the process a secret or how much it spent to develop it, the existing evidence indicates that the process was a protectable trade secret.

The violation of a duty: Anston Tool has a good argument that Bella had a duty to maintain the process in confidence. She knew it was a secret (Andrew said so expressly) and yet she specifically asked Andrew to reveal it. Her request to hear the information under these circumstances suggests an implied agreement on her part to keep the secret and use it only for the purpose for which it was revealed: evaluating whether she should contract with Anston. She should refrain from using or divulging it to others without Anston Tool's permission. She breached this duty when she revealed the secret process to Tod, and thus may be liable to Anston Tool.

Anston Tool v. Tod and Tabor Household Tool for **Trade Secret Misappropriation**

Assuming that Anston Tool's process was a protectable trade secret, it must be determined whether Tod Tabor and his company (hereafter collectively "Tabor") had a duty to refrain from using the process without Anston Tool's permission. The relevant standard is whether a reasonable person in Tabor's situation would know that the process was a trade secret and that Bella was breaching a duty in revealing it to Tabor. If so, Tabor incurred a duty to refrain from disclosing or using the secret without permission. A good argument exists that this standard was satisfied. As to notice that the process was a trade secret, Tod was a professional who had been in the business for 20 years, yet he had never heard of the process. He clearly could see that the process was valuable. These facts arguably should have put him on notice that he was hearing a trade secret, especially given the fact that Bella expressly told him that she had learned it from one of Tabor's competitors in the course of one-on-one business negotiations. In addition, the manner in which Bella learned of the process should have put Tabor on notice that she owed a duty of confidentiality to Anston, which she was breaking. At the very least, a reasonable person in Tabor's position would have made further inquiry, which would have revealed the trade secret status and breach of duty. Since Tabor had the requisite notice, and thus a duty to refrain from use, his subsequent unauthorized use of the process should lead to liability.

QUESTION 7

In October 1999, X, an American author living in New York, completed a biography of A, who was a soldier in the American Revolutionary War. The biography was the result of three years of painstaking research. It chronicled A's life from early childhood, but focused particularly on A's enlistment as a foot soldier in the American army and his remarkable rise through the ranks to the position of colonel. The book was entitled *A: The Story of a Remarkable Soldier.* On the cover, under the title, was the statement: "The true story of Colonel A and the battles that made him famous."

In January, 2000, X assigned her copyright in the book to Y Corp., a publisher. Y Corp. printed and sold over 60,000 copies, with proper notice of copyright, during the next several years.

Library records of the Dallas Public Library indicate that in April of 2010, Z, an American living in Dallas, checked out a copy of *A: The Story of a Remarkable Soldier* and kept it for four weeks. The following March, 2011, Z published his own biography of A, entitled *The Life and Times of Colonel A.*

A comparison of the two books reveals the following:

1. Unlike X's biography, Z's biography does not discuss A's childhood, but begins at the time that A enlisted in the American army. While X's book deals equally with all the seven battles in which A was involved, Z's book focuses primarily on the three most important ones. Approximately 80 percent of the facts set forth in Z's book can be found in X's book, although there are a considerable number of facts in X's book that do not appear

in Z's, relating mainly to A's childhood and the lesser battles in which A participated. In addition, Z inserted a number of facts about life in colonial America and the drafting of the Declaration of Independence and the Constitution that were not included in X's book.

2. The books are both organized chronologically.

3. In describing A's involvement in one battle, X set forth her own particular theory about A's motivation in choosing the battle strategy that he did. Z's work sets forth a similar theory.

4. X and Z have different writing styles. However, the language in two paragraphs in Z's book, describing A's relationship with his wife, are virtually identical to two paragraphs in X's book.

5. In addition, it appears that X invented a minor character named Corporal Peel, who served as A's messenger in two important battles. X depicts Corporal Peel as a buffoon and descriptions of his "services" to A introduce an element of humor to X's narrative. Even though Corporal Peel was fictional, X said nothing in her book to indicate that this was the case. In his book, Z refers to Corporal Peel as A's messenger three times, and in one place, Z purports to set forth some "facts" regarding Corporal Peel that are the same as "facts" X invented in writing her biography.

Y Corp. became aware of Z's book in January 2012, and discovered that neither it nor X had registered the copyright in *A: The Story of a Remarkable Soldier*. Y Corp. immediately registered the copyright, recorded the transfer from X to the Y Corp., and then filed a lawsuit against Z alleging copyright infringement.

Please evaluate Y Corp.'s likelihood of success.

SAMPLE ANSWER TO QUESTION 7

Infringement

In order to prevail on its infringement claim, Y Corp. must demonstrate that Z copied from its copyrighted book and that the copying constituted an unlawful appropriation.

Copying: Copying can be established through circumstantial evidence that the defendant had access to the plaintiff's work and that the two works are sufficiently similar to give rise to an inference that the defendant copied from the plaintiff. Here, Y Corp. has a pretty good case. Access is clear from the Dallas Library records. Moreover, there is considerable similarity between the works. It should be noted that for purposes of the copying issue, all similarities are relevant, even if the similarities do not involve copyrightable elements of the work. The similarities surrounding Corporal Peel are particularly compelling evidence of copying.

Unlawful appropriation: Under the second part of the *Arnstein v. Porter* test for copyright infringement, it must be determined whether the defendant's work is "substantially similar" to the plaintiff's copyrightable expression. 154 F.2d 464 (1946). It should be noted that in the case of a factual work, such as a biography, the court may apply a more stringent standard than the normal subjective "audience test" employed in *Arnstein*. For example, the court might apply a "more discerning" or even a "thin copyright" standard, which requires "virtual identicality" or a "bodily appropriation of copyrighted expression."

(1) Facts: Though Z may have copied a large quantity of facts from X's book, facts are not themselves subject to copyright protection, and thus these similarities cannot themselves support a finding of substantial similarity. Y Corp. might argue that refusal to prohibit the kind of free-riding Z took on X's research will undermine X and other authors' incentive to do original research, to the detriment of the public. However, the Supreme Court rejected such arguments in *Feist Publications, Inc. v. Rural Telephone Service Co., Inc.*, 499 U.S. 340 (1991), when it rejected the "sweat of the brow" doctrine. Facts are not original to an author. The Constitution's Patents and Copyrights Clause only authorizes Congress to protect the *original writings of an author.*

(2) Selection and arrangement of the facts: While an author's selection and arrangement of facts may be deemed copyrightable expression as a general matter, X's chronological organization is unlikely to be protected. Most works of history and biography are organized chronologically, which suggests that this form of organization may be so common as not to be original. Moreover, the chronological structure of the work may be deemed a scene a faire, because it is a standard or stock device in biography, and most authors of biographies would need to use a similar organization. While Y Corp. may argue that X's *selection* of facts to report is protectable, nothing in the facts of the question suggests that X engaged in meaningful selection, rather than essentially repeating all the facts she could discover about A. Generally, courts are not generous in finding copyrightable expression in works of non-fiction, apart from the author's literal language. If a court were to find that X's selection judgment constituted copyrightable expression, it might treat the copyright as "thin," and require a showing of "virtual identicality" or "bodily appropriation of expression" before finding that Z infringed it. Given the circumstances of the case, this might be hard to do.

(3) The theory about A's motivation: In the absence of evidence that Z tracked X's language in expressing her theory, a court is unlikely to consider Z's use of the same theory in determining the issue of infringement. The theory is an idea, or an interpretation of historical fact, and copyright does not prevent the copying of either.

(4) Similar language in two paragraphs: X's choice of language in the two paragraphs Z copied is protected expression. The similarity in this case is "literal similarity." However, two paragraphs out of an entire book is not very much. These similarities are more likely to lead to a finding of infringement if it can be demonstrated that they are particularly important, in the overall context of X's book, as opposed to mere "filler."

(5) Corporal Peel: Y Corp. may argue that since X's purported "facts" about Corporal Peel are fictitious, they constitute protected expression. However, in this case a court might refuse to consider this argument, based on an estoppel rationale. X represented to the public, both by implication (designating the work a biography — a work of nonfiction) and directly (the subtitle says the work is a true story) that all the information in the book is factual. The law permitted Z to copy facts, and he may reasonably have relied on X's representations, so that X (and as X's successor in interest, Y Corp.) now is estopped to deny that Corporal Peel is factual. Even if a court did not find an estoppel, it might question whether a character in X's work is itself entitled to protection. Y Corp. would have to demonstrate that the character was drawn in considerable detail. Since Corporal Peel was a relatively minor character in X's work, Y Corp. may not be able to do this.

On the whole, since the only copyrightable expression Z took may be the two paragraphs (and possibly selection judgment), Y Corp.'s case for infringement is not a guaranteed winner. Moreover, Z would probably raise a fair use defense.

Fair use defense: Copyright Act §107, which codifies the fair use defense, specifically lists use for purposes of research as an example of a possible fair use. However, this is not in itself determinative. Section 107 lists four factors that should be considered in determining whether an infringing use should be excused from liability:

(1) The purpose and character of the use: In this case, Z's purpose was commercial in nature, because he planned to sell the book commercially. This militates against a finding of fair use. However, since Z added some information and insights of his own to his book, Z's book could be deemed a productive, or transformative use. A finding of a transformative use would weigh in Z's favor.

(2) The nature of the copyrighted work: In this case, X's book was published and it was a work of nonfiction. Courts have found that the public has a greater need to use published works of nonfiction, and a right to copy the uncopyrightable elements, such as facts and ideas. Therefore greater leeway to copy expression may be afforded, to the extent that it is necessary in order effectively to copy the unprotectable facts and ideas. Thus, the nature of the work in this case may favor a finding for Z if his copying was necessary in order to convey unprotectable facts and ideas taken from X's book.

(3) The amount and substantiality of the portion used in relation to the copyrighted work as a whole: This factor may favor Z, because the amount of copyrighted expression actually copied in this case is probably relatively small. However, the literal copying of two paragraphs is problematic for Z. Even given Z's legitimate interest in accessing and using uncopyrightable facts from X's book, Z probably had no need to copy the literal expression of the facts here. As a general matter, the factual nature of the work (factor 2) only permits copying that is necessary to access and use the facts, and no more.

(4) The effect of the use upon the potential market for the work: The Supreme Court has indicated that this is the most important factor. If the defendant's work threatens to serve as a substitute for the plaintiff's work, and thus fill the public demand and undercut the plaintiff's market, then a court is unlikely to find a fair use. In this case, even though the focus of X and Z's biographies differ, persons who otherwise might have bought X's book now may buy Z's instead. Most readers are unlikely to purchase both books.

This is a close case. However, given that Z's use was commercial and may undercut the market for the X book, Y Corp. is likely to prevail on the fair use issue.

Remedies: Because Y Corp. did not register its copyright for several years after X's book was published, its ability to obtain statutory damages and attorney fees will be impaired by Copyright Act §412. Y Corp. might be able to enjoin further reproduction or distribution of Z's book and obtain damages for any lost sales that it can demonstrate are attributable to Z's infringement. It could also recover any of Z's profits that were not attributable to the sales counted in the calculation of Y's lost sales. In the case of Z's profits, Y Corp. need only establish the amount of Z's gross revenues. The burden would then shift to Z to prove what, if any, amounts should be deducted as expenses or costs of producing the infringing book or as attributable to factors other than his infringement.

QUESTION 8

In February 2008, X conceived of a new type of widget. He described the new widget and the way to construct it in great detail in a memorandum, which he had witnessed by his secretary and placed in a safe deposit box. He began to construct the new widget the following month. Widgets are fairly intricate machines and require custom-made parts. It took X several months to complete the first one. In May 2008, the prototype widget was approximately one-third complete, and not yet operable. Nonetheless, during that month X entered into a written contract to sell three of the new widgets to Y. The widgets were to be delivered in March 2010. X delivered the three completed widgets to Y on schedule. In July 2009, X filed an application for a patent on his new widget. X was granted a patent on the new widget in April, 2012.

X was primarily in the business of manufacturing metal products, including nails, screws, nuts, and bolts. His New Jersey factory also had a shop for making custom parts for machines. Deciding that he was not well equipped to manufacture his patented widget on a large scale, he entered into an agreement with A in April 2012. The agreement authorized A, who had a factory in Connecticut, to manufacture a total of 100 of the patented widgets per year, to be delivered to X, who would then sell them to customers. In order to manufacture the widgets, A would need to have gadgets (one of the components of the widget) custom-made. The agreement provided that A must purchase all the custom-made gadgets used in making the patented widgets from X, who would construct them in his New Jersey factory. The agreement further provided that henceforth A must purchase all nails, screws, nuts, and bolts used in his factory from X. The agreement stated that it would last for five years and could be renewed.

A commenced making widgets pursuant to the agreement. In December 2012, B, who owned an export business in New York, approached A with a proposal. B felt that there would be a strong market for X's widgets in Southeast Asia, but felt that X was charging too high a price. B suggested that A make 50 additional widgets, beyond the 100 per year specified in his license with X, that B would then sell to Southeast Asian buyers. When A protested that he could be held liable for patent infringement, B told him that she had consulted with a patent lawyer, who, upon learning the facts set forth above, had opined that X's patent might be invalid. Upon learning this, A agreed that it would be worth taking the risk.

In order to make the additional widgets, A went to C, who owned a custom machine shop, and placed an order for 50 custom-made gadgets, providing C with the proper specifications. C began work. A couple of weeks later, while at a trade convention, C mentioned her contract with A to a business acquaintance, stating that she had never heard of gadgets of the type ordered by A. The acquaintance told C that the only use for such gadgets was in X's patented widget, but that he thought A was required by license to buy all the gadgets used in the patented widget from X. After returning home from the convention, C completed the custom gadgets and delivered them to A as required by her contract.

When he received the completed custom-made gadgets from C, A incorporated them into the 50 widgets, made the finishing touches, and shipped the completed widgets to B in New York, as agreed.

Once she received the widgets, B negotiated a contract to sell 30 of the widgets to D, a Thai businessman, who would take delivery of them in Thailand for use in that country. B received payment and the widgets were shipped.

The following year X learned all the facts recited above, and communicated them to you.

  a. Please evaluate all possible causes of action for patent infringement that X might assert against A, B, C, and D, explaining your reasoning, evaluating any potential weaknesses in the case, and discussing what damages X might expect to recover and how they would be measured. Even if you conclude that X's lawsuit would not succeed due to the resolution of one issue, nonetheless discuss all the issues fairly raised by the facts.

  b. Assume that all the actions described above occurred ten years later than described, so that the Leahy-Smith America Invents Act is fully applicable. Would your response under a. change in any respect? Please explain your answer.

SAMPLE ANSWER TO QUESTION 8

1. Patent infringement causes of action against A, B, C, and D

A's potential liability: Assuming (for now) that X's patent was valid and enforceable, A should be liable for direct infringement. A was licensed to make 100 widgets yearly, using gadgets supplied by X. However, by making an additional 50 widgets, with gadgets provided by C, A engaged in an unauthorized making of the patented invention, in violation of Patent Act §271(a).

B's potential liability: B may also be liable for direct infringement, due to her unauthorized sale of the patented invention to D, the Thai importer. However, this will only be the case if the sale took place in the United States. While more detailed facts are needed in order to determine the location of the sale, it appears that the negotiations and payment may have occurred in the United States, suggesting that it might be possible to find that the sale occurred in the United States. If the sale did not occur in the United States, the question arises whether B nonetheless made an infringing offer to sell in the United States. While the law is not yet settled, some case authority suggests that even if an offer to sell occurs in the United States, it will not infringe unless the contemplated sale would itself take place in the United States. Under this interpretation, if the sale itself took place outside of the United States, then neither B's offer or sale would directly infringe X's patent under Patent Act §271(a).

Even if B is not directly liable, she may be liable for inducing A to infringe under Patent Act §271(b). B solicited and actively encouraged A's direct infringement, and assisted it by providing a market for the finished infringing widgets. She did so knowing of the existence of X's patent and that (at least if X's patent was valid and enforceable) A's actions would infringe. The issue would be whether B's belief (based on consultations with her lawyer) that X's patent might be invalid is sufficient to prevent X from demonstrating that B had the necessary knowledge or intent for inducement liability. B might argue that, as a matter of social policy, courts should encourage the testing of patent monopolies by those who have a good-faith, reasonable belief that the patent may be invalid. To do this, the court should construe the knowledge requirement strictly and find that B is not liable because she believed in good faith that there might be no infringement due to patent invalidity.

C's potential liability: C did not actively solicit either A or B to directly infringe, so she is unlikely to be liable under §271(b). However (again assuming that X's patent is valid and enforceable), C probably will be liable for contributory infringement under §271(c). The custom-made gadgets appear to be a material component of X's patented widget. C knew that the gadgets were made for use in an invention that was patented. She knew that the gadgets were not staples, were a material part of the patented invention, and had no substantial noninfringing use. The fact that she may not have known these things when she entered into the contract should not relieve her of liability, since she clearly knew them when she performed the contract of sale to A. To avoid liability, she should have declined to proceed with the transaction.

D's potential liability: D, the Thai businessman, probably is not directly liable to X, because any unauthorized sale, offer to sell, or use of the patented invention that D made probably occurred outside of the United States. X might possibly argue that in buying A's infringing widgets, D rendered himself liable for inducement under §271(b). To fully assess this possibility, more facts are needed regarding D's knowledge and actions at the time the transaction occurred.

Possible defenses: The defendants might raise a couple of defenses in this case. First, they may argue that X's patent is invalid under Patent Act §102(b). Second, A may argue that X's patent is unenforceable under the patent misuse doctrine.

Patent validity — §102 (b): Section 102(b) prohibits a patent if the invention was on sale in the United States more than a year before the application for patent was filed. In this case, X entered into a written contract to sell three widgets to Y in May 2008, more than a year prior to his application for patent (in July 2009). X may argue that this should not disqualify him because, at the time of the contract, there was no operable physical embodiment of the widget. However, under the Supreme Court's decision in *Pfaff v. Wells Electronics, Inc.*, 525 U.S. 55 (1998), the issue is whether, at the time of the contract, the invention was "ready to patent." If the memorandum X wrote in February 2008 was sufficiently detailed to enable a person with ordinary skill in the art to make or practice the invention, then it is likely that X's later contract will trigger the §102(b) statute of limitations, and that his patent will be invalid for failure to file within the one-year deadline. This would relieve all the defendants from infringement liability.

Patent misuse: Even if X's patent was not time barred under §102(b), a court might find it unenforceable under the patent misuse doctrine. In this case, X engaged in two instances of "tying" in his contract with A. First, he required that, as a condition of the license, A buy all custom-made gadgets used in the widgets A built from him. This would not constitute patent misuse, because the gadget was a material component of the invention with no substantial non-infringing use. Patent Act §271(d) expressly permits patent owners to tie licenses to an agreement to buy such components from the patentee. Second, X required that, as a condition of the license, A buy all nails, screws, nuts, and bolts used in his factory from X. Nails, screws, nuts, and bolts are staple items with many substantial, non-infringing uses. Under §271(d), this contract condition may constitute patent misuse if X has market power in the widget market. This issue cannot be determined under the facts given. While X has a monopoly in this particular type of widget, it is possible that there are so many other types of widgets (or other non-infringing substitutes) in the market that he actually has no appreciable market power. If he has no market power, then his tying arrangement will not appreciably harm competition and will be permitted. If X does have market power, and thus patent misuse is found, X will be prohibited from enforcing his patent until the misuse stops and X no longer enjoys benefits from it.

Damages: If infringement liability is found, the defendants will be liable for actual damages to X. These damages probably will be measured by the "reasonable royalty" standard, which awards the plaintiff an amount that reasonable parties would have agreed to pay and receive as a royalty for the defendants' use of the invention in an arms-length transaction. The alternative measure of damages—the plaintiff's lost sales—would be difficult to apply in this case because, in order to recover, X must show that "but for" the defendants' actions, X would have sold his own widgets to the defendants' customers. Here, X did not have the ability to make and sell the 50 widgets himself. In addition, the defendants' sales were all to foreign buyers, who might have bought from others who lawfully made and sold X's invention outside of the United States. Also, there is evidence that X charged significantly more for his widgets than A and B did, which might cast doubt on any assumption that D would have bought from X if the widgets were unavailable from A and B at their lower price.

X might also seek punitive damages against A and B for willful infringement. However, B, at least, had consulted her lawyer and had been advised that X's patent might be invalid. When parties consult with qualified lawyers prior to acting and believe in good faith that the patent is likely to be invalid, courts generally will not impose punitive damages. A did not himself consult a lawyer. However recent case law and statutory provisions hold that evidence of *failure* to consult a lawyer about an allegedly infringed patent may not be used to prove that the accused infringer willfully infringed the patent.

2. Would things change under the Leahy-Smith America Invents Act?

Assuming that no change other than the Leahy-Smith Act occurs in the ten years at issue, the results described above would not likely differ. While the Act significantly revises Patent Act §§102 and 103, the revisions would not change the outcome of A, B, and C's patent invalidity defense. As revised by the Leahy-Smith America Invents Act, §102(a)(1) prohibits a patent if "the claimed invention was patented, described in a printed publication, or in public use, on sale, or otherwise available to the public before the effective filing date of the claimed invention." Arguably X put the invention "on sale" prior to his application date. The concept of "on sale," as construed by the Supreme Court in the *Pfaff* case, will likely remain controlling, so that the question about whether X's memo rendered the widget "ready for patenting" would remain controlling.

Because it wanted to preserve the flexibility that inventors enjoyed under the old §102(b) grace period, Congress created exceptions to the new §102 novelty requirement. The amended §102(b)(1) provides that a *disclosure made one year or less before the inventor's effective filing date* will not anticipate the inventor's invention under subsection (a)(1) if the disclosure was *made by the inventor* or a joint inventor or by another person who obtained the disclosed subject matter either directly or indirectly from that inventor or joint inventor. This provision effectively gives X a year to file after placing his new widget on sale, just like before. However, if he placed it on sale *more than one year* prior to his application date, as X arguably did here, his invention is unpatentable for lack of novelty,

QUESTION 9

In 1980, Charles Callum began doing business in San Francisco as a sole proprietorship that he called "Wild West Haberdashery." Wild West Haberdashery manufactured various styles of cowboy hats and sold them wholesale and through a series of retail outlets in Northern California and Oregon. One of Wild West Haberdashery's more popular products was a 10-gallon-style hat that it sold under the trademark "Starry Night." In 1982, Callum registered "Starry Night" for hats on the U.S. Patent and Trademark Office's Principal Register. Wild West Haberdashery engaged in sporadic advertising in magazines, newspapers, and on radio stations in California and Oregon, and enjoyed a stable, profitable stream of business.

In 2005, Ted Toben began doing business in Texas as a sole proprietorship called "Wild West Outfitters." Wild West Outfitters sold, through several retail stores in Austin and Dallas, a complete line of cowboy clothing and accessories. One of Wild West Outfitters' most popular products was leather chaps that it sold under its own unregistered trademark, "Starbright." Wild West Outfitters engaged in considerable advertising over the local country and western radio stations in Austin and Dallas, and it also advertised in the local newspapers and through direct mail brochures promoting "Wild West Outfitters" and "Starbright" chaps. When Toben began doing business, he did not know of Wild West Haberdashery or Starry Night hats.

In 2010, Callum decided to expand his business. He opened a new retail outlet of Wild West Haberdashery in Austin and began selling Starry Night 10-gallon-style hats through that outlet.

Toben learned of Callum's activities two months later and immediately filed suit for Lanham Act §43(a) and state common-law trademark infringement and passing off, seeking to enjoin Callum from doing business under the name "Wild West" and to enjoin Callum's use of the trademark "Starry Night" for hats in the Austin-Dallas area.

Callum filed counterclaims for trademark infringement and passing off to enjoin Toben from operating under the name "Wild West" and to enjoin Toben from using the trademark "Starbright."

Please determine what, if any, relief each is entitled to receive and explain your answer. If you need further facts, state what facts you need and why. Apply federal law and "general common law" as appropriate; you should not try to discuss the specific state law of California or Texas.

SAMPLE ANSWER TO QUESTION 9

Rights in the "Wild West" trade name: Both Toben and Callum are using the "Wild West" designation as a trade name. The Lanham Act does not provide for registration of trade names, and the facts do not indicate that either has registered "Wild West" as a trade or service mark. Thus, the respective rights of the parties must be determined pursuant to Lanham Act §43(a) and/or under the general state common law (which is likely to be the same).

The name "Wild West" would suggest a geographic location in the western United States to most consumers. If consumers would be likely to think that the name indicates that the parties' businesses originate from that place, then the name is geographically descriptive, and the parties must demonstrate secondary meaning. If consumers are not likely to think that the businesses originate from the western part of the country, then the name is suggestive (suggesting the nature of the products, or associating the products with the western lifestyle of cowboy days) and no secondary meaning will be required. Because the outlets consumers would encounter are located in the West, and Western goods like hats and chaps are often made in the West, the name may be deemed geographically descriptive. Assuming that consumers would understand the name to be geographically descriptive of the businesses, we must examine the presence of secondary meaning. Toben has used the name in the Austin and Dallas area since 2005, and during that time he has engaged in extensive advertising through the use of that name. Thus, it is fairly likely that he can establish secondary meaning in Austin and Dallas. Callum has used the name for over 30 years in northern California and Oregon. Though his advertising has been sporadic, the advertising in combination with Callum's steady stream of business under that name is likely to be sufficient to establish secondary meaning in northern California and Oregon. However, there is no evidence that Callum has acquired secondary meaning in Texas. Two months of business under the name is unlikely in itself to be sufficient, and the facts do not suggest that he has engaged in heavy advertising of the name during that time.

Under the common law, the first person to acquire secondary meaning in a descriptive or geographically descriptive trade name acquires superior rights in it. Assuming that Callum acquired secondary meaning in California and Oregon prior to 2005, he was the first to acquire secondary meaning in an absolute sense. However, Toben was the first to acquire secondary meaning in Texas (which is geographically remote from California and Oregon) and he did so in good faith—without notice of Callum's prior use. Thus, Toben should have the benefit of the remote, good faith defense, which not only protects him against Callum's attempt to enjoin his use of "Wild West" in Texas, but also will permit him to enjoin Callum from entering his Austin-Dallas market, if he can demonstrate that Callum's use will cause a likelihood of consumer confusion.

A court would probably find that Callum's use of "Wild West Haberdashery" in Austin and Dallas causes a likelihood of confusion with Toben's "Wild West Outfitters." Only the last word of each name differs, and in this case the first two words probably make the strongest impression on persons viewing or hearing the names. Moreover, while "haberdashery" and "outfitters" do not sound alike, they both suggest a clothier. In determining the issue of confusion, the court will not assume that the consumer has the opportunity to make a side-by-side comparison of the names. In fact, the court should assume that the consumer has only an imperfect memory of one or the other. In addition, in this case, the retail businesses are similar (retail sales of Western-style clothing), and they are likely to attract many of the same customers. These customers may not be sophisticated consumers. All these considerations support a finding of a likelihood of confusion and suggest that the court should enjoin Callum from use of the name "Wild West Haberdashery" in the Austin-Dallas area.

Rights in "Starry Night" and "Starbright": Callum's mark, "Starry Night," as applied to hats, appears to be arbitrary. Thus, his rights are not dependent on the existence of secondary meaning. (In any event, given the duration of Callum's registration, the mark probably has become incontestable, thus eliminating a challenge on lack of distinctiveness grounds.)

Callum was the first to use the mark in trade and also the first to register it. Because registration served as constructive notice of prior use, and Toben began his use after Callum's registration, Toben cannot claim the remote, good faith defense. Upon registration, Callum obtained superior rights not only in northern California and Oregon—where he actually had used the mark—but also in all other areas of the United States (including Texas) where the mark was not in use at the time. Thus, if Callum's and Toben's consecutive use of their marks in Austin and Dallas will cause a likelihood of consumer confusion about the source or sponsorship of their respective products, Callum will have, by virtue of his registration, the right to enjoin Toben's further use.

The issue of confusion is a close one; but in the end, the court is likely to find that Toben's use does cause a likelihood of confusion and must be enjoined. While the words "Starry Night" and "Starbright" are different, they sound somewhat similar. The first syllable is the same and the last syllables both have the same distinctive vowel sound. Moreover, both marks evoke a similar mental image of a night sky with stars. Although the marks have a different number of syllables and look somewhat different (one word versus two), the similarities outweigh the differences. In addition, while the products the marks identify differ, they are closely related, so that a reasonable consumer might think that they were produced by the same source. Likewise, the outlets at which both products are sold probably are similar, and there will be some overlap in prospective purchasers (Western-wear fans).

Thus, a court is likely to enjoin Toben's use. However, since Toben was in fact unaware of Callum's prior use, and is not selling a directly competitive product, the court might decline to award damages. It may even consider ways that Toben could continue to use its mark, with differentiating elements and disclaimers that would avoid confusing consumers.

QUESTION 10

In 2009, Alpha Co. got a patent for a new chemical compound it had discovered (the "Alpha compound"), that is effective in killing fleas on cats and dogs without injuring the cats or dogs. Alpha markets the patented compound, mixed with water, some preservatives, and a perfume scent, in a spray can under the trademark "Fleasoff." Subsequently, Zelda discovered that if she mixed "Fleasoff" with an oil-based paint and painted a wood fence with the mixture, not only fleas, but also flies, ants, and spiders avoided the fenced-in area for up to two years. Zelda would like to apply for a patent on her discovery and exploit it commercially, using the "Fleasoff" mark on her own product label to indicate the key ingredient. Please advise Zelda of her legal rights (and potential liabilities) in this regard.

SAMPLE ANSWER TO QUESTION 10

Due to Alpha's patent, Zelda cannot manufacture the claimed Alpha compound, or sell paint containing self-manufactured Alpha compound, without a license from Alpha. However, under the doctrine of exhaustion, Zelda can purchase Fleasoff from Alpha or any other lawful distributor, combine it with paint and then resell the combination without liability (as long as Alpha has not placed any enforceable restrictions on use of the Fleasoff it puts on the market). Moreover, Zelda can truthfully advise consumers that her paint contains "Fleasoff," as long as her use of the mark is truthful and not misleading about the immediate source of the paint. Zelda may also apply for a patent on her new composition of matter, and for the process of applying it to wood as a means of keeping bugs away, assuming that her inventions are novel and non-obvious (they clearly are useful). However, even if she obtains a patent, she must obtain a license before she can produce Alpha's patented component.

Table of Cases

Table of References to the Copyright Act of 1976 (17 U.S.C. §101 *Et Seq.*)

Table of References to the Lanham Act
(15 U.S.C. §1051 *Et Seq.*)

Table of References to the Patent Act
(35 U.S.C. §101 *Et Seq.*)

Index

Flowchart illustrations are indicated by italic page numbers.